AAU-9107
UC-gradstudies

Please remember that this is a library book,
and that it belongs only temporarily to each
person who uses it. Be considerate. Do
not write in this, or any, library book.

A PROFESSIONAL ORIENTATION TO COUNSELING

SECOND EDITION

Nicholas A. Vacc
University of North Carolina at Greensboro

Larry C. Loesch
University of Florida

ACCELERATED DEVELOPMENT
A member of the Taylor & Francis Group

A Professional Orientation to Counseling, second edition

Copyright 1994 by Accelerated Development Inc.

10 9 8 7 6 5 4 3 2

Printed in the United States of America

Technical Development: Cynthia Long
                         Marguerite Mader
                         Janet Merchant
                         Julie Nelson
                         Shaeney Pigman
                         Sheila Sheward

Library of Congress Cataloging-in-Publication Data

Vacc, Nicholas A.
   A professional orientation to counseling / Nicholas A. Vacc, Larry C. Loesch. -- 2nd ed.
       p.   cm.
   Rev. ed of: Counseling as a profession. c1987.
   Includes bibliographical references and index.

   ISBN 1-55959-051-3
   1. Counseling. 2. Counseling--Practice. 3. Counselors--Training of. 4. Counselors--Professional ethics.   I. Loesch, Larry C.
II. Vacc, Nicholas A.   Counseling as a profession.   III. Title.
BF637.C6V33   1993
158'.3' 023--dc20   93-27363
                                                                        CIP
LCN: 93-27363

For additional information and ordering, please contact:

ACCELERATED DEVELOPMENT
A member of the Taylor & Francis Group
1900 Frost Road, Suite 101
Bristol, PA 19007
1-800-821-8312

DEDICATION

To
Jennie Vacc
and
Katherine Loesch

our first and most caring
teachers and counselors

PREFACE

This book is intended to serve two purposes. The first is to help students become professional counselors by providing an orientation to the profession. The second is to provide practicing professional counselors with a current review of the counseling profession and the curricular content required for the preparation of counselors.

We believe that the counseling profession currently enjoys greater and better identity among the general and professional public than it has at any time in the history of the counseling profession. This improved identity is the result of many, many significant accomplishments by and for professional counselors including advancements in counselor credentialing, improved counselor preparation standards and increased adherence to those standards, greater governmental recognition of counselors' competence, and more ethical and more accountable professional practices by counselors. Despite these recent accomplishments in the counseling profession, the need to fulfill significant professional goals of five years ago remains essentially the same for several reasons. As a profession, counseling has not yet achieved the public recognition that it should command, and professional credentialing for counselors has not yet become completely accepted nor endorsed. Also, counselor preparation is not yet standardized to the extent that there is widespread clarity of understanding about counselors' minimal competencies and professional practices, which are in accord with the highest ethical and legal standards but are not yet universal among counselors. And so, although tremendous gains have been made within the profession, there is still much to be improved. The "good news" is that professional counselors' continued efforts should facilitate relatively rapid achievement of appropriate goals.

This book is an effort on our part to assist in the evolutionary process. Our intent has been to provide an organized and clear presentation of the nature and activities of the professional counselor. Therefore, included are descriptions of the distinctive characteristics of professional counselors, the differences between professional counselors and other providers of mental health services, and the approaches, methods, and activities used by professional counselors to alleviate the problems for which they render help.

Accreditation standards for programs preparing professional counselors stipulate that new students should receive a "professional orientation." That is, they should be educated early in their programs about the roles and functions of a professional counselor and the knowledge and skill bases and professional and ethical guidelines for professional counseling. Unfortunately, this orientation traditionally has consisted of an academic experience that emphasizes establishing a foundational knowledge base for, and development of, so-called basic counseling skills. Even more unfortunately, this academic experience typically has been comprised of "bits and pieces" from a variety of professional sources, thereby failing to provide a coherent introduction and digressing substantially from the *orientation* purpose. Counselor trainees have been expected to develop a "professional orientation" and to act as "professionals" but have not had benefit of an effective explanation of these expectations in terms of activities, behaviors, and guidelines. Thus, far too often counselor trainees have emerged from their preparation experience with the *mis*understanding that having good counseling skills is the sum and substance of being a professional counselor. It is our hope and intention that this book alleviates the continuation of this misunderstanding.

A Professional Orientation to Counseling, published in 1987 under the title *Counseling as a Profession*, was developed with several goals in mind. One was to update previously presented information, particularly that concerning professional counselors' preparation and credentialing. A second goal was to add sections that would enhance the book's value for both counseling practitioners and trainees. Thus, legal, ethical, and other areas viewed by the Council for Accreditation of Counseling and Related Educational Programs as essential for high-quality counselor preparation are included. A third goal was to organize content to make the book most useful for persons who identify themselves as professional counselors.

Finally, no book is completely the product of its authors. We, like all authors, are indebted to numerous others for their contributions to our thinking. Special recognition, however, is given to the work of Craig Cashwell in researching and drafting sections of material concerning group counseling and social and cultural issues, to Pamela Sides and Sandy Ritter for their careful reviews and editing, and to the countless individuals who contributed their time and energy to helping make this second edition a reality. Our sincere appreciation is offered as a small indication of our gratitude.

June 1993
Nicholas A. Vacc, Ed.D., NCC, CCMHC
Larry C. Loesch, Ph.D., NCC

TABLE OF CONTENTS

LIST OF FIGURES

LIST OF TABLES

PART I

PROFESSIONAL
ORIENTATION

Chapter **1**

PROFESSIONAL COUNSELING: A POINT OF VIEW

Belkins (1984) described counseling as the fusion of many elements. Included are a "compassionate treatment of mental health problems . . . psychodynamic insights of Freud and psychoanalysis, the scientific scrutiny and methodology of the behavioral approach, the quantitative science of psychometrics, the humanistic perspective of client-centered therapy, the philosophical bases of existentialism, and the practical . . . applications that evolved from the vocational guidance movement" (p.19). Belkins' description of counseling remains appropriate today because it captures the comprehensiveness of the activity known as counseling. In helping clients enhance their lives, professional counselors apply knowledge, skills, and techniques derived from their studies in human growth and development, social and behavioral sciences, and counselor education. Their work may involve individual interpersonal relationships, social or small-group interactions, or community-wide involvements. They also may be involved with personal, social, familial, or vocational concerns.

And finally, they may be involved with either direct or indirect service delivery.

As a result of the comprehensiveness of counseling, specialty areas have developed attempting to delineate the broad counseling specialties. However, being distinct from one another is difficult because professional counselors with different specialties have much in common. Primarily, all counselors are concerned with helping people develop, prevent difficulties, and overcome problems. Also, broadly speaking, all counseling specialties include principles and theories of behavior. Some focus on mental-health counseling, while others are concerned with student personnel in higher education or school counseling. Finally, regardless of specialty, there is a common linkage among professional counselors: the goal of helping people "cope" and find effective solutions for problems that can arise at any point in the lives of otherwise normal people. As members of a group of mental-health professionals, counselors distinguish themselves by the applied nature of their work. A brief overview of each specialty follows.

SPECIALTIES IN COUNSELING

Mental-Health Counseling

Mental-health counseling emphasizes the provision of services in the community, in business or industry, or through private practice. Within these settings, professional counselors deliver many types of mental-health counseling services. For example, they may counsel families, adults, adolescents, and/or children; offer consultation; or help people find and achieve appropriate vocational goals and placements. Within counselor education programs, specializations in this area typically are designated community or mental-health counseling.

Marriage and Family Counseling

The specialty of marriage and family counseling views the family unit as having unique factors that require special knowledge and skill for the practice of marriage and family counseling. Professional counselors working in this specialty primarily are interested in specific problems that impede family functioning. Practice with a focus on the family includes working with couples concerning training in parenting skills, relationship enhancement, or pre-marital counseling. These areas of focus, as well as implementation of systemic intervention, are directed toward assisting a significant portion of the population (those who define themselves as part of a family whether remarried, part of a step family, a single parent, divorced, or a "significant other") achieve identity as a family unit.

Student Development Practice in Higher Education

Student development practice in higher education is based on the recognition that undergraduate and/or graduate students need to be considered in the context of the total college or university environment. Professional counselors in higher education settings have special concern for the university community and its problems. They may be occupied with recruitment (admissions), the management of a counseling program, student residence life, career planning and placement, student mental health, student activities (e.g. fraternities and sororities), special student groups (e.g., students with disabilities, international students, and students requiring educational opportunity programs), student judicial affairs, retention, advising, or student development in general.

School Counseling

Professional counselors in this specialty area view the school as a unique "community" that must be studied and understood if the people in that environment are to be assisted with their educational, personal, and social development. All school personnel (i.e., administrators, supervisors, teachers, cafeteria workers, secretaries, custodians, volunteers, and teacher assistants) are viewed as important contributors to the achievement of educational goals and to the quality of life in a school. However, the professional counselor in the school setting specializes in facilitating the development of children and adolescents, with emphases on interactions among children, school personnel, and parents.

Student personnel in higher education and school counselors share a concern for understanding the educational settings in which behavior occurs. Professional counselors in these settings bring their knowledge, skills, and techniques to the situations and apply them to problems presented within these special environments (i.e., unique places in which people live, work, and study).

Collectively, the above information provides a "sense" of what professional counselors do. Yet, it is an incomplete response to the question because it does not encompass what it is that counselors actually do in their daily activities. This remains a question that is asked often by both professionals and laypersons and, although responded to by a wide variety of professionals, is usually only incompletely answered. In an attempt to provide a complete response to this question, Loesch and Vacc (NBCC, 1993) conducted a job analysis of professional counselors. In essence, they undertook a systematic examination of the nature and/or features of professional counselors' work behaviors. Accordingly, their analyses provided information on the degree of dissimilarity or similarity in the work activities among professional counselors of all specialties. This information was useful in clarifying the congruence of activities that take place among professional counselors.

The primary purpose of the investigation was to gain an understanding of the nature of work behaviors among professional counselors. The factor analysis findings provided a scientifically meaningful description of what professional counselors do across specialties through a "simple representation" of job behaviors.

Presented in Table 1.1 are the five orthogonal factor solutions that describe counselors' work behavior frequencies. The five clusters encompassing 136 work behaviors are ordered from highest to lowest by weighing the frequency of a behavior with its importance (e.g. being able to access the potential for a client to harm self or others would be highly important). The 722 responding counselors reported that they engaged in fundamental counseling practices, counseling groups, counseling families, counseling for career development, and professional practice.

(Continued on page 9)

Table 1.1
Work Behaviors, to Include Both Frequency and Importance, for 722 Respondents.

Fundamental Counseling Practices

1. Counsel clients concerning personal change
2. Establish counseling goals
3. Assess potential for client to harm self/others
4. Evaluate client's movement toward counseling goals
5. Evaluate extent of client's psychological dysfunction
6. Counsel adults
7. Clarify counselor/client roles
8. Develop comprehensive treatment plans
9. Assist with client's evaluation of counseling
10. Reframe client's problem
11. Identify source-of-problem alternatives
12. Obtain client's informed consent prior to counseling
13. Counsel clients concerning lifestyle change
14. Inform client about ethical standards and practice
15. Clarify client's support systems
16. Assess psychosocial needs
17. Systematically observe client behaviors
18. Evaluate need for client referral
19. Evaluate existing (pre-counseling) client data
20. Conduct pre-counseling diagnostic interview
21. Use "active listening" skills
22. Maintain case notes, records, and/or files
23. Use cognitive-oriented counseling techniques
24. Self-evaluate counseling effectiveness
25. Inform client about legal aspects of counseling
26. Use behavioral-oriented counseling techniques
27. Determine DSM-III-R classification
28. Analyze cost-benefit of treatment alternatives

Counseling for Career Development

29. Assist client in understanding test results
30. Facilitate client's development of decision-making skills
31. Use test results for client decision-making
32. Use interest inventories
33. Evaluate client's educational preparations
34. Use self-report personality inventories
35. Use test/inventory results for intervention selections
36. Evaluate client's occupational skills

Table 1.1 Continued

37. Use occupational information in counseling
38. Provide career/vocational education
39. Facilitate clients development of job-search skills
40. Use achievement tests
41. Provide career counseling for adolescents
42. Use print and other media in career counseling
43. Select appraisal instruments/techniques for counseling
44. Provide career counseling for adults
45. Use non-test appraisal techniques
46. Use aptitude tests
47. Use career resources library
48. Use intelligence tests
49. Use computerized career counseling resources
50. Provide career counseling for persons with disabilities
51. Provide group vocational counseling
52. Provide career counseling for older adults
53. Provide out-placement counseling
54. Use computerized "counseling" software

Counseling Groups

55. Assist with group members' feedback to each other
56. Identify harmful group-member behaviors
57. Evaluate progress toward group goals
58. Resolve conflict among group members
59. Self-evaluate group counseling effectiveness
60. Determine group counseling termination criteria
61. Inform clients of group counseling guidelines and goals
62. Systematically observe group members' behaviors
63. Use "structured" activities during group counseling
64. Use group-centered group counseling leadership techniques
65. Use leader-centered group counseling leadership techniques

Counseling Families

66. Counsel persons in crisis
67. Counsel clients concerning substance use/abuse
68. Counsel clients concerning sexual abuse
69. Counsel adolescents
70. Counsel concerning family member interaction
71. Counsel clients concerning personality change
72. Counsel clients concerning physical abuse
73. Develop family conflict resolution strategies
74. Counsel concerning family change
75. Clarify family counseling goals

Table 1.1 Continued

76. Clarify familial behavior norms
77. Inform family members of family dynamics/roles
78. Inform family members of family counseling guidelines and goals
79. Clarify client's moral/spiritual issues
80. Counsel concerning divorce
81. Counsel children
82. Counsel concerning human sexuality
83. Counseling concerning divorce-conflict reduction
84. Interview client's significant others
85. Use Behavioral family counseling techniques
86. Counsel concerning marriage enrichment
87. Use Structural family counseling techniques
88. Use Strategic family counseling techniques
89. Use Multigenerational family counseling techniques
90. Counsel concerning pre-marriage

Professional Practice

91. Serve as a liaison with other agencies
92. Provide consultation services for ethical or legal dilemmas
93. Participate in case conferences
94. Administer counseling program
95. Conduct prevention-oriented developmental activities
96. Participate in staffing decision-making processes
97. Engage in professional/community public relations
98. Participate in continuing education/skill enhancement
99. Conduct community outreach
100. Correspond orally with others to maintain professional communications
101. Evaluate counselors' performance
102. Establish programmatic service goals
103. Read current professional literature
104. Write to other professionals to maintain professional communications
105. Participate in professional organization activities
106. Assess programmatic needs
107. Review legal statutes and regulations
108. Supervise staff
109. Provide counselor skill-development training
110. Review ethical standards
111. Provide consultation services for interpersonal skills training
112. Provide consultation services for human relationships development
113. Provide consultation services for human resource needs evaluation
114. Engage in formative evaluation of counseling program
115. Engage in summative evaluation of counseling program
116. Supervise counselor trainees
117. Provide consultation services for professional skill development

Table 1.1 Continued

118. Prepare developmental/preventative media
119. Develop program-related reports
120. Allocate financial resources for counseling program
121. Conduct self-development training for non-clients
122. Provide consultation services for organizational development
123. Provide multicultural training/education
124. Use computers for program data management
125. Engage in data analyses
126. Write communication for non-counseling, professional activities
127. Collaborate in research with other professionals
128. Engage in counseling outcome research
129. Engage in counseling process research
130. Write for publication
131. Provide career counseling for children
132. Develop appraisal instrument/technique
133. Engage in field/observational research
134. Evaluate computer software
135. Conduct fund-raising activities for program development/maintenance
136. Engage in experimental/laboratory research

Note: The above table is an adaption from *Social and Personality Development*, by Shaffer, D.R., 1988 (pp. 36-37). CA: Brooks/Cole Publishing Co.

Loesch and Vacc's (NBCC, 1993) work has provided the profession with an empirical description of counselor practice. What it does not do is provide information about the relationship of counseling to other mental-health specialties such as psychology or social work. To make comparisons among groups of mental-health professionals we must continue to rely on descriptions of roles, functions, and responsibilities.

DIFFERENCES BETWEEN PROFESSIONAL COUNSELORS AND OTHER MENTAL-HEALTH PROFESSIONALS

Mental-health professionals, other than counselors, include counseling applied and academic psychologists, social workers, marriage and family therapists, and psychiatrists. A discussion of the major focus of each professional area follows:

Applied psychologists focus primarily on psychological pathology, or on what commonly is viewed as an abnormality, illness, or disease. They typically are involved in the diagnosis of personality problems with an emphasis on personality reorganization (rebuilding the structural and functional effects of a person's personality) and are concerned with maladaptive behavior (i.e., psychopathology). *Applied psychology* is usually subdivided into school, counseling, clinical, industrial, and community psychology. In contrast, *academic psychologists* are concerned primarily with areas in basic psychology (e.g., perception, history, physiology, and experimental psychology). Typically, academic psychologists conduct research in laboratory settings on the many factors that influence animal and human behavior, and control for variables or factors that are extraneous to those being investigated. Psychologists who work in academic settings typically are concerned with obtaining data that clarify human and animal behavior and lead to generalizations.

Social workers have a special concern for community problems that may lead to psychopathology (e.g., intra-family problems, unemployment, poverty, and "urban decay"). The complex social system and delivery of social services are emphasized, usually in the context of the medical model (i.e., remediation of existing problems). Major focal points in social work are (1) "social advocacy"—social program delivery and planning, (2) "clinical practice," which typically emanates from comprehensive community mental-health hospitals and centers, and (3) mental-health consultation for community organizations, families, and individuals. In the latter context, social workers often gather and interpret pertinent information about patients' personal history and social situations, thereby providing data that may assist physicians with diagnoses and treatments.

Marriage and family therapists, a more recently developed specialty, have much in common with social workers because of their interest in the family as a unit of the community. However, they tend to be occupied primarily with family psychotherapy. Many times, marriage and family therapists are members of another mental-health professional group such as social workers, psychologists, or, in some situations, counselors. A distinction, although slight, frequently is made between marriage and family therapists and marriage and family counselors. The latter are prepared by ACA programs and the former are prepared through a variety of both academic and freestanding programs. Typically, freestanding programs are offered by agencies rather than institutions of higher education.

Psychiatry frequently is confused with applied psychology because professionals in these two areas direct their interest toward the diagnosis and treatment of psychopathology. Psychiatrists, however, are medical specialists who hold a doctoral degree in medicine (M.D.), study the characteristics of people, and explore such topics as abnormal behavior, motivation, drives, and anxiety and the medical and psychological conditions that affect these dynamics. Typically, psychiatrists conduct their work in hospital settings. In sharp contrast to psychologists, psychiatrists often use psychopharmacological drugs (i.e., medications) in the treatment of psychopathological disorders. In a few federal hospitals, some psychologists, who have received special training, have the privilege to prescribe psychopharmacological drugs.

Although to distinguish completely among various mental-health professionals is impossible, differentiation on the basis of commonly held perceptions is possible. For example, mental-health problems may be conceptualized along a continuum from rather minor "adjustment problems" for otherwise normal people to "abnormal behavior" (i.e., severe psychopathology). Similarly, the "work orientations" of mental-health professionals may be conceptualized as being on a continuum from scientist with an emphasis on theory and research, to practitioner with an emphasis on affective interactions. A combination of these continua forms a quadrant system based on descriptions of the extremes. Mental-health professionals may be placed in the quadrants as illustrated in Figure 1.1. Presently, insufficient research data are available for determining which quadrant placement would be best for a given profession, but the figure may be used to convey general, relative positions of several of the professions discussed.

Illustrative Case—Keith

The approach to a given problem varies by specialty and can be explained best through an example. Consider Keith, a 27-year-old male who is struggling unsuccessfully to advance himself within a large retail firm. According to his wife, he is very nervous and becomes tense when he leaves for work. He does not concern himself with responsibilities in the home, and he annoys his wife with unprovoked verbal assaults on their six-year-old son. Keith appears unhappy at work, and his wife is unhappy about her inability to comfort him. Despite the necessary oversimplification of this example, it can be used to illustrate certain distinctions among the various mental-health specialties.

A *social worker* most likely would view Keith's presenting problem in the context of the occurrence of various factors in a population. Consideration would be given to the kind of neighborhood in which Keith resides, his income, his educational background, and whether his wife works (i.e., socioeconomic factors). Also of interest to the social worker would be elements of the couple's life-style such as possessions, what is being purchased on installment plans, club

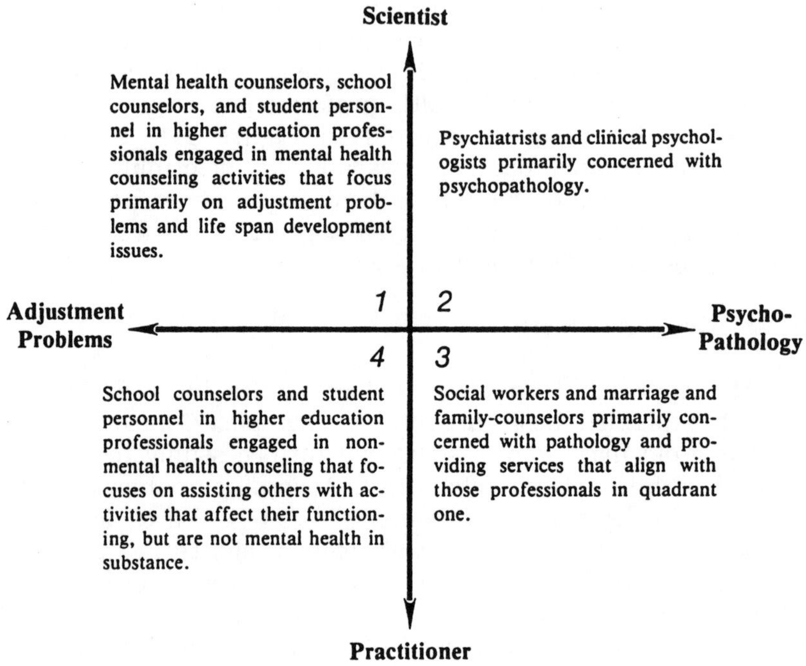

Scientist

Mental health counselors, school
counselors, and student personnel in higher education professionals engaged in mental health
counseling activities that focus
primarily on adjustment problems and life span development
issues.

Psychiatrists and clinical psychologists primarily concerned with
psychopathology.

Adjustment   *1* *2*
Problems ◄─────────────────────────────────────► Psycho-
                               4 *3*   Pathology

School counselors and student
personnel in higher education
professionals engaged in non-
mental health counseling that focuses on assisting others with activities that affect their functioning, but are not mental health in
substance.

Social workers and marriage and
family-counselors primarily concerned with pathology and providing services that align with
those professionals in quadrant
one.

Practitioner

Figure 1.1.   Mental-health service delivery continuum.

memberships, religious affiliations, childhood history, and past individual medical or psychological problems. The social worker might believe that a referral is necessary or might view the particular problem as solvable through meetings with the couple to discuss family dynamics.

Based on this information, the social worker might refer Keith to a psychiatrist and would provide the latter with a picture of generalities based on his or her knowledge of family dynamics and adult behaviors. An important role for the social worker is to contribute to the understanding of a problem by providing information about the social-psychological variables in Keith's life.

Marriage and family therapists also would consider demographic and contextual variables. However, the primary focus of their concern would be intra-family dynamics. The marriage and family therapist would arrange an interview with the couple, perhaps including the child, and would focus attention on whether their problems are with interpersonal relationships within the family or with social situations with other groups of people. The focus primarily would be on the problems of adjustment as they relate to the interpersonal relationships of the family. During therapy, the marriage and family therapist would have cogent and useful advice to offer Keith and his wife on how to improve their interpersonal relationships, based on the premise that Keith's improved interactions would be a benefit in helping his entire life.

The *psychologist* probably would interview Keith and perhaps administer a battery of psychological tests. The psychologist might view Keith's problem as hostility toward authority figures or insufficient maturation to maintain adequate control of his impulses. Keith also could be viewed as anxious because he is not achieving at an optimal level of functioning, based on self and/or others' expectations. From the psychologist's perspective, these factors may be contributing to a low level of self-esteem or valuation which creates feelings of unworthiness. This interpretation of Keith's situation is based on psychoanalytic-personality theory, although psychologists are not confined to this approach. For example, other psychologists might base their view of Keith's problem on the work of the behavioralist B.F. Skinner, using knowledge from learning theory and employing behavior modification techniques.

The **psychiatrist,** like the psychologist, initially is concerned with diagnosis. An interview with Keith would be arranged and information from significant others in Keith's life more than likely would be requested. For example, demographic information and family history, including family interactions and past occurrences of problems, could be gained from a social worker, and a psychologist could provide results of clinical psychological tests. A psychiatrist mainly would be interested in determining causes of or reasons for Keith's behavior, at the very least, gaining a good understanding of the symptoms in order that appropriate treatment could be prescribed. The treatment might be medication to reduce the anxiety and general impulsive behavior, or therapy with the psychiatrist or, more typically, with a social worker.

A **professional mental-health** or **community counselor** working with Keith would consider the same data as other mental-health service providers but would apply the data to life-span development (i.e., vocation, career, family, child-rearing, interpersonal and intragroup relationships, and the person's context of a quality life). These professional counselors would recognize the type of environment in which Keith is employed and the values associated with it. Like social workers and marriage and family therapists, professional mental-health counselors would try to understand family dynamics. However, they might depart from the procedures of the other mental-health professionals by deciding jointly with Keith to administer a battery of psychological, interest, and educational tests if insufficient information existed following interviews with Keith. The professional mental-health counselor might conclude that Keith and his wife could benefit from joint counseling or that there is a need for a referral because of the severe degree of pathology present with Keith. Whether or not a referral is made, a professional mental-health or community counselor would conduct counseling sessions with Keith to help him formulate an appropriate plan of action (i.e., appropriate referral for specific assistance or continued counseling).

In sharp contrast to the other specialists, the **professional school counselor's** involvement with Keith and his family would begin with the son. The assumption is made that the family dynamics have affected a change in the child's behavior (e.g., the child is exhibiting learning difficulty or acting-out behavior in school) and that his teacher has sought help from the school counselor. Because the focus of concern is on the child's behavioral changes, the school counselor must work closely with the teacher in order to help the child. The school counselor utilizes the same data as that considered by the mental-health or community counselor except the data are applied to the school situation. A school counselor tries to understand the student based on (1) the child's perspective, (2) prior knowledge of school experiences and teachers interactions with this child, (3) observations of the child in the classroom, (4) interviews with the child, and (5) data contained in the child's cumulative school file. Included in the latter is information concerning achievement and intelligence test data, family background, academic performance, and previous teachers' comments. However, if insufficient information is available, the school counselor subsequently may decide that an interview with the parents could be beneficial. In this situation, interviewing Keith and his wife might aid the school counselor in determining that (1) the "core" problem of the child's school learning and/or overt-behavior problems is due to interpersonal problems at home; and (2) the parents could benefit from counseling. The school counselor would focus primarily on improving the child's behavior and performance in school but also would help the child to cope with problems at home.

Of course, many overlapping areas are addressed by mental-health service providers, and the illustrations and distinctions cited above are not as clear-cut as described. For example, social workers and marriage and family therapists may be knowledgeable of and have skills in career development and testing, and some professional counselors may function as psychologists. However, what professional counselors have in common are (1) knowledge and skills in human growth and development, social and behavioral sciences (especially psychology), helping relations, group interactions, assessment and appraisal, and research methodology; and (2) a profound respect for the scientific approach.

ASSUMPTIONS FOR PROFESSIONAL COUNSELORS

The counseling profession is based on certain assumptions, some of which are definitive and fully agreed upon by professional counselors. Others, however, are implicit; they are not specifically stated or readily acknowledged and, in many instances, not clearly perceived. Two factors that most professional counselors view as important to successful practice are a counselor's (1) knowledge and skills in professional counseling and (2) personality. Without useful knowledge, a professional counselor is unable to practice effectively. Likewise, in order to practice, a professional counselor needs to be able to respond to clients in ways that promote their willingness to profit from the counselor's efforts. Relatedly, a professional counselor must exhibit personality characteristics that allow clients to be receptive to the counselor's efforts.

Knowledge and Skills

A professional counselor needs to be knowledgeable of those aspects of mental health that relate to the development, relief, and solution of an individual's emotional or career concerns which are associated with quality of life. In addition, the professional counselor must be aware of the effect biological and environmental influences may have upon an individual's behavior. Knowledge and skill development should include preparation in the following eight areas:

1. human growth and development;
2. social and cultural foundations;
3. the helping relationship;
4. group dynamics, processes, and counseling;

5. life style and career development;
6. appraisal of the individual;
7. research and evaluation; and
8. professional orientation.

These are the "core" areas recognized by the Council for Accreditation of Counseling and Related Educational Programs (CACREP) and have been found by faculty in counselor training programs to be highly relevant to preparing counselors (Vacc, 1992).

Human Growth and Development. This area involves an understanding of the nature and needs of individuals at all age levels. Included are studies in human behavior, personality theory, and learning theory. The focus of human growth and development permits the professional counselor an opportunity to gain an understanding of how psychological, sociological, and physiological factors influence behavior at all developmental levels.

Social and Cultural Foundations. Study in this area focuses on ethnic groups, subcultures, gender issues including changing roles of men and women, urban and rural societies, population patterns, cultural mores, use of leisure time, and differing life patterns. Knowledge of traditional disciplines such as the behavioral sciences, economics, and political science is emphasized.

The Helping Relationship. This area is comprised of counseling and consultation theory, development of self-awareness, and an understanding of how and why clients do what they do. Development of helping relationship skills for the successful practice of counseling is emphasized.

Group Dynamics, Processes, and Counseling. Included in this area are theories of group behavior, group practices, methods for working with groups, group dynamics, and observational and facilitative skills.

Life-style and Career Development. The study of life-style and career development encompasses vocational-choice theories, the relationship between career choice and life-style, sources of occupational and educational information, approaches to career decision-making processes, and approaches to career exploration. The intent is to enable the professional counselor to be of assistance to clients in their personal, social, emotional, and vocational choices and/or with the activities in their daily living.

Appraisal of the Individual. The particular knowledge, skills, and experiences necessary to enable a professional counselor to gather information to use in making judgments about clients and environmental settings comprise this area. Included are methods for gathering and interpreting data (i.e., use of tests), individual and group testing, observation techniques, and general skills necessary for the assessment and appraisal of individuals' behaviors.

Research and Evaluation. Effective functioning as a professional counselor necessitates a knowledge base in the areas of statistics, research design, and development of research and demonstration proposals. Professional counseling practitioners, regardless of specialty, must be able to contribute to the body of literature in the profession through research.

Professional Orientation. This area includes knowledge of the basic components of the counseling profession (i.e., professional organizations, codes of ethics, legal considerations, standards of preparation, certification, and licensing). In addition, the role identity of the professional counselor and other human-service specialists is explored.

Personality

Even the most knowledgeable and well-trained professional counselor will be unable to help others if certain personality characteristics are not evident, thus causing clients to be unreceptive to the professional counselor's behaviors. Although the qualities of personality that promote effective counseling are nebulous, researchers have identified several personality characteristics that are important in promoting a productive counselor-client relationship. Three essential characteristics are security, trust, and courage (Belkin, 1984).

Security. Prerequisites to security are self-confidence, self-respect, and freedom from fear and anxiety. Anxiety is associated with the diminished ability to attend to the client during an interview (Milliken & Kirchner, 1971). Secure counselors feel comfortable about themselves and therefore provide healthy models for their clients. The professional counselor who is suspicious and who questions everyone's motives is unlikely to be of help to others.

As a personal quality, a secure counselor is more likely to allow clients to be themselves. Counselors who are comfortable with themselves do not seek to satisfy their own needs by "shaping the client in their own image." They have the capability to allow clients to develop at their own rate and in their own direction.

Trust. Trust, in its most elementary form, is to be able to give, receive, and depend on others, a quality that is highly important in determining the professional counselor's attitude toward people. According to Belkin (1984), trust, which develops during the early stages of life, is difficult to learn if not acquired when young. In counseling, the absence of trust may cause a counselor to act in ways that do not benefit clients.

Courage. All human beings appear to have an innate desire to be loved, recognized, and respected. Within the context of counseling, however, professional counselors must be able to put aside their own need for gratification. For example, the professional counselor must be willing to absorb a client's anger or to accept a sense of "aloneness" as the client progresses and becomes autonomous from the counselor. Analogous to professional counselors working with clients is parents allowing their growing children to mature and develop. During a counseling relationship, the client initially (1) relies upon the counselor, (2) shares personal thoughts, aspirations, and behaviors that are rarely made public; and (3) seeks direction and order in his or her life. Subsequently, counselors must be emotionally capable of relinquishing their clients' dependency and allowing them to gain control of their own lives.

In summary, professional counselors need to have enough self-security, self-trust, and courage to relinquish a part of themselves when helping others.

In addition, Bardon and Bennett (1974) found that particular personality qualities affect helping professionals' behavior when making judgments about their clients. They suggested that professionals working with clients need to possess personality qualities that include genuineness, positive skepticism, and empathy.

Genuineness. As Truax and Carkhuff (1967) indicated, genuineness involves a concern for what happens to people. To understand the importance of this quality, reflect upon the role professional counselors play in the lives of their clients. Counselors are empowered to tell others what to do and they have great authority because they are viewed as experts. Such power in relationships with their clients only can be regulated or controlled by a sincere and overriding concern for the welfare of others, a value that is integral to preventing potential misuse of authority.

Positive Skepticism. Another important personality quality is an attitude of positive skepticism. Skepticism, as viewed by Bardon and Bennett (1974), reflects an understanding of the imperfections of the current state of knowledge, instrumentation, and methods. Unfortunately, professional counselors often have to act without the security offered by the exactness available in other disciplines (e.g., the "hard sciences"). However, because of the nature of their involvement with real-life situations that require assistance and because better alternatives typically are unavailable, professional counselors must act. A cautious, skeptical, and yet critical approach that makes use of past successes and failures must be an abiding value of professional counselors when assisting clients. The adjective "positive" has been included to suggest that skepticism should be linked with a willingness to persist and try new approaches. This is most important because professional counselors may encounter personal disappointments, a lack of immediate results, and uncooperative clients. Therefore, an optimistic outlook, despite discouraging encounters, is required.

Empathy. Empathy is the ability to identify with others (Truax & Carkhuff, 1967). Professional counselors on many occasions work with people whose values and life experiences are very different from their own. Also, clients often enter a counseling relationship being extremely antagonistic toward the counselor; the counselor is perceived as "threatening" and reflective of the troublesome social system that most likely prompted their seeking assistance. To function well can be difficult when people are hostile, angry, and negative. Professional counselors, however, need to develop an understanding of how their clients feel and must be able to respect those feelings even when they appear to be making the counselor's job difficult.

Although the personality qualities presented above are neither explicit nor inclusive, they are highly important in determining how the professional counselor functions. Perhaps personality qualities are more reflective of the attitude professional counselors need to take toward the nature of their work than is knowledge. Knowledge, of course, is the base upon which the practice of counseling is built, but it is ultimately more useful for professional counselors to approach problems regarding human behavior when they possess the various personality variables suggested by Belkin (1984), Bardon and Bennett (1974), and Truax and Carkhuff (1967).

The Counselor as Scientist

A final assumption about professional counselors, the *sine qua non*, is that the professional counselor is a scientist, a view that is consistent with the earlier assumption of positive skepticism as a desirable characteristic of the professional counselor. If behavior can be altered and individuals are capable of making changes as a result of the counseling relationship and process, then professional counselors must observe the effects of their procedures as they affect clients by carefully measuring and evaluating change. Professional counselors continuously are being confronted with measuring the effects of their counseling in order to derive specific conclusions. Therefore, a scientific aspect is essential in the practice of counseling.

The practitioner as scientist has been described by Barlow, Hayes, and Nelson (1984) as involving three interrelated activities or roles. First, the practitioner is a consumer of research findings that are reported in professional journals and at professional meetings. The information gained involves either new or reexamined assessments of approaches which the practitioner puts into practice. In the second role, the practitioner is an evaluator and appraiser of approaches that use empirical methods which would increase effectiveness and accountability. Finally, the practitioner is a researcher who produces and analyzes data and who reports these data to the scientific community at professional meetings and in professional journals.

Conceptually, the research basis for practice or professional activities and judgments of counselors is illustrated in Figure 1.2. A majority of what is known about human behavior is derived from research in the social and behavioral sciences, much of which is conducted under circumstances that are less than ideal. With numerous replications, however, the scientific credibility of research findings is enhanced and enables the scientist to draw conclusions. When professional counselors try to determine something about a client's behavior, they must take into account many factors or variables, some of which cannot be ignored, such as developmental level, age, gender, situational events, attitudes, personality, personal habits, and cultural considerations. Literally, the professional counselor is confronted with an almost limitless number of confounding variables when counseling.

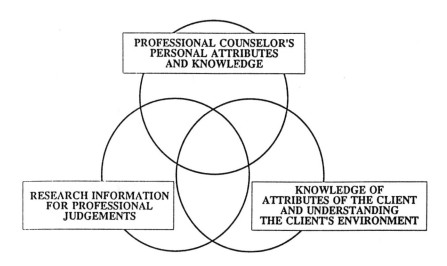

Professional counselor's personal attributes and knowledge

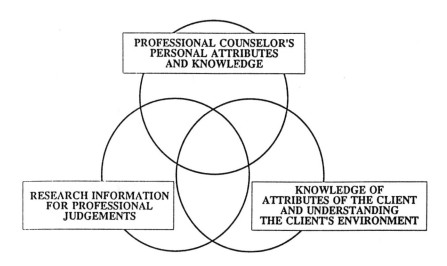

PROFESSIONAL COUNSELOR'S
PERSONAL ATTRIBUTES
AND KNOWLEDGE

RESEARCH INFORMATION
FOR PROFESSIONAL
JUDGEMENTS

KNOWLEDGE OF
ATTRIBUTES OF THE CLIENT
AND UNDERSTANDING
THE CLIENT'S ENVIRONMENT

Figure 1.2. The influence of research and practice as they affect the outcomes of a professional counselor working with clients.

Illustrative Case—John. To illustrate, consider John, an adolescent whose behavior alienates others because it is offensive. To understand John and to help him alter his inappropriate behavior, the professional counselor must understand (1) what is known about adolescent behavior; (2) how behavior is changed; (3) how John perceives his interactions with others, reactions to him, and aspects of his life; and (4) other special problems that John brings to interpersonal relationships. The professional counselor, working with John, must help by using two resources at once. One resource is the existing accumulated data that have been derived by other practitioner-scientists as established, accumulated laws or rules for people in general. The other resource is existing data that are specific to John, his behaviors, and his life situation. The first resource is termed *nomothetic,* which pertains to general laws and principles, while the second resource is termed *idiographic,* or that which is characterized as individual laws of behavior in order to explain individual cases.

THE PROFESSIONAL COUNSELOR AS PRACTITIONER-SCIENTIST

Professional counselors, to be most effective in helping individuals, must integrate information, reconcile differences, and view themselves as scientists. All evidence needs to be considered and evaluated and a decision derived through distillation of all available knowledge, information, and experiences. As a practitioner-scientist, the professional counselor is engaged in a very real sense in a scientific experiment in which questions are raised and examined, and results and conclusions are changed as new evidence becomes available. Counseling involves a series of formative evaluations and action plans. When professional counselors take a course of action or discuss what is happening during counseling, they must judge the probability of the validity of change in the client's behavior against the data.

To understand how a competent professional counselor practices, it is necessary to recognize that practice is scientific; it takes place when knowledge, both nomothetic and idiographic, is filtered by a professional counselor. Competent professional practice is also the interaction between the professional counselor and knowledge in a setting, an interaction designed to foster helpful behavior. Ultimately, professional counselors are only as useful or as valuable as the amount of knowledge they have gained. This book is dedicated to the assumption that *the content of counseling is never removed from scientific methods.*

In addition to knowledge and techniques, effective counselors must have skills in scientific inquiry, not only to enable counselors to be fully functioning professionals, but to establish counselors as self-regulating professionals. This viewpoint is neither original nor new; the scientist-professional model has long been used by counselor preparation programs approved by the American Psychological Association (APA) (Hock, Ross, & Winder, 1966).

Adoption of the APA training procedures is not being suggested for professional counselors, but the practitioner-scientist viewpoint, as opposed to the scientist-practitioner approach, makes considerable sense for the future of professional counseling. Moreover, this viewpoint is consistent with the existing *Ethical Standards of the American Counseling Association* (ACA, 1988). These Standards state that counselors must gather data on their effectiveness and use the findings to guide them in the counseling process. The spirit of scientific inquiry, therefore, must pervade the perspectives of professional counselors, with the manifestation of the spirit being the common rule rather than the exception.

Inherent in the practitioner-scientist approach is viewing scientific inquiry in counseling from a much broader perspective than has been characteristic in the past. As mentioned earlier, the core of this view is the professional counselor's development of a habitually inquiring, critical attitude about practice. Thus, scientific methods are equated with inquiry as well as traditional methods of normative data gathering. This means that professional counselors continually must engage in careful, scientific review of all their activities. Common to both scientific inquiry and practice is the necessity for a questioning attitude, a method of problem solving, a high regard for evidence, and methods for self-monitoring and improvement. The practitioner-scientist approach, then, is more than just data gathering and analysis; it is a way of approaching all professional activities.

The distinctive feature of the practitioner-scientist approach is the need for professional counselors to have competent training in knowledge and techniques associated with counseling and research methods. Being a professional counselor, therefore, means being competent in facilitating science as well as human development. Although a major part of a professional counselor's time is spent in practice or direct service, a part of the direct service must be devoted to the improvement of and subsequent changes in services as determined through scientific inquiry. An important element of the practitioner-scientist approach is that it encourages professional counselors to examine and compare client behaviors for decisions about counseling goals, intervention strategies, and effectiveness of the counseling process. The approach guides the professional counselor to promote sensitive counseling that is suited uniquely to each client. Many people view the scientific approach as a "one-time" activity. However, counseling and data gathering are continuous processes throughout a relationship with a client; they are activities that, in fact, establish direction for the counseling process. The scientific approach is a means for obtaining and using information to generate and establish counseling goals and intervention strategies and to determine the effectiveness of counseling.

The focus of this ongoing process is not to find the "truth" for working with people but, rather, to use information in a way that helps clients develop. In this respect, the professional counselor can be viewed as an experimenter who continually is assessing and conceptualizing the relationships among the information obtained, counseling goals, and counseling approach. The effectiveness of the professional counselor, therefore, is maintained by the counselor's ability to gather data in a scientific manner and to use it for making ongoing modifications to the counseling process. Without the scientific component, the counseling process becomes merely an "act of faith."

SUMMARY

Professional counselors apply knowledge, skills and techniques derived from the areas of human growth and development, the social and behavioral sciences, and from counselor education. In addition to professional counselors, there are many types of mental-health professionals (e.g., applied psychologists and social workers) who work in many settings such as private practice, community agencies, and higher education. However, as members of a group of mental-health professionals, counselors distinguish themselves by the applied nature of their work. Further differentiation among the many mental-health professionals can be made on the basis of commonly held perceptions with regard to mental-health problems. These can be conceptualized along a continuum from adjustment problems to abnormal behavior. In addition, differentiation can be made between mental-health professionals regarding work orientations that range from scientist to practitioner.

The counseling profession is based on a number of assumptions. To be successful, counselors must possess certain essential personal characteristics such as security, trust, and courage. Relatedly, counselors also are assumed to have mastered a body of knowledge and skills. Finally, the professional counselor is a scientist. This role is important, because counselors are required to evaluate the effects of their counseling and to read as well as produce research findings published in professional journals. Counseling as a profession, then, encompasses a diverse number of settings and involves basic assumptions about what is required to be successful.

Chapter **2**

EVOLUTION OF THE COUNSELING PROFESSION

To characterize fully the history of an entity as nebulous as a profession is impossible. However, some understanding of the history of the counseling profession is necessary if its current status and future are to be understood effectively. Although heritage is not destiny, destiny is in part contingent upon heritage. The question is, how can the history of a profession be explained? One possibility, and the one of choice here, is to review the history of an organization that has long served as a representative of a profession. In the current context, the American Counseling Association (ACA) (formerly the American Association for Counseling and Development [AACD] prior to 1992, and the American Personnel and Guidance Association [APGA] prior to 1983) is such an organization.

Counseling professionals who view themselves solely as "psychotherapists" might suggest that the history of the counseling profession dates to Sigmund Freud, if not farther back to the earliest "psychological healers." However, that view is parochial and inconsistent with the perspective of the counseling profession taken in this book. More typically, the history of the counseling profession traces its beginnings to approximately the turn of the twentieth century. That was when education professionals began to realize that young people in society needed help in making effective vocational decisions. The visionary efforts of professionals such as Frank Parsons and Mrs. Quincy Adams Shaw were particularly notable. In brief, they and their colleagues began a series of significant activities designed to enable teachers to help students with vocational planning and decision remaking. The significance was twofold. One, the activities marked the first attempt at formally providing psychologically-based services for "normal" people (i.e., the use of "psychological" services for persons without severe mental illness). Two, through the Vocational Bureau of Boston, they sought to train a "new" professional with the title "Teacher-Counselor" (Smith, Engels, & Bonk, 1985). Thus, they associated the title "counselor" with the provision of helping or counseling services for people who were not suffering from serious psychological disturbance.

As interest and activities in "vocational counseling" grew during the early 1900s, those involved soon recognized that a national organization would be beneficial to those sharing a common professional interest. Therefore, the National Vocational Guidance Association (NVGA) was formed in 1913, primarily as a result of the efforts of Jesse B. Davis who served as the first NVGA Secretary. NVGA retained its original name until 1985 when it became the National Career Development Association (NCDA).

Other professionals did not lag far behind those interested in vocational counseling in deciding that "normal" people had needs other than for educational or psychotherapeutic assistance. For example, the needs of students on college and university campuses, and those of the professionals who addressed college students' needs, were recognized in the second decade of the twentieth century. Thus, the National Association of Deans of Women (NADW) was formed in 1913. Soon after, the National Association of Student Personnel Administrators (NASPA) was formed in 1916. At about the same time, college and university placement officers, then called "appointment secretaries," determined that their particular professional needs and interests were not being met effectively by NVGA and that their work represented a broader professional perspective than that reflected in either NADW or NASPA (Johnson, 1985). Therefore, they established the National Association of Appointment Secretaries (NAAS) in 1924. NAAS continued to broaden its professional scope, eventually evolving into the National Association of Placement and Personnel Officers (NAPPO) in 1929 and the American College Personnel Association (ACPA) in 1931. In the late 1980s, the duality of ACPA's interests (i.e., student personnel/development administration and counseling) prompted division within the organization. Thus, the American College Counseling Association (ACCA) was formed in 1992 for those interested in counseling activities for college students.

The historical association between counseling and education also has been reflected in other ways. For example, the Teachers College Personnel Association (TCPA) was established in 1931, with the intent of focusing on testing and research activities. This focus, however, was not agreed upon unanimously within the organization, and TCPA existed both as a separate organization and as an affiliate division of the American Association for Colleges of Teacher Education (AACTE) during its first 20 years. In 1951, TCPA changed its name to the Student Personnel Association for Teacher Education (SPATE). One year later it separated from AACTE. In 1974, SPATE restructured its professional perspective and became the Association for Humanistic Education and Development (AHEAD) (Wilson & Robinson, 1985).

The value of professional preparation and supervision also has been evident throughout the history of the counseling profession. This importance was first formally recognized with the founding of the National Association of Guidance Supervisors (NAGS) in 1940. Although NAGS originally was composed exclusively of counselor supervisors, it soon attracted counselor trainers. Thus, in 1952 the name was changed to the National Association of Guidance Supervisors and Counselor Trainers (NAGSCT). Nine years later, NAGSCT changed its name to the Association for Counselor Education and Supervision (ACES).

"Strength through unity" was a common theme in the United States in the early 1950s, and this theme was reflected in the relationships among the various organizations with interests in the counseling professions. Thus, NVGA (now NCDA), ACPA (now ACCA), NAGSCT (now ACES), and SPATE (now AHEAD) joined together in 1952 to form the American Personnel and Guidance Association (now ACA). Herr (1985) aptly summarized the nature of this founding:

> The intent of these four associations was to create a unified structure that would have the collective strength to pursue goals impossible to achieve for smaller, special interest groups, as were the founding divisions at the time.

> In creating the confederation known as the American Personnel and Guidance Association, however, it was apparent that the founders were not ready to completely surrender the autonomy of their individual associations . . . . They sought common cause within the larger association umbrella, but did so with an intent to retain the capability to advance the special interests of their divisions. (p.396)

The "common bond but individual identity" theme remained evident as APGA (ACA) grew in terms of both members and divisions.

Vocational guidance continued as the major focus of "counseling" services in American schools for approximately four decades prior to World War II. However, the post World War II era fostered an awareness that "traditional" vocational counseling services were not the most appropriate for a growing segment of the school population: students planning to attend college. During the late 1940s, therefore, a large number of school counselors turned their attention to college-bound students. This schism in the professional focus of counselors working in schools prompted the need for a professional organization better suited to counselors who were less oriented to vocational counseling in schools. The result was the formation in 1953 of the fifth APGA (ACA) division, the American School Counselor Association (ASCA) (Minkoff & Terres, 1985). ASCA soon became, and remains today, the ACA division having the largest membership.

Recognition of the counseling needs of persons with disabilities also increased in the post World War II era and incited the passage of the (Federal) Vocational Rehabilitation Act (VRA) in 1954. The VRA not only symbolized the importance of the needs of persons with disabilities but also provided funds for training counselors to assist with those needs. At about the same time, a growing number of members within APGA (ACA) were becoming involved in rehabilitation counseling activities. These factors melded together during the early 1950s and led to the formation of the Division of Rehabilitation Counseling (DRC) within APGA (ACA) in 1958. In 1962, the DRC became the American Rehabilitation Counseling Association (ARCA) (DiMichael & Thomas, 1985). Although what might be referred to as a "subliminal affection for empiricism" had long been present in the APGA (ACA) membership, it did not emerge fully until the mid-1960s. A number of professionals, most of whom were already APGA (ACA) members, then moved to form a division specifically for professionals with interests in measurement and evaluation. Their efforts resulted in the 1965 origination of the Association for Measurement and Evaluation in Guidance (AMEG), the seventh APGA (ACA) division. However, formal incorporation of this division did not occur until 1968 (Sheeley & Eberly, 1985). In 1984 AMEG changed its name to the Association for Measurement and Evaluation in Counseling and Development (AMECD) to be consistent with the name change of the parent organization. In 1992, AMECD changed its name to the Association for Assessment in Counseling (AAC) to reflect more accurately its place in the counseling profession.

The recurrent vocational counseling emphasis in APGA (ACA) reemerged with a new focus in 1966 with the formation of the National Employment Counselors Association (NECA). The new focus was on employment counseling as a specialty area within the more general field of vocational counseling. Similar to AAC (AMEG; AMECD), most of the original members of NECA were already members of other existing APGA (ACA) divisions (Meyer, Helwig, Gjernes, & Chickering, 1985). In 1992, the organizational name was changed slightly to the National Employment Counseling Association (NECA) to be consistent with the name change of the parent organization (i.e., ACA).

The late 1960s and the early 1970s were times of "social consciousness raising" in the American society, and APGA (ACA) was not untouched by this movement. A large number of professionals within the association believed a need existed to recognize specifically the needs and talents of ethnic minority persons. However, opinions differed considerably about how the recognition should be manifested within a professional organization. Eventually, in 1972, the disparate ideas came together in the formation of the Association for Non-White Concerns in Personnel and Guidance (ANWC) (McFadden & Lipscomb, 1985). ANWC changed its name in 1985 to the Association for Multicultural Counseling and Development (AMCD) in order to reflect more accurately the prevalent orientation in APGA (ACA).

Although the Association for Religious and Value Issues in Counseling (ARVIC) traces its history in APGA (ACA) to 1973, the seminal activities for the division began in 1951 with the formation of the Catholic Guidance Council in the Archdiocese of New York (Bartlett, Lee, & Doyle, 1985). That beginning lead to the 1961 formation of the National Catholic Guidance Conference (NCGC) by members of APGA (ACA). The evolution from NCGC to ARVIC reflected change in the nature and purposes of the division. Bartlett, Lee, and Doyle (1985) stated:

> As an organization, ARVIC has experienced a metamorphosis. It no longer attempts to serve solely as a Catholic professional organization; rather, it attempts to fill a void within the AACD structure by providing a forum for the examination of religious and values issues in counseling. (p. 449)

Throughout most of the early history of the counseling profession, the emphasis was on "one-to-one" counseling interaction between counselor and client. However, maturation of the profession brought with it a realization that group counseling and other professional work with groups is not only effective but also economical and efficient. This realization prompted APGA (ACA) professionals who were interested in all facets of group dynamics and processes (including counseling) to form the Association for Specialists in Group Work (ASGW). It became an APGA (ACA) division in 1973 (Carroll & Levo, 1985).

A unique example of the counseling profession's responsiveness to the multifaceted needs of society is found in the Public Offender Counselor Association (POCA), which officially became an APGA (ACA) division in 1974. POCA was created to be responsive to the specific professional needs and interests of counselors who work with public offenders (Page, 1985). In the 1980s, interest grew among POCA members to broaden its focus and purposes, and, therefore, POCA became the International Association of Addictions and Offenders Counselors (IAAOC) in 1990.

The rapid growth of the American Mental Health Counselors Association (AMHCA), which officially became an APGA (ACA) division in 1978, perhaps knows no equal in the history of professional organizations. From its beginnings in 1976, AMHCA expanded exceptionally rapidly in the early 1980s, at one point having the largest divisional membership in ACA (Weikel, 1985), and it is now the second largest ACA division. AMHCA's growth reflected the fact that a considerable number of professional counselors now work in other than educational settings.

The Military Educators and Counselors Association (MECA), although not a formally recognized ACA division, was formed as an organizational affiliate of ACA in 1984. MECA was created to be responsive to the professional needs and interests of counselors who work with military service personnel and veterans, their dependents, and civilian employees of the military services (Cox, 1985).

The "graying of America" was, and is, a phenomenon that substantially impacted professional counselors as they increasingly worked with older persons. Greater attention to the counseling needs of and services for older persons was accompanied by recognition of the need to attend to the circumstances and needs of adults of all ages. Thus, the Association for Adult Development and Aging (AADA), formed as an AACD (ACA) division in 1986, is comprised of members who have as their primary professional interest counseling persons at all stages of adult development. However, the greatest emphases are given to mid-life, pre-retirement, and gerontological counseling specializations.

Concerns about the "demise of the traditional American family" have been voiced for several decades, and those concerns have not gone unnoticed by professional counselors. Commencing in the early 1980s, provision of marriage and family counseling services has become a major movement in the counseling profession. This professional movement became formalized within AACD (ACA) in 1989 with the formation of the International Association of Marriage and Family Counselors (IAMFC). While professional counselors in this group focus on the nuclear family, their interests and counseling services extend to marital and sibling problems, family subsystems, external societal influences affecting family systems, and other factors that may cause difficulties for and within families.

In 1983, APGA changed its name to the American Association for Counseling and Development (AACD). The change was symbolic of the evolving professional orientation among AACD (ACA) members, and indeed within the counseling profession. As Herr (1985) stated:

> . . .the overriding issue was that the term guidance was essentially used only in elementary and secondary school settings and was becoming an archaic and vague term even there. Although such a perception of the term guidance is questionable, the primary argument for the name change was that association members were increasingly being found in settings other than education and that what these persons did was *counseling*, not *guidance*. (p. 395)

However, the desire for clarity of professional definition did not end in 1983. Members of ACPA involved with student personnel/development administration activities increasingly became disenchanted with the counseling emphasis in AACD in the 1980s and moved to withdraw from the parent organization in the late 1980s. Consequently, the withdrawal of ACPA from AACD, the formation of ACCA, and the change of name from AACD to the American Counseling Association (ACA) became official in July, 1992. Dr. Ted Remley, ACA Executive Director, hailed the name change in stating:

> This is significant, particularly as it relates to the public outside of the profession. The new name is easy to remember and more narrowly focused and descriptive of what our members do. It also more clearly defines which profession the association represents. (quoted in Sacks, 1992, p. 10)

The evolving history of APGA to AACD to ACA thus exemplifies the broadening scope of the counseling profession as well as the continuing quest among professional counselors for distinct identity within the helping professions. In 1992, ACA membership exceeded 57,000 and continues to grow steadily. Literally every facet of the counseling professions and all types of professional counselors are represented within it. The 1992 ACA divisions, ordered by original organizational founding date, are as follows:

1952   Association for Humanistic Education and Development (AHEAD),

1953   American College Counseling Association (ACCA),

1953   Association for Counselor Education and Supervision (ACES),

1953   National Career Development Association (NCDA),

1953   American School Counselor Association (ASCA),

1958   American Rehabilitation Counseling Association (ARCA),

1965   Association for Assessment in Counseling (AAC),

1966   National Employment Counseling Association (NECA),

1972   Association for Multicultural Counseling and Development (AMCD),

1974   Association for Religious and Value Issues in Counseling (ARVIC),

1974   Association for Specialists in Group Work (ASGW),

1974   International Association for Addictions and Offender Counselors (IAAOC),

1978   American Mental Health Counselors Association (AMHCA),

1984   Military Educators and Counselors Association (MECA; an organizational affiliate),

1986   Association for Adult Development and Aging (AADA), and

1989   International Association of Marriage and Family Counselors (IAMFC).

LESSONS FROM HISTORY

Clearly the history of ACA is not a complete history of the counseling profession. Nonetheless, a professional organization, because it is composed of members of a profession, reflects the issues and trends within the profession represented by the organization. Therefore, a number of inferences about the counseling profession can be drawn from the history of ACA. And as Oliver Wendell Holmes, Jr. noted, "A page of history is worth a volume of logic."

Lesson 1: Professional counselors are identifiable and unique.

Unfortunately for professionals who refer to themselves as counselors, the title "counselor" has been used in a wide variety of contexts in the American society. The media are replete with "legal counselors," "real estate counselors," "financial counselors," "travel counselors," and the like. Overexposure to the title counselor has served to desensitize the public to the title in general, and to its application to a type of mental health professional in particular. However, regardless of the overuse of the title, a group of professionals exists who may be referred to accurately and validly as counselors. The application of the title is more than "self-anointment" by those who refer to themselves as counselors. By 1992, 32 states had licensure (or similar credentialing) laws for "professional counselors" (or corresponding titles that include the word counselor). Thus, the use of the title *professional counselor* to refer to a particular type of mental health professional is, and continues to be, grounded in law. Relatedly, although this specific use of the term *counselor* has not yet become commonly understood by the general public, such understanding is rapidly increasing.

Professional counselors also are uniquely identifiable within the counseling profession. Of course, there exists a variety of different types of professionals who do "counseling" (e.g., clinical and counseling psychologists, clinical social workers, psychoanalysts, marriage and family therapists, and psychiatrists). However, professional counselors are not "mini-psychologists," "closet psychoanalysts," "imitation social workers," or "pseudo-shrinks." Nor are they people who only give advice, tell students what courses to take, or tell people which jobs to pursue. They are, simply, professionals whose primary vocational activity is the provision of counseling and closely related mental-health services.

Lesson 2: Counseling professionals may be differentiated in a variety of ways.

Why is differentiation necessary or appropriate? An effective answer must encompass two components, one theoretical and one pragmatic. With regard to the former, there are those in the counseling profession who have alleged that "counseling is counseling is counseling" regardless of the natures of the persons receiving the counseling services, persons providing the services, locations of services, and how or with which set of techniques the services are being provided. This perspective belies the complexities of people in society and in the counseling profession, as well as the widely varying places and circumstances in which counseling services are rendered. In an "age of specialization," the needs for and benefits of specialization within the counseling profession are readily evident. To suggest that counseling is "an" activity that is applicable regardless of clientele, location, or type of service provider is to deny the effectiveness gained from years of research and development of specialized counseling activities.

With regard to the second component, the simple fact of the matter is that counseling professionals work in relatively easily differentiated settings (e.g., educational systems or institutions, private practice, business and industry, or community agencies) and/or with relatively easily differentiated clients (e.g., students, persons with disabilities, or couples and families). What follows then is that professional counselors can maximize their effectiveness by developing specialized skills specifically applicable in the settings in which they work and/or to the clients with whom they work.

Thus, to differentiate among counseling professionals is prudent both for the public and for counseling professionals because it facilitates effectiveness and efficiency in counseling service delivery. There are several ways to make the differentiations. One would be on the basis of title, as presented in Chapter 1. Others are on the basis of type of setting in which counseling services are provided, type of counseling service provided, or type of primary professional interests and activities. By relating this to the ACA history presented previously, it can be noted that the various ACA divisions also may be clustered along three dimensions. For example, ASCA and ACCA clearly relate to particular settings. Similarly, ARCA, NCDA, NECA, ASGW, IAAOC, AMHCA, MECA, and IAMFC relate to types of counseling service, while ACES, AHEAD, AAC, AADA, AMCD, and ARVIC relate to primary professional interests and activities.

Unfortunately, neither these three differentiation bases nor the ACA divisional titles listed are sufficient to differentiate completely among counseling professionals because complete differentiation actually is not possible. For example, school counselors quite obviously engage in and are concerned with vocational counseling and working with people of varying ethnicities. Similarly, other professional counselors are involved with and concerned about matters and activities beyond their *primary* professional activities. Thus, professional counselors tend to be multifaceted in terms of professional concerns and involvements. Nonetheless, to differentiate among them often is expedient for purposes of communication clarity.

Lesson 3: Professional counselors fulfill societal needs not fulfilled by other professionals.

One example of the validity of this statement is reflected in the membership of POCA (now IAAOC). Page (1985) stated that, "POCA is unique because it emphasizes the importance of providing counseling services to public offenders . . . . Other professional associations such as the American Correctional Association place emphasis on correctional concerns rather than on rehabilitation concerns" (p. 455). Other examples are also readily available. School counselors, as represented by ASCA, are the primary (and in many cases the only) providers of mental-health services to students in schools. Similarly, employment counselors, as represented by NECA, are the primary (and again in many cases the only) providers of counseling assistance in governmental employment agencies. And finally, rehabilitation counselors, as represented by ARCA, are the primary providers of counseling services to persons with disabilities.

Lesson 4: Professional counselors fulfill societal needs also being fulfilled by other professionals.

The provision of many counseling services is not restricted to professional counselors. For example, marriage and family counseling services are provided by marriage and family counselors, as represented by IAMFC, but are also provided by professionals such as social workers, counseling and clinical psychologists, mental-health counselors, and marriage and family therapists. Similarly, ACCA members provide counseling services to college and university students, but so do other professionals such as counseling and clinical psychologists, and psychiatrists. Thus, many of the professional activities performed by professional counselors also are offered by other professionals (as was shown in *Illustrative Case—Keith* presented in Chapter 1). This overlap helps to associate and involve counselors with other professional specializations and allows them to benefit from the knowledge gained from the work experiences and research of other professionals.

Lesson 5: The counseling profession reflects needs and trends in society.

The beginning of the counseling profession, vis-a-vis the earliest vocational counseling activities, is testimony to this lesson. The counseling profession literally came into existence because of societal needs that were not being met in other ways. If young people had not had a need for assistance with vocational concerns, or if such a need had been fulfilled through other means, Parsons, Adams, Davis, and others would not have found it necessary to act as they did to begin the counseling profession.

Current examples also are obvious. The formation and rapid growth of both AMHCA and IAMFC reflect the widespread and dramatically increasing need for mental-health and for marriage and family counseling services for (other than seriously disturbed) people in society. Problems such as those relating to interpersonal and family relations, stress management, life-style management and development, and vocational and personal adjustments are common to "normal" people. Counselors help people with the various manifestations of these problems, and professional concern about these problems is reflected in the professional activities of counselors and professional organizations.

The counseling profession's efforts to meet the needs of society also are reflected in the many new settings and situations in which counselors are now working. For example, the last decade has seen tremendous growth in the numbers of counselors working in business and industry settings, residential facilities (e.g., for youth or for older persons), abused-person shelters, medical facilities, and various other places where, historically, counselors have not worked. Perhaps most importantly, because of the counseling profession's responsiveness to the needs of society, the expansion of the number of settings and situations in which counselors work continues to increase.

Lesson 6: The counseling profession sometimes seems to act in opposition to trends in society.

Concerns about the rights and responsibilities of and respect for individuals have a long history in American society. However, in the so-called modern era, these concerns were most evident in society during the 1960s and early 1970s. In general, those were times in which attention was given to "individuality" as the essence of the human condition. Relatedly, they were times when empiricism, as applied to human characteristics, traits, and behaviors, was decried in society at large. However, during the same period, a resurgence of interest in empiricism occurred in the counseling profession. This phenomenon was reflected in the formation of AMEG (ACC) in the mid-1960s. Another fact to be considered is that AMEG (AAC) had its largest membership during the late 1960s and early 1970s, but as society's emphasis on "individuality" ebbed, so did the AMEG (AAC) membership.

This situation was not the paradox it seemed to be; rather, it was an example of a professional response to current conditions in society. As society clamored about "individuality," counseling professionals sought to understand better both "individuals" and "individuals within society." The counseling profession sought to gain this understanding through application of proven scientific methods. Such methods incorporate, and indeed emphasize, empiricism. Therefore, although the counseling profession appeared to be antithetical to the trend in society, it was in fact attempting to be effectively responsive to that trend. Those activities in turn lead to development of many "empirical" methods and resources for understanding individuals. As those methods and resources became available and common, ostensible interest in empiricism among counseling professionals waned.

Lesson 7: The counseling profession has a flirtatious relationship with empiricism.

Throughout its history, the counseling profession has wavered between being enamored with empiricism (vis-a-vis rigorous psychodiagnosis, assessment, research, and evaluation) and being disenchanted with empiricism (vis-a-vis almost totally unstructured approaches to counseling). The history of AHEAD (formerly TCPA and SPATE) is a classic example. Originally conceived as an organization dedicated to research and evaluation, it evolved into an organization for counselors primarily interested in humanistic perspectives. Humanism and empiricism certainly are not totally separate, but just as certainly empiricism is not a major focus within humanistic perspectives.

Other evidence of the fluctuating relationship between the counseling profession and empiricism can be found through a review of the contents of professional counseling journals. For example, the contents of ACA's *Journal of Counseling* (the *Journal of Counseling and Development* until 1992, and the *Personnel and Guidance Journal* prior to 1983) show that the journal, at times, was almost completely devoted to research but at other times almost totally devoid of research.

In more recent times, the counseling profession has sought a "balanced" relationship with empiricism. On one hand, the counseling profession has acknowledged the need for and benefits of empiricism, an acknowledgement reflected, for example, in professional preparation and ethical standards adopted within the profession. On the other hand, the counseling profession has not mandated that empirical perspectives be adopted within the profession and indeed has gone to some lengths to insure that it is not considered mandatory (also as reflected in the professional preparation and ethical standards). In general, the counseling profession seems to have taken the position that empiricism is important, but only for those counselors who deem it important.

THE COUNSELING PROFESSION TODAY

A rapidly growing understanding of, and demand for, positive mental health is evident in the American society in a number of ways. For example, "self-help" mental-health books are setting sales records, businesses and industries are allocating substantial fiscal and physical resources to employee well-being, communities are acting to alleviate various types of physical and mental abuse, prominent campaigns have been launched against drug and alcohol abuse, and "wellness" activities are being sought by millions of people. Collectively, these and other activities similar to them signify society's realization that positive mental health is desirable, and more importantly, achievable. And positive mental health is supposed to be the result of effective delivery of counseling services.

Counseling and Mental Health

Society's concern with mental health is reflected in the counseling profession; reciprocal impacts exist between the parallel mental-health movements in society and in the counseling profession. For example, these movements have fostered the realization that in order for positive mental health to be achieved, it must be present both within, across, and over people's lives. That is, both people in society and professional counselors have come to understand that positive mental health cannot be attained in one aspect of life without being achieved in other aspects of life as well, and also that positive mental health should be achieved at all age levels. This realization has in turn created demand for counseling services that relate to many different facets of people's lives. The direct effect on the counseling profession has been a greatly increased need for more, and more diverse, professional counseling services and, relatedly, for professional counselors.

The counseling profession has impacted the positive mental-health movement in society by providing literally more services than are sought. Many counseling services are provided simply to help people with existing problems, the typical view of the purpose of counseling. The counseling profession, however, takes a much broader purview of the situation and seeks to foster and promote positive mental health in a number of other important ways. For example, professional counselors engage in many developmental and/or preventive activities intended to help people cope with certain types of problems before they occur. Additionally, professional counselors frequently provide consultation services to help people helping other people with problems and concerns. And finally, the counseling profession has extended its service provision settings to many places where people typically would not expect to find them (e.g., health care centers, government agencies, or religious institutions).

These mutual impacts have resulted in the counseling profession having a rapidly growing recognition and appreciation in society. Most counselors readily acknowledge, however, that the counseling profession has not yet achieved a complete or fully recognized place in society. The counseling profession is therefore acting within itself to enhance its identity within society. These activities include trends such as development of new counseling theoretical bases and techniques, increased use of technology, promotion of professional standards, improvement of training methods, expansion of political involvements, extension of service areas, promotion of public awareness of the counseling profession, and increased attention to accountability.

Counseling and Its Theoretical Bases

The counseling profession has long been grounded in a relatively few basic counseling theories (e.g., client-centered, existential, behavioral, rational emotive, or gestalt) and has worked diligently to establish effective techniques based on those theories. However, the counseling profession also has been receptive to new theoretical perspectives (e.g., cognitive-behavioral, social learning, and systemic theories) that have evolved from the fields of psychology, sociology, education, and other related disciplines. True to the history of the profession, it also is working hard, through research, professional discourse, and experimentation, to develop effective new techniques based on these newer theories. As a result, professional counselors have before them ever expanding sets of theoretical perspectives and techniques upon which to base their counseling activities. These trends have added to the identity of the counseling profession by allowing professional counselors to provide more and better services to increasing numbers of people.

Counseling and Computers

The counseling profession also has begun to capitalize on modern technological advancements. This trend is perhaps most evident in the area of vocational counseling where a number of relatively sophisticated computer systems are regularly used to enhance vocational development and counseling activities. However, integration of technology also is evident in other parts of the counseling profession. For example, more and more counselors are using computers for data and information management in their "normal" counseling activities. Unfortunately, the use of computers to assist counseling processes and activities is by no means universally accepted or practiced. Ekstrom and Johnson (1984) aptly summarized the situation:

> Computers are a topic that counselors can no longer ignore. Computers are now being utilized to provide course and client scheduling; to improve counseling office management; to create, administer, score, and interpret tests; to provide information about careers and colleges; to assist individuals in making educational and occupational choices; to provide instruction and remediation; to provide personal and mental health counseling; as tools for research; and as aids in writing reports or papers. All of the indications point to computers being even more widely used in counseling in the future. (p. 132)

The use of computers and other so-called modern technology contributes to the identity of the counseling profession primarily by expediting the work of counselors, therefore allowing them to provide better services to more people.

Counseling and Ethical Standards

Two major types of professional standards currently are being emphasized within the counseling profession. One is ethical standards, which are standards of behavior voluntarily adopted by the members of a profession to insure the welfare of service recipients. The primary ethical standards for professional counselors are those developed and maintained by ACA. ACA's *Ethical Standards* were developed by the membership over a period of approximately 30 years and are updated periodically to reflect new needs and circumstances. Adherence to ethical standards is voluntary because they have no basis in law. However, the vast majority of professional counselors diligently strive to adhere to them because such behavior enhances society's view of the counseling profession as one that cares deeply about the welfare of its service recipients. If a counselor does engage in unethical behavior, the counselor's behavior may be subjected to peer review. For example, if an ACA member is alleged to have engaged in unethical behavior, ACA's Ethical Standards Review Committee will investigate and review the situation. Professional sanctions, such as loss of ACA membership, may be imposed on ACA members found guilty of unethical behavior. Similar processes are used by credentialing agencies. For example, the **National Board for Certified Counselors** (NBCC) has its own set of ethical standards applicable to National Certified Counselors (NCCs). If an NCC is alleged to have acted unethically, NBCC reviews the case. If found guilty of unethical behavior, the NCC's certification may be revoked.

Counseling and Counselor Preparation

The other set of standards currently receiving considerable emphasis within the counseling profession is that related to preparation practices. These "Standards of Preparation" are discussed at greater length in Chapter 3. The important points as they apply to this discussion are that counselor professional preparation standards exist and that they are widely implemented within the counseling profession. Approximately 1,000 counselor preparation programs exist in the United States and its territorial possessions (Hollis & Wantz, 1993). Standards of preparation are necessary to insure that counselor trainees receive appropriate and effective preparation regardless of the preparation program in which they participate. The implementation of standards of preparation also is particularly important in a "mobile" society where both counselors and clients frequently relocate; standardized counselor preparation helps to insure effective counseling services regardless of location. Such standardization also helps to enhance society's perception of the counseling profession as one that carefully monitors its own activities.

In addition to the implementation of standards of preparation, the counseling profession continually seeks other ways to improve counselor preparation. For example, professional journals focusing on counselor preparation are replete with research on current training practices as well as innovative ideas for new training methods. Professional meetings for counselors also emphasize new approaches to counselor preparation. Collectively, these are indicators that the counseling profession is striving, in many different ways, to improve the effectiveness of counselor preparation. This effort is being put forth because the counseling profession realizes that effective preparation has a direct result in effective services and an indirect result in enhancement of society's perceptions of the profession.

Counseling and Political Involvement

Another major thrust in the counseling profession is increased involvement in political systems. The most obvious example of this phenomenon is the widespread and increasing passage of state level counselor licensure laws. However, professional counselors also are becoming active in other political arenas. For example, state and national counselor organizations frequently employ lobbyists to promote legislation that benefits not only the counseling profession but also the people who receive counseling services. The situation is effectively summarized by Solomon (1982) who wrote:

> Counselors and other human service providers are in a pivotal position to effectively communicate the concerns of people they serve to policy makers at local, state, and national levels of government. They are in an even better position to shape legislative initiatives, bills, and laws to

more appropriately address counseling issues that directly impact the counseling profession as well as the people they serve. Most of the political successes that affect the counseling profession will depend largely on counselors themselves. (p. 580)

Political awareness and sophistication are rapidly increasing within the counseling profession, with one result being an enhanced public perception of the profession.

Counseling and Public Relations

Counseling professionals have realized that effective public relations is an important part of promoting positive mental health in society (as well as in establishing a favorable professional identity) and therefore increasingly are engaged in public relations activities. Professional counselors' public-relations activities take many forms, the most common of which are providing assistance for development of public-service announcements and other media presentations, donating time to charitable causes, and developing mental-health facilitation media that can be used without counselor intervention. In addition, increasing numbers of counselors are providing pro bono (i.e., free) services on a regular basis. Some professional organizations (e.g., AMHCA) even have suggested that pro bono work for a limited proportion of the counselor's clientele is an ethical and professional obligation.

Counseling and Marketing

Historically, counselors and other mental-health professionals were relatively "low key" in promoting the counseling profession. In fact, "advertising" is specifically prohibited in most ethical standards applicable to professional counselors. However, more recently a distinction has been made between advertising which is presumably for a counselor's personal gain, and marketing which is presumably for enhancement of the counseling profession in general. Ritchie (1989) noted that, "Marketing essentially is an exchange of goods or services. School counselors offer guidance and counseling services in exchange for public support" (p. 54). Obviously this perspective can be generalized readily from school counseling to other types of counseling.

Gilchrist and Stringer (1992) delineated the potential benefits of marketing in the counseling profession when they indicated

> Effective marketing may benefit counselors in three ways. First, marketing may help counselors maintain their position as service providers.
>
> A second benefit of marketing is that it may help enhance the image of counseling services.
>
> Third, the marketing process may help meet increasing demands for counselor accountability. (p. 156)

As Wittman (1988) summarized,

> . . . the challenge is for the counseling profession to perfect those skills necessary to remain highly responsive to the needs and demands of its clients. The health care and business professions are turning to the use of marketing skills for this purpose. It is now time for the counseling field to discover how it can benefit from the lessons learned from marketing. (pp. 308-309)

Yet, while marketing is receiving increasing attention, it is by no means universally endorsed in the counseling profession; significant controversy remains. For example, in response to Wittman's position, FongBeyette (1988) noted that existing community-based assessment and evaluation techniques and strategies that were developed for use by counselors have been proven effective. Therefore, the need is small for counselors to adopt marketing techniques which are more suitable for business and industry. Gilchrist and Stringer (1992) perhaps provided the comment that should serve as a guideline for counselors: "Counselors need the benefits of effective marketing programs, but marketing must not jeopardize professional or ethical conduct" (p. 156).

Counseling and Accountability

Awareness of the need to be accountable is increasing in the counseling profession as professional counselors realize that the benefits of their activities are not "self-evident" to persons outside the profession. Counseling is, for most people, a very private matter. Even those who benefit greatly from counseling services are not likely to share their experiences with others because of the (perceived) stigma of having had a need for counseling. Thus, few people outside the counseling profession are "singing the praises" for counselors. Professional counselors are aware that their responsibility is to prove that what they do is helpful, effective, and desirable; therefore, they have intensified their efforts to be accountable. A major thrust is being made to show that counseling results in *behavior* change among counseling service recipients. Clearly this thrust is consistent with the practitioner-scientist perspective presented earlier. More generally, however, it reflects the fact that demonstrating an ability to produce *behavior* change provides the strongest basis for the positive identity of the counseling profession within society.

SUMMARY

Over the last four decades the counseling profession has evolved from an amorphous collection of disparate professionals with vaguely defined similarities to a representation of professionals with focused and specialized preparation in a variety of counseling skills who have a relatively singular purpose: provision of effective counseling services. The evolutionary process has been both reflective of and responsive to societal, educational, legal, and political trends. Significant obstacles have been encountered and overcome. Thus, identity as a professional counselor is now more meaningful than at any point in history.

Even in light of the substantial accomplishments and advancements in the counseling profession, however, more remains to be achieved before professional counselors enjoy a clear, distinct, and fully respected identity. Fortunately, mechanisms already exist through which such an identity can be achieved. Continuing emphasis on standardized, effective counselor preparation, credentialing, and accountability will enable the noble goals to be reached.

Chapter **3**

PROFESSIONALISM
IN COUNSELING

Emener and Cottone (1989) reviewed models of professionalism and concluded that the four primary characteristics of a *profession* are (1) a body of specialized knowledge and theory-driven research, (2) professional preparation and review, (3) a code of ethics, and (4) professional identification and practice control. Similarly, Wittmer and Loesch (1986) indicated that "A profession is typically defined as a vocational activity having (1) an underlying body of theoretical and research knowledge, (2) an identifiable set of effective skills and activities, and (3) a publicly professed, voluntarily self-imposed set of behavioral guidelines" (p. 301). Support for the belief that counseling truly is a profession is provided throughout this book. For example, professional preparation for counselors is addressed in the next chapter, legal and ethical guidelines are addressed in Chapters 6 and 7, and theoretical and research bases are addressed in Part II. Yet while support can be garnered that counseling is a profession according to commonly applied criteria, those criteria do not encompass perhaps the most important part of a profession: specifically, that professionals have a distinctive orientation toward their work. It is this orientation that differentiates professional counselors from others (e.g., layperson "listeners," faith healers, palmists, advisors, and spiritualists) who purport to provide "counseling" services. Non-professional counselors, who counsel, do so on the basis of "intuition" or "natural ability" as opposed to providing counsel within professional guidelines.

Professional orientation is a rather esoteric term that defies exact definition. Addressing the counseling profession, VanZandt (1990) wrote:

> Professionalism is a complex attribute, and there may not be total agreement on its definition. Based on my reading of the literature, however, I would offer the following working definition. Professionalism is:
>
> 1. the way in which a person relies upon a personal high standard of competence in providing professional services
>
> 2. the means by which a person promotes or maintains the image of the profession
>
> 3. a person's willingness to pursue professional development opportunities that will continue to improve skills within the profession
>
> 4. the pursuit of quality and ideals within the profession
>
> 5. a person's sense of pride about the profession. (p. 244)

In general, then, professional orientation encompasses counselors' beliefs about and attitudes toward their work. Inherent in these beliefs and attitudes is the supposition that all of a counselor's behaviors should be ultimately beneficial to clients served, the counseling profession, and society, regardless of the personal advantages accrued or disadvantages endured from the behaviors. Thus, professional counselors engage in some behaviors (e.g., provision of *pro bono* counseling services, joining professional organizations, or attaining professional credentials) not because of altruistic or material personal gain, but rather because it is the *professional* thing to do. Above all else, because counselors have and adhere to a *professional orientation*, counseling is a true profession.

Counselors most frequently manifest a *professional orientation* through demonstration of respect for the dignity of their clients and the professional colleagues with whom they work in their daily activities. However, counselors also manifest a *professional orientation* in other ways, including becoming members of professional organizations and associations, obtaining professional credentials, participating in professional self-development activities, and making contributions to the theoretical and knowledge bases of the counseling profession.

PROFESSIONAL ORGANIZATIONS FOR COUNSELORS

Counselors with a good professional orientation are members of professional organizations (used here as synonymous with professional associations) for three primary reasons. First, professional organizations provide the major information and activity resources which counselors can use to improve their counseling knowledge, skills, and performance. Second, professional organizations are a primary means for counselors to associate and interact with one another. Third, professional organizations provide the most effective means for counselors to facilitate improvement of the counseling profession. Therefore, reciprocal benefits are present for counselors and the counseling profession from counselors' memberships in professional organizations; professional organizations are the media through which the counseling profession benefits individual counselors, and vice versa.

A number of professional organizations exists to which professionally oriented counselors may belong. Many counselors are members of the American Psychological Association (APA), particularly Division 17, Counseling Psychology; American Association for Marriage and Family Therapy (AAMFT); American Educational Research Association (AERA), particularly Division H, Counseling and Human Development; and/or the American Vocational Association (AVA). However, the American Counseling Association (ACA) is the primary professional organization with which professional counselors primarily affiliate. ACA has an organizational and functional structure typical of many professional organizations, and, therefore, it is described here in some detail as an illustrative example.

The ACA headquarters building is located just outside Washington, D.C. in Alexandria, Virginia. Headquarters houses the professional staff who are paid employees of the association, the ACA library, and resource and meeting rooms for association activities. Staff members in Headquarters are divided among several functional areas, such as association administration and management, budget and finance, convention coordination, membership services, and professional media and publications. In general, the headquarters staff is responsible for implementation of ACA's ongoing activities. Thus, the headquarters staff is a primary contributor to continuity within the association and the counseling profession.

In August, 1992, the ACA membership included more than 57,000 people located in the United States and approximately 50 foreign countries. Four types of ACA membership are possible: (1) **Professional,** for counseling practitioners who have graduated from counselor preparation programs (i.e., who hold a master's or doctoral degree in counseling or a closely related field); (2) **Student,** for persons currently enrolled in counselor education programs; (3) **Regular,** for persons who are not students but who are working toward fulfillment of criteria for Professional membership; and (4) **Associate,** for professionals who are associated indirectly with the counseling profession, such as test and book company representatives, program administrators, and supervisors. Professional members comprise the largest group, followed by student, associate, and regular members. Regardless of category, memberships and associated dues are on an annual basis, with unlimited renewals, except in rare cases in which membership is revoked because of ethical and/or legal misconduct. ACA has an open enrollment system which allows new members to join at any time.

In order to be responsive to the many different interests, needs, and circumstances of members, the ACA membership is partitioned into two different structures. One is a divisional structure, including the following 15 divisions and one organizational affiliate:

American College Counseling Association (ACCA),
American Mental Health Counselors Association (AMHCA),
American Rehabilitation Counseling Association (ARCA),
American School Counselor Association (ASCA),
Association for Adult Development and Aging (AADA),
Association for Assessment in Counseling (AAC),
Association for Counselor Education and Supervision
    (ACES),
Association for Humanistic Education and Development
    (AHEAD),
Association for Multicultural Counseling and Development
    (AMCD),
Association for Religious and Value Issues in Counseling
    (ARVIC),
Association for Specialists in Group Work (ASGW),
International Association for Marriage and Family
    Counselors (IAMFC),
International Association of Addictions and Offenders
    Counseling (IAAOC),
Military Educators and Counselors Association (MECA)
    (organizational affiliate),
National Career Development Association (NCDA), and
National Employment Counseling Association (NECA).

In regard to benefits received (e.g., newsletters and journals) and annual dues, membership in ACA is separate from membership in an ACA division. Counseling professionals initially may join only ACA, but must also join at least one division for second and subsequent year membership. Membership in an ACA division must be accompanied by membership in ACA, although several of the ACA divisions allow "provisional," non-dues-paying membership for one year as a trial basis for determination of interest in the division.

The second partitioning is by geographic regions. ACA's regional components are referred to as "branch assemblies" because they are composed of the branches (e.g., state-level counterparts) of ACA. The four ACA *Regional Branch Assemblies* (RBAs) are Southern, North Atlantic, Midwestern, and Western. Technically, ACA members are not "members" of one of ACA's RBAs and there are no separate dues for the RBA. Rather, the RBA structure allows for representation of ACA members by geographic region. Thus, while the RBAs have individual governance structures for their respective areas and have representation in the ACA governance structure, they do not have members in the same sense as in ACA divisions.

The ACA governance structure is unicameral. The ACA Governing Council includes the ACA President, Past-President, President-Elect, Treasurer, Parliamentarian, Executive Director (from the Headquarters permanent staff), and representatives from each of the divisions and regions. The ACA Governing Council meets at least biannually to conduct the Association's business.

The benefits of ACA membership to professional counselors are too numerous to be listed here. However, some of the major benefits can be highlighted. First, in regard to professional publications, all ACA members receive the Association's newsletter, the *Guidepost* (published 18 times per year), the *Journal of Counseling and Development* (published six times per year), and the *American Counselor* (published four times per year). Members of ACA divisions and organizational affiliates also receive divisional newsletters, typically published quarterly. Most ACA divisions also publish quarterly journals. Second, ACA provides access to a wide variety of professional resources (e.g., films, videotapes, books, monographs, bibliographic search services) to its members. Third, ACA provides a variety of insurance programs for its members, including professional liability, life, and health insurance. Fourth, ACA maintains an active political involvement system (including lobbyists) for interaction with the federal government. Relatedly, ACA has assisted with political involvement at state levels, particularly in regard to professional counselor licensure legislation. Fifth, ACA maintains a "legal defense fund" to which members can apply for funds if they become involved in work-related litigation. ACA also continues to increase member services, such as availability of an ACA credit card which has a reduced interest rate and media development services including typesetting, artwork, and printing.

Perhaps ACA's most visible benefit to its members is its annual national/international convention, which is held in the spring at a different site each year. The ACA convention is an important means for professional counselors to interact with one another; participate in professional development activities; and keep abreast of new professional activities, issues, and trends. A placement service for both students in counselor preparation programs and professional counselors also is provided at each ACA convention. In addition, the ACA convention typically attracts more than 100 exhibitors of professional materials and services.

ACA has 56 state and international branches, (i.e., geographically restricted organizations whose purpose is to represent counselors in a specific region). Each branch is a separate organization, has its own membership requirements, dues, and structure, and is defined by state or regional boundaries (e.g., Ohio Counseling Association and the European Branch Counseling Association). However, membership is usually open to any professional who wishes to join. Typically, a primary organization (e.g., North Carolina Counseling Association and Florida Counseling Association) as well as state- or branch-level divisions parallel those in ACA, although most branches typically have fewer divisions than does ACA. The activities of the ACA branches typically reflect those of ACA. For example, most hold an annual convention, are involved in legislative activities (particularly those relating to counselor licensure), publish newsletters, and provide a variety of professional resources. Some state branches (e.g., Florida and Texas) also publish their own professional counseling journals. The primary difference between ACA and its branches is of course the "scope" of their respective efforts; the ACA branches focus their activities on matters particularly pertinent to the professionals in the specific geographic area represented, while ACA focuses on national matters.

ACA has three corporate affiliates, each of which is a technically and legally separate organization but which has strong philosophical and theoretical ties to ACA. One of these corporate affiliates is the Council for the Accreditation of Counseling and Related Educational Programs (CACREP), which will be discussed in Chapter 4. The second is the International Association of Counseling Services (IACS). The primary purpose of IACS is to provide a means for accreditation of agencies (e.g., college or university counseling centers and community mental health counseling agencies) that provide counseling services. Toward that end, IACS conducts counseling agency program evaluations and publishes a directory of IACS accredited agencies. The third ACA corporate affiliate is the Counseling and Human Development Foundation (CHDF). It is a not-for-profit agency that helps the counseling profession and ACA through the management of property and financial holdings and the provision of funds for activities with special significance to the counseling profession (e.g., research).

ACA members and other professional counselors cannot "join" ACA corporate-affiliate organizations in the traditional sense; that is, these organizations do not have memberships *per se*. Rather, the counseling professionals who manage them typically are selected by the organizations themselves. However, because most of the counseling professionals who operate the corporate affiliates are ACA members, they do have strong allegiance to ACA.

The American Association for State Counselor Boards (AASCB) is another organization closely aligned with ACA. Members of AASCB are representative counseling professionals from states having, or currently seeking, counselor licensure laws or from other organizations (e.g., ACA or NBCC) with a professional interest in counselor licensure. The primary purpose of AASCB is to provide a mechanism for communication and collaboration among states having licensure laws and thus to promote and improve counselor licensure practices. Again, AASCB does not have an open membership for professional counselors but rather is composed of persons selected by state and other organizations having interest in counselor licensure to represent them.

Active membership in professional organizations is a major way for professional counselors to exhibit professionalism. Professional organization membership allows members to acknowledge to themselves and others that they are concerned about people in the world, vis-a-vis counseling services provided, and about their own competence and improvement as professional counselors. Another way that professional counselors can demonstrate their concern about professionalism in counseling is through seeking pertinent professional credentials.

PROFESSIONAL CREDENTIALS FOR COUNSELORS

Professional credentialing is usually viewed as encompassing three major professional activities: (1) academic accreditation of counselor-preparation programs, (2) certification (and the closely associated practice registry), and (3) licensure (Loesch, 1984). In general, professional counselors seek these types of credentials in order to demonstrate that they have specific knowledge and skills for certain types of counseling services and/or to be permitted to provide these counseling services. Counselors who have specialized professional credentials are presumed to be better able to provide certain counseling services.

Graduation from an Accredited Preparation Program

One "credential" a professional counselor can have is to be a graduate of an accredited preparation program. Because counselor-preparation programs exist almost exclusively within institutions of higher education, almost all of them are accredited by some accrediting agency. The question then becomes, which accreditations are most pertinent to counseling? Many institutions of higher education are accredited by a division of the Association of Colleges and Schools (e.g., the Southern Association of Colleges and Schools). Similarly, many colleges or schools of education are accredited by the National Council for Accreditation of Teacher Education (NCATE). However, these types of accreditations are general in nature and, therefore, have very little specific application to preparation for professional counseling. Thus, graduation from programs having only these types of accreditations is not a particularly strong credential for professional counselors. Comparatively, CACREP accreditation is specifically applicable to programs for the professional preparation of counselors. Therefore, graduation from a CACREP-accredited program is a much stronger professional credential for counselors. Moreover, this particular credential is increasingly providing advantages for attainment of other credentials (e.g., certifications or licensures) particularly appropriate for professional counselors. For example, graduates of CACREP-accredited (counseling) programs may participate in the NBCC's National Counselor Examination prior to completion of post-graduation experiential requirements and, if successful, become "board eligible" for NBCC certification pending completion of the experiential requirements. Similarly, some state counselor-licensure procedures are expedited for graduates of CACREP-accredited programs.

Certification

Certification is the second type of credential important for professional counselors. It is a process whereby an agency, which may be either governmental or private, attests or affirms that an individual counselor has met the minimum qualifications established by the agency. The assumption underlying any certification process is that a "certified" counselor is able to perform effectively the type(s) of counseling reflected in a particular certification (Loesch, 1984). Certification is usually referred to as a "title control" process because it only restricts the use of the title "certified"; it does not restrict who may engage in counseling activities or what types of counseling can be provided. Therefore, the primary advantage of any certification lies in the prestige associated with it. Such prestige has significant implications for professional counselors in several regards. For example, many employers give hiring preference to certified counselors. In addition, clients' initial perceptions of counselors are related to the *potential* for counseling effectiveness; the more favorable clients' initial impressions of counselors in terms of perceived competence, the more likely that counseling will be effective. Certification is one credential that usually increases clients' (initial) favorableness toward counselors (Wittmer & Loesch, 1986).

Professional certification activities for counselors have a relatively brief history, and it is only within the last decade or so that certification has been viewed as an important professional credential. Although the exact reasons for this recent emphasis are unknown, one probable reason is that only recently has arisen a need to be able to compare or "equate" counselors in a "mobile society."

The most prominent certification processes are national, and in some cases international, in scope. That is, because the minimum qualifications for such certifications are set by national agencies, they are independent of local (e.g., state-level) counselor-preparation program idiosyncracies. Therefore, all counselors certified by a particular agency are presumed to have the same *minimum* competence level regardless of the respective preparation programs from which they graduated. Accordingly, certification is one indication of minimal "equivalence" across counselors. A note may be made that this perspective is similar to the *philosophy* underlying CACREP's program accreditation thrust. The primary difference, of course, is that accreditation focuses on the program, and certification focuses on the individual.

Although the counselor-certification process implemented by the NBCC is not the oldest, it is rapidly becoming the most widely known among those specific to counselors. Therefore, the NBCC's counselor-certification processes will be exemplified here.

In the late 1970s, the Commission on Rehabilitation Counselor Certification (CRCC) and the National Academy of Certified Clinical Mental Health Counselors (NACCMHC) certified rehabilitation counselors and mental-health counselors, respectively; CACREP accredited several counselor-preparation programs, and several states passed counselor-licensure laws. These emphases on credentialing and the activities associated with them spawned interest within ACA (then AACD) in a counselor-certification process. Thus, ACA mobilized its resources to evaluate existing counselor-certification processes and to develop a plan for a broad-based counselor-certification process. In 1981, ACA sponsored several meetings to develop specific plans, which eventually led to the first NBCC meeting in April of 1982, attended by representatives from ACA, other counselor certifying agencies, a state having a counselor-licensure law, and by a member of the public. The group initiated plans for incorporation, established the initial criteria for certification, adopted an initial operating budget, developed a Code of Ethics, and established a schedule for subsequent activities. In addition, using information from a previous evaluative report that had identified deficiencies in existing assessment instruments for counselor-certification processes, the group decided to initiate the development of a counselor-certification examination specifically suited to NBCC's purposes (Loesch & Vacc, 1991).

Although both NBCC and CACREP are philosophically aligned with ACA, their respective governing bodies are constituted much differently. Whereas membership on the CACREP Council is open to representatives from various ACA divisions as well as from ACA itself, membership on the NBCC Board of Directors is not. Instead, the NBCC Board is composed of a Chairperson, Vice-Chairperson, Treasurer/Secretary, a public representative and five members elected by the Board, and one non-voting liaison from ACA, ASCA, NCDA, and AADA, respectively. The NBCC Executive Director is an *ex officio* member of the Board. NBCC also employs three consultants for technical assistance with examination development and research activities. The NBCC headquarters is located in Greensboro, North Carolina.

Counselors certified by the NBCC are presumed to have fulfilled the minimum basic knowledge and skill requirements applicable to all professional counselors. Holding a certificate from NBCC is a *generic* certification because it does not imply that NBCC-certified counselors can do a particular type of counseling, but rather that they have at least the minimum knowledge and skills necessary for any type of counseling. The generic-level competence inherent in the NBCC certification process is based on the belief that, colloquially stated, all professional counselors must both "know some things and be able to do some things" (Loesch & Vacc, 1991).

The "know some things" component of the NBCC certification is evaluated in two ways, the first of which involves consideration of an applicant's prior academic preparation. The general minimum academic requirement for NBCC certification is a master's degree in counseling or a closely related field. However, specific academic preparatory experiences, usually courses, also are required. In order to be certified by NBCC, applicants must have successfully completed academic/curricular experiences in a supervised practicum or internship, in "theories of counseling," and in six of the following areas: (1) human growth and development, (2) social and cultural foundations, (3) helping relationships, (4) groups, (5) lifestyle and career development, (6) appraisal, (7) research and evaluation, and (8) professional orientation. In essence, applicants must have had a supervised practicum or internship and coursework in counseling theories plus six of the eight "core curriculum areas" of the CACREP accreditation standards. These requirements are of course encompassed in any CACREP-accredited entry-level counselor-preparation program having a counseling emphasis (i.e., other than the CACREP accreditations of Student Affairs in Higher Education with administrative emphasis or developmental emphasis).

The second part of the knowledge evaluation component involves participation in the NBCC's National Counselor Examination (NCE). Different forms of the NCE are used for each administration because each form is developed from a large item pool. However, each form of the NCE has the same content format. That is, each form of the NCE covers the eight "core curriculum areas" of the CACREP standards. The current forms of the NCE each contain 25 questions in each of the eight areas, with 20 per area being scored for certification purposes, resulting in a total possible score of 160. The remaining 40 questions (i.e., five per area) on each form of the NCE are for item development purposes. Although subsection scores are reported, only the applicant's total score from the 160 items (i.e., the sum of the eight subsection scores) is used for performance-evaluation purposes.

The NBCC uses a modified Anghoff procedure approximately every three years to establish a "base form" minimum criterion score for the NCE. In general, this method involves having a group of counseling professionals each make a probability judgment about the likelihood of a respondent answering each item correctly, summing the estimates across items, and averaging the summed judgments across judges (Loesch & Vacc, in press). An applicant's total score is compared to the established minimum criterion score for each form of the NCE. For example, the minimum criterion score for the April, 1985 form of the NCE was 87; an applicant who scored 87 or higher on that form of the NCE "passed" the examination (Loesch & Vacc, 1991). The minimum criterion score for each form of the NCE subsequent to each base form is "statistically equated" to the minimum criterion score for the base form so that each minimum criterion score is statistically equivalent, or comparable, across forms of the NCE. Therefore, applicants do not have any particular advantage relative to surpassing the minimum criterion score in taking one form of the NCE as opposed to another (Loesch & Vacc, in press).

The NCE has been subjected to a wide variety of professional and empirical (e.g., Jaeger & Frye, 1988; Loesch & Vacc, 1991) analyses. In addition, respondents' comments about the NCE have been examined both subjectively and empirically (Vacc & Loesch, in press). And finally, NCE results have been evaluated relative to current trends and movements in the counseling profession (Loesch & Vacc, 1988). Empirical evidence and subjective opinions overwhelmingly favor the reliability, validity, appropriateness, and defensibility of the NCE for use in the NBCC counselor certification process. Thus, NBCC's conjunctive use of academic preparation analysis and NCE performance is an effective means of evaluating counselors' professional knowledge.

The "be able to do some things" component of the NBCC certification process involves consideration of an applicant's previous supervised practice and/or professional experiences. All applicants must provide documentation of successful completion of a *supervised* practicum or internship. Applicants who have not completed a CACREP-accredited preparation program also must provide documentation of successful completion of a minimum of two years post-master's degree professional counseling experience of at least 20 hours per week. This requirement is waived for graduates of CACREP-accredited (counseling emphasis) programs because of the extensive requirements for supervised counseling experience in the CACREP accreditation standards. In addition, all applicants must provide letters of reference, including ratings of specific skills, attesting to their minimum professional competence as a counselor.

In the late 1980s, NBCC implemented two procedures intended to facilitate achievement of NCC status. First, students enrolled in CACREP-accredited programs having a counseling emphasis are entitled to participate in the NCE during their last academic term of enrollment. Assuming they pass the NCE and graduate as scheduled with at least a master's degree, students exercising this option can become NCCs (almost) immediately upon graduation. Second, counselors who have completed appropriate academic requirements and graduated with at least a master's degree from a program not accredited by CACREP but who have not yet fulfilled the NBCC two-year, post-master's professional experience requirement can participate in the NCE. Assuming they pass the NCE, these counselors are accorded NBCC's "board eligible" status, which means that they will become NCCs immediately upon fulfillment of the experiential requirements. These options enable many counselors now to become NCCs more rapidly than would have been possible in the past.

NBCC certification applicants who successfully fulfill these criteria are awarded the designation *National Certified Counselor* (NCC). The initial NBCC certification period is five years, with renewal contingent upon successful completion of professional development activities. By mid-1992, approximately 17,000 counselors had been designated as NCCs.

In 1985, the NBCC incorporated the certification process previously administered by the National Council for Credentialing of Career Counselors (NCCCC). The NCCCC had been created by ACA's (then AACD's) National Career Development Association to implement a certification process specifically applicable to counselors specializing in career counseling (Sampson, 1986). The NBCC-NCCCC merger created a "two-tier" certification structure for the NBCC. Thus, the NBCC generic certification leading to the designation NCC is the basic tier, and the NBCC specialized certification leading to the designation *National Certified Career Counselor* (NCCC) is the second tier. Professional counselors seeking the NCCC status must first attain NCC status. Additional academic, experiential and reference requirements, plus an additional examination are used to evaluate eligibility for this specialized certification. By mid-1992, approximately 1,300 professional counselors had been designated as NCCCs.

In 1990, the NBCC implemented two more specialty certifications, one leading to the designation *National Certified School Counselor* (NCSC) and another leading to the designation *National Certified Gerontological Counselor* (NCGC). Similar to the NCCC, NCSC and NCGC statuses both require prior achievement of NCC status. Neither of these specialty certifications requires participation in an examination in addition to the NCE. Rather, the standard eligibility criteria for both include specialized academic coursework, two years of professional experience, and a supervised internship in the respective areas. Each also necessitates completion of a self-assessment of competence in the respective areas and competence evaluations from a supervisor and from a professional colleague with expertise in the respective area. For NCSCs, the colleague providing the competence evaluation must be an NCC or a state-certified school counselor.

Another certification appropriate for many professional counselors provided by NBCC is the *Certified Clinical Mental Health Counselor* (CCMHC). The CCMHC was started in 1979 primarily by members of ACA's (then AACD's) AMHCA division to provide a means of certifying mental health counselors. In 1992, the CCMHC specialty certification became incorporated with NBCC's. The basic CCMHC criteria include (1) graduation with a master's or higher degree from an accredited counselor-preparation program that required appropriate coursework and a minimum of 60 semester hours, (2) at least two years of post-master's, degree-relevant professional work experience that included a minimum of 3,000 client-contact hours, (3) a minimum of 100 clock hours of individual supervision by a professional counselor with CCMHC certification or equivalent credentials, (4) submission of an audio or video tape of a complete counseling session of at least 30 minutes duration, and (5) successful completion of the CCMHC's Mental Health Counselor Examination for Specialization in Clinical Counseling. The certification status awarded is *Certified Clinical Mental Health Counselor* (CCMHC).

The Commission on Rehabilitation Counselor Certification (CRCC) provides another certification appropriate for many professional counselors. The CRCC awards the designation *Certified Rehabilitation Counselor* (CRC). The CRCC was created through the joint efforts of ACA's ARCA division and the National Rehabilitation Association. CRCC eligibility includes graduation with a master's or higher degree from a rehabilitation counselor-education program accredited by the Council on Rehabilitation Education (CORE) that included a minimum

600-hour internship supervised by a CRC or from an essentially equivalent program; relevant, supervised professional work experience as a rehabilitation counselor for graduates of other than CORE-accredited programs; and successful completion of the CRCC examination. In May, 1992, more than 12,000 counselors were designated as CRCs.

The American Association for Marriage and Family Therapy (AAMFT) provides a professional credential which is similar to, but not synonymous with, a certification for counselors. This credential is AAMFT *Clinical Member* status. The eligibility criteria include successful completion of specific academic experiences as specified by AAMFT, graduation from an AAMFT-accredited program, supervised work as a marriage and family therapist, and at least two years of postgraduate-degree professional work experience in marriage and family counseling.

Registry

Registry is closely related to certification. However, the term itself may be a misnomer, because "a registry, as used in the counseling and human development professions, is a publicly distributed list of professionals who have met some identified set of minimum qualifications" (Loesch, 1984, p. 4). There is often confusion between certification and registry processes, perhaps because many certifying agencies, such as NBCC, NACCMHC, and CRCC, publish "registries" of the professional counselors they have certified. The distinguishing feature between certification and registry processes lies in the primary intent of the activity. With *certification*, the intent is to be certified, and being listed on a registry is an artifact of the certification process. With *registry*, the intent is to get on the list. However, in actuality, this distinction is picayune because both processes are used to identify those professional counselors who have fulfilled some specified level of professional competence as a counselor.

Similar to certification processes, registering processes for counselors necessitate that applicants fulfill specified minimum criteria in order to be listed on the registry. In general, the eligibility criteria typically include graduation from an accredited graduate-level counselor-preparation program, specified curricular components of preparation, appropriate professional work experience, and successful completion of an examination. Currently, Kansas and North Carolina are the only major entities implementing registry processes for professional counselors, and those processes are essentially the "licensure" laws in those states.

Licensure

Licensure is the third type of credential important for professional counselors. Distinct from certification, licensure processes are stipulated in law, implemented at the state level, and geographically restricted in authority. Licensure is a legal process whereby a state agency regulates aspects of the practice of counseling within the state. State licensure laws are legislation referred to as either "title" acts or "practice" acts. In the former, states at least regulate who may identify themselves as "licensed counselors" and, in many states, even regulate who may identify themselves as "counselors." In most states having counselor licensure "title" acts, "healers," "palmists," "readers," "advisors," and the like cannot use the word "counselor" in their advertisements. Although these individuals may perform counseling-type activities, they are prohibited by law from presenting themselves to the public as counselors. In the "practice" act, the state regulates who may engage in activities known as counseling as well as who may identify themselves as counselors. In states having counselor-licensure "practice" acts, the legislation literally defines the practice of counseling within the state. At present, the vast majority of counselor-licensure laws are "title" acts, probably because they are easier to enforce.

There is one idiosyncracy to counselor-licensure that merits digression. In general, counselor-licensure laws are intended to control the practice of counseling within a state. However, school counselors in all states are given authority to practice counseling *in schools,* through state school counselor-certification procedures. Thus, **in regard to school counseling only,** state school counselor certification has essentially the same effect for school counselors as do licensure laws for non-school counselors.

Licensure laws pertinent to the counseling profession have both commonalities and wide variations within the United States. For example, all states have licensure laws for counseling activities under the aegis of the title "psychologist." Typically, psychologist licensure laws require a doctoral degree from a program accredited by the American Psychological Association, supervised professional work experience, in-state residency for a specified period of time, letters of reference, and successful completion of an examination. Approximately one-third of the states also have license laws for marriage and family counselors or therapists, with requirements that are categorically similar to but specifically different from those for psychologists (e.g., typically a master's degree instead of a doctoral degree is required for marriage and family counselors or therapists). As of mid-1992, 37 states had enacted licensure laws for professional counselors. In the majority of those states, the title awarded is **Licensed Professional Counselor** (LPC); most others have a variation incorporating the phrase "professional counselor." Kansas and North Carolina technically have registry laws, with the awarded title of Registered Professional Counselor, but those laws are essentially licensure laws as implemented. Again, the eligibility criteria for counselor licensures are categorically similar to, but specifically different from those for psychologists.

A comparison of counselor certification and licensure processes reveals many similarities as well as a few distinct differences. Primary among the similarities is that both certification and licensure are voluntary in nature. "Counseling" can be done by many people who are neither certified nor licensed, and so these credentials are not "needed" in order to do "counseling." Rather, they are voluntarily sought by those who want to be truly "professional" counselors. Other similarities include requirements for payment of application (typically $50.00 to $350.00), examination ($50.00 to $250.00), annual renewal ($50.00 to $250.00), and miscellaneous ($25.00 to $200.00) fees; specific types of prior academic preparation (usually a master's degree from a state, regionally, or nationally accredited institution); prior supervised counseling experience; prior work experience as a counselor; lack of "negative" personal characteristics (e.g., certain types of criminal convictions); and successful completion of an appropriate examination.

In addition, certification and licensure are usually given for a specific time period, with renewal contingent upon successful completion of continuing professional development activities.

A primary difference between certification and licensure processes is the geographic region encompassed by the respective credential. Certifications are usually national in scope, while licensure is granted for a specific state. Reciprocity agreements among states, whereby one state agrees to honor all or most of the licensure criteria (e.g., performance on a licensure examination) of another state, are fairly common. However, complete "reciprocity" rarely exists between a certification and a state's licensure law even though many states use a certification examination, such as the NBCC's NCE, as (or in lieu of) a state licensure examination.

Graduation from an accredited program, certification, and licensure then are the primary credentials of professional counselors. Those professional counselors who hold such credentials do so to signify that they are interested in and actively striving toward providing the best possible counseling services. Moreover, credentialed counselors demonstrate that they are in accord with the basic philosophical premise of all professional credentialing, which is to protect the public welfare through the provision of services only by competent practitioners (Shimberg, 1982).

Developments in Counselor Credentialing

The counselor-credentialing movement continues to "roll on," and improve, in both scope and substance. For example, licensure legislative initiatives exist in most of the states not yet having counselor licensure, as well as in the District of Columbia and Puerto Rico. In Canada, discussion and plans have begun in regard to credentialing professional career counselors. And as professional counselors gain credibility for their work in more and more settings, they are becoming eligible for and included in a variety of specialized certifications, such as those for pain management, behavioral medicine, and managed health care professionals. Thus, credentialing continues to grow in value for professional counselors.

Of the 37 states having passed counselor-licensure legislation, 34 have operational licensure laws. Among the 34 having operational counselor-licensure procedures, 29 either currently use or soon will accept the NBCC's NCE for fulfillment of the examination component, and several others are actively considering use of the NCE. The widespread use of the NCE is basically attributable to its strong professional and psychometric properties and, in part, attributable to its 1990 endorsement by the AASCB as the "examination of choice" for counselor licensure. However, even in light of its widespread acceptance and use in counselor credentialing, the NCE is about to be revised substantially.

The results of a multiphase work behavior study (i.e., job analysis) for professional counselors was published in 1993 (NBCC, 1993). The study was undertaken specifically as a prelude to revision of the NCE in order to provide an even stronger professional and psychometric foundation for the examination. The initial phases of the study involved solicitation, clarification, and refinement of specific *behaviors* in which counselors engaged in their work. The result of this initial work was a list of approximately 150 work behaviors presumed to be common among professional counselors. Next, over 725 NCCs rated each of the work behaviors twice, once in regard to relative frequency in which they engaged in the behaviors, and again in regard to the importance of being able to do the work behaviors successfully in order to be effective counselors. Substantial analyses of the data were conducted, including factor analyses and analyses of differences on the bases of and relationships to demographic and professional characteristics of the respondents. Based on these analyses, 134 work behaviors were determined to be "generic" among professional counselors and therefore suitable to be represented in the revised NCE (NBCC, 1993).

Based on the results of the work behavior study, it is anticipated that the revised NCE will contain a total of 150, four-distractor, multiple-choice items allocated across five subsections: (1) General Counseling Practice (40 items, 35 scored), (2) General Professional Practice (35 items, 30 scored), (3) Group Counseling (25 items, 20 scored), (4) Career Counseling (25 items, 20 scored), and (5) Marriage and Family Counseling

(25 items, 20 scored). Thus, of the 150 items, 25 will be items under development and 125 will be scored for criterion purposes. First administration of the revised NCE is scheduled for late 1993 or early 1994. Once use of the revised NCE has begun, procedures similar to those for the current NCE will be implemented to establish the revised NCE's psychometric properties and minimum criterion scores (see Loesch & Vacc, 1991). Revision of the NCE is perhaps the most substantive change in professional counselor credentialing currently planned.

COUNSELORS' PROFESSIONAL DEVELOPMENT

Professional development is a general term used in the counseling profession to describe the activities in which professional counselors engage for the purpose of continuing to increase and improve their counseling knowledge and skills, primarily after they have become practitioners (i.e., after they have completed their counselor preparation programs). For at least three reasons, an abundance of "professional development" activities is available to professional counselors. First, many counselors who want to improve themselves participate upon their own initiatives. Second, as counselors progress through their careers, their functions and responsibilities evolve, and so they need "new" knowledge and skills to perform effectively. Third, almost all counseling certification and licensure processes have "continuing education" (i.e., professional development) requirements for recertification or licensure renewal. However, professional literature is minimal on professional development in counseling in general, what types of professional development activities are most appropriate, and which types are most effective. Indeed, although counselors' professional development "makes sense" *conceptually*, scant empirical support exists that it improves the ways counselors counsel. Why then are there so many professional development activities being conducted?

The answer most likely lies in the changing nature of society. As society evolves, so too does its impact on people. People also evolve over the courses of their lives, and their needs which can be addressed by counseling services change, and perhaps increase, concomitantly. These ongoing states of change necessitate that the counseling profession and its members be ever-improving in order to maintain competence and be effective. Therefore, even though little evidence is available to support the impact or effectiveness of professional development activities in counseling, the need for them is only too obvious; professional counselors must be constantly improving if they are to continue helping people effectively.

Perusal of the professional literature reveals that professional development activities for counselors have been suggested, developed, and implemented for literally every aspect of the counseling profession and/or for work with every type of person in society. Accordingly, addressing all the types of activities is not possible given the scope of this chapter. However, a few of the major categories of activities can be addressed.

Counseling Skill Development or Refinement

Increasing personal knowledge and improvement of personal counseling skills is by far the most common type of professional development activity in which counselors engage. Because of knowledge and skill advances derived from theory development, research, and practical experience, existing counseling techniques as well as related ones, such as consultation techniques, are continually being improved, and new techniques are being developed. Therefore, the modern professional counselor always has access to new, and presumably better, ways of doing things. Counselors extend their knowledge and improve their techniques primarily through participation in professional development activities, such as continuing education/training workshops, in-service seminars, convention programs, and self-instruction modules, or through consultation activities. Among these alternatives, the most common type is convention programs. For example, typically, over 400 different programs are presented at the annual ACA convention. Continuing education (i.e., professional development) activities, vis-a-vis convention programs, also are provided frequently at regional and state ACA conventions. Wilcoxon and Hawk (1990) surveyed ACA state branches in regard to provision of continuing education activities for their members and, among other conclusions, indicated that "perhaps the most notable finding in the study is the availability of CEU services at state levels" (p. 93). Generally, these programs are open to anyone registered for the convention, with the exceptions being those few programs for which special fees are charged. The next most common professional development activity is training workshops. These, too, are innumerable because of the large number of organizations, agencies, and individuals presenting them. An example of this type of activity is the large number of "Professional Development Institutes" (PDI's) presented by ACA at various times throughout the year and at various locations. The primary differences between convention programs and training workshops are that the latter are usually longer (e.g., one to three days versus one to three hours for convention programs) and they have larger fees (e.g., $100.00 to $500.00).

Supervision Skill Development

Another major area of professional development for counselors is supervision skill development. Supervision may be defined generally as a specific type of consultation activity in which one professional counselor critiques another's work with clients toward the goal of maximizing the supervisee's skills and effectiveness. Dye and Borders (1990) wrote:

> Over the last 10 years counseling supervision has emerged as a separate specialty within the counseling profession. [C]ompetent supervisors are not only competent counselors but are also able to convey their counseling knowledge and skills (i.e., create learning environments) in ways that promote a supervisee's effectiveness and professional identity. (p. 27)

Because more and more counselors, as well as program administrators and managers, are becoming involved in supervision activities, an increase in professional development activities focusing on supervision has occurred. Impetus for this increase also has come from licensure laws and certification policies that require supervised experience for licensure or certification eligibility and/or renewal. More than ever the counseling profession is acknowledging that supervision, like counseling, requires a strong knowledge base and proven skills in order to be effective. Thus, the counseling profession is emphasizing supervision skill development as an important professional activity for counselors.

Use of Technology

Professional development in regard to use of technology also is currently being emphasized in the counseling profession. So-called "modern technology" in general, and microcomputers in particular, have the potential to dramatically impact the counseling profession; indeed, at least one "computer therapist" already exists (Wagman & Kerber, 1984). In discussing "high technology" in relation to the counseling profession, Harris-Bowlsbey (1984) presented three valid assumptions:

> First, high technology will never replace high touch in the human resource development field. Although robots may make automobiles better and faster. . .human beings will never be better counseled or guided by robots, computers, or interactive videodiscs. A second assumption is that high technology and high touch should be viewed not as opponents, but as potential partners. . . . Third, presumably the profession's thinking about the merger of high technology and high touch is new and tentative; therefore the counselors whom we educate and supervise will need preservice and in-service training. . . (p. 7)

Harris-Bowlsbey's third assumption is apparently true in that a multitude of professional development activities concerning the uses of computers in counseling have been offered and are well-attended. Moreover, given the rapid advances in technology, this trend shows no sign of decreasing. However, use of various computer applications in counseling has not been uniformly embodied. Sampson and Krumboltz (1991) indicated:

> The availability of computer applications in counseling has increased dramatically over the last 10 years.

> These applications encompass a wide diversity of topics relating to personal, family, career, and educational counseling, as well as administrative, research, and counselor training functions.

> An examination of published literature and presentations at professional meetings, however, reveals that certain types of computer software in counseling have received much greater attention than others. In particular, computer-assisted testing and computer-assisted career guidance have been

described and researched far more often than the use of computer-assisted instruction by clients in relation to personal, social, family, and career issues. (p. 395)

Thus it is likely that use of technology will continue to be a focus of professional development activities for professional counselors.

Burnout Prevention or Amelioration

The fourth major area of professional development for counselors is burnout prevention or amelioration. A classic question in the counseling profession is, who counsels the counselors? Counseling is an emotionally taxing activity that extracts an extremely heavy toll from counselors. Thus counselors, perhaps as much or more than people in any other profession, are susceptible to "burnout"; a state of emotional lethargy wherein motivation to perform is low, and skills and talents are used inefficiently and ineffectively. Because of the increasing incidence of burnout among counselors, many professional development activities have been and are presented to help counselors avoid it. These activities are intended to enable counselors to monitor and moderate their professional (and sometimes personal) activities so that they are able to continually "regenerate their professional energies" and in so doing maintain and increase their level of effectiveness.

Participation in professional development activities is an important part of a counselor's professional orientation. It is the means by which professional counselors "keep current," improve, and remain professionally motivated. As with participation in professional organizations and attainment of professional credentials, participation in professional development activities benefits both counselors and the clients to whom they provide services.

PROFESSIONAL CONTRIBUTIONS BY COUNSELORS

The fourth aspect of professional orientation, making contributions to the theoretical and knowledge bases of the counseling profession, is much smaller in scope than the first three because, unfortunately, only a small proportion of counselors are actively involved in it. That is, the primary means by which counselors make contributions to the profession in general is through research and publication activities, and only a small proportion of counselors conduct research and/ or write for publication in professional journals. Two primary reasons have been offered for this unfortunate circumstance: (1) counselors lack substantive research skills and therefore are not comfortable, capable, or confident in conducting or publishing research, and (2) counseling research results have not been readily applicable to counseling activities and, therefore, counselors see little value in it.

Goldman (1976, 1978) suggested that counselors are "turned off" to research because, among other reasons, during their training programs they were exposed to unreasonable expectations for research activities. He stated that the counseling profession has "sanctified precision, measurement, statistical methodology, and the controlled laboratory experiment" (Goldman, 1976, p. 545) and, in so doing, has set the standards for research and publication so high that most counselors or trainees feel incapable of achieving it and, therefore, do not try. Galassi, Stoltz, Brooks, and Trexler (1987) added that "a frequent explanation for this low [research] productivity is that the research training provided in doctoral programs has been ineffective in training students to conduct and value research" (p. 40). Empirical evidence to support these positions is scant, but results of counselors' performance on the NBCC's NCE seem to suggest that research is among counselors' lesser areas of competence. That is, scores on the Research and Evaluation subsection of the NCE have been consistently lower than those for other subsections (Loesch & Vacc, 1988). Thus, possibly, counselors in general do not have great degrees of proficiency in research. However, Goldman (1977) also has argued that extensive research skill proficiency is not really necessary for counselors to conduct meaningful research. Rather, he posited that counselors should strive to conduct research that is within their realm of competence.

It is unlikely that the debate over counselors' *needed* levels of proficiency in research will ever be resolved. However, there is little reason to continue the debate. Even if counselors' research proficiency levels are low, forces within the counseling profession are present which will more than likely result in their elevation. Specifically, moderately high research proficiency levels are evident in all counselor-preparation program standards (such as CACREP's) and in counselor certification (such as NBCC's) and licensure requirements. Therefore, counselors will have to have at least minimal levels of research competence in order to achieve those credentials.

The lack of relevance-of-research results to counseling practice has been suggested by many authors, perhaps most notably by Goldman and his collaborating authors (1978). They suggested that counselors should not strive to investigate problems that fit "rigorous" research standards but rather, should adopt presumably less rigorous research approaches that fit problems with which counselors are confronted. Thus they advocate making research activities more relevant to counseling practice by focusing on the actualities of counseling situations rather than on adherence to traditional, and presumably higher, research methodology standards. Mehrens (1978) has taken an alternative position.

> Those who wish to relax rigor often seem to hope that sloppy research will increase relevance. I posit that it is seldom, if ever, the case that relevance and rigor are purely ipsative. Increasing rigor need not always demand the examination of a less relevant problem; examining a more relevant problem need not always mean that we must relax the rigor. (Mehrens, 1978, pp. 10-11)

In essence, Mehrens is arguing that the way for counselors to gain relevant information from counseling research is to use the most rigorous methods, i.e., that the best information comes from the most rigorous research methodology.

Again, further argument in this regard is unlikely to be productive. The major point is that regardless of individual approaches or perspectives posited, consensus seems to be present among authors that counselors should engage in research activities. Engels and Muro (1986) commented:

> Vacc and Loesch (1983) offered excellent general and specific suggestions and questions regarding the necessity for research as a means of self-regulation and self-evaluation, leading

to a fruitful progressing and maturing in all aspects of the profession. We join in advocating inquiry as an integral, ongoing part of preparation programs and professional practice, with dedication to scientific and human inquiry and a healthy skepticism to generate a dialectic for ongoing improvements in effectiveness and data to document those improvements. (pp. 301-302)

Martin and Martin (1989) clearly summarized how research fits within the counseling profession:

> . . .while appropriate research may not immediately change the field of counseling, the impact of research cannot be felt until clinicians accept applicable findings. Research results will never totally guide clinical practice; the number of variables is far greater than could ever be examined. However, research can be informative and help guide choices. Using research findings with sound clinical judgment helps counselors more ably assist their clients, which is the one common goal among researchers and clinicians alike. (pp. 491-492)

Thus, research (and the subsequent publication of its results by professional counselors) not only is consistent with the empirical counseling approach advocated in this book but is also the primary means by which counselors improve the counseling profession.

SUMMARY

Becoming a professional counselor is not easy. Much has to be learned, many skills have to be developed, and an appropriate orientation has to be adopted. Learning and skill development must continue across the life span, therefore *being* a professional counselor is not easy either. However, professional counselors enjoy many, many intrinsic and extrinsic rewards. These rewards are gained primarily through joining professional organizations, attaining professional credentials, engaging in professional development activities, and making contributions to the counseling profession. For the vast majority of professional counselors, the benefits gained far outweigh the efforts expended. More importantly, society and the people in it gain significantly from professional counselors participating in these activities. What greater good is there than that?

Chapter **4**

PROFESSIONAL PREPARATION OF COUNSELORS

The preceding chapters illustrate that neither singular nor simple answers exist to the questions "What is a professional counselor?" and "What does a professional counselor do?" There also is no singular or simple answer to the question "How should professional counselors be prepared?" Indeed, the question, "What should be done to produce a good counselor?" has been a source of continuous debate since the inception of the counseling profession. Given the current complexities of the counseling profession, a response to this question must necessarily be multifaceted. Further, underlying issues must be addressed before the responses can be understood.

ISSUES IN COUNSELOR PREPARATION

It is obvious from historical perspective, research, observation, and just plain common sense that professional counselors are differentially effective in their counseling activities; some counselors simply are better than others. While the effectiveness differential is readily acknowledged, causes of the differentiation are not. Some of the major issues involved can be best stated and addressed as questions.

1. Are professional counselors born or made?

The vast majority of professional counselors like to conceive of themselves as empathic, warm, caring, concerned, hopeful, and loving people whose primary goal in life is "to help other people." The professional counseling literature also promotes these qualities as necessary for effective counseling (e.g., Corey, Corey, & Callanan, 1988; Okun, 1987). Relatedly, counseling research generally shows that the greater the extent to which counselors *convey* these and related characteristics (such as those discussed in Chapter 1), the more effective they are in their professional counseling activities. Accordingly, considerable concern has been and continues to be focused upon the "personal characteristics" of potential professional counselors. The central issue is whether potential counselors must have certain types of personal characteristics *before* counselor preparation or whether they can (and must) develop appropriate characteristics during preparation programs.

From 1950s into 1980s, a substantial portion of the professional counseling literature and research focused upon the specification and/or determination of counselor characteristics associated with counseling effectiveness. This effort potentially had highly significant implications, because if personal characteristics could be shown to be definitively associated with counseling effectiveness then those characteristics could be used as selection criteria for persons wanting to enter counselor preparation programs. That is, applicants possessing the "appropriate" characteristics to the greatest extent would be admitted to counselor preparation programs, while those possessing the characteristics to a lesser extent would be denied admission and, therefore, presumably denied access to the counseling profession.

The search for characteristics associated with counseling effectiveness has covered an amazingly diverse array of counselors' personal attributes and of aspects of counseling effectiveness and has involved use of an equally diverse set of measurement and evaluation instruments and techniques and data analysis procedures. However, even though substantial effort has been invested, clear and definitive results have not been found. For example, Rowe, Murphy, and De Csipkes (1975) conducted a comprehensive analysis of the 1960 to 1974 professional literature on the relationships between counselor and/or counselor trainee *personality* characteristics and counselor effectiveness and concluded that further search for such relationships should be discontinued because the results of previous studies were "generally disappointing, often contradictory, and only tentative" (p. 241). Conversely, Wiggins and Weslander (1986) concluded that

> . . .their study demonstrated some definite differences between groups of [school] counselors rated as effective or ineffective. Ineffective counselors are rated low by the supervisors, are dissatisfied with their jobs, have low self-esteem, have a low level of tolerance for ambiguity, and are not correlated significantly with the Holland environmental code for counselors. Effective counselors are rated high by the supervisors, are happy with their jobs, have high self-esteem, have a high level for tolerance for ambiguity, and have congruent Holland codes. (pp. 34-35)

Thus, the best statement that can be made is that some professionals believe that definitive associations have been established between personal characteristics and counselor effectiveness, while others believe such associations have not been determined. Thus, many counselor-preparation programs use evaluations of applicants' personal characteristics for selection purposes, while many others do not. The search continues.

The alternative side of this issue holds that appropriate personal characteristics are developed within the context of counselor-preparation programs. Again, however, conflicting evidence exists about whether desirable changes actually take place. For example, Zahner and McDavis (1980) concluded that "The results [of their study] . . . indicate that training for both the professional and paraprofessional groups [of counselors] has minimal influence on moral development of its current or past students" (p. 248). Conversely, Schwab and Harris (1981) concluded that "The results [of their study] suggest . . . that counselor trainees do change and grow toward being more self-actualizing from the time they enter to the time they graduate from their counselor training program" (p.222). It is generally accepted that counselor-preparation programs do change the personal characteristics of the people who participate in them. However, the exact nature and extent of these changes have not yet been fully determined.

The debate about whether good counselors are "born or made" has been de-emphasized in counselor-preparation practice today for two reasons. First, the relationship between counselor trainees' *possession* of measurable personal characteristics and the ability to *convey* desirable personal characteristics has not been shown to be direct. For example, because a concept such as empathy is extremely difficult to measure validly, researchers typically have focused upon related concepts, such as altruism, and **inferred** an associated ability to be empathic. However, a counselor trainee who scores high in altruism on some personality inventory is not necessarily inherently able to convey empathy in counseling processes. Thus the search for personal characteristics associated with counseling effectiveness is thwarted both theoretically and pragmatically and has not yielded results substantial enough to warrant continued emphasis.

Second, and more importantly, most counselor preparation programs today attend to both sides of the debate. That is, most attend to initial "personal characteristics" of applicants in their student selection procedures, although the nature and extent of the attention given varies greatly. Procedures employed range from the use of specific, multifaceted evaluations (e.g., "personality" inventories and personal interviews) to the use of global indicators of applicants' personal characteristics (e.g., reference letters and applicant goal statements). Most counselor-preparation programs also incorporate activities intended to enhance participants' personal characteristics. Again, these procedures vary from very specific (e.g., "sensitivity" group activities designed to improve self-disclosure abilities) to general activities (e.g., lectures on professional commitment). Thus, a major professional issue has been de-emphasized and avoided through accepted preparation practices.

2. What selection criteria are important?

Counselor preparation programs are similar to other professional preparation programs in offering primarily graduate-level (i.e., post baccalaureate) curricula. A distinguishing feature of counselor-preparation programs is the lack of a standard undergraduate-level (i.e., baccalaureate) curriculum. For example, persons aspiring to be physicians typically must first complete a "pre-med" undergraduate curriculum and persons aspiring to be lawyers must complete a "pre-law" undergraduate curriculum. In contrast, although persons aspiring to be counseling or clinical psychologist typically must first complete a "psychology" undergraduate curriculum, no "standard" undergraduate curriculum must be completed before persons can enter counselor-preparation programs. Institutions with undergraduate-level counselor-preparation curricula do exist, but they are extremely rare. Therefore, the undergraduate programs completed by applicants to counselor-preparation programs are diverse. In fact, students in counselor-preparation programs represent extremely varied previous academic preparations, including those in the areas of the "social" and "hard" sciences, liberal arts, fine arts, and business. This situation has had, and continues to have, significant implications for the selection of students for counselor-preparation programs.

During the early years of the counseling profession, as described in Chapter 2, most professional counselors worked in educational institutions, primarily as secondary-school counselors. Persons seeking entry to counselor-preparation programs usually held baccalaureate degrees in education and frequently were working as teachers. In addition, many counseling professionals then viewed previous training and experience in "teaching" as "necessary" for becoming an effective school counselor, perhaps because most state departments of education required prior teaching experience for certification as a school counselor.

As the counseling profession has evolved and become diversified, the relevance and importance of prior training and experience in teaching has been de-emphasized for several reasons. First, the proportion of professional counselors who work in schools has decreased significantly; therefore, the potential relevance of prior teaching experience has decreased proportionately. Second, a considerable number of states now certify persons to work as school counselors who have not had teaching experience but who have completed school counselor-preparation programs. Third, research has not shown that school counselors with previous training and experience in teaching are more effective than school counselors without teaching experience; no empirical basis exists for suggesting that teaching experience is particularly beneficial in becoming an effective counselor. Even in light of these considerations, however, a substantial portion of professional counselors have completed baccalaureate curricula in education. One reason is that school counselors still constitute a significant portion of professional counselors in general, and many of them have had prior training and experience in teaching. Another is that most counselor-preparation programs are housed in schools or colleges of education within institutions of higher education, so undergraduate education majors typically have a greater probability than other undergraduate students of becoming familiar with counselor-preparation programs.

When school counseling and the associated prerequisites were preeminent in the counseling profession, counselor educators (trainers) could hold reasonable, relatively common assumptions about the previous academic and experiential backgrounds of students in counselor-preparation programs. More importantly, they could build upon those assumptions in the construction of counselor-preparation curricula. Today, however, making generalized assumptions about students' prior training and experiences is not possible, and counselor preparation programs must be constructed to accommodate students with widely varying backgrounds.

Academic performance and aptitude are perhaps the most widely used selection criteria for entry into counselor-preparation programs. Undergraduate grade point average is the most commonly used indicator of applicants' academic *performance.* The most commonly used indicator of applicants' academic *aptitude* is their score(s) on graduate-level academic aptitude tests. For example, in reference to counselor-preparation programs, Hollis and Wantz (1986, p. 55) indicated that "the most frequently used standardized test as a selection instrument is the Graduate Record Examination (GRE)." Because counselor-preparation programs are composed of graduate-level curricula, students must have sufficient academic skills and aptitude to complete satisfactorily the academic requirements. However, research generally shows that these indicators are neither substantially related to nor particularly good predictors of counseling effectiveness. Therefore, academic performance and aptitude indicators continue to be used, because they help identify students who will successfully complete counselor-preparation academic requirements, not because they are good predictors of counseling effectiveness.

Counselor-preparation programs generally require applicants to have letters of reference submitted with their applications for evaluating an individual's "character," "potential for academic success," "potential for success as a counselor," or any combination of these factors. Hollis and Wantz (1990) indicated that three letters of reference is the average requirement used by counselor-preparation programs. Unfortunately, evaluations provided in reference letters usually add little, if any, discriminative power in the prediction of either academic success or counseling effectiveness. Thus, while the practice is common, the actual benefits of requiring applicant reference letters are few.

Some counselor-preparation programs require applicants to submit a "goal(s) statement" that includes a brief explanation of what the applicant intends to do upon graduation from the program. Goal statements are used in evaluating the extent to which applicants have made decisions about their vocational aspirations. Generally, the more focused the applicant's goal statement, the more favorable its evaluation, because identification of specific goals typically facilitates delineation of appropriate preparation activities (i.e., specific work settings and/or counseling activities). Unfortunately, the nature of the counseling profession and of counselor-preparation programs detracts from the usefulness of goal statements. Many people are unaware of the many different aspects of the counseling profession until after they have been admitted to counselor-preparation programs (in part because of the lack of undergraduate programs). Thus, applicants' goal statements typically reflect a restricted knowledge base which, in turn, restricts their usefulness. However, goals statements do provide a tangential benefit in the selection process; they allow program faculty to make at least a cursory evaluation of applicants' writing abilities. Such information is of some use for making judgments about applicants' abilities to complete graduate-level writing assignments effectively.

An increasing number of counselor-preparation programs are using "personal interviews" as part of student selection processes. Typically, applicants are queried either individually or in groups by one or more program faculty about their prior educational and/or professional experiences, professional plans and aspirations, or other topics specific to particular preparation program situations. Personal interviews are useful for evaluation of applicants' verbal communication skills, language usage, general demeanor, and self-presentation.

Beyond these commonly used selection criteria (i.e., academic performance indicators, reference letters, goal statements, and interviews), there is only diversity. Indeed, additional selection criteria are almost as varied as are counselor-preparation programs. Some of these selection criteria are related to requirements for counselor certification or licensure, others to specific theoretical orientations held by program faculty, and still others to specific intended job placements for program graduates. Thus, no universal credentials exist that applicants to counselor-preparation programs must possess. Even the few commonalities that *are* shared relate primarily to academic success, rather than to counseling effectiveness. However, this situation should not be construed as negative. Rather, it is an appropriate reflection of the diverse nature of the counseling profession. Various professional counselors fulfill many different roles and functions, and, people aspiring to be counselors should have credentials as varied as their intended roles.

3. How much academic preparation is necessary?

The delicate balance between efficiency and effectiveness is difficult to define and even harder to achieve in many aspects of the counseling profession. For example, professional counselors always strive to provide the best possible services for their clients in the shortest possible time periods and with the least possible disruptions to and/or discomforts in clients' lives. In brief, professional counselors try to obtain for each client the best results as quickly and as easily as possible. An analogous situation exists for counselor preparation. The goal is to prepare effective professional counselors expeditiously. At issue is *how*.

One factor influencing the nature of counselor-preparation program requirements is the nature of the students who enroll in them. Because students enter counselor-preparation programs with widely varying backgrounds, such programs must build upon an uneven foundation; therefore, establishing a "starting point" for counselor preparation is difficult. If the starting point includes excessive pre-program requirements, many persons who otherwise might have entered counselor-preparation programs will not do so because of the perceived "extra" work necessary just to start the programs. Conversely, persons who have had relatively extensive prior preparations may find the initial counselor preparation work to be mundane or redundant and, thus, lose motivation. Typically, counselor-preparation programs respond to this situation by incorporating a few "pre-program" requirements. These are usually a few courses, such as those covering personality theories, abnormal psychology, learning theories, or basic statistics, that most applicants to the program have already completed. Students who have completed the pre-program requirements begin the "basic" counselor-preparation program curriculum upon admission. Students who have not completed the pre-program requirements are usually required to take them soon after admission, and before they begin the "basic" counselor-preparation program curriculum. Thus, counselor-preparation programs attempt to "level the foundation" by creating a "happy medium" among the diverse backgrounds of program applicants.

The length of time and amount of credit hours needed for counselor preparation also are confounded by external forces pertinent to professional practice. For example, state-level requirements for certification as a school counselor are typically less numerous than those of counselor-preparation programs because school counselor-certification requirements in most states are based on the assumption that school counselors will have had prior teaching experience. Requirements for school counselor certification in those states are often merely listings of courses, as opposed to requirements for completion of a fully integrated counselor preparation program. Conversely, in many of the states that have counselor licensure laws, the number of requirements for being licensed as a counselor is greater than that of most counselor-preparation programs (e.g., in regard to supervised counseling experience). State legislatures have taken conservative approaches to "protecting the public welfare" in constructing their counselor licensure laws by including relatively extensive requirements. In addition to forces at the state level, national counselor certifying agencies have an influence on counselor preparation programs. These agencies typically have eligibility requirements approximating those of state licensure laws and therefore tend to exceed those of the majority of counselor preparation programs. To summarize, some external forces influence increases in the length of time and amount of coursework required for counselor preparation, while others, in effect, influence decreases or, at least, maintenance of the status quo.

A third aspect of this issue relates to the academic bases for specifying the time length and/or coursework for counselor preparation. Typically, guidelines for counselor preparation have specified that programs should require a specified minimum number of academic credit hours. Although this approach allows for relatively easy *quantitative* comparisons of minimum requirements across counselor preparation programs, it is fraught with pragmatic difficulties. For example, although "quarter-hour" credits can be converted to "semester-hour" credits relatively easily, and vice versa, numeric conversions do not necessarily reflect content equivalence, even across courses having similar titles. Further, wide variations occur in minimum credit-hour requirements for similarly titled degrees across institutions within states and across states. For two counselor-preparation programs to have essentially similar *content* (or course) requirements and to award similarly titled degrees and yet to have substantially different *quantity* (minimum credit-hour) requirements is possible and, in fact, quite common. This situation becomes even more confounded when variations in individual instructional styles and emphases are considered.

That is, even when relatively specific guidelines have been presented for elements of counselor-preparation programs, individual instructors have considerable freedom in interpretation and implementation of those guidelines and elements.

Partly in response to the difficulties in attempting to equate minimum credit hour requirements and partly for theoretical reasons, some counselor-preparation guidelines specify enrollment in programs for a minimum period, as well as for a minimum number of credit hours. The former requirement is based on the idea that the development of effective counseling skills entails more than rote accumulation of knowledge. The belief is that effective counselors synthesize and apply knowledge learned in "typical" (i.e., didactic) courses and that it then takes time and practice for counselor trainees to develop applied skills. Thus, the requirement of a minimum time period for enrollment is viewed as a way of "insuring" that counselor trainees have had sufficient time to synthesize and integrate knowledge before they attempt to apply it in the actual practice of professional counseling.

Current guidelines for counselor-preparation programs attempt to be simultaneously responsive to a wide variety of factors. Accordingly, they reflect a series of compromises between what is theoretically desirable and what is practical, and between what is desirable and what is possible. Fortunately, the guidelines generally have been effective in achieving the delicate balances among these considerations, primarily through increasing the length of counselor-preparation programs in general and the supervised field-experience components in particular (Hollis & Wantz, 1990, 1993).

4. What should be the minimum degree?

Closely related to the question of what should be the minimum academic preparation necessary for counselors is the question of which academic degree should reflect that minimum preparation. Because counselor preparation is almost exclusively provided at the graduate (i.e., post-baccalaureate) level, there are basically two choices: master's or doctorate. If a broad, encompassing definition of who are "counselors" is accepted, then both degrees will have been proffered as the required minimum. For example, clinical social workers and marriage and family therapists have long operated on the belief that the *master's degree* is the appropriate minimum for "entry" into the counseling profession, while clinical and counseling psychologists have held that the *doctorate* is the necessary minimum.

A more focused definition of who "counselors" are has been presented in Chapter 1, and, within that perspective, the master's degree is clearly the accepted minimum (i.e., "entry-level") degree. Far more master's-level programs exist than doctoral-level counselor-preparation programs (see Hollis & Wantz, 1990, 1993). Further, all states having counselor licensure laws and all national counselor certification agencies stipulate that the master's degree is the required minimum for state licensure and national certification. Of course, state school counselor-certification requirements have long stipulated that the master's degree is the necessary minimum for such certification. Thus, for professional counselors, the master's degree is the accepted minimum academic degree required for entry into the counseling profession.

An interesting question associated with acceptance of the master's degree as the minimum requirement for counselors is what should be the nature and purposes of the doctorate in counseling (i.e., in counselor education, as distinguished from the doctorate in clinical or counseling psychology)? At least one prominent counselor educator has argued that the doctorate in counseling should be focused upon preparation of counselors having advanced "clinical" skills who would be best-suited for work in community agencies (Randolph, 1990). Others (Vacc, 1990; Wittmer & Loesch, 1990) have argued that such a focus would be inconsistent with perspectives held in the counseling profession and that emulation of other professionals would not be particularly fruitful for professional counselors. Lanning (1990) suggested that persons holding a doctorate in counseling should have an "educator/practitioner" orientation and fulfill four primary professional roles: (1) counselor educator/trainer, (2) counselor trainee supervisor, (3) researcher, and (4) counseling practitioner. It is unlikely that this issue will be resolved in the near future. However, regardless of debate about the issue, it is likely that the master's degree will remain the minimum academic degree for professional counselors.

5. What should be emphasized?

Two major issues are raised by this question: what content and skill areas and what method of instruction should be emphasized in counselor-preparation programs?

Counselor Education and Supervision is a professional journal devoted in part to the presentation of ideas, research, and practices in counselor preparation. Perusal of issues of this journal, for even a relatively small time span, such as a year, reveals extremely large and diverse sets of knowledge and skills with which counselors are supposed to be familiar and adept. The idea can be gained from this journal, as well as from many others, that professional counselors are supposed to know about everything, be able to do anything, and be able to work effectively with many, many different types of people. Quite obviously this is not possible, and more importantly, it is probably not desirable. Counselors, like most other professionals today, tend to "specialize," either in terms of clients to whom services are rendered or in terms of types of skills and activities used. Nonetheless, a common assumption in the counseling profession is that a "basic" body of knowledge and a set of "basic" skills should be possessed by all counselors regardless of professional specialization. Thus it is a widely held belief in the counseling profession that a "generic" base of knowledge and skills must be learned and achieved by all professional counselors.

Considerable debate has always existed over the nature of the generic knowledge and skill base for professional counseling. The recommendations for the various knowledge and skill areas to be included in this generic base are far too numerous to be elaborated here; suffice it to state that knowledge of almost all aspects of human functioning and almost all counseling skills have at one time or another been proffered as being "essential" for all professional counselors. As a result, over the last several decades, counselor trainers and professional counselors have been engaged in an effort to achieve a degree of consensus about the nature of generic preparation for professional counselors. Although some of the results of this effort were alluded to in Chapter 1, they also will be discussed further in a later section of this chapter.

Somewhat less consensus exists about relative emphases given to different methods of instruction in counselor-preparation programs. Debated is the amount of instruction which should be didactic compared with how much should be experiential. Didactic instruction involves the presentation of knowledge by an instructor through lectures and material resources to typically large groups of counselor trainees (i.e., typical classroom instruction). Experiential instruction, however, means that counselor trainees "learn by doing," typically under close supervision. Experts agree that some of each of these types of instruction should be incorporated into counselor-preparation programs, because some knowledge areas are covered most effectively through didactic instruction, and some skills are taught most effectively through supervised experiential instruction. However, the most appropriate method is not readily apparent in many areas. For example, agreement exists that all counselor trainees need to have good understandings of professional ethics. Didactic instruction is usually a good way for counselor trainees to learn the *contents* of various professional codes of ethics. However, the *applications* of professional ethics involve complex sets of intricate decisions and value judgments, and didactic instruction is probably less effective in this regard. Experiential instruction techniques, such as supervised "role-playing," are usually better for teaching counselor trainees how to *apply* professional ethics. But, the question remains, how much time should be devoted to each type of instruction? For the most part, the answer to this question has been left to the discretion of counselor trainers in the respective counselor-preparation programs.

6. How should counselor preparation be evaluated?

The evaluation of counselor-preparation program effectiveness has undoubtedly received the least attention of any of the major aspects of the counseling profession. While a considerable number of research investigations of the effectiveness of specific aspects of counselor training has been made, reports of total program effectiveness evaluations are almost nonexistent in the professional counseling literature. This unfortunate state of affairs is in direct contrast to increasing emphases on "personal" (i.e., individual) accountability for professional counselors. The professional counseling literature is replete with statements that professional counselors must be "accountable" for their professional and personal activities, but apparently counselor preparation programs are not holding themselves to similar standards.

In fairness, acknowledgement should be made that significant obstacles in conducting evaluations of counselor-preparation programs exist, not the least of which is determining appropriate criteria for effectiveness. Further, counseling professionals typically receive little or no formal preparation in program evaluation strategies or techniques (Wheeler & Loesch, 1981). Moreover, the counseling profession is not unique in these regards; few disciplines in the "social sciences" in general, or the "helping professions" in particular, have devoted much time and effort to preparation program evaluation activities. However, difficulties, lack of expertise, and common practice not withstanding, very little evidence is available to show that counselor-preparation programs achieve what they are supposed to accomplish.

Professional counselors are frequently admonished to engage in individual accountability activities so they can have control over criteria for effectiveness rather than having criteria "imposed" upon them. This appears to be sage advice. However, the counseling profession apparently has not listened to its own advice—and with predictable results. "External forces" are having a significant influence on what constitutes effective counselor preparation. The most common "forces" in this regard are state and national counselor-certification and licensure agencies. Professional counselor certification or licensure "eligibility" requirements literally define counselor-preparation program effectiveness, at least for professional counselors seeking those credentials. Professional counselors have had significant input into certification and licensure requirements and therefore have had some say in what constitutes counselor-preparation program effectiveness. However, other persons (e.g., legislators and lay persons) have had significant roles in establishing certification and licensure eligibility criteria. As a result, the counseling profession has relinquished at least part of its control over definition and/ or determination of counselor-preparation program effectiveness.

There is a "hopeful" side to this situation. Concern about the nature of counselor preparation has been increasing during the last three decades, and in the early 1980s, substantial investments of thought, time, effort, and resources came to fruition in the establishment of commonly accepted "standards of preparation" for professional counselors. The establishment and application of counselor-preparation program standards is not synonymous with counselor-preparation program evaluation. However, the standards of preparation serve to reflect the counseling profession's definition of what constitutes effective minimum counselor preparation. Thus, the movement toward application of the standards of preparation is a significant and necessary step toward evaluation of those programs.

STANDARDS OF PREPARATION

Chapter 2 described how the counseling profession evolved from a few individuals' rather inauspicious concerns about the vocational developments of adolescents into a comprehensive and complex profession that attempts to address the multitude of mental health services needs of literally all people in society. Current philosophies, practices, and trends in the preparation of professional counselors have evolved along an analogous course. In the early, formative years of the counseling profession, relatively little disagreement about the professional preparation of counselors existed, primarily because little differentiation among counselors was present and the vast majority of professional counselors were working in schools and had been teachers. Counselors had common backgrounds and common vocational goals, and preparation was "simply" facilitation of transition from one role to another role in the school. However, as more and more distinct facets, roles, and functions emerged within the counseling profession, agreement about the nature of professional counselor preparation dissipated. In fact, considerable disagreement arose about the preferred nature of counselor preparation during the 1940s and 1950s. This situation prompted some members of the counseling profession to examine both what was happening and what they would like to see in counselor preparation. Thus began the push for "standardized" professional preparation for counselors.

Historical Development

Similar to attempting to describe the evolution of the counseling profession in its entirety, to cover all the activities relevant to the evolution of current practices in counselor preparation is not possible. Therefore, the tactic of describing the evolution of one professional entity specifically concerned with counselor preparation will be used. That entity is the Council for the Accreditation of Counseling and Related Educational Programs (CACREP).

CACREP lineage can be traced to the National Association of Guidance Supervisors (NAGS). One of the reasons for the founding of NAGS was to bring together individuals (i.e., supervisors of school guidance personnel) who had common concerns. Among their concerns was how to effectively supervise and administrate counselors whose roles and functions were changing and expanding and, concomitantly, whose preparations were becoming more diverse. This latter aspect prompted counselor trainers to become interested in and involved with the issue and, in part, led to the formation of the National Association of Counselor Supervisors and Counselor Trainers (NAGSCT) in 1952. Throughout the nine-year life span of NAGSCT, interest in counselor preparation and the attention given to it were increasing. Relatedly, counselor trainers (educators) were becoming increasingly involved in the activities of the association and eventually dominated its perspectives. This shift is partially reflected in the change of the name from NAGSCT to the Association for Counselor Education and Supervision (ACES), wherein counselor education/training and supervision are transposed.

The desirability of "standardizing" counselor preparation rose to prominence within ACES in the late 1950s and early 1960s, although the prominence was in fact fostered by a relatively small proportion of ACES' membership. However, ACES' membership was generally receptive to the idea of developing "standards of preparation," and in 1963 that division endorsed an initial set of standards of preparation that would, theoretically, apply to all (graduate-level) programs preparing professional counselors. Perhaps more importantly, it also committed to continue to develop the initial (ACES') standards of preparation. An interesting note, however, is that while ACES *endorsed* the *standards of preparation and their further development*, ACES did not endorse a *requirement* that counselor-preparation programs adopt and/or abide by those standards.

As attention to standards of preparation continued to increase within ACES, other professional associations also became interested in the issues involved and initiated their own activities. For example, the American School Counselor Association (ASCA) adopted a set of specific guidelines for preparation of secondary school counselors in 1967 and another specific set for elementary school counselors the next year. Similarly, the American College Personnel Association (ACPA) in 1968 adopted specific preparation guidelines for student personnel workers. Other associations did not formally adopt guidelines but instead increased their involvement through input and feedback to the members of ACES who were most involved in the development of ACES' standards of preparation.

In response to the then relatively widespread interest in standards of preparation, ACES' "Commission on Standards and Accreditation" was created in 1971. The significance of this event was two-fold. First, it was a reaffirmation of ACES' commitment to the development of standards of preparation. Second, and perhaps more important, it was the first formal acknowledgement of ACES' intent to establish procedures for accrediting counselor preparation programs. Thus, it signified ACES' commitment to implementing a plan wherein counselor-preparation programs would be required to use and abide by the standards of preparation.

ACES' efforts relative to development of the standards resulted in the adoption of *Standards for Preparation of Counselors and Other Personnel Services Specialists* in 1973. This first set of standards delineated preparation guidelines for what is referred to as "entry-level" preparation: the minimum preparation necessary to assume a beginning position as a professional counselor. Subsequently, in 1977 ACES adopted the *Guidelines for Doctoral Preparation in Counselor Education* to be applied to doctoral-level counselor preparation programs. Both of these sets of standards were revised and, in 1979, adopted by ACES as the *Standards for Entry Preparation (Master's and Specialists) of Counselors and Other Personnel-Services Specialists* and the *Standards for Advanced Preparation (Doctoral) in Counselor Education.* Concurrent with the adoption of the 1979 revised standards, ACES began to accredit counselor-preparation programs according to those standards. ACES worked closely with the California Association for Counselor Education and Supervision (CACES), because CACES had already accredited a few programs in California using its own standards, which were similar to ACES' standards.

The initiatives shown by ACES in the development of standards of preparation and the implementation of preparation program accreditation activities were generally accepted by the counseling profession, but they also severely taxed the resources of ACES. Thus, in 1980 the ACA (then AACD) Board of Directors voted to adopt both sets of ACES' standards, to support further work on the standards, and to establish and support an entity to conduct broad-scale activities relative to counselor program accreditation. This latter commitment led directly to the formation of (CACREP).

CACREP held its first official meeting in September of 1981, at which time it officially adopted the ACES/ACA (AACD) entry-level and advanced-level standards of preparation, recognized and accepted the accreditations awarded by ACES (and therefore by CACES), and established ideological and procedural guidelines for its own accreditation process.

CACREP is currently an "organizational affiliate" of ACA. This means that it is a legally distinct (i.e., technically separate from AACD), not-for-profit organization which focuses solely on activities necessary for the accreditation of counselor-preparation programs. However, while CACREP is legally distinct from ACA and is not directly involved in ACA's functioning, it does have non-technical linkages to ACA. For one thing, CACREP, like most other accrediting agencies, is not financially self-supporting and receives some financial support from ACA for its operations. For another, CACREP's membership is aligned with the ACA divisional structure; members of the "Council" are placed there by ACA and ACA divisions. For example, in 1992, the Council included representatives from ACA's Association for Counselor Education and Supervision (ACES), Association for Assessment in Counseling (AAC), American Mental Health Counselors Association (AMHCA), American College Counselor Association (ACCA), National Career Development Association (NCDA), Association for Multicultural Counseling and Development (AMCD), American Rehabilitation Counselors Association (ARCA), Association for Specialists in Group Work (ASGW), Association for Religious and Value Issues in Counseling (ARVIC), International Association of Marriage and Family Counselors (IAMFC), and Association for Humanistic Education and Development (AHEAD). Also, a representative from ACA is on the Council (and therefore ACA is technically a *member* of the Council), a public representative, and the CACREP Executive Director who serves as an *ex officio* member of the Council. Other ACA divisions are permitted to place representatives on the Council but, as of 1992, have not done so. This configuration allows CACREP to maintain close philosophical ties with the ACA while functioning autonomously. For example, between 1981 and 1986, CACREP incorporated several relatively minor changes in the standards of preparation being applied as well as "guidelines" for several aspects of preparation without obtaining approval from ACA. Thus, today, CACREP has its own standards of preparation and accreditation processes, although they are philosophically aligned with ACA purposes and goals.

CACREP accreditation is program specific; it accredits individual preparation programs instead of the academic units (i.e., departments) in which the programs are housed. Because of the diversity of individual preparation program titles used in different academic units in colleges and universities, CACREP accredits programs only under the program titles it has adopted. The entry-level program titles used by CACREP are (1) **School Counseling (SC)**, (2) **Student Affairs Practice in Higher Education (SA)**, (3) **Marriage and Family Counseling/Therapy (MFCT)**, (4) **Community Counseling (CC)**, and (5) **Mental Health Counseling (MHC)**. Within entry-level SA programs, one of three possible program emphases is identified: (a) **Counseling,** for persons intending to become counselors in colleges and universities **(SAC)**, (b) *Administrative,* for persons intending to become administrators of college and/or university student services programs **(SAA)**, or (c) *Developmental,* for persons intending to be providers of student services other than counseling, such as financial aid, admissions, residence life, or career planning and placement **(SAD)**. The one advanced (i.e., doctoral) level program title used by CACREP is *Counselor Education and Supervision* **(CE)**.

As CACREP's activities intensified and expanded as more programs sought accreditation, CACREP received more and more suggestions from various professional groups about what ought to be covered in the respective sets of standards. The burgeoning amount of both solicited and unsolicited input about its standards of preparation prompted CACREP to adopt, in 1984, a moratorium on implementation of new standards and a plan for periodic "standards review and/or revision." CACREP therefore instituted a "five-year review cycle" for possible revision of its standards of preparation. This plan stipulates that changes in standards can be submitted for consideration by CACREP at any time, but changes can only be adopted for use at the end of (at least) a five-year period.

CACREP initiated its first standards of preparation review/ revision process in 1985, with an implementation date of July 1, 1988. The second CACREP standards of preparation review/revision process was initiated in 1989, with a target implementation date of July 1, 1993. However, because of the complexity of the process and the many inputs that had to be considered, the next CACREP standards have an implementation date of January 1, 1994. The "1994" CACREP standards of preparation have the same basic format as in the 1988 CACREP standards (e.g., "core curriculum" plus specialty standards) but will incorporate additions to and/ or changes in many of the specific standards.

The CACREP Orientation to Counselor Preparation

CACREP standards of preparation and accreditation procedures are best understood within the context of what may be called the CACREP orientation to counselor preparation. It should be noted that this orientation is not unique to CACREP;

rather, it evolved from within ACA. In general, this orientation holds that persons who identify themselves as professional counselors should have completed successfully the commonly agreed upon, or "core," curricular experiences, including learning in specified content/knowledge and skill areas and supervised counseling practice. In addition, all who identify themselves as professional counselors should have completed successfully "specialized" preparation in at least one specialization area (e.g., school counseling, community counseling, or marriage and family counseling/therapy). Thus, within this orientation, effective counselor preparation entails education and training in a specialized type of counseling for each aspiring counselor built upon core area preparation common to all counselors. Therefore, even though CACREP entry-level accreditations are given and titled by specialization area, it can be assumed that there is considerable commonality of preparation among graduates of any of the CACREP entry-level accreditation program areas.

The CACREP orientation also holds that advanced-level (i.e., doctoral) preparation should be built upon entry-level preparation. Therefore, it is possible for a counselor-preparation program to achieve CACREP advanced-level accreditation only if it encompasses all of the requirements of the CACREP entry-level accreditation standards for at least one specialization area. This tiered system helps to insure that all professional counselors have evolved from and are operating upon common content/knowledge, skill, and experiential bases.

CACREP Standards Format

The 1988 CACREP *entry-level* standards of preparation are presented in six subsections: Section I, The Institution; Section II, Program Objectives and Curriculum; Section III, Clinical Instruction; Section IV, Faculty and Staff, Section V, Organization and Administration; and Section VI Evaluations in the Program. The related CACREP *advanced-level* standards of preparation are contained in one section: Doctoral-Level Standards for Programs in Counselor Education and Supervision. Five sets of specialization standards are built upon the other (so-called "generic") entrylevel standards, including Environmental and Specialty Standards for (1) Community Counseling, (2)

Mental Health Counseling, (3) School Counseling, (4) Student Affairs Practice in Higher Education, and (5) Marriage and Family Counseling/Therapy.

CACREP Standards for Entry-Level Preparation

Section I. The first section of the 1988 CACREP entry-level standards identifies accreditation requirements for the institution and "academic unit" (e.g., department) in which the program seeking accreditation is housed. In general, this section specifies the needed "identity" of the program within the institution, as well as the needed resources to conduct the program. The standards in this section also reflect the belief that a counselor preparation program must be an "integrated program" with specifically assigned resources, rather than a "collection of courses" which students may take to obtain an academic degree.

Some of the standards in this section relate to how the program is described in the institution's published materials (e.g., graduate school bulletin or catalog) and how the program is configured within the institution's organizational structure (e.g., within a department within a school or college). Others relate to needed financial support for the program operation and for the faculty specifically involved with the program. Standards in this section also specify necessary program resources (e.g., computer, library, and media facilities) for instructional and research activities associated with the program. Finally, a standard is included which stipulates that students in the program must have access to "counseling services" other than those provided by program faculty. This latter standard is based on the belief that counseling services available to students in counselor-preparation programs should not jeopardize student's academic standings.

Section II. The second section of the standards incorporates several requirements directly related to the CACREP orientation discussed previously. For example, one standard requires that the entry-level program extend over a minimum of two full academic years, defined as either four semesters or six quarters with a minimum of 48 semester hours or 72 quarter hours of graduate-level credits required of all students. Students' participation in a small-group activity intended to enhance their self-understanding, self-analysis, and interpersonal skills is required in another standard. A third standard in this section stipulates that when evaluations indicate that a student's participation and further continuation in the program would be inappropriate, program faculty should assist the student to find a more appropriate academic or vocational placement. Another standard is provided that relates to pre-program professional requirements and their integration into curricular requirements for the program.

Other standards in the second section relate to the necessity for having clearly defined and stated program objectives and for distributing those objectives to students and others associated with the program. Similarly, standards exist relating to the development and distribution of instructional materials (e.g., course syllabi and reference lists) to students. Also, some standards in this section are intended to facilitate students' professional involvements beyond classroom instruction. For example, standards are included relating to students' participation in research activities with faculty and in extracurricular professional development activities, such as workshops, seminars, and colloquia.

The major portion of the second section delineates the eight so-called "common core" areas of academic preparation. These are the same areas that were identified and defined in Chapter 1: Human Growth and Development; Social and Cultural Foundations; Helping Relationships; Group; Life Style and Career Development; Appraisal; Research and Evaluation; and Professional Orientation.

The requirement for fulfillment of "environmental and specialty standards" within each student's counselor-preparation program also is addressed in the second section. The "environmental" portion of those standards reflects the belief that (at least minimally prepared) counselors must be knowledgeable of the general workings of the professional settings in which they work as well as specific counseling techniques and clientele characteristics. The "specialty" portion of those standards reflects the belief that professional counselors "specialize" (i.e., focus on use of particular knowledge and skills with particular clientele) within their professional activities. As delineated previously, the five possible environmental and specialty standards areas are presented separately from the entrylevel standards even though they are considered as parts of the respective program objectives and curricula.

Section III. Because carefully supervised clinical practice has been, and is, at the heart of counselor preparation, the third section presents standards relating to supervised clinical (counseling) experiences and instruction for students. Some of the standards in this section relate to students' practicum and internship experiences. The practicum experience is viewed as the student's first experience with actual clients. Therefore, the standards call for students to have relatively limited but closely supervised counseling activities in practicum. A practicum must be a minimum of 100 hours, including at least 40 "contact" hours with clients in the setting. An internship is viewed as an "advanced" clinical experience for students and is permitted only after the student has had at least one practicum experience. The standards stipulate that the student participate in the internship in a setting similar to the one in which the student intends to work. The setting for the student's internship is important, because during this experience, the student is supposed to perform the functions and duties of a "regular" employee of the setting. An internship is a minimum of 600 hours, including a minimum of 240 "contact" hours with clients in the setting.

Other standards in section three relate to the nature of clinical supervision for students in practicum or internship. Indicated is that students in *either* practicum or internship must receive both individual and group supervision on a weekly basis. Individual supervision is a weekly meeting of at least one-hour duration between the student in practicum or internship and a program faculty member or another supervisor with equivalent professional credentials. Group supervision is a weekly meeting of at least one-and-one-half-hours duration with several (typically five to seven) students in practicum or internship and a program faculty member or another supervisor with equivalent credentials. In addition, a student in practicum or internship is required to have an on-site (i.e., "host") supervisor with whom the student meets according to a schedule they determine. Other related standards in this section stipulate counseling laboratory facilities which should be available to the program for which accreditation is sought, necessary professional credentials for supervisors, and needed interactions among supervisors and program faculty.

Section IV. Needed credentials of faculty and assignments to and within the program for which accreditation is sought are described in the fourth section of the standards. For example, the standards indicate that an identified program leader or coordinator must be present so that someone has "ultimate" responsibility for the program. In addition to the program leader, at least two other faculty must have instructional assignment to the program for which accreditation is sought. Also stipulated is that program faculty can only provide instruction in areas for which they have demonstrated expertise. Expertise, as used in this context, must be demonstrated through the program faculty members' recent involvements in professional activities such as research, publication, consultation, and/or participation in professional organization activities.

Section V. The fifth section covers standards that address the operation of a program. Standards relating to required development and distribution of program informational materials and to program orientation activities for students are included. The need for clearly defined admissions policies and procedures is addressed in this section. Of particular importance here are the standards relating to the specified minimum faculty-to-student ratio within the program and maximum faculty instructional loads. Standards also are included that relate to clear presentation and effective dissemination of students' requirements for matriculation through the program. Finally, standards requiring that students have a "planned program of studies" are included to insure that students are following integrated curricula rather than just taking a collection of courses.

Section VI. The last section of the entry-level standards focuses upon various types of evaluations conducted within the program. One subset of standards in this section relates to required evaluations of students by program faculty. In general, the program faculty is charged with the responsibility for determining whether students are progressing satisfactorily in the development of their knowledge bases, skills, and professional orientation. Other standards in this section relate to required evaluations of instructional and clinical supervision activities by students and the dissemination of the results of those evaluations to program faculty. Another subset of standards in this section calls for periodic evaluation of the program by graduates of the program and dissemination of those evaluation results to all persons associated with the program. This latter subset is the only formal requirement for evaluation of the effectiveness of the program in the CACREP standards.

The standards in these six sections are applied by CACREP to all entry-level programs for which accreditation is sought; thus, they reflect the intent of "generic" or "core" preparation in entry-level programs. Concomitantly, the standards in the respective "environmental and specialty standards" subsections reflect professional area specializations.

CACREP Standards for Doctoral-Level Preparation

CACREP uses the term "advanced-level" preparation to mean counselor preparation beyond entry-level preparation. Therefore, the CACREP standards for doctoral-level preparation are used *in addition* to the standards for entry-level preparation. Again, a doctoral program in an academic unit can be accredited by CACREP even if no CACREP accredited entry-level program is included within the academic unit; however, the doctoral program must fulfill *both* the entry-level and advanced-level standards in order to be accredited. In general, the CACREP advanced-level standards extend the entry-level standards through greater emphases on supervised practice, research and statistics, and specific preparation in a professional specialization. The advanced-level standards also reflect the belief that preparation for "professional leadership" should be incorporated at this level. Therefore, specific standards are included that relate to activities presumed to facilitate development of professional leadership characteristics, abilities, and skills in doctoral students.

ACCREDITATION PROCEDURES

CACREP's accreditation process includes five "steps." First, the faculty, with assistance from students in some cases, conducts a "self-study" on the program for which accreditation is sought. The purpose of the self-study is to determine the ways the program meets, or does not meet, the applicable CACREP standards and to document the degree of compliance with each of the standards. This step involves substantial investment of time, effort, and resources because (1) each person associated with the program is supposed to be involved in the development of the self-study, (2) specific information is needed from each person associated with the program, and (3) collective, as opposed to individual, information and/ or opinions about degree of compliance with each standard is required.

During the second step, the institution's application materials and self-study are evaluated by a three-person review committee, composed of CACREP representative (i.e., council or designated) members, to determine if the program is ready for a site-team visitation. If the committee members reviewing the degree of compliance with each standard, as presented in the self-study, determine that the program (vis-a-vis the self-study) is not ready for a visitation by a site team, recommendations for needed changes and/or improvements are given, and the self-study is returned to the institution. If the committee determines that the program is ready, the third step in the process (i.e., a visitation by a site team) is implemented.

CACREP site visitation team members are counseling professionals who have successfully completed training to act in accord with CACREP's accreditation procedures. The purpose of the site team visitation is to "validate" the institution's self-study (i.e.,to determine if the self-study is accurate). Upon conclusion of the site visit, the team members compose a report of their findings, based on their review of the program's self-study and their visitation to the institution.

In the fourth step, the CACREP Executive Director returns the site visitation team's report to the institution. The program faculty, in turn, review the site visitation team's report and respond to it. This response is made only in regard to the accuracy of the site visitation team's report, not in regard to any actions taken as a result of the site visitation team's report. This response is also delivered to the CACREP Executive Director.

In the last step, the CACREP council members review the institution's self-study, the site visitation team's report and the institution's response to the site visitation team's report, and make a decision about the accreditation status to be awarded to the program.

One of three decisions may be rendered by CACREP about each program for which accreditation is sought: (1) Seven-year Accreditation, (2) Two-year Accreditation, or (3) Denial of Accreditation. Seven-year accreditation status is accorded to programs that essentially fulfill all applicable standards. Two-year accreditation status is accorded to programs that fulfill most applicable standards but need to fulfill specific requirements before seven-year accreditation status can be granted. If the program does not fulfill the stipulated requirements within the two-year period, accreditation is denied to the program. However, a program may be moved from two- to seven-year accreditation status in less than two years if the requirements are fulfilled before the deadline.

Historically, CACREP has rendered the decision "Denial of Accreditation" to programs on very few occasions. This should not be construed to mean, however, that CACREP approves almost all programs for which accreditation is sought or is that it lax in application of its standards of preparation. Rather, it is a reflection of CACREP's "philosophy" and its operating procedures. Philosophically, CACREP is dedicated to the enhancement of the counseling profession through assisting counselor preparation programs to improve their effectiveness through adherence to and application of the (CACREP) standards of preparation. This philosophy is operationalized primarily in step two. The initial review of the program's self-study provides the institution with an opportunity to delay the application for accreditation of the program until the program "substantially" meets CACREP's standards of preparation. Thus, only those programs for which a high probability exists for at least two-year accreditation status are processed through the subsequent steps in the CACREP accreditation process.

ACCREDITATION BY OTHER AGENCIES

Several agencies, other than CACREP, accredit specific counselor-preparation programs. For example, the American Psychological Association (APA) accredits doctoral-level counseling psychologist-preparation programs, the National Council for Accreditation of Teacher Education (NCATE) accredits master's-degree-level school counselor-preparation programs, the Council on Rehabilitation Education (CORE) accredits master's-degree-level rehabilitation counselor-preparation programs, and the American Association for Marriage and Family Therapy (AAMFT) accredits master's-degree-level marriage and family counselor-preparation programs. Although goals and processes of each of these agencies have distinguishing aspects, the agencies are all philosophically similar to CACREP in their desire to improve the counseling profession through implementation of standardized counselor-preparation practices.

SUMMARY

A strong movement exists within the counseling profession to improve counselor preparation through the application of "standards of preparation" within the context of program accreditation activities. For example, by the end of 1992, approximately 80 of the more than 400 academic units in the United States housing counselor-preparation programs had CACREP-approved programs. This may appear to be a relatively small proportion. However, it is substantial, given that CACREP has had formal operations for only approximately a decade. Applications to CACREP are increasing rapidly, indicating that the use of commonly-supported and widely-recognized standards of preparation is on the rise in the counseling profession. As much as any other current professional phenomenon, this movement stands to improve both professional counselors and the counseling services they provide.

5

TRENDS IN PROFESSIONAL COUNSELING

Counseling is an emergent, evolving, and dynamic profession currently experiencing rapid growth and generally positive changes. Major changes in counselor preparation and professional credentialing were discussed in the preceding chapters. The remaining changes are difficult to categorize, because they are occurring in literally every aspect of the counseling, profession. However, for discussion purposes, these changes may be subdivided into those taking place in professional counselors' work settings and those concerning the clientele with whom professional counselors work. Relatedly, changes in "where and with whom" are often associated with "how" counselors work. Therefore, some changes in methods and techniques also will be discussed.

TRENDS IN SETTINGS WHERE PROFESSIONAL COUNSELORS WORK

It has been noted that the counseling profession has its heritage in school counseling. Today, a substantial number of professional counselors still work in public and private schools, and counselor employment in schools shows every indication of continuing to increase. The value and worth of having counselors in schools is becoming more widely recognized. This recognition, in turn, has evolved from most school counselors fulfilling their roles and responsibilities effectively. There is considerable commonality in the nature of school counselors' roles and functions across school levels, but those rolls and functions are differentially emphasized across school levels (Miller, 1988). Therefore, each of the three school levels (i.e., secondary, middle, and elementary) merits some individual discussion in regard to the work of school counselors.

Secondary Schools

Historically, "counseling functions" have been fulfilled in secondary schools since the second decade of the twentieth century. In the early years of school counseling, the functions were fulfilled by teachers, administrators, support personnel, or volunteers. Today, however, almost every secondary school has at least one full-time school counselor whose *primary* responsibility is to fulfill school counseling functions. Traditionally, counselors in secondary schools focused most of their efforts on "college-bound" students, endeavored to collect "occupational information" for use by students, and spent the remainder of their time in more mundane activities (e.g., class scheduling and attendance monitoring). The current trend, however, is for counselors in secondary schools to be highly involved in activities deemed appropriate by professional associations such as ASCA, even though there is variation in the attention given to particular activities (Tennyson, Miller, Skovholt, & Williams, 1989). School counselors are increasing their emphasis on clerical and administrative functions and stressing activities that directly benefit students.

Counseling in secondary schools now emphasizes greater attention to the needs of all students, not just those who are academically talented (Moles, 1991). For example, counselors in secondary schools typically coordinate comprehensive career guidance programs suitable for students with widely varying circumstances, skills, abilities, and resources. Because such programs typically include use of computerized career development resources, most secondary school counselors also are using "modern technology," especially microcomputers, to help more students. Relatedly, counselors in secondary schools are extending their effectiveness through greater use of group counseling, presentation of "classroom guidance" units, coordination of peer counseling programs, and involvement in "teacher-as-advisor" programs. Secondary school counselors also spend a considerable amount of time in consultation roles in helping teachers, administrators, and other school personnel to assist students with academic, personal, and other types of concerns. Thus, counselors in secondary schools are now much more involved in professionally appropriate roles and functions and considerably less involved in those activities which often fostered negative stereotypes of them.

Middle Schools

School counseling functions in middle (or junior high) schools are essentially the same as they are in other school settings. However, implementation of school counseling services in middle schools is shaped by the nature of middle school students themselves. As early adolescents (sometimes referred to as "transescents"), middle school students present a wide array of personal and social characteristics and an even more diverse array of behaviors. Middle school counseling programs must be tailored to this age group. Kottman (1990) indicated as follows:

> The school counselor must design the guidance and counseling program to accommodate the attitudes and developmental needs of children in the early stages of adolescence. Active methods of counseling that require intense involvement on the part of both the counselor and students have been found to be most successful with children in junior high and middle school.

> Methods that capitalize on the characteristic attitudes, behaviors, and development of junior high and middle school students are usually active and interactive. Many procedures are appropriate alternatives for traditional "talk" therapy, which may also be too passive or threatening for working with children at this level. (p. 138)

Kottman (1990) advocated use of therapeutic game play, stories and metaphors, and role-play and simulation as primary examples of counseling interventions particularly appropriate for middle school students. These types of activities are useful interventions for remediation of middle school students' concerns and problems. However, the trend in middle school counseling is toward preventive and/or developmental counseling activities rather than remedial. Primary among activities of this nature are peer facilitator and teacher-as-advisor programs. Peer facilitator programs have been operational in schools for almost two decades and involve students using so-called "basic helping skills" to assist their peers to cope with developmental and other concerns (Myrick, 1987). Teachers-as-advisors programs are newer than peer facilitator programs and are rapidly being incorporated into schools, particularly middle schools. Describing the typical situation, Myrick (1987) wrote the following:

> Most middle schools incorporate organized guidance periods in the school schedule. Students are usually assigned or given the opportunity to choose a teacher who will be their advisor and referral base. Teachers as advisors meet with all their advisees during regularly scheduled homeroom or home base periods. The homeroom is the foundation for a group approach to guidance. In many middle schools, one or more homeroom periods a week are scheduled for group guidance activities. Students can raise questions, identify problems, and talk about their feelings, behaviors, and goals. (p. 25)

Middle school counseling programs necessitate unique approaches to students in a unique developmental stage. Fortunately, innovative and effective approaches to counseling services for middle school students are now commonly implemented.

Elementary Schools

The most significant advancements in school counseling over the last several decades have been in elementary school counseling. Substantial numbers of counselors first began working in elementary schools in the late 1960s and the early 1970s. Since then, the number of counselors in elementary schools has increased rapidly. This increase is attributable primarily to the realization that increasing the number of counselors is better for all concerned with schools (e.g., students, parents, or teachers). That is, attempting to prevent students' problems before they arise is far more beneficial than remediating problems after they have arisen. Thus, counselors in elementary schools spend most of their time and efforts focusing on preventive and/or developmental counseling activities. Myrick (1987) provided the basic assumption for the developmental approach in writing that "Developmental guidance and counseling assumes that human nature moves individuals sequentially and positively toward self-enhancement" (p. 31). He went on to clarify the primary objective of developmental guidance and counseling in schools:

> The developmental approach considers the nature of human development, including the general stages and tasks that most individuals experience as they mature from childhood to adulthood. It centers on positive self-concepts and acknowledges that one's self-concept is formed and reformed through experience and education. It further recognizes that feelings, ideas, and behaviors are closely linked together and that they are learned. Therefore, the most desired conditions for learning and re-learning are important considerations for development. The ultimate objective is to help students learn more effectively and efficiently. (Myrick, 1987, p. 32)

Classroom guidance units, small group counseling, and parent and teacher consultation are the primary methodologies used in developmental elementary school counseling. However, counselors in elementary schools also are involved in remediative counseling for students experiencing problems such as abuse, neglect, poor peer relationships, parental divorce, discrimination, or learning difficulties. In essence, elementary school counselors provide a full range of counseling services but focus upon developmental counseling activities.

Colleges and Universities

Counselors have a long history of working with college and university students in counseling centers as well as in a variety of positions involving student affair activities (e.g., admissions, residence life, student activities, and career placement). Traditionally, this conglomerate of activities has been represented in the counseling profession and in ACA by the American College Personnel Association (ACPA). However, the withdrawal of ACPA from ACA, and the accompanying exodus of professionals with primary interest in student affairs practice administration activities have changed the situation. The emergence of ACCA within ACA has clarified the counseling focus and allowed ACCA members to be more coherent in their professional views and interests. Concomitantly, ACA's International Association of Counseling Services (IACS), which accredits college and university counseling centers (among other activities), has intensified and extended its activities. Thus there is a reemerging focus within ACA and the counseling profession on the provision of counseling services in colleges and universities.

Bishop (1990) noted that college and university counseling services in the near future are likely to focus upon four broad categories of service areas: (1) crisis management, (2) career development, (3) special student populations, and (4) student retention. How services such as these are delivered and the corresponding roles and responsibilities of professional counselors in colleges and universities typically reflect the institution's size. Large colleges and universities tend to divide functions into highly specialized tasks and have staff in each area, whereas smaller institutions have a few people responsible for many different functions.

Many professional counselors work primarily in counseling centers helping college students with vocational, social relationship, and adjustment problems. However, computerized vocational development resources have done much to facilitate career counseling work. Thus, counselors recently have been able to devote more of their attention to students' "personal" concerns and problems. The growing recognition that "college students are also people" has greatly increased the types of problems to which counseling center counselors attend. For example, increasing numbers of college students experiencing problems such as parental divorce, anorexia, bulimia, marital difficulties, excessive stress, depression, or anxiety are seeking the services of counseling center counselors. Moreover, the increasing numbers of "non-traditional" students in colleges and universities (i.e., those who have returned to college after some lapse in their educational sequence) have necessitated that these counselors be able to help people with developmental and adjustment concerns. Perhaps the most dramatic change is the large numbers of college students seeking help for substance-abuse problems (Burns & Consolvo, 1992). Counselors in colleges and universities today are providing counseling services for the full range of problems evident in society, but their work is generally restricted to students.

Community Agencies

Nowhere in the counseling profession has change been more dramatic than in the relatively recent increase in counselors working in community (mental health) agencies. This increase has greatly enhanced the "identity" of the counseling profession because it has brought about the recognition that professional counselors can provide valuable services to all people in society, not just to students in educational institutions. Thus, the increase in counselors working in community agencies has allowed professional counselors to enjoy full membership status among the professions previously recognized as primary providers of mental health services.

Counselors working in community agencies are employed in many different types of agencies and involved with the provision of a wide variety of counseling services. They work in community agencies such as community mental health centers, abused and/or victimized person facilities, geriatric centers, substance abuse (i.e., drug or alcohol) programs (including both residential and out-patient facilities), crisis and hot-line centers, half-way houses, runaway shelters, vocational rehabilitation centers, nursing homes, residential facilities for the elderly, and shelters for the homeless. Within these types of settings, counselors provide counseling services in areas such as personal adjustment, marriage and family, sex, career, grieving and loss, educational, wellness, and personal development. They work with people of all ages, from very young children to very elderly people.

Traditionally, counselors working in community agencies have provided remediative counseling services. That is, people have typically sought services from the agencies after problems have arisen. Remediation is still a major emphasis in counseling in community agencies. More recently, however, counselors in community agencies also have become involved in preventive and/or developmental counseling. Further, counseling activities are now being provided in many community situations that did not previously have counselor involvements. For example, some counselors are now providing services in the context of Health Maintenance Organizations (HMOs). In commenting on the roles of counselors in HMOs, Forrest and Affeman (1986) stated the following:

> The educational model as well as the medical model provides an important vehicle for the delivery of primary prevention. Most MHCs [mental health counselors] are generally well prepared in this area. They are trained in group facilitation, and much primary and secondary prevention can be delivered in group settings . . . . The MHCs are aware that the patient's social support systems are a means of preventing physical illness, and MHCs commonly use processes for aiding in improving these systems . . . . (p. 69)

A somewhat related phenomenon is the increasing numbers of counselors working in the area of behavioral medicine. Nicholas (1988) indicated:

> Varied societal changes have opened the way for increased opportunities to further the goals of mental health counseling through behavioral medicine. Spiraling health care costs, changes in delivery and financing of health care, [and] an epidemiologic shift . . . ha[ve] emphasized the importance of individual behavior in health and disease . . . . Mental health counseling and behavioral medicine are conceptually consistent . . . . Behavioral medicine can benefit from the skills of the mental health counselor, and there are readily identifiable roles for mental health counselors in behavioral medicine. (p. 76)

Thus, counselors working in community agencies are involved in literally all types of professional activities in the counseling profession.

A relatively small, but increasing, proportion of professional counselors are working in hospitals and other medical care facilities (e.g., renal care, cardiac, or trauma centers, or hospices). The counseling services provided by counselors in these settings are almost exclusively remediative or crisis-oriented in nature, primarily because clients enter the facilities to seek services for severe medical problems. Bereavement (i.e., grieving and loss) counseling is one of the major services provided by counselors in these settings, although counselors sometimes provide other types of services such as family, stress reduction, or sexuality counseling.

Business and Industry

A trend that appears to have substantial potential for counseling professionals is the increasing employment of counselors in business and industry (Lewis & Hayes, 1984). Smith, Piercy, and Lutz (1982) stated:

> A greater employee "entitlement" attitude is one reason for the growth of Human Resource Development (HRD) activities, programs, and practices within organizations . . . . There are a number of other reasons for the expansion of HRD activities in the corporate setting. Governmental regulations. . . are external forces causing an increase in counseling and HRD personnel positions. Technological changes and competition are other reasons that companies have begun to provide more counseling and HRD services to employees. Corporations have therefore become more involved in developing systematic career development programs for employees in addition to a variety of training and development activities. (pp. 107-109)

The employment of counselors in business and industry is based primarily on the adage that "a happy employee is a good employee." That is, an employee who is free from major personal problems is likely to be productive, be punctual, have a low rate of absenteeism, and show allegiance to the employer. Counseling services in business and industry therefore are intended primarily to keep employees "happy" (i.e., functioning effectively in their work and personal lives).

Counselors in business and industry settings are usually employed within the context of human resource development (HRD) or employee assistance programs (EAPs). Gerstein and Bayer (1988) indicated:

> Clearly, counselors have the potential to play an important role in the EAP arena . . . . counselors are needed to assist with program evaluation, quality service assurance,

program administration, theory development, research, and marketing. (p. 296)

Both of these types of programs typically involve provision of services such as interpersonal and/or employee relations training, career and life-style development (including leisure counseling), stress and/or time management training, consultation about a variety of mental health concerns and, not surprisingly, "personal" (and/or familial) counseling services. More recently, primarily because of economic fluctuations and corresponding changes in employment assignments, counselors have become involved in "relocation facilitation" in response to employee (and familial) stresses resulting from geographic relocations (Ramey & Cloud, 1987). Thus, as in other settings, counselors in business and industry settings become involved in many different types of counseling service provision.

Religious Congregations

An interesting mixture of professions is evident in the growing number of clerics (e.g., ministers, priests, sisters, or rabbis) who have completed counselor-preparation programs. Members of religious congregations often turn to their respective clerics for spiritual guidance and "counseling" about problems in their lives. Many clerics have realized that some of these people need assistance that is not readily amenable by religious/ spiritual guidance alone; thus, they need to provide counseling services in accord with the interpretations used throughout this book. The types of counseling services provided by clerics are many, but three seem to be most prevalent. One is bereavement (i.e., grieving and loss) counseling. In the difficult times following loss situations (e.g., deaths of loved ones), members of congregations typically seek solace from clerics. Facilitation of the bereavement process is therefore a common counseling activity for clerics. A second is marriage and family counseling. Again, in times of marital and/or family problems or "crises," clerics are among the first to whom members of congregations turn for assistance. A third counseling activity for clerics is referral. That is, when people have problems, they often approach their respective clerics first, probably because they are aware that their clerics will maintain confidentiality about the problems. In these situations, clerics are instrumental in deciding whether the problems can be resolved through religious/spiritual guidance, counseling provided by the clerics themselves, or counseling services from (other) professional counselors. If the latter option is selected, these clerics also have to decide to whom to refer the people and how to facilitate the referral process. Given the large numbers of people with whom clerics typically work, referral activities are quite common for them. Thus, counseling, in some relatively restricted forms, thus is common in many religious congregations.

Legal Systems

A small, but growing, segment of professional counselors is working in criminal justice and other parts of legal systems. For example, counselors working in correctional institutions primarily provide personal adjustment and career and life-style counseling for incarcerated persons, particularly those for whom release is imminent. Counselors working in other offender rehabilitation programs, such as those for sex offenders or spouse (or other family member) abusers, focus primarily on remediation of the dynamics and/or situations underlying the offenses, but offer other types of counseling for problems related to the offenses. More recently, some professional counselors have become involved in providing counseling services within another part of the legal system: divorce litigation. These counselors are employed by the legal system (i.e., employed by a court as opposed to being employed by either of the litigants) to provide "divorce mediation" services prior to trial. The goal of counseling in such situations is to enable the litigants to achieve a mutually accepted marriage dissolution agreement, instead of having it decreed by a judge. In essence, divorce mediation counseling is a very specialized form of marriage and family counseling.

Private Practice

The establishment of counseling "private practices" is an obvious trend in the counseling profession today. Weikel and Palmo (1989) wrote:

> Probably the most exciting aspect of the expansion of mental health services has been the broadening of private practice

> to include all of the core providers [of counseling and/
> or therapeutic services], and not merely psychiatrists and
> psychologists. For MHCs [mental health counselors], this
> expansion has provided new opportunities for demonstrating
> their skills. . . . (p. 17)

Although the vast majority of counselors still are employed by agencies or educational institutions, the number of self-employed, and usually self-incorporated, professional counselors has increased significantly within the last few years. The increase is likely to continue, primarily due to the fact that a substantial number of professional counselors are able to be financially solvent, and in a few cases financially affluent, from the proceeds of their private practices. This financial solvency is in part linked to professional credentialing. That is, more and more professional credentials (e.g., licensures, certifications) of counselors are being recognized as indicators of professional competence. In turn, as the status of their credentials increases, so do the costs of their services and the willingness of people and/or agencies to pay those costs. For example, a rapidly increasing number of insurance company policies now cover the services of professional counselors who are (usually) licensed and/or certified. Payments by entities other than counseling service recipients (e.g., insurance companies) are known as "third-party payments." Similarly, a growing number of companies and corporations are providing third-party reimbursements to (usually) credentialed counselors in private practice for services rendered to company employees, because it is often less expensive for the companies to pay private practitioners than to provide "in-house" counseling services.

The counseling services provided by various counselors in private practice run the gamut of the various services found in the counseling profession. Private practitioner counseling services can be found for any imaginable human mental health need. However, the vast majority of counselors in private practice have focused their counseling activities on children, marriage and/or family issues, substance-abuse, or "personal adjustment" counseling. In addition, most counselors in private practice are heavily involved in consultation activities, particularly those relating to the facilitation of human and interpersonal relations development, and in the provision of training workshops. Thus, most counselors in private practice are involved in diverse professional activities in order to generate income.

These then are the major trends in the settings where professional counselors work. Collectively, they reflect the general trend in the counseling profession of counselors working in almost all types of settings. Indeed, identifying settings where counselors do *not* work is difficult.

TRENDS IN CLIENTELE WITH WHOM COUNSELORS WORK

Just as the number of settings in which counselors work has expanded greatly in the last two decades, so too has the number of different types of people with whom counselors work. This general trend is, of course, partially a function of the increase in the number of settings. Therefore, professional counselors are actively involved themselves in a greater variety of counseling services in order to serve effectively more and different types of people. Thus, professional counselors have been and continue to be proactive in their efforts to serve increasing numbers of people. The people served can be categorized in several different ways, one of which is by their stage in the life span.

Preschool Children

One of the newest client groups for professional counselors is that of preschool children. The counseling profession's emphasis on developmental counseling in elementary schools has prompted some counselors to extend the emphasis to children before they enter school. There are potentially significant advantages to working with children before they enter formal educational systems. Hohenshil and Brown (1991) wrote:

> Prekindergarten children are at an age when interventions have the best probability of success . . . . From a developmental perspective, the earlier the interventions are begun, the better the success rate whether children are at risk or not. This is the fundamental rationale upon which prekindergarten programs rest. (p. 3)

Accordingly, some counselors are now providing services such as learning skills training, interpersonal-relationships facilitation, and social skills enhancement to very young children. Relatedly, because some young children have problems which need remediation, some professional counselors use techniques such as "play" counseling and "art therapy" to help these children. Counselors working with young children also often work with the children's parents to help the parents develop better parenting, behavior management, and child motivational skills. In general, counselors' efforts with very young children often are intended to help the children "get a good start" in life and overcome problems (e.g, abuse and/or neglect) they have already encountered.

Elementary School Age Children

The vast majority of elementary school age children receive needed and/or desirable counseling services from counselors working in schools. However, counselors working in community agencies and private practice increasingly also are providing services to elementary school age children. Several reasons exist for this trend. One is that school counselors simply work with too many children to provide effective services for all who need them. As a result, some parents are seeking other sources of assistance for their children.

A second reason is that some parents fear (inappropriately) that a stigma will be attached to their child(ren) if they are counseled in the school setting and so seek "less public" counseling services for their child(ren). A third is that because school counselors must be able to provide many different types of counseling services, it is difficult for them to "specialize" in particular types of counseling; counselors in community agencies or private practice typically "specialize" and therefore may be able to provide better services.

A third, though less frequent, reason is that "court-ordered" counseling for children is increasing as more and more judges come to understand the nature and benefits of counseling services for children. An example of this trend is the increasing number of children who are being required by courts to receive counseling for problems resulting from parental divorce. Typically, judges order such counseling services to be provided by counselors in community agencies or by counselors in private practice who have contractual arrangements with the judicial system.

Middle School Age Children

Thornburg (1986) listed eight developmental tasks, across three developmental areas, with which counselors could help transescents (i.e., middle school age children).

Physical development
Becoming aware of increased physical changes

Intellectual Development
Organizing knowledge and concepts into problem-solving strategies
Making the transition from concrete to abstract symbols

Social Development
Learning new social and sex roles
Identifying with stereotypical role models
Developing friendships
Gaining a sense of independence
Developing a sense of responsibility (pp. 170-171)

In borrowing counseling techniques from those appropriate for elementary school age children and adolescents, as well as in developing techniques specifically appropriate for transescents, counselors have made great strides in providing effective counseling services for middle school age children. In so doing, they have done much to facilitate transescents' successful passage through an often difficult developmental period.

Secondary School Age Students

For reasons similar to those for elementary and middle school age children, increasing numbers of secondary school age children (i.e., adolescents) are being counseled not only by school counselors but also by professional counselors in community agencies or private practice. Adolescence is a difficult period in any person's life because of "normal" problems such as emerging sexuality, changing peer relationships, academic pressures and strains, identity development, career exploration, disengagement from family and parents, and value conflicts. Adolescents today also are increasingly confronted with problems related to drug and alcohol abuse, delinquency, depression, parental divorce, step-family acclimation, physical or sexual abuse, and a host of societal problems such as unemployment, discrimination, or threat of nuclear holocaust.

Many, many parents are unable to help their children through the difficulties of adolescence and so seek professional counseling services for their children. In addition, many, many youth themselves also are seeking counseling assistance with problems. In extreme cases, youth with severe problems receive counseling services from "crisis centers" or residential treatment (e.g., substance abuse) facilities. However, more typically, they receive counseling services from counselors in community agencies or private practice who specialize in working with youth.

Persons in Mid-Life

Among the newer groups for whom counseling services are being provided more frequently is the group of persons in "mid-life." The term "mid-life" is difficult, if not impossible, to define in terms of age range because of changes in human longevity. Conflicting interpretations about to which "life" it applies further complicates definition; is it the middle of actual life, marital and/or family life, or career life? Generally, the term mid-life applies to a person's situation in life, and is usually applied to people who have established relatively stable life-styles, careers, familial situations, and behavior patterns and who are not yet preparing for "retirement." Some people in this situation are so stable that "stability" becomes a problem for them. Consequently, these people are asking themselves "Is this all there is?" The general disenchantment experienced by many people in mid-life is typically caused by such problems as identity confusion, depression, marital and/or familial strife, career dissatisfaction, and substance abuse. Accordingly, these people seek counseling for a variety of purposes and generally want to find "new" directions for themselves and their lives.

Older Adults

The "graying of America" is a colloquial phrase used to reflect the rapidly increasing average age of people in society, an increase that is attributable to increasing human longevity and to the associated increase in numbers of "older people" in society. The graying of America has brought greater attention (overdue) to their life situations, needs, and problems. Riker (1981) stated:

> . . .the need for help is great among older citizens in this country. Even a cursory look at statistical information regarding alcoholism and suicide among older persons highlights some of the extremes of mental health problems. Less extreme, but certainly suggestive of a general mental health problem of older persons, are the results of a 1980 nationwide study of 514 randomly selected Americans, 60 years of age and older. This study places those interviewed in three descriptive categories, as enjoyers (27%), survivors (53%), and casualties (20%) . . . . The designation for each category seems to be self-explanatory, with casualties referring to those experiencing major difficulties in areas such as health, finances, or living conditions. For whatever reasons, the majority of this older population sample are survivors, while an additional 20% are facing major problems. The range of the problems is considerable, the intensity varies, but the extensiveness among older persons seems inescapable. (pp. xvii-xviii)

Part of the response to this situation has been a rapid increase in counseling services specifically suited to older persons, which is often referred to as gerontological counseling. Older persons experience the myriad problems experienced by younger persons, but with at least one major confounding factor: the perception of not having enough time left in their lives to resolve the problems. Moreover, the counseling needs of individual older persons tend to be generalized within their respective lives; if they have needs for counseling, they tend to have the needs in many aspects of their lives as opposed to in specific parts of their lives (Myers & Loesch, 1981). Thus, counseling services for older persons need to be comprehensive in scope, and professional counselors who work with older persons must be able to provide a variety of types of counseling services.

Intellectually Gifted and Talented People

In addition to life span divisions, the clientele for professional counselors also can be categorized by other human characteristics. Some of these characteristics describe groups of people who would not ordinarily be expected to need counseling services. For example, Myers and Pace (1986) summarized the relevant professional literature and found the following problems to be evident among various intellectually gifted and talented people: depression, underachievement, perfectionism and overachievement, suicide, delinquency, peer relationship problems, career development problems related to potential for multiple careers, problems in making long-range plans, difficulties in dealing with deferred gratification, early career closure, and value conflicts with peer groups, family, and society. More recently, McMann and Oliver (1988) indicated that the presence of a "gifted" child in a family may cause significant intrafamilial difficulties. However, Myers and Pace (1986) noted that "Significant information is starting to accumulate on the needs of gifted persons, but there is very little experimental documentation of effective counseling and guidance strategies" (p. 550). Thus, gifted and talented persons are a group for whom individual, group, or family counseling services are often appropriate, but also a group to whom professional counselors have only recently turned their attentions.

Culturally Differentiated Populations

Recognition of the unique characteristics of persons from various cultural groups (sometimes referred to as ethnic minorities or persons of color) has prompted the counseling profession to be responsive to their needs through the provision of "multicultural" counseling services specifically suited for them. Of course, culturally differentiated persons experience any of the problems for which counseling services are generally appropriate. However, they also may experience problems associated with their unique characteristics and life situations. Because of cultural differences, counseling service delivery modes appropriate for persons in society's "majority" may not always be appropriate for culturally differentiated persons. Vacc, Wittmer, and DeVaney (1988) stated:

> Our belief is that helping professionals may hold the key
> to the process of reducing, if not eliminating, the social
> and emotional barriers which prevent many of America's

subgroup members from becoming secure American citizens. To do this, helping professionals must make a concerted effort to approach the different subgroup members among their clientele, with a cognitive understanding over and above the affectual . . . . [I]f helping professionals are inexperienced in the values and conduct of special populations, these professionals will be less effective than they would be when operating with an accurate, cognitive understanding of the total milieu of these individuals. (p. 4)

Similarly, Pedersen (1991) noted:

> There are as many different approaches to direct service delivery as there are culturally differentiated populations requesting that service. It is important . . . [that] the direct service provider match the right treatment with the right client in the right way. It is important for counselors to approach both the problem and the solution through a multicultural lens that accommodates both similarities and differences. (p. 205)

Thus, professional counselors who provide counseling services for culturally differentiated persons must be thoroughly knowledgeable of both the characteristics of various cultural groups and counseling approaches and techniques effective for working with them.

Genders

Provision of gender-specific counseling services is another major trend in the counseling profession. The need for such specialized counseling services first became evident with recognition of women's changing roles and status in society. As women entered the labor force in increasing numbers and as they pursued redefined (i.e., "nontraditional") roles in familial and interpersonal situations, they encountered problems which often made the transitions difficult. Westervelt (1978) stated:

> Counselors know that [women's] changed or changing perceptions of self and society generate new sources of conflict and ambivalence and of guilt and shame, as well as new sources of motivation and new patterns of aspiration. (p. 2)

Counseling services and techniques specifically for women evolved from women's unique needs and situations, particularly the need to achieve their potentials and adjust effectively to new behavior patterns. Counseling services and techniques specifically for men evolved for similar reasons (i.e. changing roles and life situations), but at a slower rate. Scher (1981) stated:

> Most men are hidden from themselves and from others. Pressures from intimates and society, however, as well as self-engendered possibilities, are creating a slow push toward greater openness to new potentials. The conflicts and problems that this push creates will and have brought men to counseling. (p. 202)

In summarizing the current state of affairs, Scher and Good (1990) wrote:

> . . .it is necessary to examine what we know about the intersection of conceptions of gender and counseling. We believe that conceptions of gender have a powerful effect on the counseling process. This is caused by the gender roles of the participants, the gender role history of the client, and the expectations of our culture as to how members of each sex are to behave, think, and view the world. (p. 389)

In general then, gender specific counseling helps males and females contend with the respective problems and difficulties associated with their sex-role developments.

Persons Differentiated by Sexual Orientation

Recognition of the rights of persons differentiated by sexual orientation is increasing in society and, concomitantly, in the counseling profession. However, counselors must learn much in order to effectively counsel such persons. Dworkin and Guiterrez (1989) presented the challenge which confronts the counseling profession:

> In order to counsel gay, lesbian, and bisexual clients, counselors must become familiar with the culture of their clients and the "folkways" that are pertinent to these people's lives, from the client's perspective, so that "these continuous methods of handling problems" that they learn in the

counseling session are relevant. Just as counselors would not use the same method to treat Anglos as to treat Blacks, a counselor cannot always use the same methods that work in a heterosexual context to counsel clients living in and existing within a gay, lesbian, or bisexual context. (p. 6)

While the counseling profession has demonstrated increased sensitivity to issues involved in counseling individuals differentiated by sexual orientation, few specific techniques have been developed and little research has been done on what is effective in counseling such persons. Thus, the counseling profession is just beginning to develop specialized counseling approaches for persons differentiated by sexual orientation.

Abused Persons

Another subset of clientele groups receiving increased attention and greater services from professional counselors includes persons having particular types of problems. One of the most striking subgroups in this category is comprised of abused persons. Abuse usually refers to physical abuse (i.e., battering), but also may refer to verbal abuse or neglect (i.e., necessary attention not provided). Abused persons include those from the very young to the elderly, all ethnicities, and both genders. The incidence of abuse is staggering; "every five years, the number of deaths of persons killed by friends and acquaintances equals that of the entire Viet Nam War" (Wetzel & Ross, 1983). Although abuse occurs among all types of people, women are by far the most frequently abused persons. Abuse against women most frequently occurs in two forms: physical abuse (e.g., by a spouse) and sexual assault (e.g., rape).

Victims of *any* type of abuse experience psychological trauma, if not an associated physical trauma. Thus, counseling for abused persons is primarily remediative in nature. Counseling abused persons also typically necessitates that professional counselors work in collaboration with other professionals such as physicians, law enforcement officers, and attorneys. Of the different counseling services offered, counseling abused persons is among the most difficult, yet it is one in which more and more professional counselors are becoming involved.

Substance Abusers

Substance, typically alcohol and/or drug, abuse is another major problem for which increasing numbers of people are seeking counseling. Humans at literally any age after conception may encounter substance abuse problems. Indeed, substance-abuse problems are so pervasive that almost everyone in society will be touched, either directly or by close association, by these problems. Professional counselors are increasing and intensifying their counseling services for substance abusers. Both remediative and preventive counseling services and strategies are being used in the effort to combat substance-abuse problems.

Traditionally, substance abuse counseling was most prevalent in community (mental-health) agencies, schools, and residential treatment facilities. However, substance abuse counseling is increasingly being provided by counselors in private practice or as a part of employee assistance programs (EAPs) in business and industry. A wide variety of counseling approaches and strategies have been used in the attempt to alleviate substance abuse problems. Unfortunately, no clear patterns of effectiveness have appeared. Thus, although professional counselors are making concerted efforts with regard to the provision of substance abuse counseling, proven tactics have not yet been established, and counselors must continue to explore and use a wide variety of counseling methodologies to help people with substance abuse problems.

Wellness/Holistic-Health Proponents

Counseling services are being provided frequently for people interested in holistic health. Gross (1980) stated:

> Holistic health is an approach to well-being of people that includes the prevention of illness, alternative ways of treating illness, and the means by which good health and the full enjoyment of life can be achieved. The term holistic . . . means whole in the sense that a living entity is more than the sum of its parts. It also connotes an interdependent

system in which a change in one part of the system makes for changes in all other parts of the system. The application of holism to health is an attempt to overcome the mind/body dualism that has long characterized Western science and medicine. (p. 96)

Myers (1991) provided the context for counselors to assist in such an approach to well-being when she wrote:

Wellness refers to the maximizing of human potential through positive lifestyle choices. This holistic paradigm offers a philosophical base for counseling and development that provides guidelines for intervention and at the same time emphasizes the uniqueness of our approach as counseling and human development professionals to mental health concerns. (p. 183)

A number of different terms have been used to refer to counseling aimed at facilitating holistic health, including wellness counseling, health counseling, and holistic counseling. Regardless of the term used to describe this kind of counseling, the goal is to help people achieve better mental and physical health through greater reliance on their own innate physiological and psychological maintenance systems. To achieve this end, professional counselors typically use some remediative activities (e.g., help people stop smoking) and some preventive activities (e.g., stress management training). Such counseling is provided by counselors in a variety of settings and is especially common in employee assistance programs. Unfortunately, the potential for holistic/wellness counseling has not yet been achieved fully, primarily because the focus in "wellness" programs has been on *physical* well-being. Myers (1991) indicated:

The mental health component of existing wellness programs is probably understated. The strong link between physical and mental health leads to emotional benefits as a by-product of wellness programs. Ultimately, the potential exists for mental health to be a direct target of wellness interventions. The foundation exists; it needs only to be further developed and implemented. (p. 189)

Individuals with Sexual Problems

People with problems related to human sexuality form another major clientele for professional counselors.

Unfortunately, the number of professional counselors who are able to provide effective sexuality counseling is limited. Schepp (1986) commented that only a few counselor-preparation programs offer a specialization in sexuality counseling and that "to enter the field, one must usually obtain general professional preparation first and then take additional sexuality courses and [sexuality counseling] supervision" (p. 183).

In general, clients with problems related to sexuality may be divided into two subgroups: heterosexuals and persons differentiated by sexual orientation. Clients from the first subgroup usually seek counseling for problems that relate to sexual functioning, such as inability to achieve orgasm, premature ejaculation, or painful intercourse. Clients from the second subgroup usually seek counseling for problems that sometimes relate to sexual functioning, but more often relate to sexual identity confusion, guilt, or generalized anxiety from generally unexpressed sexual preferences. Accordingly, professional counselors providing human sexuality counseling must be competent to counsel with regard to both the physical and psychological aspects of human sexuality.

Individuals with Marital and/or Familial Problems

Finally, the fastest growing clientele for professional counselors is comprised of persons experiencing marital and/or familial difficulties. Based on their longitudinal study of counselor preparation programs, Hollis and Wantz (1990) indicated that marriage and family counseling is one of the fastest growing specializations among professional counselors and the most popular academic program major among students in counselor preparation programs. Because of the currently high level of interest in marriage and family counseling among both professionals and students, the growth trend in this area is likely to continue for quite some time.

Movement by professional counselors into the realm of marriage and family counseling is by no means complete, and neither has it been nor will it be accomplished without difficulty. Historically, persons involved in marriage and family counseling aligned themselves with the American Association for Marriage and Family Therapy (AAMFT), an organization that some (e.g., Everett, 1990a) still believe to be the only appropriate professional organization for marriage and family counselors. More recently, a significant number of ACA members have provided marriage and family counseling services, a situation which led to formation of the International Association of Marriage and Family Counselors (IAMFC). The existence of two organizations representing marriage and family counselors has led to considerable debate, with both philosophical and pragmatic components most effectively represents marriage and family counselors. The debate has both philosophical and pragmatic components. In regard to the philosophical concerns, AAMFT has put forth the proposition that marriage and family therapy [counseling] is a profession onto itself whereas IAMFC (and therefore ACA) has viewed marriage and family counseling as a specialty built upon generic counseling expertise (cf. Everett, 1990a, 1990b; Brooks & Gerstein, 1990a, 1990b). In regard to the pragmatic concerns, both CACREP and AAMFT have sought accreditation from the Council on Post-Secondary Accreditation (COPA) for their marriage and family counselor-preparation programs. However, historically, COPA rarely has approved two accrediting agencies to accredit similar professional preparation programs. The significance of COPA approval is great because most educational institutions neither desire nor would be able to afford two accreditations for the same program.

Regardless of the outcomes of the debates about which organization best represents marriage and family counselors and/or should be allowed to accredit their professional preparation programs, at least one significant commonality is among marriage and family counselors: adoption of a "systems theory" approach to counseling. Everett (1990a) wrote:

> The application of systems theory in understanding family behaviors and dynamics represents both the foundation and integrating force in marital and family therapy [counseling].

> Family systems theory identifies the interactional milieu of the family as central to emotional development, behavioral patterns, and values and loyalties for individual members. The appearance of symptomatology is an expression of systemic dysfunction. Such dysfunctions, or imbalances,

may appear in an early generation and be passed across numerous generations, displayed variously as symptoms in individuals, marriages, or parent-child relationships. (p. 499)

Using this generalized framework, professional counselors conduct counseling with entire families to attempt to resolve problems of one or more family members. However, as Grunwald and McAbee (1985) reported,

> Counselors are finding that an increasing proportion of families coming for help can be classified into special categories, i.e., different from the usual father, mother, and children family unit. One in five children are living with a single parent. The divorce rate is well over forty percent and even greater for some ethnic groups. Live-in [unmarried] mates . . . are common. All of these situations present some special problems for the family counselor as these special families seek assistance. (p. 245)

The problems addressed are myriad, including marital disharmony, singleparenting, drug abuse, children's delinquency, alcoholism, step-family adjustments, sexuality, and physical and sexual abuse. Counseling for these areas may be provided by counselors in various settings, however, it is primarily provided by those in community agencies and in private practice.

SUMMARY

The preceding discussion has highlighted some of the trends in the major settings in which counselors work and in the clients with whom they work and has alluded to some of the methods used by professional counselors. Of course there are other settings in which professional counselors work, many other types of people for whom they provide services, and many more specialized counseling activities. However, primary descriptors of the counseling profession today would be expansion and extension in positive directions. Because of these trends, the counseling profession's benefits to society also are increasing.

Chapter **6**

LEGAL CONCERNS IN COUNSELING

The stature of the counseling profession has improved dramatically within recent years, primarily because of implementation of credentialing processes, expansion of counseling service realms, increased effectiveness of counseling services, and more focused conceptualizations of who counselors are and what they do. However, these gains have not been, and further gains will not be, achieved without difficulties. As counselors' *professional identity* improves, they and their activities are subject to increased scrutiny by their clients, the general public, and other audiences. Now more than ever professional counselors must be mindful of the implications of their behaviors and be attuned to pertinent ethical and legal considerations. Remley (1988) wrote:

> Ethical and legal considerations are important to us [i.e., counselors], but not because we need help in protecting ourselves from suits filed by the clients we serve. Instead, adherence to ethical and legal standards are vital if we are to take our place as full partners in the practice of mental health counseling.
>
> Many counselors are confused about the similarities and differences between their relationships with family, friends,

and acquaintances and their professional relationships with clients. This confusion leads to a multitude of ethical and legal problems. (p. 167)

Professional legal and ethical issues are quite frequently intertwined, and it is often difficult to separate them in examining the potential inappropriateness of any particular counselor's behavior. However, they are separated here for the sake of clarity of presentation. Legal issues in counseling are covered in this chapter, and ethical issues are addressed in the next chapter.

The legal system of the United States is based primarily on *case* (i.e., decided by a court) law, and thus is referred to as a *common law* system. In such a system, legislative bodies may create (statutory) laws, but judicial processes determine the validities and appropriate applications of those laws. Judicial decisions have the "force of law" because they determine the conditions and manners in which statutory laws will be applied. Judicial decisions, within the context of a common law system, reflect "the common thought and experience of a people" (Fischer & Sorenson, 1985, p. 2). Fischer and Sorenson noted the following:

Legal principles and rules . . . arise out of social interaction, as people form beliefs and habits that are shared and eventually become customary. Some of these customary beliefs and habits are later formulated into legal principles or rules that further reinforce the relative stability of antecedent customary beliefs and habits. (p. 3)

There are two primary implications from the use of a common law system. One is that the legal system of the United States is by no means static; "the common thought and experience of a people" change over time, and interpretations of law change accordingly. A classic example is the prohibition era, in which consumption of alcoholic beverages was legal, then illegal, and then legal again. The second implication is that interpretations of law are often situationally contingent. This is why seemingly self-evident laws are continually tested in the courts based upon the nuances of the circumstances in which the laws are being applied.

The common law system and the implications of its use are of significant importance to counselors. They necessitate that counselors be particularly cognizant of (a) local (usually state) laws and legal issues applicable to their counseling activities and situations and (b) laws and legal issues for their clients. Therefore, for the sake of clarity, the legal aspects of counseling of which counselors should be aware can be divided into those for counselors and those for clients.

LEGAL CONCERNS FOR COUNSELORS

The topics presented below were selected because they are prominent or are frequently overlooked by counselors. However, they are by no means the only ones which could have been presented. Effective professional counselors are always "on the lookout" for legal concerns about which they should be knowledgeable.

Informed Consent

Counseling can begin easily—a "client" comes to the counselor for "help" and the counselor begins "counseling." Even though a common occurrence, it creates a potentially significant legal issue for counselors. A counseling relationship is only one of several types of (verbal or other) relationships that two, or a small group of, people may have. Counselors are well aware of what is involved in a counseling relationship, but most people in society are not. Thus, there exists potential for misunderstanding about the nature and method of provision of the "help" to be provided. If the difference in perspective is great enough, there may be grounds for legal recourse by the client.

The way for counselors to avoid misunderstandings about the nature and methods of provision of counseling services is for them to obtain informed consent for counseling from prospective clients. Technically, the client gives informed consent to the counselor to be counseled. Robinson (1991) provided three criteria for informed consent for counseling, paraphrased as follows:

1. The client (or in the case of a minor, the child's parent) must be capable of engaging in rational thought to a sufficient degree to make competent decisions, including initiating participation in a counseling process.

2. The client must receive relevant information about counseling as the counselor perceives it in a manner that the client understands. That is, it is the counselor's responsibility to insure that the client understands counseling as the counselor will conduct it.

3. The client (or in the case of a minor, the child's parent) must give the consent voluntarily.

Rinas and Clyne-Jackson (1988) noted that informed consent may be either *implied* (behavioral) or *expressed* (written or verbal with witness). Implied consent for counseling is given when clients engage in behaviors that could be interpreted as informed choice. For example, informed consent usually would be implied when clients voluntarily seek counseling services with the expectation to pay for services rendered from a counselor in private practice. Expressed consent for counseling is given when clients have received an explanation of counseling from the counselor and either acknowledge consent in the presence of a witness or sign a document (i.e., informed consent form) indicating consent.

The obvious key to informed consent for counseling is the explanation given to the client. Rinas and Clyne-Jackson (1988) indicated the following:

> It is generally accepted that the description given to the client should consist of the following elements: diagnosis of the client's presenting problem(s), a description of the recommended treatment approach, benefits that should result as well as probability of such benefits, possible adverse effects that could follow the intervention with an estimation of their likelihood, [and] alternative treatment approaches with their incumbent risks and benefits. (p. 76)

Thus, clients should be told "what they are getting into" *and* the alternatives available to them in a manner and language they understand.

Informed consent is a term that counselors usually associate with the research and/or data-gathering processes, but it is equally applicable to counseling practice. It is always good professional practice for counselors to obtain informed consent for counseling, and in some cases it is imperative (e.g., when information obtained from counseling will be disclosed to persons not involved in the counseling process). Counselors should obtain expressed consent whenever they foresee that the client's implied consent might not be self-evident.

Duty to Warn

As professionals with specialized training and skills, counselors are expected to be able to interpret *and predict* human behavior effectively. Usually, such interpretations and predictions are about relatively innocuous behaviors, but not always. Among the most difficult decisions counselors have to make are those about the seriousness of clients' stated intentions to harm others or themselves. Because ethical standards call for counselors to divulge information when they believe a client will carry out a stated intention to harm, a professional basis exists for such disclosure. Also a legal basis exists for such disclosure, known as *duty to warn.*

The legal basis for counselors' duty to warn evolved primarily from the case of *Tarasoff v. Regents of the University of California* (1974). In the Fall of 1969, Posenjit Poddar was a student at the University of California at Berkeley and a client at a university mental health facility. He informed his psychiatrist that he harbored anger against Tatiana Tarasoff and that he intended to kill her. The psychiatrist notified the campus police who detained Poddar for a short time but later released him. On October 27, 1969, Poddar killed Tarasoff. Thereafter, Tarasoff's parents sued the psychiatrist and his employer (as well as a supervising psychiatrist and the university's police department). Tarasoff's parents claimed that, among other things, the psychiatrist had been negligent by not informing their daughter of Poddar's stated intention. A lower court ruled in favor of the defendants, but the California Supreme Court subsequently ruled in favor of the parents. The court held:

> . . .a psychotherapist treating a mentally ill patient. . . bears a responsibility to use reasonable care to give threatened persons such warnings as are essential to avert foreseeable danger arising from his [her] patient's condition or treatment. (p. 559; cited in Hummel, Talbutt, & Alexander, 1985, p. 34)

A critical element of the *Tarasoff* ruling was that, although the psychiatrist had informed the campus police, he had not gone far enough in his duty to warn; he also should have informed the intended victim.

In subsequent cases the courts broadened the interpretation of counselors' duty to warn to include situations even where there is not a specifically identifiable intended victim. For example, the *Lapiri v. Sears, Roebuck, & Co.* (1980) case involved a patient who had been receiving inpatient, and then outpatient, treatment at a VA hospital. The patient purchased a shotgun, just prior to terminating treatment against his psychiatrist's advice. Later, he entered a nightclub and began shooting, killing Dennis Lapiri and seriously injuring Lapiri's wife. The court held that the psychiatrist had a duty to warn even though there was not a specific intended victim. In regard to this case, Herlihy and Sheeley (1988) noted that "The court stated that there were ways other than alerting the victim to act on the duty to warn, such as attempting to detain the patient" (p. 147). Thus counselors' duty to warn potentially extends to a wide variety of situations.

In summarizing results and implications from several cases related to duty to warn, Hummel, Talbutt, and Alexander (1985) concluded that:

> These cases clearly indicate that therapists have a duty to warn victims; that the facts must be clear enough for the therapist to know the intended victims; and that there is a duty to warn even when victims are not named if their identities are clear. Although these court cases deal with therapists, counselors should assume that the same standards apply to them. (pp. 74-75)

The nature of counselors' duty to warn is complicated when a client indicates intent to do harm to self, including physical injury or suicide. Sheeley and Herlihy (1989) offered the opinion that school counselors likely would be immune from liability for a student suicide outside of the school setting. However, Pate (1992) provided a report of a case recently upheld by the Maryland Supreme Court in which a school counselor was held responsible for a student's suicide because the school counselor allegedly was aware of the student's intent but did not notify the student's parents.

The ruling described by Pate (1992) may portend a trend of holding school counselors liable in cases of student-client suicide. Whether or not duty to warn in cases of potential suicide extends to other types of counselors is unknown. However, there is a tendency to treat all mental health service providers as if they had equal skills and competence (Sheeley & Herlihy, 1989). Therefore, it is likely that counselors' duty to warn in cases of potential suicide will encompass all counselors.

If a counselor becomes aware of a client's intention to harm someone, the counselor is required to inform appropriate persons. The question is, "Who are appropriate persons?" Unfortunately, only general guidelines can be given. If a specific intended victim is identified, that person (or a parent/legal guardian) should be told. In the case of potential suicide, effort should be made to insure that the client is monitored and/or restrained by others (e.g., family members). If a specific group of people is identified, they should be told. If no specific intended victims are identified, attempts should be made to obtain legal restraint of the client. And in any case, the police should be told. A counselor also would be well-advised to consult with other professionals, including attorneys, about who should be informed. It is likely that such actions will damage, if not terminate, the counselor's counseling relationship with the client. However, preventing injury must be the highest priority.

Disclosure

When a counselor's duty to warn is applicable, a relatively clear legal mandate is that the counselor must disclose information received from a client without the client's permission. Other situations exist in which counselors are admonished to disclose information from clients, but the legal basis for such disclosures is not always as clear.

Another situation which necessitates disclosure by counselors is *suspected* child abuse and/or neglect. Fischer and Sorenson (1985) provided the definition of child abuse contained in the 1974 National Child Abuse Prevention and Treatment Act (PL 93-247):

> Physical or mental injury, sexual abuse or exploitation, negligent treatment, or maltreatment of a child under the age of eighteen or the age specified by the child protection law of the state in question, by a person who is responsible for the child's welfare, under circumstances which indicate that the child's health or welfare is harmed or threatened thereby. (p. 182)

Although child abuse is not a crime under federal law, each state has created a definition of child abuse for use in its child protection legislation. Most state definitions are in accordance with the definition in PL 93-247, which creates a semblance of a national standard concerning child abuse.

All states and the District of Columbia have enacted legislation that make it legally mandatory for school counselors to report suspected child abuse (Fischer & Sorenson, 1985; Hummel, Talbutt, & Alexander, 1985; Sandberg, Crabbs, & Crabbs, 1988). Likewise, the legal responsibility to report suspected child abuse has been extended to other types of counselors in most states (Hummel, Talbutt, & Alexander, 1985). Thus, as a general rule, counselors have legal responsibility to report suspected child abuse.

Although counselors are required to report suspected child abuse, they are not required to provide substantive evidence of child abuse; they simply must have good reason to suspect it. However, upon reporting suspected child abuse, counselors likely will be asked to defend the basis of their allegation. Sandberg, Crabbs, and Crabbs (1988) suggested that the best basis for supporting an allegation of child abuse is good record keeping, particularly in regard to notation of child behaviors (including verbalizations) and observation of physical abuse symptoms.

State child abuse-reporting laws offer legal protection for persons who report suspected child abuse, and therefore state laws provide "encouragement" to report suspected child abuse. Further, counselors may be subject to civil or criminal legal action if they fail to report suspected child abuse (Hummel, Talbutt, & Alexander, 1985). Thus, counselors have a strong legal obligation to report *suspected* child abuse. In effect, suspected child abuse situations provide legally mandated and protected reason for counselors to disclose information obtained from clients without their permission.

The situation may seem more complicated for counselors when they suspect child neglect and/or psychological abuse. However, it is not necessary for counselors to distinguish clearly between physical (including sexual) abuse and neglect and/or psychological abuse (Fischer & Sorenson,1985). Again, counselors are required to report child neglect and/or psychological abuse *suspected from their professional judgements and interpretations of child behaviors, verbalizations, or psychological states* (Fischer & Sorenson).

Many other situations exist in which a counselor's legal obligation to disclose information without a client's permission is far less clear-cut. For example, having knowledge of clients' criminal or substance abuse activities poses complicated legal (and ethical) dilemmas for counselors. A situation which increasingly confronts counselors is working with clients who are HIV-positive or have AIDS (Acquired Immune Deficiency Syndrome) and are sexually active with one or more partners who are unaware of the clients' medical condition. Unfortunately, definitive legal precedents, requirements, or guidelines for disclosure in such situations have not been established. Therefore, counselors involved in such situations are advised to seek legal consultation immediately upon finding themselves confronted with legally complicated disclosure circumstances.

Record Keeping

The very real limitations of human memory in combination with large case loads highlight the need for counselors to keep notes and records about clients. Unfortunately, such record keeping presents potential difficulties for professional counselors, and there are only a few circumstances in which clear guidelines are available.

Concerns about (a) the nature of educational records kept and (b) who had legitimate access to those records led to the Family Educational Rights and Privacy Act of 1974 (FERPA), also known as "the Buckley Amendment." The FERPA was enacted to regulate (among other things) who had legitimate access to the educational records of students in public schools. In general, the FERPA stipulates that school personnel (i.e., employees) have legitimate access to information in students' records to facilitate educational and/or learning activities. More importantly, FERPA stipulates that parents or legal guardians have access to the information kept in their child's records and that *the information must be made available to them in a manner in which they can understand.* Thus, test data, teachers' notes, demographic information, and any other information kept in students' records must be accessible to students' parents or legal guardians.

Employed school counselors have legitimate access to information in students' records when they use the information to facilitate students' educational processes and progress. Similarly, they can add information to students' records for such purposes. However, complications arise when school counselors maintain "case notes" for counseling purposes. If school counselors maintain such case notes in students' records, the provisions of the FERPA apply, and parents or legal guardians and other school personnel presumably have legitimate access to those notes (Fischer & Sorenson, 1985; Hopkins & Anderson, 1990). However, whether or not case notes maintained in school counselor's personal files are subject to the provisions of the FERPA and/or accessible by others (e.g., by subpoena) has not been clearly determined.

Legal standards and practices in regard to record keeping by counselors in other professional settings are even less clear. In general, school and other counselors' professional records (e.g., case notes) are considered a form of "communication" between counselors and their clients and so are subject to laws related to privileged communication (to be covered subsequently). Therefore, counselors' professional records are "protected" (i.e., need not be disclosed without client permission) **only** in situations in which clients are receiving counseling in circumstances where they have right to privileged communication, and those circumstances are relatively rare.

Because counselors only infrequently provide counseling in situations in which their professional records or case notes are *not* subject to access (e.g., by subpoena), the best advice that can be given is that counselors should maintain professional records and case notes as if they will be reviewed by others. This does not mean that such records and case notes cannot contain professional judgments, but it does mean that the bases for the judgments indicated should be clearly indicated in the records or case notes. Remley (1992a) wrote:

> Attorneys who are asked to defend counseling actions taken, or to explain actions not taken, are delighted if the counselor has extensive written materials that help prove his or her version of the controversy. Notes are extremely good evidence that attorneys can use to help counselors substantiate their positions. (p. 31)

Thus, counselors who maintain records and case notes should keep comprehensive and exact notes that allow for detailed clarifications or explanations of counselors' or clients' behaviors, including their respective verbal behaviors.

Criminal and Civil Liability

Counselors may be held liable for their professional actions and behaviors within either of two legal regards. The first regard is **criminal liability,** which arises when a counselor is charged with participation in and/or aiding and abetting criminal activity. In general, criminal liability involves a counselor's participation in a crime against society, rather than against an individual (Fischer & Sorenson, 1985). The most common examples of situations in which counselors are at risk for criminal liability include (a) being an accessory to a crime such as theft, assault, or fraud, (b) civil disobedience, and (c) contributing to the delinquency of a minor (Fischer & Sorenson, 1985; Gladding, 1988; Hopkins & Anderson,

1990). Fortunately, criminal liability prosecution of counselors is relatively rare.

The second regard in which counselors may be held liable is *civil liability.* In general, civil liability involves a "crime" against an individual (Fischer & Sorenson, 1985). Civil liability is rooted in the concept of *tort,* "a wrong that legal action is designed to set right" (Hopkins & Anderson, 1990). Hummel, Talbutt, and Alexander (1985) indicated:

> The basic concept of tort . . . is that each individual has a legal and social obligation to protect other individuals in society. If one person breaches or twists the relationship and someone is injured, then the injured party may sue and be compensated for the injury. The injured party has been diminished; and the only means we have, as a society, to make the person whole again is through a monetary settlement. (p. 68)

Although there are a number of facets of civil liability in which counselors could become involved, most frequently counselors' involvements are in regard to *malpractice.* Hummel, Talbutt, and Alexander (1985) wrote that, *"Malpractice in counseling* can be defined as harm to a client resulting from professional negligence, with *negligence* defined as departure from acceptable professional standards" (p. 70).

Talbutt and Hummel (1982) and Slimak and Berkowitz (1983) identified the following areas of potential malpractice for counselors:

1. making a faulty diagnosis, such as attribution of a physically-based problem to a psychological condition;

2. failing to take action when someone other than the client is in danger;

3. improperly certifying in a commitment proceeding;

4. engaging in behavior inappropriate to accepted standards of the profession, such as unethical behaviors;

5. failing to take adequate precautions for a suicidal client;

6. providing services for which competence has not been demonstrated, established, or proven;

7. breaching confidentiality;

8. promising a "cure"; and

9. taking advantage of the counseling relationship for personal gain, monetary or otherwise.

Among these various possibilities, the most common one for which malpractice suits are brought against counselors is the latter category (i.e., taking advantage of the counseling relationship). Within this category, the most frequently presented basis for malpractice suits against counselors is sexual harassment and/or misconduct. Counselors even may be found guilty of malpractice for having a sexual relationship with a former client if the basis for the sexual relationship can be established as having been initiated during the counseling relationship (Hummel, Talbutt, & Alexander, 1985). Counselors must refrain from sexual relationships with current and recent clients if they are to avoid this type of malpractice suit.

Provision of Services

Two other aspects of law are in regard to the provision of services in which counselors may become entangled. The first is contract law, and in particular, breach of contract. Counselor and client "contracts" for provision of counseling services may be either *expressed* or *implied* (analogous to the situation for informed consent). An expressed contract is one that is written, verbal, and/or witnessed by a person not involved in the counseling relationship. An implied contract is one that is situationally evident from the client's and counselor's behaviors and/or verbalizations. Hopkins and Anderson (1990) noted the possible subtleties of establishment of a contract, such as when counselors "rather casually" communicate to clients that they will provide treatment for a certain number of counseling sessions, a certain number of hours, or a particular fee, or that they will use particular techniques. If counselors fail to provide counseling services *as presented to clients*, they can be held liable for breach of contract. In general, then, counselors who wish to avoid suits for breach of contract must provide counseling services of the nature and under conditions as presented to clients (Brown & Srebalus, 1988).

The second aspect of law relative to provision of services is what has sometimes been legally construed as fraud. Because of the relative recency of professional counselor credentialing procedures such as licensures or certifications, counselors frequently have not been recognized by health insurance companies as eligible for direct (i.e., "third-party") payments. In order to be paid by insurance companies for their counseling services, some counselors have provided their services under the "supervision" of professionals eligible for third-party payments. Coven (1992) wrote:

> An accepted standard of practice which has prevailed within the mental health provider community for many years has been for services to be actually rendered by a "lesser" trained provider such as a counselor; to be "supervised" by a "better qualified" provider such as a psychologist or psychiatrist; and for the health care or insurance forms to be "signed off, on, by" the supervising "more qualified" provider. Frequently the supervising provider had no face-to-face contact with the patient. (p. 1)

Although the practice may have been common, it is unlikely to continue much longer. Coven indicated that "Since 1983 some health care providers and insurance companies have challenged the standard of "nonapproved" providers collecting monies under the supervision and signature of the supervisor, even an approved provider" (p. 3). The basis of the challenge is that the collection of monies for the provision of counseling services by persons other than those who actually provided the services is fraud. Scant legal precedent exists to support this challenge at present. However, it seems likely that such precedents will accumulate rapidly. Thus, counselors should be cautious about entering into arrangements in which payments for services rendered are not made directly to them.

Expert Witness Testimony

An increasing number of counselors are being called upon to provide expert witness testimony, a new and relatively lucrative activity for professional counselors. Remley (1992b) stated the following:

> An expert witness is an objective and unbiased person with specialized knowledge, skills, and/or information, who can assist a judge or jury in reaching an appropriate legal decision. (p. 33)

Unfortunately, many counselors believe they have "specialized knowledge, skills, and information" simply because they have graduate-level training and/or experience in counseling. This naive perspective belies the intricacies and complexities of forensic psychology. Ill-prepared, unskilled, or un- or misinformed counselors who become involved in provision of expert testimony are at risk at least of embarrassment and at worst of legal repercussions. Rinas and Clyne-Jackson (1988) summarized the common scenario succinctly:

> When involved in a court situation, the mental health professional is typically in a foreign arena. In court settings, for example, the consultant [i.e., expert witness] is frequently confused as to what constitutes a "mental health" opinion versus a legal conclusion. In cases of criminal responsibility the mental health expert may be asked "whether individuals have acted with appreciation of the nature of their acts or with free will to avoid violations of the law if they so choose." Such legalistic terms have no real meaning to the mental health professional who unsuccessfully struggles with trying to translate these terms into language he or she understands, for example, what does the legal profession mean by the expressions "appreciation," "nature of the act," and "free will." (p. 119)

Thus, counselors who provide expert witness testimony must have highly specialized knowledge (e.g., of psychopathology, personality assessment, or both), specialized skills (e.g., for working with persons known to have a particular mental disorder), and extensive relevant professional experience.

Some counselors also believe that they have "specialized skills, knowledge, and information" about their clients and therefore would be "good" expert witnesses on behalf of those clients because they have provided counseling services. However, Remley (1992b) pointed out:

> After a witness has been recognized by a judge as an expert . . . the witness is given the opportunity to state an opinion about the matter before the court . . . . The attorney for the side that is harmed by the expert's testimony is given the opportunity to discredit the expert's testimony.

> One of the most effective methods of overcoming the damaging effect of an expert witness opinion is to convince the court that the expert is biased and, therefore, his or her opinion cannot be trusted. (p. 33)

It is highly unlikely that counselors can serve as "unbiased" expert witnesses for their clients. In general, only counselors who have documented evidence of specialized knowledge, skills, and information, as well as substantial relevant experience, should provide expert witness testimony. Counselors who choose to develop such expertise should realize that it most likely will significantly limit the scope of their professional activities.

Marketing and Advertising

A variety of definitions have been provided for the concept of marketing as applied to the counseling profession. For example, Ambrose and Lenox (1988) defined *marketing* as "structuring programs to meet clients' needs after identifying their beliefs and attitudes," whereas Ritchie (1989) defined it as "an exchange of goods for services" noting that counselors exchange counseling services for public support. In general, marketing involves the promotion of counseling services to the public with the intent that the public subsequently will partake of those counseling services more frequently and to a greater extent. *Advertising* (along with selling and public relations) is the primary communication method elements of marketing (Wittman, 1988).

Whether or not counseling professionals should engage in marketing has been the subject of much debate. Ritchie (1989) and Wittman (1988), for example, proposed that the counseling profession has much to gain (e.g., improved public image and more clients) from use of marketing principles and strategies. However, Fong-Beyette (1988) and Stadler (1988), for example, proposed that marketing is basically unprofessional, and that counselors should not and do not have reason to engage in marketing. It is evident in these writings, and others like them, that the respective authors are not all using the same definition of marketing. Therefore, the debate is likely to continue.

To look at marketing from a positive perspective, it may be defined as those activities intended to promote the counseling profession as a whole. Marketing within this context would be used not to benefit particular counselors, but rather to enhance the image of the counseling profession as well as of counselors in general. Advertising, in contrast to marketing, can be conceived of as a process intended to achieve gain for particular counselors. Clearly these are not technically correct definitions or distinctions. However, they do allow the generality that marketing counseling is "good" and that advertising counseling is not.

Gilchrist and Stringer (1992) identified three potential benefits of marketing counseling: (1) maintenance of counselors' positions as service providers, (2) enhancement of the image of counseling services, and (3) fulfillment of demands for counselor accountability. Obviously, achievement of goals such as these would greatly increase and improve the professional identity of the counseling profession. Therefore, movement toward these goals is being pushed by the leadership of the counseling profession. As Beverly O'Bryant, 1992-1993 ACA President, wrote:

> It is our responsibility to change the present. It is our responsibility to represent the future and make the discipline of counseling understood, recognized, and appreciated among the mental health professions and laymen as well.
>
> Each of us must provide accurate information about all of our specialties to a multitude of publics. We must publicize our services more and participate in government relations initiatives locally and nationally. (O'Bryant, 1992, p. 36)

In order to be responsive to O'Bryant's charge, counselors will have to "market" the counseling profession through effective public relations programs including various promotional, and communication activities.

Advertising, at least within the perspective presented previously, is quite another matter. Advertising has been viewed with disdain within the counseling and related professions. Indeed, most professional organizations for counseling service providers have policy statements that place severe restrictions on advertising of professional services. Rinas and Clyne-Jackson (1988) summarized current allowable practices:

> . . .professionals are prohibited from soliciting clients directly. They are entitled to send out announcement cards to potential referral sources but, even in doing this, restrictions are imposed. In general, the private practitioner must limit the information on the card to such items as name, address and phone number, highest level of education achieved in field of practice, office hours, type of clientele serviced (e.g., adolescents), and a brief description of the services available (e.g., family therapy, diagnostic assessments).

> In addition to sending out announcement cards, the new practitioner is also allowed to be appropriately listed in the telephone directory . . . . (p. 12)

Many state counselor credentialing laws also provide specific regulations for "advertising" by credentialed counselors. Thus, counselors are well-advised to be "conservative" in regard to advertising, and to verify locally allowable practices before engaging in advertising.

Defamation (Libel and Slander)

Counselors have access to "personal" information about clients by virtue of the very nature of the counseling process. They also necessarily form opinions about their clients, some of which are based on emotional reactions such as surprise, anger, or frustration. If counselors disclose information or opinions inappropriately, they could be subject to charges of defamation. Hummel, Talbutt, and Alexander (1985) wrote:

Counselors, because of the nature of their work, have many opportunities for defamation that could result in litigation. They are privy to conversations, records, and personal information and they communicate with a range of individuals who may pressure them to reveal confidential information. (p. 85)

In the legal sense, there are two types of defamation: libel and slander. *Libel* is defamation expressed in a written form, and **slander** is defamation expressed in a verbal form (Hummel, Talbutt, & Alexander, 1985; Talbutt, 1988). In either case, in order for a counselor to be found guilty of defamation, it must be shown that written or verbal statements made by the counselor were (1) false, (2) brought hatred, disgrace, ridicule, or contempt to another person, and (3) resulted in damages (Hummel, Talbutt, & Alexander, 1985). In other words, the communication must be proven to have been *malicious*. Recognize, however, that a communication may be judged malicious *even though there was no malicious intention*. The plaintiff in a defamation case does not necessarily have to prove that a communication was intended to be malicious, but merely that it was malicious in regard to the three criteria listed above.

The pressure on counselors to disclose information inappropriately is sometimes social, sometimes professional, and sometimes both. For example, if a teacher refers a student to a school counselor because the student is misbehaving and otherwise having difficulties in class, the teacher reasonably might later ask the school counselor, "What's wrong with the student?" A school counselor responding to such a question would be well-advised to avoid describing the student in terms of perceptions of the student's characteristics. Counselors also sometimes "just talk" about their clients in social and/ or informal professional situations. Such "talk" could become the basis for a defamation suit against the counselor.

Talbutt (1988) provided four guidelines for counselors to follow to avoid allegations of defamation:

1. Always act in good faith and keep all communications free from malice.

2. Report behavior objectively and factually, and avoid use of psychological jargon that could be misconstrued.

3. Communicate about clients only in response to requests and only when a duty to respond exists.

4. Communicate only what is believed to be true and supported by facts.

These guidelines reflect a basic tenet of good professional practice: counselors should communicate about clients only in professional manners and only in professional contexts.

These, then, are the major legal concerns with which counselors should be familiar and for which they are specifically accountable. However, they are not the only legal concerns of which counselors should be aware. Counselors also should be aware of the legal concerns particularly applicable to their clients.

LEGAL CONCERNS FOR CLIENTS

Clients usually have all the legal rights of other members of society, perhaps the only exception being those clients who are convicted felons. Clients also sometimes have additional, specific legal rights by virtue of being clients. Some of the major legal concerns for clients applicable to counseling situations are provided in the paragraphs that follow.

Right to Treatment

Clients' legal right to treatment concerns for counselors actually encompass several different legal rights: (1) right to treatment, (2) right to least intrusive (or least restrictive) treatment, and (3) right to adequate treatment. Although these client rights are often interrelated, they are presented here separately for clarity.

Increasing numbers of counselors are working in residential "mental health" facilities, particularly those operated and managed as state agencies. Typically, state-operated residential mental health treatment facilities have large populations, few professional staff, and minimal operating budgets. Because of these conditions, people in such facilities often have been "warehoused" (i.e., provided custodial care only in terms of basic physical needs). It is in regard to clients in such residential facilities that clients' right to treatment has been most frequently challenged in the courts.

Most right to treatment cases have been brought before courts for three major groups of people: (1) those with diminished intellectual capacity, (2) those with severe psychological disturbances, and (3) those with physical disabilities. In general, the courts have held that all these types of clients have legal right to psychotherapeutic/counseling services (Rinas & Clyne-Jackson, 1988). That is, the courts have ruled that these potential clients cannot just be ignored; they must receive treatment/services in regard to their *psychological* conditions and/or situations (e.g., in residential facilities). Unfortunately, although court rulings generally have been in favor of such persons, provision of counseling and related psychological services continue to be withheld from many of them (Robinson, 1991). What progress has been made for underserved clientele has been primarily for persons (particularly students) with physical disabilities (Brown & Srebalus, 1988).

The courts have generally held that clients have the right to the least intrusive treatment that will alleviate the condition for which treatment was sought. The "least intrusive" treatment (i.e., counseling intervention) is that which will achieve treatment goals with the least number of undesirable side effects. For example, use of psychotropic drugs is obviously more intrusive than use of a verbal-interaction counseling treatment. Counselors, of course, rarely recommend use of psychotropic drugs, however, the principle still holds. Drug therapy is not the only type of treatment that is occasionally deemed too intrusive. For example, family counseling might be considered unduly intrusive if individual counseling is deemed sufficient to achieve desired treatment goals. In commenting on evaluation of treatment intrusiveness, Rinas and Clyne-Jackson (1988) noted:

> In determining the degree of intrusiveness of a particular intervention, the professional should take into consideration

a number of different factors. First of all, the therapist should consider the permanence of any change that could result from a particular procedure . . . . Another characteristic to consider is the "foreignness" of the change to the client, that is, the degree to which the modified behavior differs from the behaviors typically manifested by that client. The therapist should also consider the scope of the behaviors that could possibly be changed as a result of the intervention, the speed with which changes are likely to occur, the duration of the change, and the client's ability to resist such change. (p. 88)

Perhaps the most significant aspect of clients' right to treatment for counselors is clients' right to *adequate* treatment (i.e., treatment by a competent professional). A substantial number of court cases have been brought against counselors in which the primary allegation was incompetence on the part of the counselor (Rinas & Clyne-Jackson, 1988). In general, what is alleged in these cases is that the counselor attempted to use therapeutic or counseling interventions for which the counselor could not demonstrate and/or verify professional competence. No clear trend has been established in the outcomes of such cases. However, some counselors have been found guilty of attempting to use interventions for which they were unqualified. Counselors never should use interventions beyond the limits of their competence. Unfortunately, it is not always easy to determine the limits of competence. For example, is a counselor who was trained specifically in marriage and family counseling necessarily competent to do individual or small group counseling? Probably not. Conversely, counselors specifically trained to do small group counseling probably are not competent to do family counseling. Robinson (1991) wrote:

> If you are not qualified to treat a certain client problem, what should you do ethically? Your first choice is to refer the client to someone who is more qualified to help him or her. If there is no one available (which would be the exception rather than the rule), then it is incumbent on you [i.e., the counselor] to get continuing education, to devour library books and articles on the presenting problem, and to seek supervision. You do not just proceed as if what you know can generalize to every client problem. You are responsible for the welfare of that client, and it is your professional and ethical responsibility to find for

that client the best services possible - be it from you or
from someone else. (pp. 452-453)

Robinson's advice to counselors is good from professional
and ethical perspectives. However, probably only her first
recommendation (i.e., make a referral) is valid *legally*. That
is, once counseling has begun and the counselor has made
a personal judgment of professional competence insufficiency,
he or she probably could not garner needed knowledge and
skills rapidly enough to present a defensible position in a
court of law. While counselors generally are well-advised to
continue to increase their professional knowledge and skills,
attempting such improvements *during* a counseling process
for a client who has a problem that exceeds the counselor's
current competence is not advisable from a legal perspective.

Access to Records

The legalities of clients' right to access records kept on
them are, at very least, complicated and confusing. In regard
to the educational (i.e., academic) records, FERPA serves as
the basis of laws covering clients' right to access. As mentioned
earlier in this chapter, FERPA stipulates that parents of school
children have legal right to the information maintained in
their children's educational records. However, parents of children
generally do not have a legal right to access "personal" notes
or records maintained by school counselors for their counseling
activities with children (Hummel, Talbutt, & Alexander, 1985).
But when do personal notes and records become part of
educational records and thereby permit parental access to
them? Personal records become educational records when
a (school or other) counselor shares his or her personal notes
or records with other school personnel (Hummel, Talbutt,
& Alexander, 1985). Thus, the act of sharing of the counselor's
"personal" information, either in writing or verbally, negates
the counselor's strictly personal use of those notes or records
and makes them accessible to parents.

Conditions of FERPA also generally apply to college students.
If they are more than 18 years of age, they (not their parents)
have the right to access their educational records. However,
there are several access restrictions in FERPA specific to college

students. For example, they do not have right of access to parental or familial financial information maintained by the postsecondary institution. In regard to letters of reference, students have the right to waive access to those letters. Before the letter is submitted, potential contributors of reference letters must be informed of whether or not the student for whom the letter is to be written has waived the right to access. If right to access is waived, students cannot subsequently review those letters, except when the letters are later used for a purpose other than the originally intended one (Hummel, Talbutt, & Alexander, 1985). School and other counselors asked to submit letters of reference should note waiver of right of access status and adjust the content of their letters accordingly.

Right-to-access legislation is somewhat less clearly defined concerning records other than those held in educational settings. Rinas and Clyne-Jackson (1988), in discussing records other than those for student clients, indicated that counseling clients generally have right to access their records. However, they also noted that most counseling facilities attempt to discourage clients from accessing their counselors' records. Rinas and Cline-Jackson further noted the considerable professional and legal argument over whether clients have right to access their counseling records if the information in the records is potentially "harmful" to the clients. The issue of debate is what is harmful to clients and, more importantly, who decides what is harmful. Unfortunately, although legislation has been passed in some states which gives clients right to access to their records, there is substantial variation in that legislation. In addition, there have been very few judicial decisions regarding clients' right to access their records in settings other than educational settings. To avoid impinging upon or violating clients' to access, counselors should carefully review any client right to access legislation in the states in which they practice.

Right to Due Process

As citizens, student and other clients cannot have their Constitutional rights denied, withheld, or restricted arbitrarily or capriciously. In other words, counselors in schools or in other circumstances cannot capriciously deny clients rights of freedom of speech, assembly, or association. However, clients rights may be restricted or denied under certain circumstances, if due process procedures have been followed.

In the case of *Tinker v. Des Moines* (1969), the United States Supreme Court held that students had the same fundamental rights as other citizens and that they could express those rights in a variety of ways as long as the methods did not "materially or substantively" interfere with the rights of others or of educational processes (Hummel, Talbutt, & Alexander, 1985). For example, students have the Constitutional right to express their opinions (i.e., have freedom of speech), but they cannot express those opinions as a means of blocking other students' access to classes. Similarly, although the United States Constitution gives citizens the right to bear arms, students may be prohibited from bringing weapons to schools, because those weapons constitute a significant potential danger to others.

Hummel, Talbutt, and Alexander (1985) listed the basic elements of due process for a person, summarized as follows:

1. The person must be given notice; in other words, the person must be apprised that a behavior is prohibited before procedures are instituted against the person.

2. A hearing must be held in which the person has the opportunity to refute the charges made.

3. An impartial person or persons must preside at the hearing.

4. The person has the right to counsel. For students, the "counsel" may be an adult, not necessarily an attorney.

5. The person has the right to question witnesses and/ or to bring forth witnesses.

6. Any decision must be made on the basis of evidence presented, and not on the basis of factors extraneous to the case at hand.

Counselors could become involved in due process procedures in any of several capacities, and therefore should know the due process requirements for the circumstances in which they work.

Sexual Misconduct

Allegations of sexual misconduct against counselors, as well as lawsuits based on such allegations have increased dramatically in recent years (Coleman & Schaefer, 1988; Nelson, 1992). Sexual misconduct may be overt and direct, such as in the case of sexual intimacy between counselor and client during or as a result of counseling, or covert and indirect, such as in the case of verbal harassment or sexual hugs and fondling. Counselors' sexual misconduct in either form has long been considered ethically and professionally inappropriate (Coleman & Schaefer, 1988). In recent times, it has been declared not only inappropriate but illegal. An increasing number of states are passing legislation specifically prohibiting sexual intimacies between counselors and their clients during or after counseling relationships. Further, an increasing number of state counselor licensure boards are incorporating statutes against counselor and client sexual intimacy, with the penalty being revocation of licensure (Coleman & Schaefer, 1988).

Advice for counselors contemplating sexual intimacy with clients is really very simple: don't. Sexual intimacy with clients is at least unethical and unprofessional, and at most illegal.

Privileged Communication

Privileged communication is usually thought of as the legal counterpart to confidentiality. That is, counselors frequently speak or write about privileged communication as *their* legal right not to disclose information obtained from clients during a counseling relationship. However, contrary to this commonly held perception, "...privileged communication is a legal term that indicates that the client's communications cannot be disclosed in a court of law without the client's consent. The privilege belongs to the client, not the counselor...." (Robinson, 1991, p. 455). Herlihy and Sheeley (1987) provided the technical distinction between confidentiality and privileged communication when they wrote:

> *Confidentiality* is an ethical standard that protects clients from disclosure without their consent, whereas *privacy* is an evolving legal concept that recognizes individuals' rights to choose the time, circumstances, and extent to which they wish to share or withhold personal information. *Privileged communication,* a narrower concept, regulates privacy protection and confidentiality by protecting clients from having their confidential communications disclosed in court without their permission. (p. 479)

More simply, ". . . standards on confidentiality have evolved to protect the client's communications outside the courtroom whereas privileged communication protects the client from having private information divulged within the courtroom" (Rinas & Clyne-Jackson, 1988, p. 56).

Various authors (e.g., Fischer & Sorenson, 1985; Hopkins & Anderson, 1990) have listed the four legal criteria typically used to determine whether or not communications should be considered privileged:

1. The communications must have originated with the assumption of both parties that the communications would be held in confidence.

2. Confidentiality of communications between the two parties must be viewed as essential to maintenance of an effective relationship between the parties.

3. The type of relationship must be one which is valued by members of the community and society.

4. The damage done to the relationship by disclosure of the information communicated under the assumption of confidentiality must be judged to be greater than the benefit derived for the litigation process.

The first two criteria are clearly reflected in the ethical standards of the counseling profession. The applicability of the third and fourth criteria clearly increases with improvements in the professional identity of the counseling profession.

Unfortunately, the majority of states currently do not give clients the right to privileged communication in their counseling relationships with counselors (Herlihy & Sheeley, 1987). However, the number of states providing counseling clients' right to privileged communication is increasing, primarily because of increasing and evolving counselor licensure laws and other improvements in counselors' professional identity.

In states where counseling clients have the right to privileged communication, counselors involved in clients' litigation do not have to decide whether right to privileged communication should be invoked in a court of law. Rather, that right, and the responsibility for decisions related to it, belongs to the client. Indeed, with the exception of circumstances in which counselors' *duty to warn* (e.g., requirement to report child abuse and/or neglect) comes into play, counselors are legally prohibited from disclosing counselor-client communications without the client's express permission. If clients release counselors to disclose counselor-client communications in a court of law, counselors can, and probably must, respond to inquiries about counselor-client communications (Fischer & Sorenson, 1985; Hopkins & Anderson, 1990; Hummel, Talbutt, & Alexander, 1985). In legal proceedings, counselors generally are responsive to clients' decisions about right to privileged communication; counselors do not make decisions about that right.

Even in states where counseling clients have the right to privileged communication, at least two circumstances exist in which that right cannot be applied directly. The first concerns child counseling and the second concerns group and/or marriage and family counseling. In regard to counseling children (i.e., persons under the age of 18), the client's right to privileged communication "passes" to the parent(s) or legal guardian(s). Thus, the parent(s) or legal guardian(s) make decisions about disclosure in courts of the child's communications during counseling (Rinas & Clyne-Jackson, 1988). In regard to group and/or marriage and family counseling, Fischer and Sorenson (1985) wrote:

> The historical view of the courts has been that if more than two people are involved in the conversation, the privilege

is lost to all, since there is no confidentiality intended. Although this view makes little sense in group counseling or therapy, counselors should realize that there is a significant lag between developments in their professional techniques and law. (p. 21)

Thus, the presence of a "third party" is in and of itself sufficient to negate the right to privileged communication in any counseling context (Rinas & Clyne-Jackson, 1988). In general, then, privileged communication may be assumed to apply only to communications between a professional and one other adult.

The goal of enabling counseling clients to have the right to privileged communication throughout the United States is a frequently espoused and noble one, because the achievement of such a goal would do much to enhance the credibility of the counseling profession. However, counselors should be aware that even if that goal were achieved, significant legal intricacies would remain in various privileged communication statutes, and counselors would not have *carte blanche* to withhold counselor-client communications. In any case, counselors should make every effort to understand fully the nuances of clients' privileged communication statutes in the locations where they practice.

LEGAL RESOURCES FOR COUNSELORS

Increasing legal complexities for counselors and for their clients necessitate that counselors be proactive in regard to legal concerns. That is, counselors must act in ways that will enable them to avoid legal problems. Remley (1992a, 1992b); Hopkins and Anderson (1990); Hummel, Talbutt, and Alexander (1985); and others all have indicated that the best way for counselors to prevent themselves from becoming embroiled in legal problems is to act in accord with accepted professional standards; that is, to act ethically. Certainly that is good advice, but it is not complete advice, because it is based on the assumption that ethical standards cover all legal situations and that counselors know what the accepted standards of the profession are. The former assumption may not be true in general and the latter may not be true in regard to legal concerns.

There are at least two behaviors (in addition to acting ethically) in which counselors can engage to protect themselves from legal problems. Each is facilitated by membership in a professional organization such as ACA. The first is to increase their knowledge of legal concerns, issues, and practices. For example, ACA makes available a wide variety of resources (including books, visual media, and professional development activities) designed to increase counselors' knowledge of the law. The second is to obtain professional liability insurance, such as that available at reasonable costs through ACA. Good counselors strive to improve continually their knowledge of the legal aspects of their profession. Even better counselors know that no matter what they do, they may be subject to legal involvements and they need to act so as to protect themselves as much as possible.

SUMMARY

Today, legal concerns for counselors and their clients encompass many aspects of law and almost all human interactions, conditions, and situations. When the counseling profession in general, and counselors in particular, were less well-known, the likelihood of counselors' involvements in legal matters was far less than it is now. Increased recognition brings with it increased scrutiny and increased responsibility. Thus, counselors now need to devote substantial time and effort to becoming knowledgeable of the legal concerns, issues, and intricacies applicable to their work with clients. They also must make concerted effort to act in ways that are ethically, professionally, and legally defensible.

Chapter **7**

ETHICAL CONCERNS IN COUNSELING

The legal considerations for the counseling profession not withstanding, counseling is essentially a self-regulating profession. That is, although the number of litigations in which counselors are involved is increasing, the fact remains that a relatively small proportion of counselors are involved in litigations. Although counseling activities must be conducted within applicable legal standards, little legal precedence regarding counseling related litigation exists; thus, counselors must look primarily to professional rather than legal guidelines for their counseling activities. The professional guidelines which serve as the basis for counseling activities are known as *ethical standards.*

THE NEED FOR ETHICAL STANDARDS

Indicated previously was that "a publicly professed, voluntarily self-imposed set of behavioral guidelines" is one of the characteristics of a profession. More simply, no amount of training, preparation, or personal wisdom will enable counselors to know what is "the right thing to do" in some of the situations they will encounter in their counseling activities. Therefore, ethical standards are needed to facilitate counselors' decision making in those situations. However, ethical standards are only guidelines. Van Hoose (1986) wrote:

> All the psychological helping professions have ethical standards in one form or another. These standards reflect professional concerns and define basic principles that should guide the professional activity of the practitioner. Ethical codes help to clarify a counselor's responsibilities to clients, and they are an aid in ethical decision making.
>
> Ethical codes are quite helpful, indeed essential, but they do not answer all ethical questions. (p. 168)

Thus, ultimately, counselors have at least some personal responsibility for their decisions about appropriate behavior.

In general, a set of ethical standards is a reflection of the collective values and belief system of the members of a profession. Ethical standards are created, in part, to reduce the need for counselors to have sole responsibility for their professional decisions (i.e., to minimize personal responsibility for decision making). However, Mabe and Rollin (1986) wrote:

> A responsible member of the counseling profession must look to various sources for guidance. We fear that many professions may see a code of ethics as the sole basis for explicating responsibility for its members. The code is clearly a central part, but only a part, of the basis for explication of professional responsibility. A professional code is necessary but not sufficient for the exercise of professional responsibility. (p. 294)

Thus, codes of ethics do not provide "absolute rules" which will absolve counselors of decision-making responsibility in every situation. For example, Mabe and Rollin provided six problem areas in which ethical standards may not provide clear guidelines for decisions, including that (1) some counselor personal values issues cannot be handled within the context of a code of ethics, (2) some aspects of a code of ethics are difficult to enforce, (3) not all the interests of affected persons (e.g., counselors, clients, and representatives of agencies or institutions) can be effectively represented in a code of ethics, (4) there is a limited number of topics that can be covered in a code of ethics, (5) there may be multiple (e.g., professional versus legal) forums in which topics need to be addressed, and (6) different codes of ethics may conflict with one another. However, even when a set of ethical standards does not provide *explicit* guidelines for decision making, it may provide *implicit* guidelines through its inherent value orientation.

In addressing the limitations of attempting to make decisions simply on the basis of ethical standards, Van Hoose (1986) differentiated between ethical standards and ethical principles, and wrote:

> Counselors who are unable to find direction in ethical codes may find answers to ticklish questions in some fundamental principles of helping. Ethical principles provide a more solid framework for decision making than do ethical codes or statutes. The fundamental principles of counseling include autonomy, beneficence, nonmaleficence, justice, and fidelity. (p. 168)

"Autonomy" is used in this context to mean that clients' right to make their own decisions should be respected (except in certain very specific situations). "Beneficence" means that counselors should always attempt to act in the best interests of their clients. "Nonmaleficence" means that counselors also should make every effort to avoid doing harm to their clients. "Justice" means that counselors should treat people as equals (i.e., not discriminate on the basis of gender, race, economic situation, or other personal characteristics). "Fidelity" means that counselors have loyalty to their clients. In essence, Van Hoose was describing a moral-reasoning orientation which counselors should use to make decisions, an orientation which is reflected in many sets of ethical standards but which may not be stated explicitly in them.

Ethical standards are needed basically because counselors need guidelines for making decisions about some of their counseling activities. While ethical standards do not absolve counselors of personal responsibility in making professional decisions, they do reflect the prevailing ethical sentiment of the profession and, in so doing, suggest the professional standards to which counselors should adhere. Therefore, ethical standards set the course for professional behavior while allowing, and requiring, that counselors be integrally involved in making specific decisions about how to follow the course.

PROFESSIONAL PREPARATION FOR
ETHICAL PRACTICE

Although it can be inferred that many counselor education students value the five "fundamental principles of counseling" described by Van Hoose (1986) by virtue of their selection of a potential profession, the extent to which they adhere to those principles is unknown. Therefore, it is incumbent upon counselor education programs to instill or enhance those principles in counselor education students. In addition, it is incumbent upon counselor education programs to insure that counselor education students have thorough knowledge of applicable ethical standards. These goals are widely recognized and accepted as appropriate. For example, Engels, Wilborn, and Schneider (1990) wrote that "Because circumstances requiring moral and ethical choice pervade our increasingly complex society, it is clear that ethics overtly and deliberately needs to be taught in any counselor education program" (p. 111). The question is how they should be taught.

In discussing ethical practice training for counselor education students, Engels, Wilborn, and Schneider (1990) provided six curricular goals, including

> . . . (1) to facilitate student self-awareness, with attention
> to personal assumptions, values, biases, strengths, and
> limitations; (2) to facilitate student awareness of the pervasive
> nature of ethical issues in life and society . . . ; (3) to
> foster commitment to personal and professional ethical action
> and responsibility for action; (4) to facilitate broad ethical
> knowledge and reasoning skills . . . ; (5) to heighten student
> appreciation for the complexity and ambiguity of ethical
> principles and standards; and (6) to foster sensitivity to
> cultural and other issues [in ethical practice] . . . . (pp.
> 113-114)

Kitchener (1986) proposed that ethical behavior is essentially a type of morality and therefore that ethical practice preparation for counselor-education students should give them abilities to (1) interpret potential ethical dilemma situations as moral ones, (2) formulate a moral course of action, (3) be able to decide what to do, and (4) implement a course of action. These comments suggest that in order for counselor-education students to become ethical practitioners, they must become knowledgeable of their own ethical principles, of pertinent ethical standards, and of the interaction between these principles and standards, and they need effective ethical decision-making skills.

One issue in counselor education student ethical practice preparation is whether such preparation should be a singular curricular experience (e.g., a course) or integrated into the various curricular experiences in the counselor-education program. The latter option is clearly the one of choice (Engels, Wilborn, & Schneider, 1990). A wide variety of models for ethical practice preparation in this regard have been proposed. For example, Pelsma and Borgers (1986) presented an experience-based model built upon four learner abilities: (1) concrete experience (affective/feeling), (2) reflective observation (perceptual/watching), (3) abstract conceptualization (symbolic/thinking), and (4) active experimentation (behavioral/doing). They recommended that counselor education students be presented with various ethical dilemmas and asked to "solve" them. Pelsma and Borgers wrote:

> Each ethical dilemma experienced forms the basis for additional concrete experience (affective). Given the opportunity to reflect on and observe (perceptual) the situations, values, and ethical principles involved, the individual can then assimilate this experience into a theory (symbolic) from which new implications for ethical action are deduced and chosen. These implications then serve as guides for the creation of ethical practices (behavioral). These practices, in turn, re-create new experiences that bring the learning process full cycle. (p. 312).

Thus, effective preparation for ethical practice of counseling involves consideration and reconsideration of a wide variety of possible ethical dilemmas and situations so that a personalized pattern of ethical decision making is established.

Tennyson and Strom (1986) indicated that counselors must move beyond mere understanding of ethical standards to development of professional *responsibleness*. They wrote that "Counseling is a moral enterprise requiring responsibleness; that is, action should be based on careful, reflective thought about which professional response is right in a particular situation" (p. 298). Perhaps most importantly, they emphasized that development of professional responsibleness (in regard to ethical practice) should not stop with the end of a counselor-preparation program; such development should continue throughout each counseling professional's career. They advocated use of professional development activities involving discourse among professionals about ethical issues and concerns, such as workshops and convention programs, as the best means to foster continued development of professional responsibleness. Tennyson and Strom wrote:

> The continuing development of a professional, like the continuous maturing of a field, requires critical self-awareness and self-criticism . . . . Because value judgments are implicit in their practice, counselors exercise moral responsibleness when their beliefs, attitudes, and actions are grounded in reasons that are openly examined through critical reflection. This reflection can be pursued independently, but it is enhanced through rational discourse with professional peers. (p. 302)

OVERVIEW OF THE 1988 ACA ETHICAL STANDARDS

Ethical standards applicable to professional counselors have been created by large professional associations such as ACA, APA, and AAMFT, as well as by counselor-certification agencies such as NBCC, CRC, and NACCMHC. A number of the divisions of ACA (e.g., ASGW, ASCA, and NCDA) also have created sets of ethical standards specific to their respective professional interest areas. Thus, there are quite a few sets of ethical standards to which counselors should adhere. However, because the ACA and NBCC *Ethical Standards* are the ones most commonly espoused by professional counselors and because they are typical of sets of ethical standards, they are the ones presented here.

Members of ACA have always advocated adherence to professional ethical standards. However, ACA (then APGA) did not publish its own ethical standards until 1959 (Engels, Wilborn, & Schneider, 1990). Prior to that year, ACA recommended adherence to other sets of ethical standards, particularly those of APA. The (APGA, then AACD, and now)

ACA *Ethical Standards* have been revised several times since their original publication, with the most recent version being the 1988 *Ethical Standards of the American Association for Counseling and Development.* These became *Ethical Standards of the American Counseling Association* concurrent with the organizational name change in July, 1992.

The 1988 version of the ACA *Ethical Standards* contains the same subsections as the 1981 version. However, the 1988 version incorporated new or revised statements related primarily to concerns about use of computers in counseling, sexual harassment, assessment, various counselor interventions, and advertising (Allen, Sampson, & Herlihy, 1988). A few statements from the 1981 version were deleted in the 1988 version. These changes reflect the evolving nature of the counseling profession as well as of life in society. The 1988 ACA (AACD) *Ethical Standards* are presented in Appendix I.

The large number of statements in the ACA *Ethical Standards* precludes comment upon each one. Therefore, following are comments on the eight subsections in general. Changes noted between the 1981 and 1988 versions of the ACA *Ethical Standards* can be referenced to Allen, Sampson, and Herlihy (1988). Some of the particular statements within the subsections are addressed specifically in the subsection of this book on areas of ethical concern, which follows discussion of the NBCC *Ethical Standards.*

Part of the **Preamble** of the ACA *Ethical Standards* explains why they were created:

> The specification of ethical standards enables the Association to clarify to present and future members and to those served by members, the nature of ethical responsibilities held in common by its members.

Again, by definition, ethical standards reflect value, moral, social, and professional judgments. Thus, they are intended to communicate to both counselors and clients the value judgments, reflected in behavioral statements, made by professional counselors about how counselors should behave and how counseling should be practiced.

Section A: General

The first subsection of the ACA *Ethical Standards* covers the following facets of counselors' responsibilities: (1) development of the counseling profession in general, (2) communication of boundaries of competence and professional qualifications, (3) provision of professional services, and (4) clients, colleagues, and employing institutions. Added for the 1988 version was a specific prohibition against sexual harassment (defined as "deliberate or repeated comments, gestures, or physical contacts of a sexual nature) by counselors. A charge to counselors to respect "a client's individual rights and personal dignity" also was added.

Section B: Counseling Relationship

The second section provides guidelines for the conduct of individual and group counseling processes, on topics such as confidentiality, record-keeping, client selection, and computer-assisted counseling. The 1988 version incorporated five new statements pertaining to computer applications in counseling, as well as the specific declaration that counselors should avoid all types of sexual intimacies with clients.

Section C: Measurement and Evaluation

Because assessment and appraisal (i.e., measurement and evaluation) often are components in counseling processes, guidelines relating to these topics are covered in Section C: Measurement and Evaluation. This section presents guidelines for selection, administration, and disclosure of results; for interpretations of assessments; and for client orientation and counseling in regard to assessments. The limitations and appropriate uses of computer-assisted assessments also are addressed in this version.

Section D: Research and Publication

This section presents guidelines for the conduct of research and publication by professional counselors, including a guideline concerning the need to protect the rights and privacy of individuals participating in research processes.

Section E: Consulting

The importance of consultation as a professional activity is reflected in the ethical guidelines given for it in Section E: Consulting, which includes coverage of the nature and parameters of consulting relationships. Neither of these sections was changed significantly in the 1988 version.

Section F: Private Practice

Because of the increasing incidence of counselors with "private practices," Section F: Private Practice provides guidelines specifically applicable to this type of counseling service provision. Changes in this section included incorporation of guidelines for advertising and for public presentation of credentials.

Section G: Personnel Administration

This section includes guidelines for administration and/or management of counseling program activities. A noteworthy change for the 1988 version is the requirement for counselors to inform clients of the nature of confidentiality provisions if they intend to disclose client information to a supervisor.

Section H: Preparation Standards

The importance of effective preparation for professional counselors is reflected in Section H which emphasizes the general need to provide effective learning and self-development environments for counselor education students. The responsibility of counselor-preparation programs to monitor access to the counseling profession through ongoing evaluations of students' knowledge, skills, and suitability for the profession also is covered in this section.

Summary

The ACA *Ethical Standards* are intended to provide guidelines for the ethical practice of counseling in general. Therefore, although they were created by and for specific application to ACA members, presumably they are applicable to all who identify themselves as professional counselors. More importantly, however, they provide guidelines for ethical decision making. Therefore, all professional counselors are well-advised to review periodically the ACA Ethical Standards in order to make ethical decisions effectively and thereby provide the best professional counseling services for clients.

THE NBCC ETHICAL STANDARDS

Whereas the ACA *Ethical Standards* are intended for application to ACA members in particular and to professional counselors in general, the NBCC *Ethical Standards* are intended for application to the subset of professional counselors who are National Certified Counselors (NCCs). Indeed, formally indicating agreement (vis-a-vis signature) to abide by the NBCC *Ethical Standards* is a prerequisite to becoming an NCC. The NBCC *Ethical Standards*, as amended in 1989, are presented in Appendix II.

The similarity of the philosophical and professional orientations between ACA and NBCC is reflected in their respective sets of ethical standards. The NBCC *Ethical Standards* were developed originally from the 1981 ACA (then APGA) *Ethical Standards* and have evolved to address most of the same topics. Indeed, the first six sections of the NBCC *Ethical Standards* have the same titles as the first six sections of the ACA *Ethical Standards*. Differences between the comparable sections primarily concern different configurations and/or groupings of the two organizations.

The NBCC *Ethical Standards* do not contain sections covering "personnel administration" or "professional preparation," because NBCC certification is for the practice of counseling only and is not intended to have specific applicability to management or administration of counseling programs or to the preparation of counselors. However, the NBCC *Ethical Standards* do have an Appendix which includes ethical statements relating to participation in the NBCC's National Counselor Examination. Statements in the appendix emphasize that NBCC applicants must not (1) have falsified information relative to eligibility to participate in the examination, (2) aid or be aided by others during participation in the examination, or (3) disclose any information from the examination following participation.

Because of the similarity of the ACA and NBCC *Ethical Standards*, the following discussions of areas of ethical concerns for counselors are presented only in reference to the somewhat more general ACA *Ethical Standards*. However, counselors again are advised to review periodically the NBCC *Ethical Standards* in order to keep abreast of pertinent ethical considerations and practices, and to provide effective counseling services.

PROMINENT AREAS OF ETHICAL CONCERNS

Although literally any counseling activity can result in an ethical dilemma for counselors, some areas of counseling practice have been identified as common sources of ethical concern and/or areas in which ethical decision making is particularly difficult. These areas merit attention and so are addressed in the following subsections.

Clients Intending to Harm Others

Maintenance of confidentiality by counselors in regard to information gained from clients is generally considered to be the primary ethical principle underlying the ACA (as well as other, related) *Ethical Standards* even though, surprisingly, confidentiality is not explicitly defined in those ethical standards. Given the preeminence of the principle of confidentiality, it is not surprising that perhaps the most widely known specific ethical standard is the one that allows exception to the principle of confidentiality:

> 4. When the client's condition indicates that there is clear and imminent danger to the client or others, the member must take reasonable personal action or inform responsible authorities. Consultation with other professionals must be used where possible. (ACA *Ethical Standards*, Section B: Counseling Relationship, 1988)

This standard, of course, must be considered in relation to the one which holds that "The member's [i.e., counselor's] primary obligation is to respect the integrity and promote the welfare of the client . . . " (ACA *Ethical Standards*, Section

B: Counseling Relationship, 1988). In regard to a client's potential danger to others, one complexity that arises in mutual application of these two ethical standards is in deciding when the welfare of members of society must supersede the welfare of the client.

Gross and Robinson (1987) wrote:

> Definitions of client welfare are not included in the ethical standards, which is perhaps understandable when one views the existing codes as guidelines, not laws or statutes directing the behavior of individuals. Legal definitions of client welfare also do not exist but must be extrapolated from the various laws and statutes that have been established in each state. (p. 340)

Similarly, there are no ethical, legal, or statutory definitions of the welfare of members of society. Presumably, the welfare of members of society at least includes protection from physical injury or death. However, members of society also can be harmed psychologically or socially. Therefore, when a client indicates intention to "harm" other members of society, which of course also has significant implications for the client's welfare, the counselor must somehow define the welfare of the client and of members of society. This task is by no means easy, but it must be accomplished effectively in order to decide the appropriate priority (i.e., the welfare of the client or of members of society).

A second, and integrally related, complexity lies in deciding upon the seriousness of the client's stated intention. Gross and Robinson (1987) wrote that "assessment of clear and imminent danger . . . lacks definition and seems to be based on the assumption that the mental health professional is able, because of his or her education, training, or experience, to make this determination" (p. 341). The assumption that counselors can make this determination effectively is tenuous at best, because most counselors simply have not been trained to assess what may be called a client's **lethality potential** (i.e., the seriousness of the client's stated intention to cause harm to others).

What should a counselor do if a client makes even a veiled threat to others? First, the counselor must take seriously *any* statement of intention to harm others. Second, in accord with the ACA *Ethical Standards*, the counselor must seek appropriate consultation with other professionals, such as other counselors, law enforcement officials, or attorneys. Consultation in regard to determining and using effective methods to evaluate the seriousness of the client's stated intention is crucial. Third, in accord with both the ACA *Ethical Standards* and the legal principle of *duty to warn* (see preceding chapter), the counselor must inform appropriate persons, such as potential victims and/or law enforcement officials, that the client has indicated intention to harm others.

Clients Intending to Harm Themselves

The ethical (and legal) issues, dynamics, and decisions to be made that arise when a client indicates intention to harm him- or herself are similar to those for situations in which a client indicates intention to harm others. In brief, the counselor must evaluate the seriousness of the stated intention and then act accordingly.

Evaluating the seriousness (i.e., **lethality potential**) of a client's intention to harm self involves consideration of at least 10 factors, paraphrased here from Fujimara, Weis, and Cochran (1985):

1. *Previous suicide attempts.* The best indicator of a person's intention to harm self.

2. *Sleep disruption.* Disrupted sleep patterns are associated with greater seriousness.

3. *Definitiveness of plan.* Having a specific plan of how to harm self is more serious than having a vague plan.

4. *Reversibility of plan.* Intention to use an "irreversible" method, such as a gun or jumping from a high place, is more serious than intended use of a "reversible" method, such as taking pills.

5. *Proximity of others.* Intention to harm self in relative isolation is more serious than intention to harm self in proximity of others.

6. *Giving possessions away.* Having discarded personal possessions and having "arranged one's affairs" is indicative of serious intention.

7. *History of severe alcohol or drug abuse.* Greater use/abuse is associated with greater seriousness.

8. *History of previous psychiatric treatment or hospitalization.* Previous treatment for intention to harm self is associated with greater seriousness.

9. *Availability of resource or support systems.* Feelings of lack of personal and social support are associated with greater seriousness.

10. *Willingness to use resource and support systems.* Unwillingness to get help from support systems is associated with greater seriousness.

Although counselors may be aware of factors such as these to be considered in evaluating a client's intention to harm self, awareness alone is insufficient for effective evaluation. Again, because most counselors simply do not have the training or experience to make lethality potential evaluations effectively, they are well-advised to seek professional assistance when the need to make such an evaluation arises.

If a client indicates *any* intention to harm self, the counselor must act, and act quickly, to attempt to prevent the client from self-inflicted harm, for both ethical and legal reasons. Fujimara, Weis, and Cochran (1985) wrote:

> When applying legal and ethical concerns in working with the suicidal client, the counselor needs to take action to prevent suicide. This is the case when the counselor can reasonably anticipate the situation in the counseling relationship. Liability generally arises as a result of the counselor either (a) failing to act in a way to prevent the suicide (e.g., being negligent in the diagnosis of the client's

mental and emotional state) or (b) doing something (e.g., breaching a damaging confidence) that directly contributes to the client's suicide. (p. 615)

Again, counselors confronted with such situations should consult with other professionals, such as other counselors and/or law enforcement officials. Consultation with and use of the services of professionals from local crisis intervention agencies is particularly recommended.

Clients Who Have AIDS

No other situation in the history of the counseling profession has raised such complex and complicated ethical and legal issues as has counseling persons with AIDS (Acquired Immune Deficiency Syndrome). Persons with AIDS (PWAs, used here also to include persons who are HIV positive) are confronted with a terminal illness, but one which does not always follow a predictable course of progression. Ostensible debilities from the infection may not manifest themselves for many years after the infection is contracted initially. Thus, many PWAs do not exhibit observable physical symptoms, and so are free to lead relatively normal lives, which include engaging in sexual activity. However, knowledge of having AIDS is, of course, difficult for PWAs, and many seek counseling services for help in coping with the psychological stress associated with their condition. This counseling situation raises significant ethical and legal issues for counselors, particularly in counseling interactions with PWAs who are sexually active with partners who are unaware of the client's medical condition.

What is at issue when a counselor becomes aware that a PWA is sexually active with an "unknowing" partner is whether or not the counselor has responsibility to break confidentiality and inform the unknowing partner to protect the welfare of members of society. Again, this issue is the ethical counterpart to the legal concept of *duty to warn*. Unfortunately, no clear legal precedent exists to suggest appropriate ethical behavior. Although there have been a few legal challenges concerning the need for medical doctors and other professionals to disclose knowledge of AIDS, these cases apparently have been decided upon the idiosyncracies of each case; no trend in the results of such cases is evident. Thus, no clear legal basis or example exists from which counselors can develop corresponding ethical standards or appropriate ethical behaviors.

Thoughtful and substantive arguments have been presented in the professional literature about when confidentiality should be broken (i.e., disclosure should be made) in regard to counseling clients who are PWAs and sexually active with unknowing clients. For example, Kain (1988) presented the case for caution in making such disclosures for two major reasons. First, not all sexual activity permits transmission of the AIDS virus; therefore, counselors need to be aware of the *specific* sexual behaviors in which the client is engaging before considering disclosure. Second, not all clients who may be thought to have AIDS actually have it; therefore, counselors should have *medical* evidence and/or confirmation from the client that the client actually is infected before considering disclosure.

The cautions provided by Kain (1988) are appropriate and always should be considered in deciding whether or not to disclose a client's medical status to an "unknowing" sexual partner or to others. However, assuming that the counselor *knows* that the client has AIDS (or is HIV positive) and is engaging in at-risk behaviors for transmission of the disease, almost all authorities and authors advocate disclosure to unknowing partners and/or appropriate others. For example, Cohen (1990) provided a cogent philosophical argument that disclosure under such circumstances is necessary for the protection and welfare of members of society. Gray and Harding (1988) advocated that counselors implement a program including education, consultation, and active support in an attempt to get the client to disclose before the counselor is "forced" to disclose the client's medical status to partners. Finally, Erickson (1990) provided guidelines for decision making in regard to disclosure under such circumstances. An important recommendation in her guidelines is that the state public health agency should be informed when unknowing sexual partners of clients who are PWAs cannot be identified specifically.

Clearly favored in the professional literature is that counselors with clients who are known to be PWAs and to be sexually active with unknowing partners disclose the information to the partners and/or appropriate others. Whether this perspective will be supported by law under the principles of counselors' *duty to warn* is not yet certain. However, given that it is becoming the accepted standard of practice, the legal basis for disclosure likely will follow. Thus, counselors should disclose, vis-a-vis breaking confidentiality, if clients who are PWAs and sexually active with unknowing partners cannot be persuaded to disclose by themselves.

Counseling Other Than Dyadic

The increasing evidence for the effectiveness and efficiency of group counseling for many client concerns has led to the rapidly increasing use of couples and/or family counseling methods. Thus, counselors increasingly are involved in client relationships that are not one-to-one (i.e., dyadic). In any interaction between the counselor and a single client in a group counseling session, there is always at least one "third party" to the counselor-client interaction. The presence of a third party to the interaction has significant implications for the application of ethical standards to the counseling process, particularly in regard to confidentiality issues.

In general, the legal right to privileged communication does not apply to clients in group counseling, even in states where clients have right to privileged communication in individual counseling (Hopkins & Anderson, 1990). This legal situation exists primarily because of the recognized difficulty in maintaining privileged communication when counseling is extended beyond dyadic interactions. If confidentiality is viewed as the ethical counterpart of privileged communication, similar difficulty exists in regard to it. That is, it is difficult to hold one client responsible for confidentiality in regard to information learned about another client during group counseling.

How does a counselor handle confidentiality issues in group counseling? Unfortunately, there is no precise answer. The ACA *Ethical Standards* stipulate that a group counselor is to "set a norm of confidentiality regarding all group members' disclosures" (ACA *Ethical Standards*, 1988). Thus, group counselors should at least explain carefully the principles of confidentiality in counseling to the group members and encourage them to abide by those principles. However, it also is incumbent upon group counselors to explain that confidentiality in the traditional sense cannot be guaranteed (even within legal limits) as it can be in dyadic counseling situations. In effect, group counselors should not promise confidentiality to group members, but they should encourage them to maintain confidentiality in the best interests of the counseling process. Of course, group *counselors* should maintain confidentiality regardless of whether or not the group *members* do.

Couples and/or marriage and family counseling encompasses the same confidentiality issues as group counseling but includes other issues as well. Corey, Corey, and Callanan (1993) noted that most couples and/or marriage and family counselors engage in individual counseling sessions with couple or family members before or concurrent with couples or marriage and family counseling. Assuming that couple or marriage and family counseling is intended to be the *primary* counseling modality in such situations, what is at issue is whether or not information garnered during the individual (i.e., dyadic) counseling sessions should be disclosed by the counselor during couple or marriage and family counseling sessions. Strict adherence to the ethical standards for confidentiality would mandate that the counselor not disclose information obtained during the individual sessions. However, if such information is deemed by the counselor to be crucial to the effectiveness of the couple or marriage and family counseling process, then withholding the information violates the ethical standards related to provision of the best possible counseling services for clients. Again, there is no precise guideline or clearly established practice. Some couples and/or marriage and family counselors maintain confidentiality about information obtained during individual counseling sessions conducted in conjunction with couple or family counseling sessions, and some do not, choosing instead to inform clients prior to individual counseling that any information obtained may be discussed subsequently in couple or family counseling. Corey,

Corey, and Callanan (1993) advocated the latter approach, with the provision that the counselor inform the client that the information will be disclosed by the counselor during couple or family counseling only if the counselor deems it in the best interest of all concerned.

Strein and Hershenson (1991) indicated that although counseling is ostensibly only between the counselor and client directly involved, it is often not strictly dyadic in another sense. Even when a third party is not directly involved in the actual counseling sessions, third parties often exist who potentially have a legitimate right to know what is happening in the counseling process. Strein and Hershenson wrote that "much of the thinking underlying counselor-client confidentiality is rooted in the implicit assumption that counseling consists of an individual relationship between two parties, each acting singly" (p. 312). Examples of situations in which this assumption is not valid include

> (a) counseling done as an integral part of a multidisciplinary team approach to treatment, in which the counselor may function as a case coordinator or simply as one member of the team; (b) coordination of services, referral, and placement; (c) mandated evaluations or services; (d) clinical or administrative supervision that requires the sharing of case material; and (e) advocacy on behalf of a client to a group of non-counselors. (Strein & Hershenson, 1991, p. 312)

When "third party" individuals have legitimate need for and access to information from counseling sessions, counselors cannot provide the usual "guarantees" of confidentiality. Instead, they must inform clients of the limitations of confidentiality at the beginning of counseling. Strein and Hershenson noted that although counselors may feel awkward presenting "conditions" for disclosure (i.e., breaking confidentiality) to clients, it has been found through research that such *conditional* confidentiality generally has little impact on subsequent counseling effectiveness. Strein and Hershenson wrote:

> A variety of creative methods exist to reduce the awkwardness of this disclosure, including use of written handouts, a separate precounseling session led by either the counselor or an associate, or a discussion of the client's expectations

about and need for confidentiality as part of the counseling process. In summary, honesty about the limits of confidentiality, more than absolute confidentiality itself, seems to be the ethical imperative. (p. 315)

The recommendation that clients be given honest and accurate precounseling information about the limits and/ or conditions for confidentiality would seem to be appropriate for any counseling situation that is not dyadic. Presentation of limits or conditions allows clients themselves to decide whether or not counseling should proceed, or at least what to divulge to counselors, and, therefore, generally absolves counselors of the need to make difficult decisions about whether or not to violate confidentiality.

Computer-Assisted Counseling

Sampson (1990) wrote that "Computer technology is now a common resource that counselors and clients use to collect, process, and disseminate information" (p. 170). Computer applications in counseling are increasingly varied, and range from counselors' rather simplistic uses of word processing software; to electronic gathering, storage, manipulation, and transfer of client data; to emulation of counselor functioning through interactive computer programs. The diversity of potential computer applications in counseling is associated with an equally diverse set of potential ethical concerns. Unfortunately, because of that diversity, only major categories of potential ethical concerns can be covered in this chapter.

Sampson (1990) identified seven major areas of potential ethical concerns related to computer applications in counseling. Following are brief summaries of those areas.

Confidentiality. A primary advantage of the use of computers is the capability of storing incredibly large amounts of information in incredibly small storage areas (e.g., on diskettes or on hard drives). However, this capability also can be a disadvantage because of the difficulty of controlling access to data stored electronically. Counselors who use electronic storage of client data need to be careful about who has access to what information.

Counselor Interventions. The increasing use of computer-assisted counseling interventions necessitates that counselors (1) prescreen clients' suitability for computer use, (2) properly orient and instruct clients, and (3) follow up with clients so that clients use the technology and interpret the results correctly. Computer software used for counseling purposes should never be the sole counseling intervention; such programs are intended to assist the counseling process, not replace it. Invalid and/or inappropriate use of computerized assistance for counseling is unethical.

Assessment. The two major ethical concerns in this area are use of notfully-validated computerized assessments and overdependence on computer-based test-interpretation systems. As with any type of assessment, the counselor has an ethical responsibility to use validated techniques only and to provide fully effective interpretations of assessment data.

Quality of Computer-based Information. Clients quite frequently seek specific information from counselors then make important decisions based on the information provided. Counselors now use computers for information storage and retrieval for clients' purposes. As has been true historically, counselors are ethically responsible for the accuracy of the information given to clients.

Use of Computer-assisted Instruction. Counselors have an ethical responsibility to insure that clients do not become misled by unreasonable expectations and/or become overdependent upon computers in lieu of more effective professional interventions.

Equality of Access to Computer Applications. Access to the potential benefits of computer-assisted counseling should not be denied to special client populations. Counselors have an ethical responsibility to insure that all clients have equal access to effective counseling, including all possible counseling aids.

Counselor Training. Computer applications in counseling can be used effectively only if counselors have the knowledge and skills appropriate to those applications. As is the case in any counseling activity, for counselors to use computer applications in ways for which they are not qualified is unethical.

Computer applications for counseling will continue to increase, probably at a rate faster than ethical standards can be developed to guide use of those applications (Sampson, 1990). Therefore, counselors must consider carefully and thoroughly the possible ethical implications of computer applications. Determination of analogies between computer applications and other processes extant in counseling may be particularly helpful for ethical decision-making.

Multicultural Counseling

A fundamental precept of the ACA *Ethical Standards* (1988) is that counselors have responsibility for "the enhancement of the worth, dignity, potential, and uniqueness of each individual . . . ." In a complex, multicultural society, this precept means that counselors must be sensitive to the particular situations and characteristics of culturally different persons and must provide counseling services built upon such cultural sensitivity. Ibrahim and Arreondo (1990) noted that, while the counseling profession in general has made advancements in this regard, the ACA *Ethical Standards* have not been revised to reflect the need for cultural sensitivity and specificity of counseling practice. Likewise, Burn (1992) wrote:

> Although the 1988 revision of the [ACA Ethical] Standards attends to some of the cultural issues surrounding technology and testing, more significant ethical issues relative to multicultural counseling are not addressed. A paradox between the upholding of ethical guidelines and the delivery of competent transcultural counseling services still persists today. (pp. 578-579)

Thus, the concerns relative to the ACA *Ethical Standards* are not in regard to particular standards or their appropriate applications but rather are in regard either to standards that have not been included or to modifications of that need to be made.

Ibrahim and Arredondo (1990) and Burn (1992) provided thoughtful and comprehensive expositions on possible revisions of the ACA *Ethical Standards* that would make them more culturally sensitive. Unfortunately, the number and subtleties of their suggestions are too great to be presented here effectively, and interested readers are referred to the source documents. In general, these authors recommended that the ACA *Ethical Standards* be revised to stipulate that ethical practice necessitates that counselors be sensitive to and understand thoroughly the *worldviews* of their culturally different clients. Providing counseling within the context of the *client's* worldview is recommended as the only way to counsel culturally different persons effectively.

Burn (1992) aptly summarized the situation surrounding ethical concerns and multicultural counseling when he wrote:

> The professional literature contains an abundant supply of strategies and proposals for defining specific ethical principles in regard to serving culturally unique clients. If the counseling profession truly aspires to meeting the needs of the heterogeneous groups that constitute "society," it must institute principles that facilitate thorough counselor training, thus maximizing the capacity to serve effectively.

> The development and implementation of clear and specific cross-cultural ethical guidelines would be a significant step forward. (p. 582)

Clinical Supervision

Clinical supervision in counseling involves one counseling professional, the supervisor, who presumably has greater counseling expertise and experience, working with a fellow or aspiring counseling professional, the supervisee, who presumably has lesser expertise and experience, to facilitate development and enhancement of the supervisee's counseling knowledge, skills, and abilities. Clinical supervision in counseling is typically provided for one of two kinds of people: (1) for counselor-education students involved in practica or in internships as a part of counselor-preparation programs or (2) for counselors who have achieved minimum credentials (e.g., an academic degree in counseling) but who need additional supervised experience to achieve a professional credential such as certification or licensure.

The necessarily close working relationship between supervisor and supervisee, in conjunction with the supervisor's third-party status in the supervisee's counseling processes, give rise to a number of different ethical concerns. Professional literature (e.g., Bernard, in Borders & Leddick, 1987; Corey, Corey, & Callanan, 1993; Kurpius, Gibson, Lewis, & Corbet, 1991), has addressed ethical concerns in regard to supervisor's qualifications and competence, informed consent, confidentiality, dual relationships, evaluation, client welfare, and payment for services. These and many other important ethical concerns in clinical supervision merit the attention and understanding of counselors and counselor trainees. However, only two ethical concerns inherent in the supervisor-supervisee relationship can be covered here: (1) responsibility for client welfare and (2) provision of counseling to supervisees.

In the typical clinical supervision situation, supervisees discuss their work with their clients during supervision sessions with their supervisors. It also is typical for supervisees to share audio or video tape recordings of their counseling activities with their supervisors to facilitate discussions and allow for specific suggestions. In this typical situation, the supervisor is a "third party" who has indirect, and often direct (vis-a-vis tape recordings), access to psychological, emotional, and other information from the client. Therefore, inherent in the clinical supervision process is the responsibility on the part of the supervisor for the client's welfare which is similar to the responsibility of a counselor.

Corey, Corey, and Callanan (1993) indicated that "Supervisors are ultimately responsible, both ethically and legally, for the actions of their trainees [i.e., supervisees]" (p. 195). Bernard (1987) noted that, legally, although supervisors may incur liability if they fail to make recommendations because they are unaware of the client's intentions (e.g., in the case of a client intending to harm others), they probably would not incur liability for making incorrect recommendations. The law does not require infallibility, only awareness and action. Unfortunately, currently there are not ethical standards available which specifically address the supervisor's responsibility for client welfare. However, because of the legal premise, it is likely that pertinent ethical standards will be developed soon.

In the interim, supervisors and supervisees should assume that it is ethically required that supervisors assume ultimate responsibility for the welfare of their supervisee's clients.

Although supervisors have ultimate responsibility for the welfare of their supervisees' clients, supervisees are not absolved of responsibility. Indeed, supervisees, like other counselors, have responsibility for their clients' welfare, and for all ethical standards attendant thereto. Supervisees also have the additional ethical responsibility to keep their supervisors fully apprised of important client information in order to preclude the creation of ethical and legal problems for their supervisors.

Borders and Leddick (1987) suggested that the supervisor-supervisee relationship is similar to the counselor-client relationship in that both require a "close" working relationship in which personal dynamics play a role. Historically, a few models of supervision have been proposed in which supervisor counseling of supervisees is an integral part of the supervision process, based on the assumption that development of the supervisee's personal sensitivity and insight is essential to the development of effective counseling skills. However, more recently, the generally accepted recommendation is that supervisees should not be counseled, either during supervision or otherwise, by supervisors. Unfortunately, as Whiston and Emerson (1989) noted:

> . . .in practice, there are few guidelines for supervisors to ensure that promoting insight, sensitivity, and personal growth in trainees [i.e., supervisees] does not become counseling. This becomes particularly difficult when the supervisor suspects that trainees' [i.e., supervisees'] personal problems are the cause of their ineffectiveness with clients. (p. 321)

Nonetheless, it is now considered unethical for supervisors to counsel supervisees as a part of the supervision process (Corey, Corey, & Callanan, 1993; Davenport, 1992; Whiston & Emerson, 1989). This ethical principle is based upon the fact that supervision necessarily involves an evaluation function; counselors, including supervisors, are ethically prohibited from counseling persons about whom they must make evaluations (see ACA *Ethical Standards*, Section B: Counseling Relationship).

Sexual/Intimate Relationships with Clients

The ethical standards of all major professional organizations and associations for counselors, as well as those of all major counselor credentialing agencies, specifically stipulate that counselors should not engage in sexual intimacies with their clients. However, this is the most commonly violated of all ethical standards (Vasquez & Kitchener, 1988). Why is this the case? Perhaps it is because the nature of counseling is such that the step from compassion to passion often is a very small one. Vasquez and Kitchener wrote:

> The counselor-client relationship is typically a highly intimate and special one. Counselors often experience a natural sense of emotional satisfaction from their role in the counseling experience. The natural caring, warmth, and regard for clients may evolve into more erotic feelings. Indeed, attraction to clients is pervasive. (p. 214)

Clearly clients can become entrapped in a similar way. Kitchener and Harding (1990) wrote:

> Clients entrust their vulnerabilities, pain, inner thoughts, feelings, and hopes to a presumably wise and healing counselor or therapist. The therapeutic relationship is one of support, warmth, and trust. It creates a natural intimacy that may evolve into sexual feelings. (pp. 148-149)

Thus, both counselors and clients are susceptible to feelings of sexual attraction as an outgrowth of a counseling relationship which is highly personal. However, establishment of the limits of psychological and behavioral boundaries, including refraining from sexual intimacy, clearly lies with the counselor.

Counselor-client sexual intimacy can only lead to negative consequences for clients, regardless of whether it evolves from a "natural" attraction between the counselor and client or is instigated under the pretense of therapeutic benefit for the client. Pope (1988) identified potential negative consequences for the client including feelings of guilt; a sense of emptiness and isolation; sexual confusion; impaired ability to trust; identity, boundary, and role confusion; emotional lability; suppressed rage; increased suicidal risk; and cognitive dysfunction. Obviously, many significant negative repercussions for clients result from sexual intimacies with counselors.

Negative repercussions for counselors have professional and legal, as well as emotional ramifications. Vasquez and Kitchener (1988) wrote:

> Therapists [or counselors] who engage in sex with their clients court negative consequences to themselves as well. They may lose certification and licensure, be dropped from membership of professional organizations, lose or be restricted in insurance liabilities, be dismissed from jobs, be sued in civil or criminal court, and in some states be convicted of a felony. (p. 214)

Thus, counselors must refrain from sexual intimacies with clients for their own welfare as well as that of their clients. Kitchener (1988) emphasized that counselors not only must be *aware* of the potential for these negative repercussions but also must *act* intentionally to avoid situations in which they might arise.

Clients who have been victimized through sexual intimacy with a counselor frequently seek help from another counselor so as to be able to cope with the negative consequences from the sexual interaction with the previous counselor. In addition to providing counseling help, the subsequent counselor should inform such clients of the options available to them in regard to the previous counselor (although the subsequent counselor should not endorse or criticize any particular option). Hotelling (1988) listed three major types of redress available to such clients: (1) *ethical*, including filing charges of unethical conduct with professional organizations against the previous counselor, (2) *administrative*, including filing grievances with pertinent certification and/or licensing agencies and with the previous counselor's employer, and (3) *legal*, including filing a civil or criminal lawsuit against the previous counselor.

Vasquez (1988) noted that facilitating counselors' abilities to refrain from sexual intimacies with clients must begin in counselor preparation programs. She wrote:

> Educational programs must provide a climate in which students can acknowledge, explore, and discuss . . . feelings of sexual attraction [to clients]. Teachers who are critical

or rejecting of such feelings will undermine the potential for effective education. A successful training program will provide a safe environment in which the value of honest and forthright discussions of sexuality and sexual attraction, sexual socialization issues, and other relevant topics may be explored. (p. 240)

Extension of Vasquez's recommendations to professional association activities is obvious. If the frequency of counselor-client sexual intimacy, and the resultant ethical, legal, and professional difficulties, are to be reduced, then the entire profession must be open to effective dialogue about the issues and circumstances involved.

Counselor Competence and Impairment

The concept of counselor competence encompasses a variety of ethical standards and practices. In a general sense, a counselor who violates *any* ethical standard can be considered less than fully competent. However, the term counselor competence typically is used to refer to *qualifications* (i.e., the level of a counselor's knowledge, skills, and abilities to perform a particular type of counseling effectively). The ACA *Ethical Standards* specifically prohibit counselors from engaging in counseling activities they are not qualified to perform:

Members must recognize their boundaries of competence and provide only those services and use only those techniques for which they are qualified by training or experience. (Section A: General, 1988)

Common examples of counseling activities counselors may attempt that exceed their basic qualifications include using projective assessment methods, counseling abused persons, evaluating suicide lethality, counseling substance abusers, using art therapy techniques, counseling married couples and families, counseling culturally different persons, and counseling individuals exhibiting severe psychopathology. Attempting to implement these and other specialized counseling activities without specific training and supervised experience in their use is unethical. Unfortunately, counselors often attempt to use counseling activities for which they are unqualified from a sense of compassion for their clients. However, as Gilbert (1992) wrote:

> It is misguided kindness, as well as being ethically
> unwise and legally risky, to attempt to carry out a treatment
> mission with inadequate resources [i.e., competence] out
> of compassion for the client. (p. 698)

Counselors must be ever mindful of the limits of their qualifications and refrain from attempting to exceed those qualifications.

Counselor impairment is a concept closely related to counselor competence. Counselors are impaired when they are experiencing emotional, psychological, or physical symptoms which prohibit them from performing a counseling activity effectively, *even though they may have the requisite qualifications to perform the activity.* The most commonly cited types of counselor impairment result from physical and emotional handicaps (e.g., stress reactions to divorce or death of a significant other), alcohol and chemical dependencies, sexual intimacies with clients, mental illness, or suicidal orientation (Stadler, Willing, Eberhage, & Ward, 1988).

Stadler (1990) provided a poignant comment on the results of counselor impairment when she wrote:

> It would be the rare counselor who never experienced
> a frustrating day, a difficult client, or an emotional overload.
> But counselors who are functioning well can put these
> experiences into perspective; their skills remain intact and
> their personalities remain stable. On the other hand, impaired
> counselors have lost the capacity to transcend stressful
> events. They no longer function as well as they once did.
> The therapeutic skills of impaired counselors have diminished
> or deteriorated. (p. 178)

Clearly, impaired professionals cannot provide effective counseling services. Unfortunately, however, they often continue to provide services when they are not cognizant of their own impairment. They may even rationalize that work (i.e., providing counseling services) is "therapeutic" for them and will help them overcome their impairment.

Counselor impairment raises complex ethical issues, both for the impaired professional and for his or her professional peers. Stadler, Willing, Eberhage, and Ward (1988) wrote:

The injunction to do no harm to clients, their families, society, the profession, and the impaired practitioner is an ethical obligation. Pitted against this concern for the welfare of others is the autonomy of the impaired professional—the professional's capacity to determine his or her own course of action. When counselors become impaired and threaten the welfare of others, their autonomy—their capacity to determine their professional practices—should be questioned. (p. 259)

Implicit in this quote is that counselors have an ethical obligation to monitor their professional peers and to attempt to prevent impaired professionals from practicing. The decision to attempt to curtail a peer practitioner's counseling activities is by no means made easily. However, given that *beneficence* and *nonmaleficence* (i.e., promoting client welfare and doing no harm) are the two primary ethical principles of the counseling profession, counselors are ethically obligated to "do something about" impaired counseling practitioners.

Processing Complaints of Unethical Practice

The ACA has established a formal statement of procedures for an organizational response to a charge of unethical practice by an ACA member ("Policies and Procedures for Processing Complaints of Unethical Practice," available from ACA). In general, these procedures are designed to allow investigation of the alleged charge(s) within the context of "due process" (see preceding chapter). Thus, although ACA's process for consideration of an allegation of unethical behavior is not a legal process, care has been taken to respect the personal, professional, and (potentially applicable) legal rights of all involved. The major elements of the process are that a formal, written complaint, which notes the particular ethical standard[s] alleged to have been violated, must be made against an ACA member to the ACA Ethics Committee. The complainant may present verbal or other evidence in support of the allegation, and the accused member may present verbal or other evidence to refute the allegation. After these proceedings, the ACA Ethics Committee makes a decision about an appropriate response to the allegation (i.e., about what, if any thing, should be the repercussions for the accused member).

The ACA Ethics Committee noted that many complaints are not processed after initial presentation. The Committee (AACD Ethics Committee, 1991) wrote:

> A particular complaint may not go through the entire review process for several reasons: (a) the complainant may not elect to pursue the formal complaint process (e.g., he or she decides to resolve the issue directly with the accused and/or institutional [employer] channels); (b) the case may be under civil or criminal litigation (the Committee cannot act on these complaints until the litigation is completed); or (c) AACD [now ACA] legal counsel may advise that it is not appropriate for the Committee to review the complaint (e.g., the complaint is based on standards other than the AACD [now ACA] *Ethical Standards*). (p. 278)

Another reason that complaints sometimes are not processed is that if the accused is not an ACA member, ACA has no "jurisdiction" over the complaint.

Once the review of a complaint has been completed, the ACA Ethics Committee may reach one of three possible decisions: (1) No violation has occurred and the allegation(s) should be dropped, (2) The member's behavior was unethical and the member should be asked to voluntarily cease and desist in the behavior, or (3) The member's behavior was unethical and sanctions should be imposed. In the event that sanctions are to be imposed, the ACA Ethics Committee may (a) reprimand with recommendations for corrective action, (b) assign probation for specified period of time, (c) suspend ACA membership for specified period of time, or (d) expel the member from ACA. If either of the latter actions are taken, the ACA Ethics Committee also notifies the general ACA membership, the ACA divisions to which the expelled member belonged, the NBCC, and the appropriate state licensing board(s) (AACD Ethics Committee, 1991).

Quite obviously, allegations of unethical behavior by members are taken seriously by ACA—as they should be. Because adherence to ethical standards is considered fundamental to the effective practice of counseling, effective monitoring of ethical behavior is crucial to promotion and improvement of the counseling profession. Therefore, ACA must fulfill the function of effectively monitoring ethical behavior effectively in order to succeed in its role as the major representative of the counseling profession.

FUTURE DIRECTIONS IN ETHICAL STANDARDS FOR COUNSELORS

Promotion of ethical practice remains a prominent thrust in the counseling profession. This emphasis reflects not only a noble professional orientation but also the reality of increasing number of allegations of unethical behavior by counselors. Indeed, the numbers of charges of ethical violations by counselors has increased dramatically in recent years (AACD Ethics Committee, 1991; Herlihy, Healy, Cook, & Hudson, 1987; McGowan, 1991). In addition, research on counselors' understanding of applications of ethical standards consistently has reported that while most counselors do have good understanding of ethical practices, a substantial proportion do not (Fuqua & Newman, 1989). Improvements in ethical practices in counseling will result from more and better ethics research, ethics education for counselors, and revision of ethical standards.

Fuqua and Newman (1989) addressed the status of ethics research in the counseling profession and concluded that most of the existing ethics research has resulted from surveys of adherence to ethical standards and/or applications of ethical standards in hypothetical situations. Fuqua and Newman noted that "Adherence by professionals to ethical guidelines is, and should continue to be, a fundamental concern of the profession. But this kind of information reveals little, if anything, about why ethical and unethical behavior occurs" (p. 86). They also wrote:

> It is fundamental and necessary to strive toward an understanding of *why* professionals behave as they do in various situations or *how* they arrive at their decisions to respond to situations in particular ways. The answers to questions such as these have significant implications for promoting the ethical development of counseling professionals. (p. 85)

The points made by Fuqua and Newman are important. Knowing counselors' relative abilities to apply ethical standards does facilitate understanding of professional practices. However, such data are not sufficient in and of themselves to suggest how counselors should be prepared for ethical practice or how ethical standards can be made more relevant to counselors' ethical decision-making processes. Research clarifying the why and how of counselors' ethical decision making is needed to facilitate fully effective counselor preparation and ethical standards revision.

Robinson and Gross (1989) investigated practicing counselors' abilities to determine whether ethical violations had occurred or which ethical standards were applicable in a series of hypothetical situations. One of the independent variables in their study was whether or not the respondents had had formal (i.e., academic course) preparation in professional ethics. Robinson and Gross wrote:

> Perhaps the most relevant finding was that having a course in ethics significantly improves practitioners' ability to recognize which ethical standard is being violated and to suggest appropriate ethical behaviors to correct those situations. Having a course in ethics, however, did not increase the ability to recognize whether a situation involved a violation of professional standards. (p. 295)

Wilcoxon (1987) reported on a related study in which it was found that marriage and family counselors who had had a course in professional ethics were better at applying ethical standards than those who had had only workshops or other kinds of less rigorous preparation. These conclusions suggest that, while counselors' academic preparation in professional ethics certainly enhances their ethical behavior, the preparation it has focused upon ethical standards at the expense of ethical decision making. Thus, while counselors' preparation in professional ethics should include applications of ethical standards, it also should facilitate development of counselors' ethical *principles*, such as those described by Van Hoose (1986), and *responsibleness*, as described by Tennyson and Strom (1986).

At the time of this writing, the ACA had initiated procedures intended to lead to another revision of its *Ethical Standards.* It is anticipated that these revised ACA *Ethical Standards* will be published in 1994. The nature of the revisions is, of course, unknown. However, revisions proposed for consideration include (1) incorporating all the ACA *divisional* ethical standards statements into the *main* ACA *Ethical Standards;* and (2) developing new and/or additional standards covering counselor education professor-student relationships, private practice, couples and family counseling, and clinical and administrative supervision of counselors (ACA Plans, 1992). Changes such as these should lead to significant and comprehensive improvements in the ACA *Ethical Standards* and thereby substantially increase counselors' abilities to practice their profession ethically.

SUMMARY

Ethical practice in counseling is paramount because only through effective adherence to and application of ethical principles and standards will counselors command the professional respect to which they are entitled. Although there are numerous complexities and idiosyncratic considerations in understanding and effectively applying professional ethics, it is incumbent upon counselors to devote the time and energy necessary to become extremely proficient in these regards. To do anything less is to demean the counseling profession and to do disservice to those who could benefit from counseling. Counseling in accord with high ethical standards is not necessarily "good," but "good" counseling is necessarily in accord with high ethical standards.

PART II

CURRICULAR
EXPERIENCES IN
COUNSELOR TRAINING

Chapter 8

LIFE-SPAN
DEVELOPMENT

Human development encompasses many features, but it generally has been recognized as anatomical, physiological, and psychological change that represents growth, maturation, and learning; changes that begin at birth and continue until death. The nature of these changes is important to counselors, because it forms a basic framework to be used when assisting others. If professional counselors were to remove clients from the context of human development and isolate only feelings, attitudes, and behavior, they would have only a partial picture of the individuals. As a result, the potential to understand and assist another person would be diminished. Change is a continuous process of transaction between a person's biological organism and the socio-physical environment. Any counselor who does not consider both elements will have a somewhat distorted representation of an individual's needs. A human-development orientation provides the professional counselor with a better understanding of the relationship that exists between nature (genetic "unfolding") and a person's environment.

With the vast amount of information that is available in the field of human development, particularly in the area of child development, one chapter cannot provide the reader with adequate information concerning change across the life span. Accordingly, the purpose of this chapter is to assist the reader by identifying topical material generally included in textbooks which focus on human development. As authors, we have tried to maximize information and directness by summarizing concisely the main points of theoretical approaches to life span development cited within the context of professional counseling literature. A brief glance at the topics will indicate that the focus is that of social developmentalism.

This chapter features the major theoretical underpinnings and implications of human, social, and personality development while placing a limited emphasis on the physical development of individuals.

THE PSYCHOANALYTIC PERSPECTIVE OF DEVELOPMENT

Psychoanalytic theory has played an important role in counseling and human development. Two individuals most frequently associated with the this perspective of human development are Sigmund Freud and Erik Erikson. Succinct summaries of the contributions of each are presented in the paragraphs that follow, along with those of a much more recent contributor to the psychoanalytic perspective, Arthur Chickering.

Sigmund Freud

Many of the ideas about human, social, and personality developments stem from Sigmund Freud's psychoanalytic theory. His approach characterizes human beings as "blueprinted" from inborn biological needs (i.e., innate or inborn determinants of personality and social behavior).

Much of the theory of Sigmund Freud, a physician whose practicing specialty was neurology, evolved from observations of his neurotic patients. These observations led him to believe that human beings are born with two types of urges or instincts: **eros**, the life instincts, and **thanatos**, the death or destructive instincts. Freud concluded that these instincts are the source of all psychic or mental energy which individuals use to think, learn, and perform other mental functions that satisfy their inborn goals or motives.

Freud's point of view was that a newborn infant has an undifferentiated personality consisting of instincts (eros and thanatos) and some basic reflexes. These instincts are divided among three components of one's personality: id, ego, and superego. The *id* component of personality represents all of one's basic needs, wishes, and motives. The *ego* is formed as psychic energy that involves cognitive processes, such as perception, learning, and logical reasoning. These processes are designed to assist in finding realistic methods of gratifying the instincts. The *superego* is the ethical component of personality which develops from the ego. Its function is to determine whether the ego's method of satisfying the instincts is moral.

According to Freud, the social and personality development of an individual progresses through a series of five psychosexual stages: oral, anal, phallic, latency, and genital. These psychosexual stages parallel the maturation of sex instincts. Freud assumed that the activities and conflicts that emerged at each psychosexual stage would have significant influences on personality development over time.

Erik Erikson

A student of Freud, Erik Erikson extended Freud's theory by concentrating less on sexual instincts and more on social cultural determinants of human development. Erikson (1968) advocated that individuals progress through a series of eight psychosocial stages; an individual must successfully resolve the particular social conflict or crisis characteristic of each stage in order to develop in a healthy manner. The first five stages correspond with Freud's five psychosexual stages. The last three stages, which occur during young adulthood, middle age, and old age, are significant extensions of Freud's developmental approach. A comparison of Erikson's developmental stages and Freud's psychosexual stages are

(continued on page 210)

TABLE 8.1   Salient Elements of Erikson's and Freud's Stages of Development

Approxi-mate age	Erikson's stage or "psychological crisis"	Corresponding Freudian stage	Erikson's viewpoint: Significant events and social influences
To year 1	Basic trust versus mistrust	Oral	Infants need to learn to trust others to care for their basic needs, with the key social agent being the parent(s) or primary caregiver. If rejected or if care is inconsistant, infants may view the world as an unsafe place with untrustworthy or irresponsible people.
1 to 3 years	Autonomy versus shame and doubt	Anal	Children need to learn to be autonomous in caring for themselves with the key social agent continuing to be the parent(s). Children who are unable to achieve this autonomy may doubt their own abilities and feel shameful.
3 to 6 years	Initiative versus guilt	Phallic	Children will try to act grown up and accept responsibilities beyond their capabilities. This may produce conflict with parents and other family members who are key social agents, making the children feel guilty. Children need to maintain a sense of initiative while not impinging on the rights, privileges, or goals of others.

Age	Stage	Psychosexual stage	Description
6 to 12 years	Industry versus inferiority	Latency	Children need to master important social and academic skills with key social agents being their teachers and peers. Success results in becoming self-assured. Failure can result in feelings of inferiority.
12 to 20 years	Indentity versus role confusion	Early genital	In the transition from childhood to adolescence to young adulthood, the key social influence is one's peers. During this stage, individuals struggle to establish basic social and occupational identities or remain confused about their roles as adults.
20 to 40 years	Intimacy versus isolation	Genital	At this stage, strong friendships are formed including a shared identity with another person. Failure in this area may result in feelings of loneliness or isolation. Lovers, spouses, and close friends are key social agents.
40 to 65 years (middle adulthood)	Generativity versus stagnation	Genital	Adults become productive in their work, raise their families, and look after the needs of young people. Those not assuming these responsibilities become stagnant and/or self-centered. Spouse, children, and culture norms are key social agents.
Old age	Ego integrity versus despair	Genital	As one reflects, life will be viewed as either meaningful, productive, and happy or a major disappointment, based on one's life experiences.

presented in Table 8.1. As indicated earlier, Erikson's developmental stages, which are continuous, do not end at young adulthood as do Freud's stages.

Arthur Chickering

Arthur Chickering (1987) proposed a developmental model that builds upon Erikson's stages and outlines sources of impact in the college environment. Chickering saw the traditional-age college student as a person in a distinct psychosocial phase defined by the emergence of certain inner capabilities and needs which interact with the demands of the environment. Chickering expanded Erikson's identity stage to include seven vectors or dimensions of development that occur in young adulthood. These include developing competence, managing emotions, developing autonomy, establishing identity, freeing interpersonal relationships, developing purpose, and developing integrity. These vectors characterize the primary concerns the student will have, the tasks that will confront him or her, and what will be the sources of preoccupation or worry. Chickering postulated that existing within each vector are a series of developmental tasks, a source of concern, and a set of outcomes. Chickering further postulated that development along each dimension or vector involves cycles of differentiation and integration; during each of the seven vectors, the student continually apprehends more complexity and shifting. More differentiated perceptions and behaviors serve to create a coherent picture of the student. Accordingly, growth along the vector is the result of stimulation rather than of simple maturational unfolding. Students do not develop identically; they are developmentally diverse.

SOCIAL LEARNING THEORY

John Watson has generally been accepted as the most significant early proponent of behaviorism. Strongly influenced by Pavlov's work concerning the conditioning of animals, Watson applied Pavlov's findings to children's development by demonstrating the classical conditioning of a 11-month-old child who was afraid of a rabbit. Classical conditioning has been illustrated with older children as well as with infants, and its power to instill complex meaning and social attitudes has been demonstrated by researchers. Watson also was a proponent of the concept that newborn infants are "tabulae rasae," and are conditioned by their environments to become socialized (e.g., feel, think and act in certain ways). Watson believed that children's learned associations between stimuli and responses or habits are the building blocks of human development. Consistent with this approach, social and personality development was viewed as a continuous process marked by the gradual acquisition of new and more refined behaviors. These behaviors were viewed by Watson as habits that may be acquired by repeated exposure to a stimulus through classical or operate conditioning, or observational learning.

Since Watson's work in the early 1900s, various theorists have built upon his explanations of social and personality development. These efforts have been made by various groups such as that of the Neo-hullian theorists, who assumed that one's personality consists of a set of habits, each of which were formulated through learned associations. Neo-hullians also advocated that human behavior is motivated by primary and secondary drives and that behaviors which reduce drives become learned and are established as habits; the Neo-hullian goal is to help children acquire habits that are socially acceptable.

Another school of theorists who left a tidewater mark in the behaviorism movement was the school of Skinnerian, or operate learning theorists who advocated that drives play little or no role in human social learning. Instead, Skinnerians posited that the probability of individuals' actions is a function of the consequences. Accordingly, human behavior is controlled by external stimuli through reinforcement or punitive events rather than through internal stimulation.

More recently, Bandura (1977) has been the principal proponent of cognitive social learning theory which attributes habits and personality to responses acquired by observing the behavior of social models. Bandura viewed learning as a cognitive activity that occurs as an individual attends to activities even before the behavior is reinforced. According to Bandura, reinforcers and punitive events are performance variables that motivate learners to engage in activities that they have already learned. Proponents of Bandura's point of view believe that children play an active role in their own socialization and that they regulate their own behavior by rewarding acts that are consistent with learned standards of conduct. This process of socialization is a continuous and reciprocal interaction between personal, behavioral, and environmental elements. In effect, the environment affects the child and the child's behavior affects the environment. The importance of Bandura's contribution has been demonstrated by common acceptance of his belief that an individual's environment and development mutually influence each other.

Appealing elements of the social learning approach to development are its objectivity, its practical applications, and the amount of information it has helped generate about developing children and adolescents. Perhaps the greatest criticism of the social learning approach is that it discounts, or only minimally emphasizes, the importance of biological and cognitive contributions to the personal and social development of individuals.

COGNITIVE-DEVELOPMENTAL THEORY

The major contributor to cognitive-developmental theory has been Jean Piaget. Piaget and his students view children as curious, active explorers who respond to the environment according to their understanding of its essential features. From this perspective, different groups of children might react very differently to some aspect of the same environment because each group might interpret it differently. Accordingly, to predict how a child would respond to a nurturing mother, a scornful police person, or an authoritarian teacher, one would need to have knowledge of how the child would perceive or construe the event.

According to Piaget (1964), the term **cognitive development** refers to the changes that occur in mental abilities over the course of an individual's life. Piaget advocates four major stages of cognitive growth between birth and early adulthood, with each successive stage representing a new and more complex method of intellectual functioning. Piaget describes children as active, inventive curiosity-seekers who are constantly construing a "schemata" to conceptualize what they know.

and modifying these cognitive structures as their knowledge is extended. The latter activity involves "organization" (i.e., rearranging existing knowledge into higher order schemata), "adaption" (i.e., adjusting to the environment which occurs through either assimilation and accommodation), "assimilation" (i.e., the process by which a child tries to interpret new experiences within the framework of existing schemata), and "accommodation" (i.e., modifying one's existing schemata in order to interpret or cope with other new experiences). Intellectual growth results from the interplay of assimilation and accommodation, which in turn create a need for further assimilation and accommodation.

The stages in which growth takes place, according to Piaget (1964), are defined as **sensory motor** (birth to 2 years old), **preoperational** (between ages 2 to 7), **concrete operations** (ages 7 to 11), and **formal operations** (ages 11 to 12 years and older). During the sensory motor period, infants gain knowledge and understanding of objects and events by acting on them. Infants engage in the behavior of adapting to their surroundings and eventually internalize their findings by forming mental symbols which enable them to understand the permanence of objects (including people), imitating the behavior of others, and solving simple problems. The sensory motor period is followed by the pre-operational period whereby symbolic reasoning becomes increasingly apparent. During this time children begin to use words and images in their activities in inventive ways. Children become more and more knowledgeable about the world in which they live, but their thinking is quite limited in comparison to that of adults. During this period children are described as very egocentric, because they view events from their own perspective and have difficulty understanding another person's point of view. Also, their approach is characterized by "centration," which is the ability to focus on only one aspect of a situation rather than the ability to evaluate or merge several pieces of information simultaneously. During the concrete operation stage, children begin to think logically and systematically about concrete objects, events, and experiences. This period is characterized by ability to perform arithmetic operations mentally and to order physical actions and behavioral events in sequence. The final stage, formal operations, is characterized by rational, abstract, and deductive reasoning. During this period individuals are able to think about cognitive processes and to explore ideas.

Piaget made tremendous contributions to science, not only by making known his theoretical point of view, but also by legitimatizing qualitative study. However, his theory is not without critics, mainly because of its lack of specificity relative to movement through stages and insufficient rationale for and exploration of a child's progression from stage to stage.

As analyzed by King (1978), Piaget's contributions to cognitive development can be summarized in four statements. First, the development of individuals proceeds at irregular rates, movement from one stage to the next involves two phases: a readiness phase during which a person gathers prerequisites and for the next stage and an attainment stage during which a person becomes able to employ the behavioral characteristics necessary for the next stage of functioning. Second, there exists by stages a process of within-stage development whereby the capacity of an individual to use the highest elements within that stage of operations is gradually expanded to encompass a wider range of content areas. Third, Piaget identified a "state of mind" that appears to accompany phases of the developmental process. This state of mind involves an element of the self-consciousness that seems to develop when a person takes on new tasks or operations of higher stage. Fourth, as a person moves forward in development and is able to deal with higher order stages, the developmental process is accompanied by "decentering," or a shift of focus from self to the larger world.

Lawrence Kohlberg

Influenced by Piaget, Lawrence Kohlberg is recognized for his accomplishments in detailing development better. Kohlberg (1966) used Piaget's theory as a conceptual framework for theorizing about social phenomena such as emotional attachment, social ability, gender identity, sexual typing, and moral reasoning, and he stressed that cognitive and intellectual development are interrelated. He perhaps is best known for his prescriptions relative to *moral reasoning*. Kohlberg viewed social and personality development through a sequence of qualitatively distinct stages that are influenced by the child's level of cognitive development and the kinds of social experiences the child encounters.

William Perry

Perry (1970), who initiated a model that originated from the work of Piaget, outlined both ethical and intellectual development of traditional college students. He postulated a nine-position scheme which characterizes the development in students' thinking concerning the nature of knowledge, truth, and values and the meaning of life and responsibilities. In a manner similar to that of Piaget, Perry described steps in which a college student moves from a simplistic, categorical view of the world of right and wrong to the realization of the congruent nature of knowledge. He addressed the issue of the interrelationship between (1) the development of intellect or understanding of the world and the nature of knowledge and (2) the determination of an individual's identity relative to the meaning of his or her role in the world (i.e., How do I know who I am and can be?).

In essence, Perry's theory represents a continuum of development divided into nine positions or sequences that are characterized into four general categories, the first of which is *dualism* (positions 1 and 2). During the dualistic period, students are able to understand other people, knowledge, and values by viewing the world in discrete, concrete and absolute categories; in their world, elements exist absolutely. Such students have not yet acknowledged alternative perspectives, and their views and evaluations are stated as if they were selfevident.

The second category is *multiplicity* (positions 3 and 4), which is characterized by students' capability to view the world from multiple perspectives and to accept others who hold different beliefs. In contrast to dualism, which is characterized by single or dichotomous answers, multiplicity is characterized by multiple answers. During this level, students have difficulty evaluating points of view and tend to view all opinions as equally valid and, therefore, not subject to evaluation.

Category three is *relativism* (positions 5 and 6). At this level, students recognize that knowledge is contextual and relative in contrast to their view during the level of multiplicity when the existence of different perspectives was simply acknowledged. In relativism, different perspectives are seen as pieces which fit together into a gestalt. The relativism level is sometimes characterized as "students seeing the big picture". During this period, students are able to think analytically, to evaluate their own ideas as well as others' ideas, and to accept the authority and value judgments of others. However, during this level students typically resist decisionmaking.

Commitment in relativism (positions 7 through 9), category four, is characterized by traditional college students taking responsibility in a pluralistic world and establishing their own identity in the process. Such personal commitments as marriage, religion, and career are made and/or renewed, and students begin to establish their own identity and lifestyle in a way that is consistent with their own personal views, values, and themes.

EARLY GROWTH AND DEVELOPMENT

Although individuals share many attributes that emerge in the course of their development, each individual also possesses unique characteristics that are influenced by both heredity and environment. Of course, each individual begins his or her unique path of development at the moment of conception, when an ovum and a spermatozoon join to form a zygote or fertilized egg. As with all cells in the human body, the reproductive cells include chromosomes that contain thousands of genes. The genes, segments of deoxyribonucleics (DNA), possess the genetic information which in essence is the road map for development. Most human cells contain 23 pairs of chromosomes. Accordingly, fertilization results in 23 pairs of chromosomes with corresponding genes in the zygote. The fertilized ovum develops by rapid cell division known as mitosis. An ovum developing into two identical cell masses results in monozygotic, or identical, twins. However, if two different ova are fertilized at the same time by two different spermatozoa, the result is dizygotic, or fraternal, twins. The developing human is then called an embryo and is sensitive to numerous conditions that affect the mother and her behavior, such as rubella and dietary intake.

Studies of premature infants have shown a relationship between low birth rate and low IQ, as well as physical and neurological defects. These findings have caused the health profession and social policy makers to focus increasing attention upon the conditions that affect the mother prior to the infant's birth.

Some general principals that have been accepted concerning the physical development of infants include the following: (1) growth and functional development occur both from head to the tail region (cephalocaudally) and from the center axis toward the extremities (proximodistally), (2) body size shows especially rapid growth during infancy and early childhood and again during adolescence, (3) an individual's growth follows a biologically determined curve which permits some prediction of its course and extent, (4) motor and perceptual development is characterized by an initial increase in simple motor skills and differentiation in later hierarchial integration of simple actions into more complex units, and (5) maturation does not insure skilled development. Most studies have confirmed that skills are usually optimally learned at times of maximum biological readiness. It is fairly apparent that the basic structure of growth is predetermined through genetic determinants which form a structure and on which the social environment may later capitalize. The capitalization of events in the environment is referred to as learning.

The word *learning* has multiple meanings. As it relates to human development, however, it is generally viewed as a process through which an activity originates or changes based on situations encountered in the environment. Embedded in this definition is the exclusion of reflexes, maturation, or temporary states occurring to the organism. Critical to development are associative, instrumental, and observational learning. The concept of classical conditioning introduced by Pavlov (1927) is a type of associative learning. For example, Pavlov discovered that if a dog is presented with meat powder (**unconditional stimulus** [UCS]) and a metronome (**conditional stimulus** [CS]) simultaneously, the dog will eventually salivate (**conditional response** [CR]) upon presentation of the metronome alone. Pavlov also reported that such acquisition of a conditional response can be **extinguished** by prolonged presentation of the conditional stimulus without the unconditional stimulus. As cited earlier, Watson (1930) demonstrated that classical conditioning could be employed with infants as well as with older adults. Thorndike (1932) focused much of his work on instrumental learning and formulated the **Law of Effect** which states that reoccurrence of an act depends upon the positive or negative consequences it has caused in the past. Building on Thorndike's earlier work, Skinner (1938) designated instrumentally conditioned acts as **operants**. He is widely recognized for many of the principles of instrumental learning. As a result of Thorndike's and Skinner's earlier work, it has been generally designated that behavior is positively reinforced if the satisfaction of a basic need is accomplished or if a secondary reward achieved. Behavior is negatively reinforced if an adverse stimulus is removed, reduced, or avoided. In either situation, the probability of reoccurrence or extinction of the behavior increases accordingly when reinforcement is no longer present. Reinforcement may occur on a continuous or partial schedule depending upon whether the reinforcer follows every stimulus response or just select ones. Partial schedules of reinforcement, which may be either fixed or variable, have been demonstrated to be more effective in maintaining behavior than have continuous schedules.

THE PRESCHOOL YEARS

During the preschool years, a child's personality becomes richer, more complex, and more highly differentiated. During this period of time, new personality characteristics and motives may emerge, and previously established ones may modify simultaneously. The forms and amounts of various behavior characteristics depend on the child's social experiences. For example, factors affecting the establishment of aggressive behavior include the type of reinforcement received for such behavior, the observation and imitation of models, and the degree of anxiety or guilt associated with aggressive behavior. Frustration is frequently associated with increased aggression, but children differ widely at this age in the ability to tolerate frustration and in the intensity of their reactions to it. Researchers have demonstrated that children who tend to be highly aggressive during the preschool years are also likely to be highly aggressive in later adulthood.

Although dependency tends to be a relatively constant characteristic during the preschool years, situational factors, such as social context, influence the expression of dependency. That is, children who are highly dependent on their mothers are apt later to generalize their dependency responses on others. Many attributions have been given to dependent children; one that appears in the literature with some frequency is the syndrome of "withdrawal of love" (i.e., significant others giving love and affection to children when they behave "appropriately" and withholding these rewards when they behave in an "inappropriate" way). The withdrawal of love syndrome tends to produce children who frequently manifest dependent behavior at home.

Dependency, autonomy, and independence tend to be characteristics that are formulated in the preschool years but remain evident through later childhood, adolescence, and adulthood. Research has demonstrated that mature, confident, and independent preschool children have family settings that are highly consistent, warm, loving, and generally secure. Such family situations give children a degree of independence but maintain firm lines relative to expectations.

DEVELOPMENT IN MIDDLE CHILDHOOD

During the middle childhood years, a child is exposed to an ever increasing number of influences outside the family. A child's family remains important, but children are also greatly influenced by peers and others in their social environment. Also, during this period, a child's personality tends to be maturing and becoming more stable.

Middle childhood years are reflective of a critical period in the developmental continuum of children. According to Piaget, prior to age 7 or 8, a child's concept of justice is based on rigid and inflexible notions. However, between the ages of 8 and 11, a progressive equalitarianism develops and, beginning about age 11 or 12, the element of equity comes into play. Ethnic, racial, and religious identifications become fairly well established during the middle childhood years, with prejudicial experiences having serious consequences for the child's personality development and self concept. It is generally accepted that attitudes of children during the middle childhood years are learned primarily from parents, peers, and society.

Depending on how children interact with their surroundings, social environment can expand markedly during the middle childhood years. An important force in this expanded social environment is a child's peers. The peer group provides an opportunity for middle age children to learn to interact, to deal with hostility and dominance, to relate to a leader, to lead others, to work with social problems, and to further develop self-concept. Peer groups may become more "formal," as with the formation of "gangs." Also, there is a general tendency for children to conform to the values and attitudes of other members of their peer group, although wide variations exist in the strength of these tendencies. While we often unquestioningly view conformity as an indication of maladjustment, it is a normal adaptive process during middle childhood years.

ADOLESCENCE

Adolescence has been viewed traditionally as a critical period in the developmental process. Many behavioral scientists have tended to agree that, in our society, adolescence represents a period of particular stress. Influencing this stress are such factors as the adjustment required by the physiological changes associated with puberty including increase in sex hormones and changes in body structure and function. Strictly speaking, puberty begins with the gradual enlargement of the ovaries and related organs in females and of the prostate grands and seminal vessels in males. Other contributors to stress for adolescents are cultural demands of our society concerning interdependence; sexual adjustment; peer adjustment; and vocational, career, and educational choices. It should be noted, however, that in other cultures adolescence is not viewed as a particularly stressful period of adjustment.

An important part of becoming a mature adult is developing a sense of one's identity. Yet, in adolescence, establishing one's identity becomes particularly problematic as a result of the rapid physical changes and of the increasing and changing social demands. The task of developing identity is further complicated by dependence upon the values, expectations, and opportunities of the social structure in which the adolescent is functioning.

Physiological Changes

Among the most dramatic of developmental events to which all youth must adjust are the interrelated physiological and sociological changes occurring during the early adolescent period, which roughly extends from ages 11 to 15. Many of these changes are due in part to an increased output of activating hormones by the anterior pituitary gland, which is located immediately below the brain. The pituitary hormone stimulates the activity of the gonad, or sex glands, and increases the production of sex hormones (including testosterone in males and estrogen in females) which combine with other hormones and stimulate the growth of bone and muscles.

The accelerated rate of increase in height and weight that occurs with the onset of adolescence is often referred to as a "growth spurt." The growth spurt varies widely from one child to another in intensity as well as duration and in age of onset. These variations frequently cause concern to adolescents and their parents.

As is the situation with the height and weight growth spurt, the age of onset of puberty varies considerably from adolescent to adolescent. The beginning of sexual maturation for girls ranges from approximately 8 to 13 years of age and for boys from the ages of 9 to 14.

Sociological Changes

Because adolescent development is so complex, it is difficult to describe the process in any easily understandable manner. However, one way to conceptualize development in general is to describe the task and concomitant adjustment typical of a particular stage or period in the progression through life. Havinghurst (1972) summarized the kind of demands and adjustments that people at different points in their lives need to meet if they are to be satisfied and successful. As mentioned earlier, one of the transitions of adolescence is puberty, which brings noticeable physical changes. Physical maturation also has social consequences because males who develop early experience immediate social advantages. During adolescence, cognitive changes also are occurring and, according to Piaget, formal operations emerge. Erikson described this period as a time of critical struggle during which adolescents discover who they are and what they are to become. Erikson views this period as one involved in endless discussion, fantasy playing of various roles, and hero-like worship of others. As researchers have indicated, peer group participation becomes very important and, concomitantly, identification with the family and acceptance of its norms and values seem to decrease. Peers continue to play a significant role in other adolescents' lives as each adolescent "emerges." They provide a same-age standard and an opportunity for wider experience to support some forms of institutionalized behavior. Unfortunately, the influences of peers on occasion lead to behaviors defined as juvenile delinquency: behavior that violates sociocultural codes. Also during the adolescent years, the use of drugs, including alcohol and psychoactive drugs, seems to increase.

ADULTHOOD AND OLDER ADULTS

As an individual grows older, physiological and psychological changes continue to take place. Commencing in adulthood, some physical decline becomes evident in a variety of systems. However, as during the early years of life, changes differ among individuals and systems. As individuals mature, they tend to evaluate their physiological state relative to their age. Acute illness can appear at any age and throughout the life span, although it is accepted that chronic illnesses increase with age. Contrary to stereotypes, mature and older adults can and do retain interest and engage in sexual behavior, despite the fact that their reproductive systems decline. For example, most menopausal women report no change in sexual behavior, and it has been reported by some researchers that sexual activity in later years seems to correlate with that of the earlier years.

Although there are many physiological changes during adulthood and older adulthood, intelligence seems to remain constant. Some researches have demonstrated a slight decline in IQ scores which occurs perhaps at age 65, a change that has been attributed primarily to a decline in the ability to perform perceptual-spatial tasks. Otherwise, little change or decline is evident in intelligence.

Changes are made in older adults' life-styles because their living circumstances, including vocational position, economics, and residence, usually change as their needs change; children are out of the house, more disposable income is available, and less energy is directed toward tasks of achieving or acquiring wealth and toward the desire to "experience" life. A critical aspect of the aging process is retirement, which seems to be more difficult for professionals (people with white-collar jobs) than for non-professionals (those who are classified as blue collar workers).

Work plays a very significant role in adults' lives, and meanings and income associated with work have a great deal to do with how adults think of themselves (self-esteem). In addition to its effect on self-esteem, economic well being is consequential because it affects health-care opportunities and the ability to engage in activities as well as in some social situations. The importance of social interaction in adulthood varies, but it appears that there is a correlation between number of friends and outlook on life.

A significant aspect of aging is the adaption to death. The frequency of death thoughts tends to increase with age, especially when physical illness is present. Obviously death means different things to different people (i.e, a new life, a sensation of life, being reunited with those already dead, being isolated from others, or being rewarded). Some individuals even welcome death, and the ability to cope with the prospect of death is influenced many times by religious beliefs and by close relationships with family. Individuals face death by a variety of methods, including such things as denial, rationalization, and suppression or withdrawal, and by attempting to master it through cognitive acceptance.

SUMMARY

In this chapter we have examined some of the issues concerning human growth and development. In doing so we provided cursory overview of life span development theories and trends and of the effects of environment on them. Also discussed were some fundamental concepts concerning learning. An important generalization emerging from the information presented in this chapter is that differences exist among individuals within the broad framework of human development.

9

MULTICULTURAL AND DIVERSE POPULATIONS: SOCIAL AND CULTURAL ISSUES CONCERNING COUNSELORS

CURRENT TRENDS

As a *USA Today* headline (Usdansky, 1992) reported " 'Diverse' Fits Nation Better Than 'Normal'." In essence, *USA Today's* article reported that the social structure of the United States is changing and becoming increasingly diverse. These changes are most notable in individual life span, education, employment, families, and diverse cultural groups in our population.

Life Span

America is becoming a nation with a rapidly expanding population of older persons because its citizens are living longer. Life expectancy for Americans has grown from 68.2 years in 1950 to 74.9 years in 1988 (Wattenberg, 1991). The Census Bureau projects that the average age of American citizens will have risen from its current level of 32 to 41 years of age by the year 2030 (Fosler, Alonso, Meyer, & Kern, 1990). The 75 to 85 and older age group is the fastest growing segment of the population, while the 18 to 64 year old group is expected to grow only slightly over the next 20 years and then begin to decline (Butler & Lewis, 1982; Fosler et al., 1990). These changing demographs will have an enormous impact on social policy makers and on economics because of the effect these changes will have on the nation's tax base and, consequently, on entitlement programs such as health care, social security, and education.

Education

In addition to the life span change, more persons are receiving high school and college educations than ever before. Among persons aged 25 to 29 in 1988, 14.1% were high school dropouts, which is a considerable decrease from a rate of 50% among 25 to 29 year olds in 1950. During this same time period, the percentage of persons aged 25 to 29 who completed four or more years of college increased from 8% to 22.7% (Wattenberg, 1991).

Employment

Herr (1989) has suggested that the United States work-force and employment opportunities will grow in virtually all occupations through 1995. However, jobs will require more education and the availability of such jobs will increase with a concomitant decrease in positions requiring less education and training. Women will account for more than 60% of the growth in the labor force through 1995, due to the increase of two-worker families and the growing tendency of all women, regardless of marital status, to enter the work force.

Families

The family unit has also undergone change in recent years. As a result of marital disruption among first marriages, approximately half of the children in American society will live at least part of their childhood years in a single-parent family (Bumpass, 1990). The majority of these children will be products of divorce and will remain in a mother-only family for the balance of their childhood (Bumpass & Sweet, 1989; Castro Martin, & Bumpass, 1989).

A change in the formation of marriages also has profound implications for family life (Bumpass, 1990). The percentage of first marriages preceded by cohabitation increased from 8% in the late 1960s to 49% in 1985-86. It is likely that 50% of 30 to 40 year olds have been in a cohabiting relationship and that more than 50% of recent marriages were preceded by cohabitation.

Additionally changes in number of children, when to have them, single versus dual parent, and concepts related to rearing of children also have affected the structure of the family. The proportion of children born to an unmarried mother has doubled from 1970 to 1987 (Bumpass, 1990). Currently, more than 25% of the population's children are born to unmarried mothers, two-thirds of whom report the birth as being unplanned. The unusually high birth rate among unmarried teenage mothers, soaring from 5.9% in 1950 to 30.2% in 1987, is an important consequence of unplanned fertility (Bumpass, 1990; Trussell, 1988; Wattenberg, 1991).

Cultural Diversity

In addition to the structural changes of American society over the past three decades, the United States has moved into an era of cultural pluralism (Lee & Richardson, 1991). In 1990, the composition of the United States population was, categorically, (1) white, non-Hispanic—76%, (2) African-American—12%, (3) Hispanic— 9%, and (4) Asian and other— 3% (Usdansky, 1992). It is expected that change in ethnic diversity of American society will continue into the future. Wattenberg (1991) estimated ethnic changes in the population from 1990 to 2080 to include a shift in the (1) white, non-Hispanic population from 77% to 55%, (2) Hispanic population from 8% to 19%, and (3) African-American from 12% to 16%. These projected population shifts indicate a need for professional counselors to be knowledgeable of issues concerning cultural diversity.

IMPACT ON PROFESSIONAL COUNSELORS

Fosler et al. (1990) listed several points of stress created by the current demographic trends. Current points of stress include (1) rising health care costs for the over-85 population, (2) a diminishing and poorly prepared pool of young employees and (c) a chronically unemployed or underemployed lower class. Future stress points include (1) the increasing number of poorly educated children who could expand the size of the "under-class" and debilitate the work force and (2) the large projected increase in both the number and proportion of elderly people after the year 2010. Because these points of stress impact the professional counselor's role, understanding diversity and developing an awareness of barriers and biases that can affect a counselor's effectiveness are essential.

Understanding Diversity

Knowledge concerning diverse populations, as a "starting point," is required for counselors to function effectively in the 1990s. It is important for counselors to have a working knowledge of terms used in reference to various groups and populations. For example, counseling professionals have often used the terms race, culture, and ethnicity interchangeably. However, helping professionals need to understand and be able to differentiate among such terms. Several of these are presented below.

Culture. Pedersen (1988) defined culture as a "shared pattern of learned behavior that is transmitted to others in the group" (p. 54). Different ethnic groups in a single racial group may have different cultures, and there may be different cultures within a single ethnic group.

Race. This term refers to biological differences of physical traits or genetic origin that might distinguish one group from another. Differences in race include the biological requirements of differentiation and genetic relationships. Race, however, does not include or explain differences in social behavior.

Ethnicity. The term ethnicity is used to identify the customs, language, religion, and habits one generation passes to the next, thus providing a social and cultural heritage (Pedersen, 1988). Persons preserve ethnic group values, beliefs, and behaviors when ethnic identification is strong (Hernandez, 1989).

Minority. Atkinson, Morten, and Sue (1989) defined the term minority as "physically or behaviorally identifiable groups that make up less than 50 percent of the United States population" (p. 7). This definition encompasses racial and ethnic minorities, aged persons, poor persons, gay and lesbian persons, persons with handicaps, substance abusers, and prison populations (Atkinson et al., 1989).

Prejudice. Prejudice has been defined by Axelson (1985) as "preconceived judgment or opinion without just grounds or sufficient knowledge . . . an irrational attitude or behavior directed against an individual or a group, or their supposed characteristics" (p. 120).

Cultural Relativity. This term refers to the idea that any behavior must be appraised in the context of the culture in which it occurs.

Discrimination. Axelson (1985) defined discrimination as "the creation of unfair or unjust competition . . . when categories of people are differentially treated on arbitrary grounds without reference to their actual behavior . . . [that] serves to perpetuate or maintain social distance . . . [which] may include isolation and segregation or may include personal acts growing out of prejudice" (p. 131).

Racism. Axelson (1985) defined racism as "the belief that some races are inherently superior to others" (p. 132). According to Axelson, racism exists in three categorical forms: individual, cultural, and institutional.

Characteristics across Cultures

To write about characteristics of a given culture is to risk perpetuating stereotypes about that culture. Thus, the purpose of providing the following descriptors of various subgroups within American society is to provide a baseline-reference point for working with persons of a different culture. However, it is worth repeating that more individual differences exist *within* groups in our population than can be identified *between* groups.

African-Americans. African-Americans are presently the largest ethnic minority group in the United States. The African-American population totaled 29.9 million in 1987 compared with 26.8 million in the 1980 census. The African-American population growth will, in all likelihood, continue to be greater than the Anglo population growth because of the relative youth of the African-American population (Baruth & Manning 1991).

In examining the strength of the African-American family, McDavis and Parker (1988) identified the role of the extended family, filial piety, respect for elders, and socialization of children as strong points. Extended family members are often accepted and cared for when life circumstances dictate. Filial piety refers to the high level of devotion that many African-American children hold for their parents and siblings. Elderly African-Americans are important in the family. It is not uncommon for African-American grandparents to raise their grandchildren while the parents of these children gain more education or work experience. Additionally, elderly family members play a vital role in passing on cultural values, customs, and traditions to AfricanAmerican children.

Hispanic-Americans. Included among the Hispanic-American population are Mexican-Americans, Chicanos, Spanish-Americans, Latin-Americans, Mexicans, Puerto Ricans, Cubans, Guatemalans, and Salvadoreans. While all of these groups are recognized as Hispanic and share many values and goals, certain aspects of their culture suggest a highly heterogeneous population (Baruth & Manning, 1991; Gonzalez, 1989; Ruiz, 1981). The number of Hispanic-Americans increased from 6.9 million in 1960 to 20.9 million in 1990 (Wattenberg, 1991). From 1980 to 1987, the Hispanic population increased by 34% or by approximately 5 million people (Baruth & Manning, 1991). Demographers estimate that the Hispanic population in the United States, based on its high rates of immigration and fertility, will exceed the African-American population in about the first decade of the next century (Herr, 1989).

A review of the literature by Atkinson et al. (1989) suggested that the Hispanic population is seriously underrepresented among mental health clientele, despite the overrepresentation of stressors in the lives of many Hispanics (especially those of low income) that aggravate the need for more extensive mental health care. Atkinson et al. (1989) cited a number of high stress factors which include (1) poor English skills; (2) the poverty cycle — limited education, low income, depressed social status, deteriorated housing, and minimal political influence; (3) the survival of traits from a rural agricultural culture that are relatively ineffective in an urban technological society; (4) the necessity of seasonal migration for some; and (5) the stressful problem of adapting to a prejudiced and unfriendly society.

Asian-Americans. The Asian-American population increased 70% from 1980 to 1987 (i.e., from 3.8 million to 6.5 million) and currently comprises almost 3% of the U.S. population (Wattenberg, 1991). Asian-Americans include persons from a variety of Asian cultures such as Chinese, Japanese, Korean, and Asian Indian. The inflow of Southeast Asians over the past 20 years has advanced the diversity of Asian culture. Southeast Asians, originating from countries such as Vietnam, Cambodia, Laos, and Thailand, are different from persons of the more populous Japanese and Chinese groups. Also, the Southeast Asian groups differ greatly among themselves. As with Hispanic-Americans, Asian-Americans constitute a richly diverse and heterogeneous group (Baruth & Manning, 1991).

The prevailing stereotype of Asian-Americans is that they are model minorities and problem-free (Sue & Sue, 1988). Also, a notion exists that Asian-Americans are non-assertive. However, as Pederson (1985) reported, this stereotype has not been supported, although Asian-Americans may be more inhibited in many situations than their white counterparts would be. As reported by Sue and Sue (1985), Asian-Americans display a bimodal distribution composed of a highly educated and successful group and by a group typified by little formal education and limited success. The stereotypes concerning Asian-Americans have resulted in limited financial and moral support from the government, despite the fact that Asian-Americans, as a group, are confronted with many of the same problems that confront other minority groups. The problems that many Asian-Americans encounter include (1) overcrowded living conditions in urban areas, (2) unemployment, (3) economic exploitation, (4) limited access to health care, (5) concerns over immigration status, (6) educational stress caused by strange surroundings and a lack of competence with the English language, and (7) conflict created by continual exposure to majority values and norms. Also, Asian-American students have reported more feelings of isolation, loneliness, and distress than have been reported by white students (Sue, Ino, & Sue, 1983). The problems faced by this minority group are further complicated by a sense of shame that exists about sharing personal problems with others, a factor that is not uncommon among minority group members.

Native Americans. Unlike other groups mentioned here, the population of Native Americans is showing a downward trend, with a decrease from its highest point of about three million to just above one million currently (Atkinson et al., 1989). Roughly 50% of the Native Americans in the United States live on Native American lands, while the other half live in urban areas or in other predominately Anglo geographical regions (Axelson, 1985).

Baruth and Manning (1991) suggested a number of problems and concerns of Native Americans including (1) difficulties in overcoming myths that their culture is evil, savage, and inferior; (2) negative effects of injustice and discrimination; (3) negative effects of a "culture of poverty"; (4) differing cultural characteristics; (5) high suicide and low life expectancy rates; (6) language problems, including "on-reservation" and "off-reservation" languages and the majority culture's misinterpretation of nonverbal idiosyncracies; (7) problems associated with mid-life, such as the effects of aging, marriage crises, and developmental tasks; (8) problems with alcohol or drugs; (9) poor self-concept and feelings of rejection; and

(10) low educational level. Other characteristics frequently reported concerning Native Americans include:

> passivity, shyness, a tendency to avoid assertiveness..., reverence for the person rather than possessions, respect for elders..., adherence to fairly specific sex roles, noninterference with others, humility, an inclination to share, and a reluctance to criticize the Native-American culture. (Baruth & Manning, 1991, p. 240)

However, as with other ethnic groups, Native-Americans as a group may be characterized as much by diversity and differences as by cultural homogeneity.

Barriers and Biases

Minorities have criticized current counseling approaches, many of which were developed by and for the majority culture (Atkinson et al., 1989; Jackson, 1985). The concern for cultural differences by the counseling profession in general, and ACA in particular, has enhanced the availability of appropriate counseling services for multicultural and diverse populations, although change in the counseling profession has not occurred without some "growing pains."

According to Bacon (1990), counselors must overcome barriers that often prevent recognition of diversity and provision of culturally sensitive services. These barriers include (1) attempts to deny racism or racial elements as factors in our society, (2) interactions with minorities based on myths or negative stereotypes and generalizations about minority groups based on just a few minority persons; (3) acceptance of the myth that services from the majority community are not needed because "they take care of their own," (4) lack of adequate exposure to persons of different cultures, (5) lack of understanding and respect for cultural diversity, and (6) lack of knowledge of the minority community's program service needs and fear of approaching those needs. Barriers which members of minority communities themselves must surmount include (1) lack of knowledge about available services (due, in part, to inadequate advertising of such services) and (2) feelings of unwelcomeness about participating in program services. Each of these two sets of barriers potentially stands between the counselor and culturally sensitive service delivery.

Baruth and Manning (1991) also reported a number of barriers to effective multicultural counseling. These barriers include (1) counselor assumptions, such as the premise that everyone should "Americanize"; (2) the class-bound nature of many professional mental health services and, in some cases, counselors' attributions of mental health disorders to a client's culture or social structure; (3) language differences; (4) counselors' stereotypes of culturally different clients; (5) counselors' encapsulation; (6) counselors' lack of understanding their own culture; (7) client reluctance and resistance; (8) differing world views and lack of cultural relativity; (9) counselors' labeling of women, multicultural populations, and poor people, (10) lack of understanding of clients' reasoning structures; and (11) anticipation that culturally diverse clients will conform to Anglo standards and expectations. Failure to address these barriers may profoundly impede efforts in counseling multicultural and diverse populations.

COMMON CHARACTERISTICS
ACROSS DIVERSE GROUPS

A hazard of counseling individuals who differ from the majority is the risk of assuming that all people from a specific group are the same (Lee & Richardson, 1991). However, as mentioned earlier, differences within groups can be greater than differences *between* groups. Professionals striving to attain cultural sensitivity often overlook this possibility. The challenge for the counseling professional is to integrate *individual awareness* with *cultural awareness*.

Both within-group and between-group differences exist, yet common characteristics that are important to the counseling process exist across cultures. Axelson (1985) noted numerous features that are present in every extended culture, including family units, marriage, parental roles, education, medicine, forms of work, and forms of self-expression. Even though these similar features exist, differences in basic feelings and emotions also exist within cultures and diverse populations. The recognition of differences is a growing affirmation of cultural pluralism, in which individuals are recognized and respected for their individual and cultural uniqueness. This shift towards cultural pluralism has paralleled a shift in societal perspectives on diverse ethnic populations. The great "melting pot" model of acculturation of American values and customs that once prevailed has largely been succeeded by the "salad bowl" model in which diverse ethnic groups strive to preserve their individual cultural identities.

PREPARATION FOR COUNSELORS

As reported by Vacc, Wittmer, and DeVaney (1988), a number of assumptions with which counselors need to concern themselves are basic to working with diverse groups:

1. an individual focus rather than mass methods is needed when working with individuals;

2. the individual is a person primarily and a member of a group secondarily;

3. the social aspects of an individual's life, including his/her environment at home, at school, and at work, are important;

4. accurate information is a necessary foundation for providing services; and

5. counselor preparation concerning social and cultural issues is essential.

The foundation for effectively assisting diverse groups is a counselor's knowledge of diversity and possession of good counseling skills. Counselors must be able to recognize and accept diversity. Riker and Myers (1988), in discussing the counseling of older persons, pointed out the importance of (1) general counseling skills, including communication skills, knowledge of counseling theories and techniques, and understanding of vocational development theories; (2) methods of assessment; and (3) group counseling strategies. Techniques for working with diverse populations must be built on this foundation of general counseling skills and knowledge.

Loesch (1988) proposed four particularly important skills in counseling diverse populations. These skills are active listening, individual and group appraisal, vocabulary adjustment, and confrontation. Regarding active listening, the counselor needs training in directive and nondirective approaches as well as in determining which approach is the most appropriate. Counselors working with diverse populations also need to be able to discern whether standardized testing procedures are appropriate for a given population or if some other procedure should be used. Regarding vocabulary adjustment, the counselor needs an understanding and appreciation of the differences in both verbal patterns and nonverbal behavior interpretations among different groups. Finally, counselors need thorough skills in use of confrontation. While confrontation is often a powerful intervention strategy, it must also be used cautiously with diverse populations because of the greater possibility for communication misinterpretation.

ETHICAL ISSUES

Ethical issues exist concerning counselors' behavior related to their ability to work with diverse populations. Counselors are ethically responsible to provide services to only those individuals and groups with whom they can work competently. A lack of knowledge of multicultural and diverse populations can have a negative impact on clients. Therefore, it remains the responsibility of each counselor to develop the necessary awareness, knowledge, and skills needed to provide effective services to multicultural and diverse populations.

SUMMARY

ACA has made a concerted effort to direct its members to meet the counseling needs of diverse groups. Increased knowledge concerning the diversity of society and the integration of this knowledge into counselor education curricula is being implemented. Yet, the challenge remains for counseling research and practice to meet the needs of diverse populations more effectively.

Chapter **10**

COUNSELING THEORY AND PRACTICE

All people have "problems" in their lives. However, a problem perceived as a major crisis by one person may be perceived as a minor annoyance by another. Consider the following examples. Joan cannot concentrate on her job during her husband's serious illness. Jack is confused about several career opportunities available to him. When the noise level of a class prevents Kim from hearing what the teacher is saying, she has difficulty learning. Jerry is having trouble adjusting to the requirements of fatherhood. Most people are able to solve problems like the above through their own resources and activities, but others are unable to do so and seek a professional counselor's assistance.

In addition to problem-oriented counseling, professional counselors help people by providing preventive and developmental counseling. Developmental and preventive counseling, which emerged in the 1950s in reaction to emphases on counseling for adjustment, focus upon exploring attitudes and values as they affect maturity. Developmental and problem-centered counseling differ in emphasis only; they do not differ in substance. Professional counselors help individuals with issues and concerns in a variety of ways, either on an individual (i.e., one-to-one) basis or in a small group. The professional counselor's assistance could be to (1) listen carefully and then offer suggestions and advice; (2) help persons understand the origins of their current concerns, thereby enabling them to "reconceptualize" their past actions with the goal of changing future behaviors; (3) offer support through empathic listening and attending to concerns; (4) establish and help persons implement a program of behavior modification; or (5) use a combination of approaches. Professional counselors vary widely in the ways in which they counsel clients, the kinds of client concerns with which they work, and the settings in which they conduct their work. Although variation exists, commonalities are present in the counseling process for all clients.

Among the general populace, counseling holds a variety of meanings because of the use of this term within different professions (e.g., "legal counselors," "real estate counselors," and "financial counselors"). Even among professional counselors, definitions of counseling vary and range from those concerning the facilitation of wise choices to those promoting individuals' adjustments to society (Tyler, 1969). Approaches used by professional counselors depend on their training and experience and are tempered by their personal beliefs and values, which are always involved in professional counseling, whether individual or group. Beliefs and values vary from counselor to counselor, although certain ones are universally held among counselors. Examples of commonly-held beliefs are that the worth, significance, and dignity of individuals must be recognized; that individuals benefit from a particular form of the helping relationship; and that the personal autonomy and self-direction of individuals are valuable.

Regardless of differences among counselors, both individual and group counseling require the use of identifiable communication skills and theoretical models, as illustrated in Figure 10.1. Communication skills are verbal and non-verbal techniques used by counselors to help people. Professional counselors distinguish themselves from other people and other professionals (e.g., media broadcasters) who use "communication skills" by applying a theoretical counseling model when working with clients. A counseling theory provides an integrated treatment of behavior and of interpersonal relationships so that decisions can be made about helping people. The counseling process necessarily involves use of both communication skills and counseling theory.

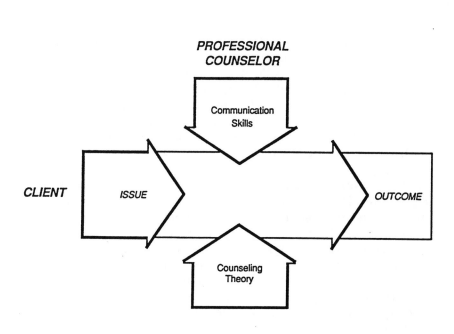

Figure 10.1. An illustrative diagram of the influence of communication skills and counseling theory upon a client's problem.

COMMUNICATION SKILLS

Several schema exist for delineation of individual (so-called "basic") communication skills that are used in counseling. For example, Carkhuff (1974) used Carl Rogers' presentations on psychotherapy and identified skills that need to be used by all counselors; Ivey (1971) reported a highly atomistic approach for training counselors in communication skills under the label *micro-counseling*; and Kagan and Krathwohl (1967) and Egan (1986) developed *micro-skill* approaches. Both micro-counseling and micro-skill approaches involve simplifying the process of communication into basic skills (e.g., learning the basic skills of speech that are judged to be helpful and practical for more effective communication).

Important communication skills when counseling a client include clarification, reflection, use of "open" questions, concreteness, and summarization. However, recognition that use of communication skills does not in and of itself constitute professional counseling is essential. These same skills are used by many indviduals in the community (usually under the aegis of being a good friend, having a good chat, or sharing with someone), but not necessarily in the systematic way in which they are used by professional counselors.

Two additional elements differentiate professional counseling from other forms of communication and conversation: (1) professional training including subsequent endorsement from the profession through certification and/or licensure and (2) subscription and adherence to professional standards. Thus, communication within professional counseling differs from that used by many in society, because it is guided by an explicit theoretical rationale, is developed in the context of specialized training, and is conducted within the context of professional standards.

THEORETICAL MODELS

By virtue of professional preparation, a counselor beginning a counseling process has a theoretical model in mind, no matter how vague, ill-formed, or undefined it may be. As clients' problems become clearer, so too does the theoretical model to be used by the counselor; the theoretical model provides direction for the counseling process. Although this "direction" may be quite hazy initially, it exists in every counseling situation and ranges from a clearly articulated single model to one in which the counselor has "merged" two or more models.

Several theoretical models describe the development of and are suitable for both individual and group counseling. Such models typically necessitate that professional counselors have comprehensive knowledge of personality and human development in order to use them. Equally effective counseling outcomes can result from many different theoretical models. However, no professional counselor is equally effective with each theoretical model. Because little is known about how professional counselors can be most effectively matched with particular theoretical models, the selection of a theoretical model is at the discretion of the counselor. Regardless of the model(s) selected, theories serve as maps for helping clients by providing direction and goals, clarifying the counselor's role, explaining what takes place during the counseling process, and evaluating the effectiveness of counseling.

Hopson (1982) discussed five "schools" of thought for classifying most of the theoretical models used by professional counselors: psychoanalytic, client-centered, behavioral, cognitive, and affective. The theories within each school that are used most frequently by professional counselors are briefly summarized in the following sections.

Psychoanalytic Models

The psychoanalytical model, in its general form, was the first counseling model. Approaches based on it concentrate on the past history of the client, the dynamics of the person's personality, and the relationship between the client and the counselor.

Freudian Psychoanalytic Theory. Sigmund Freud (1911) based this theory on the fundamental principle that an individual's behavior is controlled by desires to seek pleasure and to avoid pain, with the "mind" functioning as an expression of these conflicting forces. This "pleasure principle" is viewed as operative throughout life but experienced mainly during an individual's early years.

According to Freudian psychoanalytic theory, an individual's present mental functioning is causally connected to past experiences, and current behaviors are determined by antecedent conscious and unconscious forces and/or events. Of importance are the effects which unconscious forces have upon an individual's mental processes and activities; mental elements are evaluated in terms of the individual's degree of consciousness or repression. The latter is especially important if an individual is repressing selected mental elements to avoid pain or displeasure. Consideration also is given to the manner in which libidinal (i.e., thought to be primarily sexual) drives interact with aggressive drives and to the effect that this interaction has upon an individual's behaviors. Freud's psychoanalytic approach proposes that an individual's behaviors can be traced to important experiences and events in childhood and to subsequently generated fantasies, wishes, and dreams.

Proponents of Freudian psychoanalytic theory view a person's ultimate personality structure as influenced and determined by a culmination of biological factors and experiences. This culmination includes the development of libidinal drives through the oral, anal, and phallic phases of development as well as through the latency and adolescence periods of life. The oral phase, from birth to approximately 18 months of age, involves libidinal gratification through the mouth, lips, and tongue. Libidinal gratification during the anal phase (i.e., approximately 18 months to 3 years of age) involves activities related to the retention and passing of feces. During the phallic phase (i.e., approximately 3 to 6 years of age), the genitals become the central focus of libidinal gratification. Beginning with the latency period, which exists from the phallic phase to puberty and adolescence, the final development of an adult identity is initiated through socialization and education with significant others in the environment. Dominant within this developmental period are the *id* (i.e., the effect of libidinal and aggressive desires upon the mind), *ego* (i.e., the individual's self-identity), and *superego* (i.e., conscience).

Counseling based on Freudian psychoanalytic theory encourages the client to make rational responses and choices in response to unconscious conflicts, rather than to respond automatically to the conflicts. Clients learn to control their lives through self-knowledge of their neurotic symptoms and behaviors which represent manifestations of their unconscious conflicts.

Counseling using this theory includes four main phases, all of which are related to transference: opening, developing, working through, and resolving. *Transference* involves feelings and expectations of the client that a counselor elicits by engaging the person in a therapeutic process. The client casts the counselor in a role (e.g., parent, spouse, or sibling) that meets the client's needs. A closely related phenomena is *countertransference*, which occurs when the counselor's own needs become entangled in the client's needs. Countertransference may be reflected in the counselor's attraction to or dislike of certain clients.

Adlerian Theory. Adlerian theory, which is also referred to as *individual psychology*, focuses upon the belief that behavior exists only as the process of individuals interacting with each other. Of importance in this theory are the concepts that behavior takes place in a social context and that individuals cannot be studied or understood in isolation (i.e., without understanding the social context of the individual). An individual's behavior may change throughout life depending on the constancy of his or her life-style and on the alternatives with which the individual is confronted. Through self-determinism, individuals can choose goals to pursue. Heredity and environment, which are viewed in the context of how an individual uses them in reaching goals, do not cause a person's "being" or determine a person's behavior. Instead, individuals focus on "becoming" through striving for mastery and superiority in self-selected goals (Adler, 1972), in completion (Adler, 1958), and in perfection (Adler, 1964). Individuals face challenges through solving the "life tasks" of society, work, and sex, with the key element being interdependency; for "the benefit of the society," individuals must learn "to work together" with members of the "other sex." In Adlerian theory, all individuals are *"mitmenschen,"* or equal, fellow human beings.

The Adlerian theory approach to counseling is based on the premise that individuals give their own meaning to life and behave according to their self-selected goals. As a result, individuals have control in shaping their respective internal and external environments and assume appropriate attitudes toward the outcomes of their selections. Individuals are viewed as being creative, self-consistent, and capable of change.

In Adlerian theory, the primary social environment for children is the *family constellation*. By observing, exploring, and seeking feedback from their environment (i.e., home and family), individuals learn what is right and wrong, and what fosters their personal success. To be successful in attaining goals, an individual has to solve the various life tasks, or compensate in some way for unresolved tasks. A counselor following the Adlerian approach examines with the client his or her "life-style" and aims to change behaviors within the client's existing life-style rather than changing the life-style.

Analytical Psychotherapy. Developed by Carl Jung, analytical psychotherapy (counseling) focuses upon the relationship between the conscious and the unconscious. These two subsystems form the "psyche," a self-regulating system that controls an individual's behaviors. Analytical psychology emphasizes the need to become more aware of the conscious and of one's "being" by developing a greater understanding of the unconscious. The unconscious subsystem is viewed as contributing greatly to direction and meaning and as enabling one to be creative. Neglect of the unconscious can create problems for the individual.

Jung advocated that an individual's behavior is both consciously and unconsciously motivated, with the two subsystems compensating each other. If an individual consciously develops a strong attitude in a given direction, the counterpoint attitude becomes strongly developed in the subconscious. These differences become evident through observation of relationships with others, communication skills, work habits, and analysis and interpretation of messages from the unconscious provided through dreams.

Proponents of analytical psychotherapy believe that each individual experiences instincts of hunger, thirst, sex, and aggression, as well as of individuation, which is striving to achieve a true self or the attainment of wholeness based on conscious and unconscious factors. A person's behaviors are influenced in part by current experiences and in part by what may happen in the future as a result of the present behaviors. While conscious forces are evident and available to an individual, unconscious forces are available only through symbols which are interpreted as guiding messages. During counseling based on this model, individuals experiencing difficulties or conflicts are helped by appropriate translations of the symbolic messages provided through their dreams.

Counseling from the analytical psychology perspective is concerned with the purposeful and prospective functioning of the "psyche," which is composed of the ego, personal unconscious, and nonpersonal unconscious. While past experiences are important in the development of personality and individuation because of the effect they may have upon present functioning, future outcomes also must be considered. Conscious elements are referred to as the ego. Previously conscious elements that can be readily retracted to consciousness are considered the personal unconscious. The final component of the psyche, the nonpersonal unconscious, is composed of factors (i.e., archetypes) that are unavailable to consciousness, but which affect behaviors. Examples of nonpersonal unconscious elements include the hero archetype, the Wise Old Man, rebirth, that which we do not want to be, feminine and masculine principles, and the needs to experience centeredness, wholeness, and meaning in life.

Counseling within the context of analytical psychology is viewed as a process of helping clients find self-knowledge, achieve self-education, and/or reconstruct their personality. Individuals with conflicts experience unconscious messages that need to be addressed. After a complete analysis of an individual's consciousness, the unconscious is explored, mainly through dream interpretation, with a focus not only on antecedent causes, but also on future behavior. Enlarging upon given data through interpretation enables a client to perceive previously unconscious connections, motivations, and feelings. The goal is to make the client aware of the unconscious as much as is possible.

Client/Person-centered Model

Person-centered counseling, which was originally termed client-centered counseling, focuses on developing "self-actualization": an individual's inherent tendency to develop all capacities in order to maintain or enhance him- or herself. Developed by Carl Rogers during the 1940s, this model and its adaptations are based on an "if-then" principle and place substantial faith in the client's problem-solving abilities. If the counselor conveys genuineness, accurate empathic understanding, and unconditional positive regard, and the client perceives these attitudes, then the client will achieve beneficial change by moving toward self-actualization and overcoming self-internalized restrictions.

Counselors who use the person-centered theoretical approach to counseling assume the role of "being themselves" with their clients; their inner experiencing is permitted to be present during the counseling relationship with the client. Through inner experiencing of the counselor's own feelings (genuineness), an understanding of the client's feelings is achieved (empathic understanding). This is accompanied by an acceptance or respect for the client's individuality (unconditional positive regard) which is derived from a trust in the self-directed capacity of the client. As the client's awareness of inner experiencing develops, positive changes come from within the client.

Within person-centered counseling, present experiencing is important and provides the resources for the client's personal growth and change. The counselor assumes the role of facilitator and helps clients establish and attach meaning to their inner experiencing. Any expression that could be interpreted as evaluative in nature is avoided by the counselor, as are probing questions and descriptions of the client.

Person-centered counseling fosters a relationship with the client that includes warmth and responsiveness from the counselor, freely expressed feelings influenced by a permissive climate, and the absence of coercion or pressure. In the relationship, the counselor is often referred to as the "helper" and the client is the "other."

As stated earlier, an important assumption in person-centered counseling, is that people are born with a tendency toward self-actualization: a basic motivation to enhance the organism. With growth, the client develops an ability to discriminate between positive and negative inner experiencing and to acquire a sense of self. Thus, the client's self-concept and sense of self-regard develop. Self-regard is affected by the reactions of others and by the introjections of conditions of worth. Conflict can arise when a client's self-regard is incongruent with his/her organismic needs and desires as they relate to the interactions with significant others in the environment. If negative organismic needs persistently prevail over self-regard needs, intervention may be needed. The intent of person-centered counseling, therefore, is to enable individuals who are experiencing conflict to incorporate previously denied organismic urges into their self-concept.

Behavioral Models

Within behavioral models for counseling, principles of learning and/or behavior modification are applied to the resolution of clients' problems. Two widely used approaches based on this model are behavior therapy and multimodal therapy.

Behavior Therapy. Changes in the principles of behavior therapy have been occurring continually since the therapy's beginnings in the 1950s, primarily because of updated research findings. As a result of research, four conceptually different approaches have been developed for use in behavior therapy (i.e., applied behavior analysis, neobehavioristic stimulus-response, social learning theory, and cognitive behavior modification). However, the primary hypothesis for behavior therapy remains unchanged; behavior modification techniques are used for treating all abnormal and/or maladaptive behaviors. In contrast with previously discussed models, behavior therapy clients' prior thoughts are considered to be of little or no value in counseling, as are unconscious conflicts. Rather, the patient's present causes of behavior are the focal point, with treatment techniques varying according to the client's needs.

All behavior therapy is based on an educational model of human development as well as on a commitment to scientific methodology. With the *applied behavior analysis* approach, behavior is viewed as a function of its consequences. This approach focuses on actual behavior rather than on cognitive processes and uses the behavior modification techniques of stimulus control, reinforcement, punishment, and extinction. The *neobehavioristic stimulus-response* model of counseling focuses on anxiety. Intervention techniques involve systematic desensitization and covert conditioning for the purpose of extinguishing the underlying cause(s) of the anxiety. Overt behaviors and covert processes are assumed to follow the same laws of learning. Cognitive mediational processes, external stimuli, and external reinforcement are three focal points in counseling based on *social learning theory*. Current behaviors, cognitive processes, and environmental factors are viewed as interacting influences upon behavior. Cognitive processes, which are affected by environmental events, determine the treatment for environmental influences as they affect the individual. The client, however, determines what behaviors will or will not be changed, with behavioral change being directly related to the client's self-directed capabilities.

Another behavior therapy, *cognitive behavior modification*, emphasizes cognitive restructuring. This process involves using techniques for the purpose of gaining an understanding of individuals' interpretations of their experiences as they affect their respective behaviors. Alteration of irrational ideas, perceptions, and interpretations of significant individual experiences is emphasized.

Success within behavior therapy is dependent upon the client's willingness to make changes and upon the interactions between counselor and client. The client is an active participant in the process and is encouraged by the counselor to be completely involved in determining and setting goals. The counselor's initial responsibility is to identify the existing concern. Toward this end, assessment techniques may be used, including psychological tests, behavioral observations, self-reports and self-monitoring, role-playing, and imagery. Techniques used for treatment may include training in social skills and/or assertiveness; in such self-control procedures as progressive relaxation and biofeedback; and in real-life, performance-based techniques, such as behavior modification programs used in classrooms.

Multimodal Therapy. Arnold Lazarus developed multimodal therapy during the 1960s and 1970s. With this model, behavioral psychology is extended to include assessment procedures and interactions between sensory, imaging, cognitive, and interpersonal factors. Central to multimodal therapy is individual behavior which is determined through the "BASIC ID," an acronym for *b*ehaviors, *a*ffective processes, *s*ensations, *i*mages, *c*ognitions, *i*nterpersonal relationships, and *d*rug/biological functions. Emotions and feelings, and reactions to these two elements, are included under "affective processes." Personal awareness of reactions to bodily sensation (e.g., pain or pleasure) is considered under "sensations." Imagination is addressed through the "images" component, and an individual's analytical, planning, and reasoning skills are comprised in the "cognition" component. Relationships with others and the amount of emphasis placed on these by an individual are addressed by the "interpersonal relationships" component. Finally, the general health and physical well-being of an individual are addressed under "drug/biological functioning," which also includes biochemical/neurophysiological elements such as personal hygiene, exercise, diet, and medications used.

Multimodal counselors believe that a client's abnormal behavior is due to a multitude of problems (e.g., conflicts, unhappy experiences, and social deficits) that need to be treated using a multitude of intervention techniques (e.g., biofeedback, imagery, bibliotherapy, audiotherapy, assertiveness training, and/or role-playing). Because each individual is unique, therapy is approached through an individualized intervention plan based on the central concern of "who or what is best for the respective individual." Counselors base individual intervention plans on analysis of the interactions among modalities within the client's BASIC ID, and on external influences upon behaviors. During the initial interview, a *Modality Profile* (i.e., list of problems and prospective interventions) is charted based on excessive and deficient modalities across the client's BASIC ID. Once the counselor determines problem areas, he or she employs bridging and tracking procedures. The counselor first addresses the client's preferred modality and then gradually bridges (i.e., leads/guides) the client into other modality areas that need attention. The direction of these bridges and the appropriate intervention technique selected for each problem are determined by tracking the preference order of modalities exhibited by a client. The preference order, referred to as *firing order*, varies across individuals and across situations. The counselor's role is to help clients understand influential antecedent factors affecting their respective behaviors and to use appropriate interventive techniques. The counselor also conducts an ongoing assessment of the client's progress and adjusts the Modality Profile accordingly.

Cognitive Models

Approaches based on cognitive models focus on how clients conceptualize and cognitively organize their worlds. The common goal is to help clients change conceptualizations and, subsequently, their associated feelings and behaviors. Three widely used approaches based on this model are rational-emotive therapy, reality therapy, and transactional analysis.

Rational-Emotive Therapy. Albert Ellis, who developed the theory of rational-emotive therapy during the 1950s, advocated that emotional consequences are mainly created by an individual's belief system and not by significant activating events. Within his theory, the focal point of an individual's intrapersonal and interpersonal life is his or her growth and happiness. An individual is born with an innate ability to create or destruct, to relate or remain isolated, to select or not select, and to enjoy or dislike. These abilities are affected by the individual's culture/environment, family, and social reference group. Primary goals in rational-emotive therapy are to help (in rational and emotive ways) individuals desire rather than demand, to help them alter elements of their beings that they would like to change, and to help them willingly accept aspects of their lives that are beyond their control.

Ellis identified that several main propositions of rational-emotive therapy. He purported that individuals have innate abilities to be both self-preserving and self-destructive as well as to be both rational and irrational. Being influenced by others is most pronounced during the early years; therefore, individuals are greatly influenced by their early-life family environments. Because an individual is able to perceive, think, emote, and behave at the same time, cognitive, connotative, and motoric behaviors co-exist. Both normal and abnormal behavior are viewed as functions of perceptions, thoughts, emotions, and actions; therefore, these elements are essential in any rational-emotive therapeutic relationship between the counselor and client. Also important is the need for the counselor to be accepting of a client and yet to be critical of the client's behaviors, pointing out deficiencies where necessary and strongly stressing self-discipline and autonomous functioning if the client is remaining dependent. Finally, the strong cognitive emphasis in rational-emotive therapy makes it unnecessary to establish a "warm" relationship between client and counselor. With the purpose of helping individuals achieve deep-seated cognitive changes that could involve alterations in basic values, rational-emotive therapy uses a variety of methods, including didactic discussion, behavior modification, bibliotherapy, audiovisual aids, activity-oriented homework assignments, role-playing, assertion training, desensitization, humor, operant conditioning, suggestion, and emotional support. Rational-emotive therapy includes a general form, which involves learning rationally appropriate behaviors, and a preferential form, which involves learning how to internalize rules of logic and scientific method while also learning how to dispute irrational ideas and inappropriate behaviors. Typically, general rational-emotive therapy is included as a part of preferential rational-emotive therapy. Eliminating emotional problems involves disputing disturbance-creating ideas through logical and empirical thinking. The "real" cause of an individual's problems is viewed as the dogmatic, irrational, and unexamined beliefs that need to be exposed through objective, empirical, and logical evaluation. Individuals who are experiencing difficulty need to be made aware that the problem (1) is the product of their beliefs rather than of antecedent causes or conditions, (2) will continue unless addressed, and (3) can be extinguished or minimized through rational-emotive thinking and actions.

Rational-emotive therapy is a highly active-directive approach that views the client holistically and stresses biological components of personality development. When necessary, counselors strongly challenge clients' irrational beliefs. Their major goal in so doing is to help individuals minimize their self-defeating outlooks through developing more realistic and acceptable philosophies of life. Identifying the client's basic irrational beliefs is of immediate importance to the counselor who then proceeds to expose the same irrational beliefs to help the client develop more rational points of view.

Reality Therapy. Developed by William Glasser, reality therapy embraces the theory that the brain functions as a system that controls behaviors by fulfilling needs built into the environment. Individuals experiencing difficulties do so because they are unable to control or act upon elements in their environment in a satisfactory manner. The goal of reality therapy, therefore, is to help individuals focus upon choosing actions that are appropriate for satisfying the basic needs of staying alive, reproducing, having power, being free, and having fun.

Reality therapy views behavior as an integration of an individual's feelings, thoughts, and actions as they relate to personal needs and the behavior of others in the environment. Behavior is generated within the individual and is dependent upon the needs to be satisfied. According to reality therapy, antecedent experiences and outside forces are not consequential because the focal points of the therapy are present experiences and the client's awareness of how better choices of behaviors can be made. That each individual and society has a set of personal standards is a basic concept recognized by proponents of reality therapy and is an important consideration in helping clients who may be working contrary to society's or their own sets of standards. Also of importance is teaching individuals to gain control of their environments (i.e., to choose more effective behaviors). In essence, reality therapy views teaching as therapeutic, since the end result of therapeutic teaching should be greater fulfillment of the client's needs.

Eight basic steps are included in the practice of reality therapy. After establishing a relationship and making friends with the client, the counselor seeks input from the client about what he or she is "controlling for" (i.e., what the client wants). Second, the counselor determines what the client is currently doing to achieve what he or she wants. The third step involves aiding the client in evaluating the effectiveness of what he or she is doing relative to achieving what is desired. Then the counselor in step four aids the client in making a plan to achieve more effective control of the situation or environment. For the latter to work, the counselor gets a commitment from the client to follow through on the plan (step five) and then does not accept excuses from the client if the plan is not carried out (step six). Step seven concerns consequences, where possible, when a plan is not fulfilled. Reasonable consequences such as temporary restrictions of freedom or temporary removal of privileges are involved. The final step in reality therapy is not giving up; this involves not allowing the client to control the counselor. If a client is persistent in not following through on a plan, then the counselor helps the client attempt another plan which can be implemented, and the cycle continues until the client gains effective control of his/her life. Glasser acknowledged that gaining control of one's life may take a long time. However, he believes that the process must eventually be successful, because the individual controls the environment; the environment does not control the individual.

Transactional Analysis. Often referred to as TA, transactional analysis was developed by Eric Berne during the 1950s. The focal points of this theory are the child, the adult, and the parent: three independent and observable ego states that exist within every individual. These ego states are characterized by experiences and feelings that correspond to patterns of behavior. During the child ego state, an individual of any age behaves *emotionally* like a child. During the adult ego state, however, an individual reacts *unemotionally* to stimuli, primarily by using logic and factual data. The parent ego state involves behaviors that in essence replicate those exhibited by a parent. Moral attitudes, beliefs, and values are the concern of individuals in the parent state. Such an individual may attempt to influence, control, and/or evaluate the development of others.

A second fundamental concept of TA is a transaction, or a unit of communication between individuals. Two levels of transaction are involved: the overt social level and the covert psychological level. Diagramming transactions (a counseling function within transactional analysis) provides both the counselor and the client with a pictorial illustration of the client's interactions with significant others in his or her environment. Circles containing a(n) P, A, or C to represent the respective ego states of parent, adult, and child are connected by arrows according to the type of transaction involved. A solid-line arrow depicts a social transaction and a broken-line arrow represents a psychological transaction. Illustrations utilize three other types of transactions. During a complementary transaction (i.e., parallel arrows), an exchange is direct and overt: a definite communication between individuals. When a transference transaction (i.e., crossed arrows) occurs, exchanges are covert and discussion on a specific topic ceases immediately. The final form, an ulterior transaction (i.e., a solid-line arrow is parallel to a broken-line arrow and represents a dual-level exchange) involves an exchange between individuals during which both levels of transaction are actively and simultaneously in operation. With these "game"-type transactions, both the social level and its corresponding psychological message need to be used during interpretation and evaluation of an individual's behavior.

According to TA principles, social interactions between persons are based upon their respective needs for recognition, presented in the form of "strokes." Strokes, which are learned and are essential for growth, range from positive (i.e., approval) to negative (i.e., disapproval) to none at all (i.e., not caring). Strokes shape individual personalities and vary from family to family. Individuals develop a system of stroking through their interactions with others, thus forming the basis of their acceptance of being OK or not OK and of whether others are OK or not OK. This developmental patterning is referred to as a *life script* and is illustrated with an *epogram.*

Five psychological forces are included in the epogram, representing the critical-parent, nurturing-parent, adult, free-child, and adapted-child functions that comprise an individual's personality. Personalities are formed according to the differing contributions of each psychological force. The critical-parent finds fault, makes and enforces rules, and strives for individual rights. The nurturing-parent fosters growth and development. The adult is nonjudgmental, precise, and nonemotional. Spontaneity, eagerness, and creativity are some of the energies found in the free-child, whereas the adapted-child is conforming, flexible, and easy to get along with. The goal of transactional analysis is a well-balanced energy system which forms a bell-shaped epogram; the energy extended by the psychological forces is approximately normally distributed. Also included are the concepts of time and energy as extended in an ego state; if raised in one state, time and energy will be decreased in another state.

Affective Models

Approaches based on the affective model include Gestalt therapy and Existential psychotherapy. These therapies contain the belief that problems accumulate and have to be discharged before the client can think clearly again.

Gestalt Therapy. Gestalt therapy, which was developed by Fritz Perls, focuses on the process of helping individuals become increasingly aware of the effect of their immediate, current experiences upon their present behaviors. Past and future experiences or behaviors are not emphasized. The process, undertaken collaboratively by the counselor and the client, emphasizes the development of the client's self-awareness and involves basic concepts of phenomenology, field theory, existentialism, and dialogue. The *phenomenological perspective* systematically analyzes only current client experiences with the intent of helping clients increase self-awareness. With the *field theory perspective*, a behavior is viewed as a function of the person's life space or field. Meaning is given to a situation based on what is currently observed: the here-and-now, which may include antecedent experiences if they affect such related elements as beliefs. The third perspective, *existentialism*, focuses on the individual who is doing the perceiving and on the truth of the individual's relation to the environment. The fourth perspective is *dialogue* and *contact* with others in the environment. This perspective involves inclusion (i.e., experiencing another's situation as much as possible without losing one's own identity), presence (i.e., the counselor expressing his or her self to the client), commitment to dialogue (i.e., permitting contact to happen instead of making it happen and controlling the result), protecting the integrity of the client's experiences, and experiencing dialogue rather than talking about it.

Holism and multi-dimensionality are central to Gestalt therapy. Individuals exist with a clear boundary between themselves and others; therefore, they need to understand themselves as a function of their environment. Abnormal behavior results from problems in delineating the boundaries between oneself and others in the environment. The abnormal behaviors may be confluence (an absence of distinction between self and others), isolation, withdrawal, retroflection (a split between aspects of the self), introjection (lack of discrimination or assimilation of new information gained), projection (confusion of self and others), and deflection (avoidance of contact with others). Solutions to problem behaviors are achieved by dialogue and phenomenology concerning the client's present experiences. Therefore, a strong working relationship between counselor and client is important, with the client assuming responsibility for "what is." The goals for the client are to develop complete self-awareness through direct contact with the counselor and through self-regulation of a whole existence that is comprised of integral parts. These goals involve "good Gestalt" (i.e., a whole that is clearly organized and in good form) and "creative adjustment" (i.e., establishment of a balance between self and the environment). According to Gestalt theory, self-regulation can be achieved through phenomenology or here-and-now experiences and experimenting; dialogue through direct contact with the counselor; and awareness of the whole-field concepts of what is done, how it is done, and why it is done. The client focuses upon what he or she is aware of experiencing at the present time and then experiments with changes by using imagery, body techniques, or visualization.

Existential Psychotherapy. The goal of existential psychotherapy is for the client to find a true "sense of being." Authors closely associated with this theory include Victor Frankl, Irvin Yalom, and Rollo May. The approach concerns feelings of love, creativity, anxiety, despair, isolation, anomie, grief, and loneliness. A basic component is the "I-Am," or ontological, experience: realizing that humans are living and experiencing individuals who are able to choose their own being. When an individual's existence or values are threatened, anxiety is experienced. Therefore, existential psychotherapy emphasizes the reduction of anxiety and concentrates on aiding individuals to be tolerant of the to-be-expected anxieties normally experienced in daily being. Of major concern to the existential psychotherapist is the client's "neurotic anxiety," an anxiety that is inappropriate to a given situation. Also of concern is the "neurotic guilt" experienced by an client due to fantasized transgressions or self-guilt due to an inability to live up to potentialities. As with anxiety, guilt also may take a "normal" form. The expectation is that individuals will experience some guilt in their daily being and, therefore, need to be tolerant of this to-be-expected form of guilt.

According to existential psychotherapy theory, an individual's world is comprised of the *Umwelt*, or the biological (i.e., natural) world (also referred to as the environment), which addresses an individual's drives, needs, and instincts. The *Mitwelt*, or personal community, is concerned with interpersonal relationships. Self-awareness and self-relatedness are included in the third mode, *Eigenwelt*, which is concerned with one's relationship with self. The dimension of time is also significant in existential psychotherapy. Whether a client is able to recall important antecedent events is dependent upon his or her commitment to the present and future. Without the latter, past events have little relationship or effect upon the difficulties the person is experiencing. Relatedly, an individual's ability to transcend antecedent events to the present and future is important. Through **transcendence**, individuals are capable of continually emerging from the past to the present and the future; they are able to transcend over time and space because of the ontological nature of human beings.

Difficulties can arise when individuals experience conflicts with the ultimate concerns of existing. One essential concern or source of anxiety is freedom, or being responsible for one's existence (e.g., actions and choices). A second concern is existential isolation: a gap between oneself and the world and/or others. Death is a third concern. A fourth concern is meaninglessness: a lack of values that give meaningful direction to existence.

Existential psychotherapy counselors view their role as that of helping individuals experience conflict in order to (1) identify unconscious anxieties and maladaptive defense mechanisms being used and (2) develop alternative strategies or mechanisms for coping with the identified anxieties. The counselor's role entails identifying methods being used by the client to avoid coming to terms with his or her own anxieties, and helping the client identify and terminate anxiety-inducing situations.

SUMMARY

This chapter defined the process of counseling through a discussion of communication skills that are common to all helping and theoretical approaches that guide professional counselors. Then, important concerns of individual and group counseling were presented, and, finally, the more established counseling theories were reviewed. Several approaches were not included in the review, some of which are "off-shoots" of the ones presented and others of which are unique. All counseling approaches, whether described here or not, have been designed to help people attain a higher level of personal competence. In helping people become more autonomous and competent individuals, professional counselors seek the most effective counseling theories and methods available. At this time, no single theory has been established as the quintessential approach to professional counseling, and counselors use a variety of theories in their work.

Chapter 11

CONSULTATION

Jack Wooten, a social worker, recently returned from a site visit at a community mental-health center located in a neighboring state. As a result of his visit, he wants to integrate new ideas into his employment setting, but he is unsure whether or not some of the activities will work. Jack believes he could clarify his concerns and plans by talking with another person who shares his interest.

Martha Sanders, an employee of the telephone company, is missing more and more days, and she frequently leaves work early complaining of back trouble and headaches. At work, she often becomes frustrated and "lashes out" at people. Jane Martin, Martha's supervisor, recognizes that Martha's behavior has changed, that Martha is unhappy, and that something needs to be done. However, Jane is unsure what to do. She would like to discuss the situation with someone else who is knowledgeable of human behavior.

In each of the above vignettes, the individual can benefit from a counselor serving as a consultant. For a more specific illustration, we present the example of Laura Gordon.

Laura needs help. She is a first-grade teacher in an elementary school. Currently, Laura is experiencing some problems in her classroom for which she is unprepared. The students like her, and she feels comfortable in the school environment, but frequent classroom disturbances are hindering the children's learning process. Several of the students disrupt the class by constantly talking to themselves at a level that is barely audible, but is still distracting. Two other children in Laura's class move around the room at times when all the children are supposed to be seated. The children's disorderly conduct also occurs outside the classroom: in the hallways, the lunch room, and the playground area. The principal senses that Laura is losing control of the class and believes the children are not learning. Laura, who wants to be a successful teacher, recognizes that the principal is unhappy. She has tried "threats," has sent children to the office, and has contacted parents about their child's inappropriate behavior — all to no avail. As a result of the situation, Laura is having serious doubts about her choice of teaching as a career and about whether or not she will be able to finish the academic year in her present assignment. Unhappy, fatigued, and disillusioned, she is unsure what to do. She views quitting as the only solution but is afraid that she may be unable to obtain another teaching job because of the poor evaluation she will receive from the principal.

Laura's situation has reached an intolerable level, for her, as well as for the principal and the children. She is in need of the assistance of a professional counselor who, acting in a consulting role, helps others with possible solutions to professional problems by listening and responding, providing assurance and relief, and helping reduce stress. In this consultation process, the professional counselor would help Laura solve her problems with the children in her class. Thus, the focus of the process actually would be on helping the children as opposed to helping Laura, as would be the case in counseling.

Consultation involves a process of helping other professionals (i.e., individuals, groups, or personnel in agencies) cope with their problems so they can function more effectively and feel more satisfied with their work. Consultation may be referred to as an "indirect" function for professional counselors because the counselor helps others (i.e., the consultees) in working with still others (i.e., the persons/clients receiving the services provided by the consultees). The helping function of consultation is an important part of the professional counselor's role, because assisting other professionals to function more effectively is ultimately the most efficient and far-reaching use of the professional counselor's skills, efforts, and time. Through the provision of consultation services, professional counselors are able to impact far more people than they could impact directly. The consultation process is most comprehensively effective when it is used for preventive purposes: when the counselor helps consultees help others to avoid future difficulties.

The most efficient time for consultation is when professionals (i.e., consultees) are not under excessive stress and want to explore possible alternative behaviors or discuss their ideas with someone else before they try them. The provision of consultation in these situations creates more confident professionals. Laura's situation, however, has gone beyond the point at which preventive efforts could be implemented. With problems similar to Laura's, the professional counselor as a consultant must provide an opportunity for the consultee to "think aloud" and must aid in reducing stress and providing relief so that the consultee can choose appropriate courses of action.

Consultation is not a specialty with a single professional identity; it is an activity practiced in almost every profession. Surprisingly, however, the literature on research in and practice of consultation is almost nonexistent. In particular, evidence of successful consultation as a preventive intervention, other than anecdotal or descriptive analysis, is hard to locate. A related and unfortunate problem is the numerous meanings and connotations attached to the term consultation. For example, as used by physicians, consultation means meeting with a patient to discuss the patient's medical condition, but in many businesses, the term means being engaged in work-related conversation with another person. Then too, attorneys use the term in reference to meetings with clients. None of these examples, however, adequately reflect the use of the term consultation within the counseling profession.

The use of consultation in mental health activities (i.e., counseling) was pioneered by Caplan (1970), who wrote that consultation is a voluntary, nonsupervisory relationship between professionals for the purpose of helping the consultee(s) improve professional functioning. Caplan further stated that this relationship may involve helping a consultee with current work problems related to a specific client or program or with anticipated future concerns. Caplan suggested that consultation reduces areas of misunderstanding so that consultees may be able to cope more effectively with the same type of problem in the future.

A somewhat more expansive view of consultation has been provided by Bindman (1964):

> . . . Consultation is an interaction process of interpersonal relationship that takes place between two professional workers, the consultant and the consultee, in which one worker, the consultant, assists the other worker, the consultee, to solve a problem of a client or clients, *within the framework of the consultee's usual professional functioning* . . . . A secondary goal of the process is one of education, so that the consultee can learn to handle similar cases in the future in a more effective fashion, and thus enhance his [her] professional skills." (p. 367)

As specified by Caplan's and Bindman's definitions, the consultee-consultant relationship is voluntary and collegial, and the focus of the consultation activity is professional as it relates to the consultee's client or problem. Blocker (1975) described consultation as a process of helping that occurs between a professional helper (consultant) and a help seeker (consultee) who has a professional responsibility for another person (client). It is a temporary cooperative relationship that is concerned with a current or potential work problem.

Indicating what consultation performed by the professional counselor is *not, might* be helpful. Within the counseling profession, consultation is not therapy, advocacy, liaison with agencies, direct service, or administrative control over the consultee. Nor is it collaborating or working with (i.e., as in co-counseling) parents or colleagues jointly to provide a direct service to their child or client, respectively. These components violate the construct of consultation as used in this book and as viewed by many professional counselors. For example, assisting parents in resolving problems concerning their child is providing a direct service to parents; parents are the target of the service (and are not professional helpers or consultees).

Kirby (1985) defined consultation in terms of relationship conditions. She identified four conditions:

> . . . the consultant-consultee relationship is voluntary, the focus of consultation intervention is in a work situation or role of responsibility of the consultee, the consultant is functioning outside of the structural hierarchy, and the consultant is perceived as an expert in the area in which consultation is offered. (p. 5)

She operationally conceived consultation as:

> . . . a process whereby the consultant helps the consultees achieve their goals. Thus, the consultant facilitates the consultees' problem-solving process and, at times, guides, leads, or directs consultees as they use the consultant's expertise in their goal-seeking behavior. (p. 11)

Although consultation focuses on professional problems, an awareness of the consultee's coping skills and personality assets and liabilities is required. The integration of these characteristics is illustrated in Figure 11.1 which provides a conceptual view of the components and process of consultation.

Some of the communication skills associated with the counseling process are also part of the consultation process. Therefore, differences between counseling and consultation are dictated primarily by the theoretical framework of counseling and the model approach of consultation, as well as by their respective intentions. The term **model** is used to describe the structure of consultation because, unlike counseling, consultation has not obtained a level of sufficient substance to warrant use of the term "theory."

One major difference between counseling and consultation is that the consultant-consultee relationship is more objective

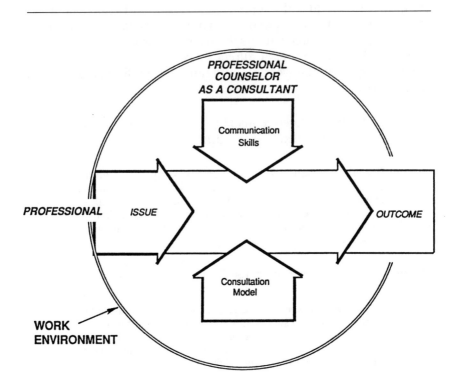

Figure 11.1. Conceptual view of the components and process of consultation.

and emotionally external than is the counselor-client relationship, which is more personal and involves disclosure of emotions. In addition, the target of consultation is problem-solving as it relates to professional functioning, whereas the target of counseling is primarily personal adjustment.

The professional counselor's consultation role in individual consultation can be more easily understood by reviewing five often-used models: training-workshops, mental-health, process, behavioral, and a theoretical problem-solving consultation. Of course these models often will be modified, combined, or varied in some way to more adequately meet the individual needs of the professional consultant.

TRAINING-WORKSHOPS CONSULTATION

Training workshops are a type of consultation in which selected traditional educational methods are used to provide information and to develop skills as a basis of prevention. A distinction needs to be made between training and teaching. In contrast to teaching or educational programs, wherein people are usually passive listeners, training workshops encompass a form of consultation that involves considerable experiential learning by the participants. For example, training-workshops consultation typically involves putting participants in dyads or triads to learn and practice new skills.

To effect training-workshops consultation, mental-health agencies, schools, and college and university offices of student affairs often have one- or two-day "retreats." More common, however, are designated periods of time (e.g., "office," "work," "in-service," or "conference" days), during which clients are not seen, classes are not held, and offices are not open. Instead a variety of professional activities take place in the context of a training workshop conducted by a consultant.

Approaches to training workshops and staff participation vary by setting. For example, with clinical mental-health counselors, one-way mirrors can be used to permit observation of (usually simulated) counseling sessions. The consulting professional counselor conducts the sessions while other counselors observe through the one-way mirror, and consultant-led group discussions follow the sessions.

The professional counselor's training and experience in communication skills and knowledge of consulting models and mental health often are used to enable groups of professionals (e.g., teachers, administrators, ministers, and social workers) to function more effectively. For example, counselors may hold training workshops for groups of concerned teachers to discuss ways of working with behavior problems, substance abuse, and adolescent suicide. A professional counselor also might work as a consultant with a group of vocational rehabilitation counselors or residence-life staff members to improve their communication skills.

Most training workshops conducted by professional counselors have clearly defined purposes and are preventive in nature. They are usually held to enable other professionals to share "here-and-now" (i.e., current and immediate) problems and to obtain help with practical solutions. Also, these solutions may be used with problems that could be encountered in the future. If problem areas have not been determined before the counselor is called to run the training workshop, the consulting professional counselor typically surveys the group members to determine their concerns. A professional counselor who serves as a training-workshop consultant has the potential to benefit other professionals enormously, but only if he or she knows their specific needs.

The following example provides a typical sequence of events during a training workshop on substance abuse. A professional counselor was asked to conduct a training workshop concerning substance abuse interventions for college-age students because a group of university residence-life directors felt insufficiently skilled to help people with problems in this area. Also, the directors were ambivalent about whether or not they should have to do something about the problem. The professional counselor surveyed the group and found that the primary concern was how to handle certain aspects of drug prevention without causing unfavorable reactions from students. A secondary concern was that the other student-development staff members and parents felt that the directors were, at a minimum, ambivalent about the problem, if not neglectful. The professional counselor's survey further revealed an unexpected amount of ignorance about drugs and physiological effects of substance abuse.

With this basic information, the counselor formulated and planned the training workshop to contain two parts. For part one, a pharmacologist was engaged to give instruction on the most commonly abused drugs and their psychotropic effects. For part two of the training workshop, which followed the more formal didactic presentation of the pharmacologist, the counselor-as-consultant divided the participants into small groups of five or six. Then, role-playing was used, during which one participant assumed the "helper's" role and the others became the "helpees." The helpees were given directions to assume the role of "badgers," asking every conceivable question about drugs, such as "Is it harmful?", "What does snorting mean?", "Is 'crack' any worse than smoking pot?", or "How do you know that drug use relates to poor grades?" The helper assumed a supportive role as well as trying to be specifically helpful to the helpee asking the question. During the session, much anxiety was generated when the helper was not familiar with the terms used and had no well formulated response to such questions. However, through role-playing, helpers were able to practice making accurate responses to questions, without implying value judgments. Once the helpers had the opportunity to become more familiar with the often asked questions and commonly used slang words and terms, their initial anxiety decreased and their abilities to provide effective responses increased.

MENTAL-HEALTH CONSULTATION

Caplan's (1970) mental-health consultation is the prototype of most consultation models used in the counseling profession. Caplan based his model on psychodynamic assumptions about human behavior and purported that predictable deficit areas of professional behaviors include the professional's lack of skills, self-confidence, knowledge, and objectivity. The model emphasizes the process of a triadic relationship in consultation: consultant, consultee, and client. In Caplan's approach, four kinds of consultation exist: client-centered case, consultee-centered, program-centered, and consultee-centered administrative.

Client-centered case consultation is the classical triadic approach which involves a consultee seeking assistance from a consultant about a client. The focus is on the client, although the consultant does not have direct contact with the client; any assistance afforded a client from the consultant is effected through the consultee.

Consultee-centered consultation concentrates on the consultee's professional problem. The process and focus is usually dyadic (i.e, the consultant and consultee), with the target being the consultee.

Program-centered consultation involves a consultant helping with an organization's problem. This approach is also dyadic, except that the focus is on the organization.

Consultee-centered administrative consultation has as its goal either improving administrators' problem-solving skills or helping them in the broad area of skill deficit and/or emotional entanglement with an issue(s).

An important component of, and typical impetus for, mental-health consultation is the consultee's loss of professional objectivity. Caplan suggested that loss of objectivity is created when a consultee has identified with the problem (e.g., the client reminds the consultee of an event or person in the consultee's past) or it may be due to a much more severe problem (e.g., the consultee has a characterological disorder such as being paranoia, histrionic, or avoidance). Caplan described this situation as "theme interference," wherein the consultee creates a syllogism in which the client is placed in a previously determined unconscious category and linked to an inevitable outcome. For example, a consultee who perceives a client as "passively demanding" may see the client's success in working with coworkers as doomed to failure. Because of the unconscious syllogism, the consultee subconsciously does not believe that the counseling really can be effective. To help the consultee with theme interference, Caplan suggested (1) "unlinking," which involves alleviating the consultee's subconscious perception, or (2) "theme-interference reduction," which involves trying to help the consultee construct other possible outcomes.

PROCESS CONSULTATION

The process-consultation model emphasizes behavioral, group-dynamic dimensions within an organization by examining the effects of communication on each strata of the organization as it pertains to the attainment of its goals. The origin of the process-consultation model, which is frequently identified with Schein (1969), rests in social psychology. It is primarily a group problem-solving approach that seeks to make people more aware of the interpersonal communications that are negatively affecting their work productivity and attitudes. Process consultation also is known as *organizational development* (OD) and is frequently used to improve organizational functioning by concentrating on and working with small groups of employees. The process consultation attempts to strengthen the organizational system by optimally using existing personnel to produce and enhance a growth-oriented environment. A counselor-as-consultant using the process consultation model seeks to help members of the organization to understand the interactional patterns interfering with the goals of the organization.

Schein (1969) suggested that interactional patterns that interfere with an organization's functioning include inconsistent decision-making styles, hidden personal agendas, poor leadership skills, inappropriate agenda setting, "scapegoating," and inappropriately high levels of competition. Consultants using this approach need also to be sensitive to problems with the structural system and/or managerial procedures within the organization.

Schein (1969) recommended the following seven interacting and overlapping steps for process consultation: (1) initial contact with the client organization; (2) definition of the consultation relationship, including both the formal and psychological contracts; (3) selection and setting of a method of work; (4) data gathering and diagnosis; (5) intervention; (6) involvement reduction; and (7) termination. Process consultants are seldom experts within the organizations or industries for which they are providing consultation. Instead, they are usually professionals whose expertise and interest are on the "how" of the interpersonal process within an organization. In summary, process consultation is oriented toward manifesting and facilitating the many levels and potentially effective modes of communication that exist in an organization.

BEHAVIORAL CONSULTATION

The behavioral model of consultation is based heavily on the assumption that changes in an environment will necessarily change the behaviors of people in that environment. This approach is particularly well suited for consulting with professionals employed in settings such as schools, prisons, hospitals, and other controlled and regulated environments.

Like the mental-health consultation model, the behavioral-consultation model is a problem-solving approach. It is based on social learning theory, with client and consultee problems conceptualized as having evolved from direct or vicarious previous learnings. The consultant's goal is to ascertain what the problem or target behavior is, determine and isolate environmental variables that foster or support the target behavior, and suggest environmental changes that will diminish the probability of the behavior continuing. A consultant who employs this model utilizes the principles and traditional behavioral techniques of behavior modification (e.g., shaping, chaining, successive approximation, or modeling) to produce new behaviors. In addition, the behavioral-consultation model may include other learning principles and models such as roleplaying, homework assignments, and feedback.

Although behavioral consultation may be applied in any setting, the usefulness of behavioral techniques in schools is particularly well documented. Perhaps this is because teachers feel more comfortable with consultants who suggest techniques and interventions consistent with the learning principles with which teachers are familiar.

ATHEORETICAL PROBLEM-SOLVING CONSULTATION

Myrick (1977) suggested an atheoretical approach to consultation which he believed is particularly well suited for professional counselors. The approach relies heavily upon communication skills described as "facilitative" (Wittmer & Myrick, 1974).

Myrick's (1977) consultation approach, which he has recommended for both individuals and groups, is a systematic set of procedures that follow seven steps. The first step focuses on identifying the consultee's problem. In the second step, the consultant clarifies both the emotional and behavioral aspects of the consultee's situation, primarily through encouraging the consultee to talk about feelings, specific behaviors that influenced the consultee's current ideas and situation, consultee expectations for achievement, previous attempts to correct the situation, and positive attitudes and behaviors already present in the situation. Step three involves identifying the goal(s) or desired outcome(s) for the situation.

In step four, relevant behaviors applicable to the situation are observed and recorded by the consultee and possibly by the consultant. In step five, the consultant and consultee develop a plan of action together, with the expectation that the consultee will play the major role in carrying out the plan. Step six is the initiation of the plan by the consultee under the "supervision" of the consultant. Step seven is follow-up: examining what has happened to determine whether the plan is working and/or whether changes, if any, need to be made in the plan. This model is straight forward, progresses systematically, and involves many already familiar skills and behaviors. Therefore, the problem-solving approach appeals to many professional counselors, particularly those working in school systems.

Myrick (1977) purported that the model is helpful with crisis, preventive, and developmental consultation. *Crisis consultation* is defined as assisting the consultee who is experiencing an urgent problem, such as an agency director who has a concerned board member coming in at the end of the day and is unsure how to approach the conference. *Preventive consultation*, the second type, is used when the consultee believes that an urgent problem is imminent. In this situation, the consultee has received signals that a problem will be developing if the situation is not handled correctly now. Finally, *developmental consultation* involves helping the consultee help others develop skills and behaviors that will either prevent problems in the future or enable them to cope effectively with problems should they arise. A current example of developmental consultation is the school counselor who helps teachers help students develop ways to avoid involvement with substance abuses.

AN EXAMPLE OF INDIVIDUAL CONSULTATION

Many times a professional counselor is approached for consultation in a rather informal manner. Other professionals, who want consultation but are uneasy about making a formal request for it, often seek out professional counselors, who have established themselves as consultants, in informal atmospheres such as in a staff dining room or lounge area or at a social event. The following illustrates such an exchange.

"I hate to disturb you now with shop talk, but could I ask you about a case of mine—Marion? I don't think I am making as much progress with the case as I would like. She's immature, but I believe her behavior is a method to avoid taking responsibility for her actions. I have been seeing her weekly since October, and during our sessions she has been timid, quiet, and generally nonresponsive— the very behaviors that prompted her to see me. And, she is concerned about keeping up with her responsibilities at the insurance company where she works. She's a great person, and I don't think there's anything seriously or pathologically wrong with her. Yet, I am worried that if I continue seeing her and she doesn't make any progress, she may think that she has a serious problem that can't be helped, and she may lose her job."

The professional counselor, in a consultant role, responded, "Yes, it's always a problem deciding if you are doing the right things with a client. What can you tell me about Marion?"

"She's young—just turned 18 in May. She graduated early from a small high school—just after she reached 16."

"What other people are closely involved in Marion's life? Others can sometimes play an important role in determining behavior. How about her parents or friends?"

"I'm not too sure. I have been focusing counseling pretty much as a job-related motivational problem."

"What approaches have you tried?"

"Primarily some time-management schemes: homework-type assignments on time use. I've also been having her practice speaking to others at work. I thought that if I got Marion to interact with others she might come out a bit more and be less timid and quiet and do a better job at work."

By this time the professional counselor has helped the consultee to formulate the problem and has learned what has been done. The consultant continued, "*What other directions might you take?*"

The consultee was relieved not to have been admonished by the counselor. "*I could explore with Marion the influence that others in her life are having on her— specifically her parents. I recognize that she is young and, you know, maybe too much pressure is on her to keep up with those older employees.*"

The counselor-as-consultant replied, "*Specifically, how do you think you can approach Marion during your next session?*" This question helps the consultee to think aloud about a plan of action.

"*Well, I think I will tell Marion that I have been reviewing our sessions and believe that I would like to explore some new avenues which might be helpful. Also, if the parents are a dominant factor, as I now think they may be, I might suggest that we have a session or two which includes them.*"

"*How do you think Marion will feel about that? Sometimes parents unwittingly can make it difficult for their child, even a young adult.*"

"*Oh, I don't believe there would be a problem. I somehow sense the family is close.*"

"*Try it and call me—let me know after your next session with her what's happening.*"

A week later, the professional counselor received a call from the consultee indicating that the last session went well and that, indeed, Marion was feeling pressured into employment and marriage by her parents. In addition, a session had been established with the parents and Marion together.

The above example, in which the process of consultation has been considerably abridged, shows how the professional counselor and consultee interact as co-professionals and not as an authority and subordinate. The consultee actually made the important decisions and the professional counselor, as consultant, primarily helped to clarify and provide support for the consultee's decisions. In effective consultative relationships, consultees perceive counselors-as-consultants as persons who respect and understand them, and who are responsive to their needs.

The professional counselor, as a consultant, usually tries to respond to a consultee's request about a problem by helping the consultee to determine alternate solutions. However, although other professionals may ask a professional counselor for assistance with a problem in the work place, they are not always receptive to assistance. They want the situation to be different, but they prefer not to have to rely on others — a natural human tendency. Alternately, consultees sometimes want someone else to make the needed changes for them. This, of course, has to be resisted by consultants because then they leave the role of consultants and become providers of direct services. If this happens, the skills of consultees are not being further developed so they can respond more effectively with future cases, and efficiency is not being obtained within the agency (i.e., the "ripple effect" is nonexistent).

Professionals within a given field may vary as much as professionals from different fields. Professional counselors, for example, differ in the amount and quality of training they have received, mainly because of variations in the college and university programs from which they graduated. They may vary in intellectual functioning, personality characteristics, skills and abilities, and performance. In addition, even the most capable, enthusiastic and well-trained professional counselors frequently will find themselves incapable of handling all the problems with which they are confronted in a work setting. Situations may be encountered where a counselor lacks the skills, insight, or knowledge to work effectively with a given problem. At these times, boundaries for feelings of inadequacy are nonexistent, and so counselors need to remember that counselors, too, may need consultation services.

Consultation is a dynamic process. It is a problem-solving activity, inherent in which are the elements of internal change, external demands, and the interface of both. Not only are the consultee and client affected, but the organization(s) for which they work also is(are) affected. Blake and Mouton (1983) noted that, "Education and consultation are probably two of the most important factors behind the forward movement of society" (p. iii). They suggested that consultation may be the more meaningful factor because it has an even greater potential for widespread effect. When professional counselors-as-consultants help consultees, consultees then can be successful with many, many people with whom they work and they can make far greater progress in the way they work. Thus, the potential of consultation as a professional counselor function is unlimited. Its need is ever present because of the constant concomitant need for new and better ways to solve a wide range of problems.

SUMMARY

Consultation is a process for helping other professionals improve professional functioning and therefore improve services to the consultee's clients. Consultation services differ from counseling services and are able to impact far more people than counselors could impact directly. One major difference between counseling and consultation is that the consultant-consultee relationship is more objective and emotionally external than is the counselor-client relationship. In understanding the professional counselor's consultation role in individual consultation, five often-used models can be considered. They are training workshops, mental health, process, behavioral, and atheoretical. Each of these models has a different focus in approaching the consultation situation.

The professional counselor and consultee interact as co-professionals and not as an authority and subordinate. From this perspective, the consultant must be sure to not leave the role of consultant by making decisions for the consultee thus negating future skills development for the consultee. In this way, consultees can be successful with many people, and therein lies the enormous potential of the counselor as consultant.

Chapter **12**

GROUP COUNSELING

A very practical problem for professional counselors, particularly those working in institutional settings, is having adequate time to provide counseling services to all the people who desire them. When, for example, school counselors decide to see students for individual counseling, they make a substantial commitment of time (typically weekly or bi-weekly) and thereby decrease the time they have available for counseling services for others. The professional counselor has to decide whether such a large portion of time is appropriately spent working with individual students. An alternative is group counseling, which evolved from individual counseling as counselors realized they were limited in the amount of time available to individually reach all persons who desired help (Kemp, 1970).

The familiarity of the construct group counseling is well known, so much so that few individuals would seek the assistance of a dictionary to determine its meaning. However, the term does not have an equivocal connotation among professionals. Perhaps this situation exists because group counseling is an outgrowth of individual counseling (Vander Kolk, 1985) resulting in many different approaches.

Graduates from most counselor education programs have been required to complete one or more courses in group counseling because of its helpfulness with diverse client populations. As Gazda (1978) indicated, through prearranged meetings that focus on a commonly agreed-upon purpose, the interaction between a collection of individuals can result in enhancing the members' personal growth/enrichment or preventing or remediating difficulties they may be encountering.

Although group and individual counseling are applied in many settings, practical considerations such as time, resources, and costs make group counseling particularly suitable for schools, businesses, and some community agency settings. Group counseling can be designed in a variety of ways to serve the needs of either homogeneous or heterogeneous groups. With the former, the group is comprised of similar individuals (e.g., adolescents, young adults, or single parents) who have a common concern (e.g., interpersonal relationship difficulties, self-development, or self-awareness). With the latter, different individuals (e.g., older adults, adolescents, married couples, and the bereaved) with individual manifestations of their respective concerns are brought together for discussions. The counselor facilitates the development of common goals among members of a counseling group. Thus, a feeling of "safety in numbers" often develops in group members, along with the feeling that they and their concerns will be accepted by the group (Trotzer, 1989).

Because counseling groups consist of individuals with diverse backgrounds, interests, and life situations, each group becomes a social laboratory in which many beliefs, coping strategies, and practices are shared, compared, and examined. Through observation and experimentation under the leadership and facilitation of the group counselor, members of a group have the opportunity to learn and/or improve interpersonal, behavioral, and social skills that closely approximate those in society, e.g., caring, challenging, intimating, and refuting (Corey, 1981).

Group counseling usually permits a counselor to make more effective use of time by working with several people simultaneously. The rationale is that counselors are able to expand their sphere of influence beyond that which is possible in individual counseling by drawing upon the resources of group members and channeling them appropriately. Recognition must be made, however, that some situations and/or problems do not readily lend themselves to rectification through a group counseling process. In fact, individual counseling is by far the most predominant form of counseling used by professional counselors. It is often characterized as a relationship between two people and is defined by terms such as *personal* and *face-to-face*. The major difference between group and individual counseling seems to be the number of persons (clients) being helped in a given block of time. In addition, all elements of what is thought of as counseling in groups take place within individual counseling except for interactions among members (clients). Individual counseling does have the advantage over group counseling of providing a setting which is perceived by many as "safer." Therefore, counseling may progress more quickly because the client has maximum personal contact with the professional counselor. In summary, both individual and group counseling are very important activities for professional counselors.

The effectiveness of group counseling depends on many components, including communication within the group, the group process, the model or theoretical approach followed, and legal and ethical issues. A discussion of each of these components follows.

COMMUNICATION WITHIN GROUP COUNSELING

Group counseling typically involves use of some of the communication skills employed in individual counseling. However, counseling more than one individual simultaneously makes some elements of the group counseling process much different from those of individual counseling. Professional counselors doing group counseling must consider special and often additional issues that are of little or less concern when counseling a single client, e.g., selection of group members, size and composition of the group, initiation of the group, and duration of the counseling process.

Group counseling is often considered to be counseling *by* the group (i.e., rather than counseling *in* the group), thus forming a major difference between individual and group counseling. With group counseling, group members learn to accept responsibility for helping others within the group as well as themselves (Ohlsen, 1970). In this perspective, productive change can take place within individuals as a result of the behaviors of the individual, the group counselor, and the other group members. Trotzer (1989) referred to this composite phenomenon as constructive influence through harnessing the power of the peer group.

As with most small-group situations, powerful norms usually develop in the group. Group counselors strive to facilitate development (as opposed to imposition) of "helpful" norms within a group. One typically sought norm for the purpose of resolving problems is **open communication** while another is **collaboration among group members**. Thus, in group counseling not only are opportunities available for members of the group to be helped but also opportunities exist for members to be helpers for others, a condition rarely present in individual counseling. As members witness others giving and receiving help, they become more willing to do both themselves. This "spectator-type" counseling process increasingly enhances each group member's opportunities for feedback and assistance. Group members develop the ability to think and perform for the good of others and to ask for feedback for themselves, with the group leader reinforcing the right of and necessity for members to make their own decisions (Kemp, 1970; Trotzer, 1989).

GROUP PROCESS

The group process is complex given the composition of a group and factors which influence what happens as the group strives to achieve its goals. Therefore, consideration needs to be given to procedures for establishing a group and to various group dynamics including size and format, length and frequency of sessions, voluntary or involuntary participation, developmental stages of groups, and roles of the various participants.

Establishing a Group

Unfortunately, the establishment of a group is often underemphasized. Yet, careful consideration needs to be given to the screening and selection of group participants. A primary criterion in determining the make-up of a group is whether the potential members will contribute to the group or be counterproductive. Thus, a pre-group interview with each prospective member is stressed by both the American Counseling Association (ACA) (1988) and American Specialists in Group Work (ASGW) (1980). Through this procedure, members who might be counterproductive can be identified, i.e., individuals who are hostile, aggressive, self-centered, suicidal, sociopathic, or highly suspicious, individuals who like to dominate others or lack ego strength. A pre-group interview also provides an opportunity for potential members to become familiar with the group leader. Finally, this procedure enables the group leader to acquaint prospective members with (1) the group's orientation and goal(s) and (2) their rights as a group member.

Knowing the group's expected composition is a prerequisite for the screening and selection procedures. For example, a heterogeneous group often enhances participants' perspectives and stimulates interpersonal interactions whereas homogeneous groups generally tend to be more helpful in addressing specific issues. Thus, the composition of a group is influenced by its goals.

As an illustration, a group comprised of adult children of alcoholics would appear to be a homogeneous grouping. Yet, adult children of alcoholics may comprise a diverse group whose members have a range of presenting issues that involve different developmental levels in addressing their resolution. For a group of this nature, the composition is both homogeneous and heterogeneous which is often useful in promoting social learning among members.

Group Dynamics

What happens within a group has an effect upon the group's success in meeting its goals since various group dynamics can be either beneficial or harmful to the group process. According to Jacobs, Harvill, and Masson (1988), 12 factors that affect the efficiency of a group include the setting or environment, size, length of session, composition of group, members' attitudes toward each other and toward the leader, leader's attitude toward members, interaction patterns among members and leader, group's level of progression, levels of goodwill, degree of commitment, and extent of trust. Some specific considerations concerning group dynamics are discussed in the following paragraphs.

Setting or Environment. For a group to be effective, consideration needs to be given to the environment in which the group meets. A comfortable and quiet setting is needed so that members will have a sense of privacy and an opportunity to interact freely with each other.

Size. Large groups (i.e., more than 10 to 12 individuals) make the attainment of goals more difficult and sometimes impossible. Determining how many members should comprise a group, depends on several factors including the purpose of the group, the leader's background and experience, and age and developmental level of group members (e.g., whether the group will be comprised of children or adults). As Corey (1990) stated, a group needs to be large enough to permit sufficient interaction but small enough to enable everyone to be an active participant and to feel a part of a group.

Format of Group. A decision that needs to be made before starting the group or during the first session is whether new members can join the group as space becomes available (i.e., an *open group*) or whether the group will maintain its original composition throughout its prearranged time period (i.e., *closed group*). While the latter is a means of maintaining stability and thus encouraging trust and effective interactions among members, the overall effectiveness of the group can be problematic if too many individuals terminate their association with the group prior to the prearranged conclusion date. An open-group format is a means of addressing this concern since new members can have an invigorating effect. However, as Corey et al. (1988) indicated, individuals joining a pre-existing group may find it difficult to become part of the group. Likewise, the trust and cohesion that has been established within a group may be disrupted by the introduction of new members.

Duration and Frequency of Groups. The duration of a group meeting and the frequency of meetings affect group dynamics. With closed groups, a termination date should be established during the first group meeting. With regard to the duration and frequency of meetings, adults usually find one and one-half to two-hour weekly meetings suitable. Adolescents and children, however, generally benefit from shorter sessions that meet more frequently.

Self-initiated or Required Participation. Another factor that can affect the dynamics of a group is whether members are required to participate or whether they are attending based on their own self-interest. While the membership in a majority of groups is voluntary, some individuals participate because a mental health center or other institution has mandated them to do so. This required membership may result in a lower degree of motivation which, as Yalom (1985) indicated, may be the most important criterion for inclusion in a group. When membership is involuntary, motivation can be enhanced through adequate preparation during the pre-group interview and by permitting ventilation of feelings about being required to attend group sessions (Corey & Corey, 1987; Corey, 1990).

Developmental Stages. Typically, groups progress through stages that have predictable dynamics, although each group generally remains unique across stages. The first stage involves the group's formation, identification, and establishment of goals and objectives. With this foundation in place, the focus during stage two moves to ways to address the goals and objectives. Stage three is often referred to as the working stage; members assume responsibility for goal attainment, and focus on changing behavior(s). Within the final stage, members' efforts are directed toward terminating the group since the group's goals and objectives have been attained.

Members' Roles. Various roles assumed by group members can either impede or facilitate the group process. These can generally be divided into three groups: (1) group building and maintenance roles which are considered positive social-emotional roles, (2) group task roles which help facilitate the group's progress, and (3) individual roles which are considered negative social-emotional roles. As outlined by

Hanson, Warner, and Smith (1980), positive roles include being (1) facilitators or encouragers who ensure that everyone feels comfortable, (2) gatekeepers or expediters who makes certain that the group functions as proposed, (3) harmonizers or conciliators who strive to reduce group conflict, (4) compromisers or neutralizers who want to address differences through cognitive solutions, (5) group observers who provide feedback to other members by summarizing the content or process, and (6) followers who express much agreement with the group but may be unsure of themselves.

Roles that are instrumental to the group's tasks include (1) initiators-energizers, (2) information or opinion seekers, (3) information or opinion givers, (4) elaborators and/or coordinators, (5) orientators-evaluators, and (6) procedural technicians.

Negative or anti-group roles include (1) aggressors who generally disagree with others' beliefs; (2) blockers who contradict the wishes of others; (3) playboys whose behaviors express non-involvement; (4) help seekers whose dependent behaviors focus mainly on own personal problems; (5) monopolists whose incessant talk interferes with the sense of equality among participants; (6) recognition seekers whose behaviors attract self-attention at the expense of others; (7) do-gooders who are always right, particularly on moral issues, and who imply that others are wrong; (8) self-confessors who disclose information that distracts group members from concentrating on their tasks; (9) informers who share information about another member's behavior outside the group; (10) hostile members who use intimidation or sarcasm as a means of self-protection; and (11) nonparticipating, withdrawn, or silent members who avoid interactions with others (Hanson et al., 1980).

Group Leader's Role and Characteristics. The most important attributes accounting for any group's success are (1) the role assumed by the leader and (2) the leader's characteristics (Corey & Corey, 1987). As can be expected, the role is partially defined by the leader's level of competency that include knowledge competencies as well as skill competencies. The former competencies include knowledge of major theories, basic principles of group dynamics, strengths and weaknesses of individual members, ethical and professional issues, research, roles and behaviors of group members, logistical factors including appropriate time to meet and the meeting environment, group stages, group interactions, and counselor roles. Skill competencies include an ability to assess clients' readiness for group participation; define group counseling; diagnose group members' self-defeating behaviors and intervene appropriately; model appropriate behavior; interpret nonverbal behavior; use skills productively; employ major techniques, strategies, and procedures related to group counseling; promote therapeutic factors; work with a co-leader; conclude group sessions; establish and terminate groups; and employ assessment and follow-up procedures.

Several personal characteristics appear to be helpful to a group leader. An effective leader can be described as being willing to model behavior and seek new experiences; believing in the group process; being open, nondefensive, and creative; having courage, stamina, a sense of personal power, a caring attitude, and a sense of humor; and exhibiting goodwill and self-awareness.

Finally, a leader's role is affected by the type of group or group model and the theoretical approach(es) employed. A discussion of these factors follows.

GROUP MODELS

Because group counseling is an outgrowth of individual counseling, many different models exist. Several attempts have been made to classify these models by types of counseling. Saltmarsh, Jenkins, and Fisher (1986) grouped the different models by nature of management and nature of group process. Their resulting four groups focus, respectively, on tasking (i.e., volunteer, mission,, goal, and working groups), relating (i.e., staff development, relationship skills, theme-defined, and in-service groups), contacting (i.e., therapy, encounter, laboratory, and mutual concern groups), and acquiring (i.e., resource, discussion, discovery, and education groups).

Gazda (1989) provided an orientation that views the different models on a continuum with three main categories which include overlapping goals. The **preventive and growth engendering category** (i.e., group guidance and life-skills training groups) overlaps the **preventive-growth engendering-remedial category** (i.e., group counseling, T-groups, sensitivity groups, organizational development groups, encounter groups, and structured groups including life-skills training and social-skills training groups), which in turn overlaps the **remedial category** (i.e., psychotherapy groups and life-skills [social skills] training groups).

In addition to the type of counseling provided, different models are grounded in specific theoretical frameworks. Thus, the focus and goals of each may vary depending on its affiliated theoretical constructs. Several of the models included in both the Saltmarsh et al. (1986) and Gazda (1989) classifications are discussed briefly on the pages that follow. For more detailed descriptions of these models, see Corey (1990) and Vander Kolk (1985). Also, the reader is referred to Chapter 10 for an in-depth discussion of a specific model's theoretical framework.

Encounter Groups

The term **basic encounter groups** was originally introduced by Rogers (1970), and later shortened to **encounter groups**. Members of encounter groups generally focus on personal development, emotional experiences, and awareness of the behavior of others (Eddy & Lubin, 1971; George & Dustin, 1988; Gladding, 1991.) Rogers (1971) and Johnson & Johnson (1987) postulated that persons would like and understand themselves more and would allow themselves to explore ways of changing if they were provided a "safe environment" in which to discuss their problems. Encounter groups are a means of meeting this need.

Task Groups

Task groups are goal-oriented. Rather than an emphasis on changing one's behavior, task groups focus on a successful performance or a finished product resulting from the collaborative efforts of group members (George & Dustin, 1988).

T-groups

Within T-groups, which originated as training groups following World War II, the focus is on interpersonal relationships and personal growth with an emphasis on how one is perceived by other members of the group. Thus, group members have the dual benefit of being better able to understand group process, in general, and their own style of relating to others within a group, in particular (Shaffer & Galinsky, 1989). The goal of T-groups is to foster a climate of openness and understanding, and to help group members become more cognizant of how their actions are interpreted by others.

Psychodrama Groups

An experiential approach to group counseling is provided within psychodrama groups, which involve a complex form of group role-playing, i.e., group members act out their concerns within the group context (Moreno & Kipper, 1968; Vander Kolk, 1985). Through personal enactment designed by the group leader, members encounter suppressed feelings or new experiences which in turn help facilitate change in or the development of behaviors.

Self-help Groups

Many types of self-help groups exist, but they all have the primary purpose of assisting members in reducing psychological stress and taking control of their lives. Ones that are established and maintained by professional organizations or individual professionals generally are referred to as support groups. Representative of this type of self-help groups are Alcoholics Anonymous, Parents Without Partners, and support groups sponsored by the American Cancer Society. Other self-help groups usually grow out of a desire by individuals in a given geographical area to address a common concern or problem (e.g., parents who have adopted children from a foreign country, or parents of children who are HIV positive).

TA (Transactional Analysis) Groups

A uniqueness of TA groups is that they originated with a group-counseling focus rather than extending an individual-counseling basis to include groups. As a result, the framework for TA Groups is fairly well established and structured, including specific terminology.

The emphasis of TA Groups is on an open relationship and equality among all members, who do not have to meet a certain criteria before joining the group, and between members and the leader. Members assume responsibility for examining and reexamining their previously made decisions for the purpose of making new ones based on their own personal awareness. As part of this process, members identify specific goals, clarify how they will attempt to reach the goals, and determine how goal achievement will be determined. Within TA Groups, the leader is responsible for teaching concepts and terminology to members and facilitating members' self-examination. Individuals are helped to understand cognitively their own and others' behavior through the analyses of "life scripts," which include four categories: I'm OK and You're OK, I'm OK and You're Not OK, I'm Not OK and You're OK, and I'm Not OK and You're Not OK (Harris, 1967).

Rational-Emotive Therapy (RET) Groups

RET Groups are based on rational-emotive therapy, which focuses on identifying members' basic irrational beliefs and helping them develop more rational points of view. The assumption is that members are responsible for their own problems and concerns which result from their own irrational beliefs and evaluation. Thus, the goal of RET Groups is to replace a member's irrational and self-defeating perspective with a more rational and tolerable point of view.

During group sessions, one person's problem is generally addressed at a time. It is the leader's responsibility to identify the irrational and/or self-defeating beliefs of a member and, along with the other group members, confront, challenge, or persuade that member accordingly. Through this process, all members of the group are provided opportunities to reflect upon and compare their own beliefs that may be irrational and/or self-defeating.

Reality Therapy Groups

Reality therapy, as with transactional analysis, originated through work with groups. Since the assumption of this model is that an individual's choice of behaviors results from internal needs, the focus of reality-therapy groups is developing an identity of success based on realistic and responsible behavior. Members are encouraged to make value judgments about their own behaviors and to develop a plan of action for change.

The leader's role is to help members focus on the reality of their respective situations with an emphasis on selecting actions that are appropriate for attaining success and, as cited in Chapter 10, satisfying the basic needs of staying alive, reproducing, having power, being free, and having fun. This is achieved through eight steps that involve helping group members (1) establish meaningful relationships, (2) focus on present behaviors, (3) determine whether their present behaviors are achieving what they want, (4) develop a positive plan to do better, (5) commit to the positive plan, (6) formulate another plan rather than make excuses if the positive plan failed, (7) learn to live with the consequences of a failed plan without punishing themselves, and (8) remain committed to the goal of change, realizing that achieving change can take time.

Gestalt Groups

Gestalt groups comprise individual counseling within a group environment with the responsibility for change resting more on the individual group member than on the group leader. The focus is on helping members increase their own awareness of how their immediate, current experiences affect their present behaviors. As a result, past and future experiences or behaviors are not emphasized.

The goal for group members is to develop complete self-awareness (through direct contact with the counselor and others in the group), which includes self-reliance, self-regulation, and self-support. Members focus upon what they are aware of experiencing at the present time and then experiment with changes through the use of various techniques such as imagery, role-playing, body techniques, or visualization.

Behavior-therapy Groups

Within behavior-therapy groups, behavior is viewed as a function of its consequences, and members' actual behaviors rather than cognitive processes are of concern. As a result, the focus is on modifying observable and measurable behaviors through behavior modification techniques. Members' previous thoughts as well as unconscious conflicts are considered of little or no value in counseling. Rather, current causes of behavior are emphasized with treatment techniques varying according to members' needs.

The leader's role is to help group members change maladaptive behaviors by learning new and more effective behaviors. This process may involve the use of behavioral techniques such as stimulus control; shaping; partial, positive, and/or negative reinforcement; punishment; modeling, and extinction.

Adlerian Groups

Adlerian groups focus on exploring life-styles of members since the underlying premise is that behavior takes place in a social context: behavior exists as the process of individuals interacting with each other. The constancy of members' life-styles and the alternatives confronting them affect whether their behaviors change across the life span. Thus, the focus of Adlerian groups is on *becoming*, which is accomplished through striving for mastery and superiority in self-selected goals.

The group leader's role is to help members recognize that through self-determinism they have choices about goals that they can pursue. Members are encouraged to accept full responsibility for the life style they have chosen and any subsequent changes they wish to make. This involves helping members recognize their strengths and their power to change, as well as uncovering suppressed feelings associated with past events that are affecting present behaviors.

ETHICAL AND LEGAL ISSUES

All ethical and legal issues that apply to the profession of counseling, in general, are relevant to group counseling. Yet, some issues exist that are unique to group work. These are outlined in the following material:

1. Because of the involvement of multiple clients, the opportunity for confidentiality to be broken is increased. That is, members within the group may not honor the confidentiality code as it applies to the group setting.

2. In establishing a group, potential members need to be provided sufficient and relevant information so that they can make informed decisions about participating in the group. Included should be information concerning the group's purpose and goals, length and duration of sessions, services that can and cannot be included, the leader's qualifications, and procedures that will be followed.

3. In addition to the group leader's qualifications and experience, a group's success is dependent upon the contributions of its members. Therefore, potential members need to be screened in an attempt to determine whether they will contribute to the group's purpose and goals. Sometimes, a group member can have a detrimental effect upon the group and thus limit its effectiveness. Therefore, identifying, prior to the group's establishment, potential members who might be counterproductive to a group is essential.

4. If a potential member has been receiving services from another mental-health provider, that professional needs to be informed of the potential member's plans to participate in the group.

SUMMARY

As a result of being able to meet a greater number of clients' needs, the use of group counseling has increased significantly in recent years. However, because it has developed as an extension of individual counseling, a variety of group counseling models are being employed. Several of these have been presented as well as the various components that need to be considered when establishing a group. The chapter has concluded with ethical and legal issues that are relevant to group counseling.

Chapter **13**

CAREER DEVELOPMENT
AND COUNSELING

All animal species on earth engage in "work." In the so-called lower order animal species, work is almost exclusively associated with the gathering and/or cultivation of food and the development and maintenance of protective habitats. Work in those contexts is physiologically and biologically necessary for the continued existence of the respective species. The same is of course true for human beings; they must work to have the food and shelter necessary for continued life. However, an additional psychosocial dynamic is associated with work for humans. Among people in most societies of the world, work has value and meaning beyond fulfillment of subsistence needs; it has potential to fulfill psychological and social needs as well. Indeed, concern about and attention to this uniquely human psychosocial aspect of work are the bases of large portions of human social, economic, political, educational, and legal systems. Particularly pertinent here is that these needs are the basis for a large portion of mental health. That is, for most people in most societies, the nature of a person's work is integrally related to what the person *is*.

Attention to work as an important part of the human experience not only spurred the beginning of the counseling profession (as discussed in Part I) but also remains a major focus in counseling. The historical antecedents within the counseling profession, in combination with preeminent values attributed to work in contemporary society, have prompted counseling theorists, researchers, and practitioners to explore thoroughly the nature of work, its roles and functions in the human condition, and, most importantly, ways for people to find and attain the work that is best-suited to and most satisfying for them. For example, Peterson, Sampson, and Reardon (1991) identified four "lines of inquiry" that have been focused upon in the development of career counseling, including ways of helping individuals to (1) acquire self-knowledge; (2) become knowledgeable of the world of work; (3) relate interests, abilities, and values to occupations; and (4) integrate self and occupational knowledge.

These types of activities are likely to continue. For example, Gysbers (1984) identified four major trends in understandings of career development and, therefore, of career counseling. Summarized, they are as follows:

1. The meanings given to career and career development continue to evolve from simply new words for vocation (occupation) and vocational (occupational) development to words that describe composite human work experiences (careers) in terms of life roles, life settings, and life events that develop over the life span.

2. Substantial changes continue to occur in the economic, occupational, industrial, and social environments and structures in which the human career develops and interacts and in which career guidance, education, and counseling takes place.

3. The number, diversity, and quality of career development programs, tools, and techniques continue to increase rapidly.

4. The populations served by career development programming and the settings in which career development programs and services take place also continue to increase rapidly.

One of the by-products of the attention given to work and its place in the human condition has been the generation of a subset vocabulary within the counseling profession. Therefore, some of these terms must be clarified before the career development and counseling activities of professional counselors can be discussed further.

The world of work may be configured along a system of levels. For example, a *position*, or placement, may be defined as a set of tasks performed by one person in a workplace, whereas a *job* is a set of similar positions in the workplace or, more generally, a set of identifiable and specific functions for which a person is paid. Because essentially similar jobs are performed by different people in different settings, an *occupation* may be defined as similar jobs found in different work settings (Herr & Cramer, 1988). The term *vocation* is often used as synonymous with occupation, but sometimes implies a psychological commitment to the occupation as well. Relatedly, because individuals usually have more than one occupation in the course of their lives, the term *career* may be defined as a lifelong sequence of occupations.

Some authorities view the definition of career as "a series of occupations" as too restrictive and therefore have broadened the definition. For example, Zunker (1986) wrote that, "Career is not only used to indicate the activities and positions involved in vocations, occupations, and jobs, but also includes related activities associated with an individual's lifetime of work" (p. 3). In a now considered classic conceptualization of career development, Super (1976) defined the concept of career as follows:

> The course of events which constitutes a life; the sequence of occupations and other life roles which combine to express one's commitment to work in his or her total pattern of self-development; the series of remunerated and non-remunerated positions occupied by a person from adolescence through retirement, of which occupation is only one; includes work-related roles such as those of student, employee, and

pensioner together with complementary avocational, familial, and civic roles. (p. 4)

Super's definition of career is noteworthy in several regards. For one, it suggests the centrality of work in people's lives and therefore reflects values typically held in society. For another, it conveys the diversity and complexity among the many life factors associated with work. One of the factors which has recently received more attention is leisure. Herr and Cramer (1988), citing Super (1976), used the term *avocational* (in place of the term leisure) to refer to "an activity pursued systematically and consecutively for its own sake with an objective other than monetary gain, although it may incidentally result in gain" (p. 17). The term avocational also reflects the centrality of work in peoples' lives and therefore has been favored by some career development theorists. However, some authors (e.g., Bloland & Edwards, 1981; McDaniels, 1984) have proposed that leisure exists apart from work and, therefore, that the term leisure is preferable over avocational. This perspective also is reflected in not-related-to-work definitions of leisure, such as one by Loesch and Wheeler (1982) who defined it as, "Any activity an individual knowingly (i.e., consciously) chooses to define as leisure" (p. 36) or one by Neulinger (1974) who stated that "any activity carried out freely, without constraint or compulsion, may be considered to be leisure" (p. 15). In any event, regardless of the term used, leisure is now viewed as an integral component of the term career (McDaniels, 1984).

In attempting to help people achieve success in jobs, occupations, and careers for which they are best suited and which will be most meaningful for them, professional counselors are concerned with facilitating individuals' *career development* (used here as synonymous with occupational or vocational development). Peterson, Sampson, and Reardon (1991) defined career development as, "the implementation of a series of interrelated career decisions that collectively provide a guiding purpose or direction in one's life" (p. 21). Herr and Cramer (1988) defined career development as "the total constellation of psychological, sociological, educational, physical, economic, and chance factors that combine to shape the career of any given individual . . ." (p. 16). These definitions emphasize both the complexity and enormity of the task with which counselors must contend; facilitating career development amounts to life counseling.

Professional counselors' career development facilitation activities primarily consist of fostering the development of one major characteristic or trait (i.e., career maturity) and two major skills (i.e., decision making and career management) in their clients. The characteristic, career (or vocational) maturity, may be viewed as a developmental, multidimensional construct. Peterson, Otten, Burck, and Loughead (1989) defined *career maturity* as the ability to make independent and responsible career decisions based on integration of knowledge of self and the world of work. Super (1957) presented a widely accepted set of components, or dimensions, of vocational (career) maturity, including (1) orientation toward work (attitudinal dimension), (2) planning success (competency dimension), (3) consistency of vocational preferences (consistency dimension), and (4) wisdom of vocational preferences (realistic dimension).

The first skill area, *decision-making*, encompasses problem solving, which is defined as the thinking process in which information about a problem is used to determine a course of action, as well as affective and other cognitive processes that allow a chosen solution to be transformed into action (Peterson, Sampson, & Reardon, 1991). The second skill area, *career management*, was defined by Herr and Cramer (1988) as, "The personal state of actively and consciously participating in shaping one's career and accepting responsibility for the activities and choices made toward those ends" (p. 17). Taken collectively, the greater the extent to which an individual develops this characteristic and these skills, the greater the likelihood that the individual will achieve an appropriate and satisfying career.

Several terms have been used to provide descriptions of professional counselors' career-development facilitation activities. The broadest term used is *career guidance*, which was defined by Herr and Cramer (1988) as, "A systematic program of counselor-coordinated information and experiences designed to facilitate individual career development and, more specifically, career management . . . " (p. 18). The general set of activities that fall under the rubric of career guidance is typically subdivided into the categories career education and career counseling. As generally conceived, *career education* involves integrating career development concepts and activities into educational curricula or other structured learning activities. Toward that end, Peterson, Sampson, and Reardon (1991) noted that, "Career education represents an ambitious effort to utilize a systems approach to facilitate change in public policies, educational institutions, public service agencies, and communities" (p. 192). Typically, the primary purpose and focus of career education is the organized and systematic provision of information about various aspects of the world of work so that individuals can make informed and therefore, theoretically, intelligent job, occupation, and career choices.

Career counseling often includes the provision of information but extends beyond career education in the attempt to help individuals use and act upon the information provided. For example, Healy (1982) stated:

> Career counseling is specialized counseling focused on career implementation and planning. The career counselor helps a client to generate and use personal and career information, to obtain and to interpret experiences relevant to careers, to set goals and to solve problems, and to evaluate progress. (p. 173)

The NCDA Professional Standards Committee (1992) provided a comprehensive perspective:

> . . . career counseling is defined as counseling individuals or groups of individuals about occupations, careers, life/career roles and responsibilities, career decision making, career planning, leisure planning, career "pathing", and other career development activities (e.g., resume preparation, interviewing and job search techniques) . . . . (p. 378)

Both career education and career counseling will be discussed at greater length later in this chapter. However, before either of them can be fully understood, the major theoretical perspectives underlying career development used in the counseling profession must be addressed.

THEORIES OF CAREER DEVELOPMENT
AND COUNSELING

Herr (1986) summarized the purposes of and alluded to the diversities among theories of career development:

> The theory and speculation encompassed by the term career development (used interchangeably with the earlier term vocational development) includes a variety of emphases and approaches. In general, these approaches attempt to describe why career behavior is different among individuals, how it comes to be that way, and the importance of such behavior in people's lives. (p. 175)

Other authors (e.g., Osipow, 1983; Sharf, 1992; Whiteley & Resnikoff, 1978) generally agree with the purposes stated by Herr. Clearly the different theories of career development have different implications for career counseling. However, there is a commonality among them. McDaniels and Gysbers (1992) indicated:

> . . . career theories provide the foundation knowledge from which counselors draw useful concepts to explain client behavior. They offer a framework within which client behaviors can be examined and hypotheses formed about the possible meanings of that behavior. (pp. 27-28)

Perspectives on career development theories vary considerably. For example, Herr (1986) described six different systems just for classifying theories of career development. All of these systems have their respective merits and limitations. Therefore, selection of a classification system is primarily a matter of personal preference, and no one classification system is necessarily better than another. Presented following are some illustrative examples of approaches to career development (and counseling) in a classification system useful for purposes here.

Trait-and-Factor or Matching Approach

Osipow (1983) presented a simplified and historical perspective on this approach to career counseling when he wrote:

The oldest theoretical approach has been known by a variety of names, most commonly by the name of the trait-and-factor approach. This system assumes that a straightforward matching of an individual's abilities and interests with the world's vocational opportunities can be accomplished and once accomplished, solves the problems of vocational choice for that individual. (p. 9)

Attributed primarily to Williamson (1939), the basic purpose of the trait-and-factor approach to career counseling is to "match" the characteristics of a client to jobs which require those characteristics and, in so doing, identify the jobs which are, theoretically, most appropriate for that client. The "trait" portion of the trait-and-factor approach refers to client characteristics; in order to use this approach effectively, counselors must have extensive and valid information about their clients' characteristics. The "factor" portion refers to characteristics of various jobs; in order to use this approach effectively counselors also must have extensive knowledge of the world of work and the requirements for specific jobs and/or occupations. Accordingly, trait-and-factor career counseling has been referred to colloquially as the "know the client, know the job" approach.

A significant question within this approach is what information about clients needs to be known by professional counselors? Herr and Cramer (1988) have identified ten major types of client attribute information usually sought by professional counselors, paraphrased here as follows:

1. **Abilities**--clients' general intelligence and specific aptitudes. Cognitive abilities are important to the types of work clients are able to perform, the education and/or training for which they are eligible and in which they are likely to succeed, and their potential levels of success and attainment in various occupations.

2. **Needs and Interests**--clients' psychological needs and vocational interests. Psychological needs are important in that appropriate work must fulfill some, and probably many, of clients' needs. Similarly, clients are not likely to find their work attractive, enjoyable,

and satisfying if their jobs are not consistent with their vocational interests.

3. **Stereotypes and Expectations**--clients' perceptions of the natures of particular jobs and occupations. Clients often act upon stereotypic perceptions and expectations about jobs regardless of the accuracy of their perceptions and expectations (unless presented with information which "corrects" their perceptions and expectations).

4. **Significant Others**--people in clients' lives who are viewed as important and valued and/or who serve as role models. Clients' significant others potentially have strong influences on clients' training, occupational choices, and career aspirations.

5. **Values**--clients' internalized beliefs about the worth of various aspects of life in general, and work in particular. Clients' values also are potentially strong influences on their occupational choices and aspirations.

6. **Residence**--clients' living situations and life-styles. The realm of clients' environments, life-styles, and experiences in part determines their educational and occupational possibilities and their perceptions of the world of work.

7. **Family**--persons perceived as closely related to a client. Family members typically exert strong influences on clients' values, life-styles, experiences, and personal characteristics, and therefore on the courses of their careers.

8. **Adjustment**--clients' levels of adaptation in the world. Clients who are not personally well-adjusted in the world are not able to make effective work-related decisions or to perform occupational activities effectively.

9. **Risk-taking**--clients' abilities and desires to engage in probability-based decision-making. Clients' risk-taking abilities are influential in determining career opportunities potentially available to them.

10. **Aspirations**--clients' vocational and personal goals. Aspirations are viewed as primary determinants of clients' achievement and success motivations.

This list is extensive, but not exhaustive. However, it does illustrate the comprehensiveness of the information sought within this approach.

In order to obtain efficiently and effectively the desired comprehensive information about clients, professional counselors using the trait-and-factor approach to career counseling use tests and inventories extensively. Historically, the relatively early development of trait-and-factor career counseling was a primary impetus for the development and use of tests throughout the counseling profession. Tests and inventories that have been developed are typically subdivided into five general categories: intelligence, aptitude, achievement, personality, and interest. "Purist" trait-and-factor career counselors use tests or inventories from each of these categories in their career-counseling activities. More typically, however, professional counselors following this approach only use tests or inventories to obtain information which cannot be obtained expeditiously from other sources (e.g., the client, academic or employment records, or counselor observation).

A second significant question within this approach is what information about jobs needs to be known by counselors? Responses to this question have resulted in a plethora of job/occupation/career information systems and of activities related to the use of these systems, some of which will be discussed later in this chapter. In general, these systems at least provide information on the activities specific to a job, preparation and/or training necessary for entry to the job, the "nature" of the work involved (e.g., levels of involvement with data, people, or things), and future trends and possibilities in the career of which the job is a part. More sophisticated systems provide information about characteristics and abilities of people who have been successful in and are satisfied with the job and suggest methods for determining suitability for the job. Sharf (1992) identified three aspects of occupational information to be considered for use within the context of trait-and-factor career counseling: (1) type of information (e.g., description of work functions, conditions, and salary), (2) classification system (i.e., how is the information organized), and (3) occupational requirements (e.g., what are the characteristics and attributes of persons in the occupations). The provision of occupational information within the context of trait-and-factor career counseling is viewed as essential not only to the client's understanding of the world of work but also to the counseling process itself.

The trait-and-factor approach to career counseling in the manner proposed by Williamson and others is not particularly popular among counselors today. This decline in popularity is attributable to widely held perceptions that trait-and-factor career counseling is based on a static model of career choice, too directive, overly dependent on test data, and difficult to use because of the increasing complexities of the world of work, occupational information systems, and society. However, Chartrand (1991) poignantly argued that these stereotypic perceptions of trait-and-factor counseling are ill-founded, ill-conceived, and generally erroneous. She explained that trait-and-factor career counseling is now more accurately characterized as a dynamic process of attempting to achieve a person-by-environment (P x E) fit. Acknowledged within this newer conceptualization is that congruence between personal characteristics, including cognitive, behavioral, and affective attributes, and environmental characteristics must be achieved before trait-and-factor career counseling is successful. Thus while many of the components from previous conceptualizations of trait-and-factor career counseling have been retained, far greater attention is given to human and environmental congruence and, therefore, to human sensitivities in the P x E trait-and-factor approach to career counseling. Perhaps this newer conceptualization will improve professional counselors' receptivity to trait-and-factor career counseling.

Decision Approaches

In contrast to the trait-and-factor approach, decision approaches to career development and counseling focus on the process of how career-related decisions are made. The major supposition in these approaches is that people will have effective career development only if they are able to make decisions efficiently. Two fundamental assumptions underlay this supposition. The first is that people strive to *maximize gains and minimize losses* through the work-related decisions they make. In this context, gains and losses are not necessarily monetary; they may be in terms of life-style, success, prestige, happiness, security, or any of a variety of other psychosocial and environmental factors or conditions. The second assumption is that at any choice-point, people have several *alternatives* available to them. One alternative is, of course, to "do nothing." Another is to "do something," and this assumption holds that several "somethings" always can be done. In a broad sense, then, the purposes of decision approaches to career counseling are to help people to (1) understand their own decision-making styles, (2) identify choice-points and options, and (3) enhance their decision-making skills and abilities.

Sharf (1992) indicated:

> Although there are many approaches to career decision-making, the models or theories can be divided into two categories: descriptive and prescriptive. Descriptive theories are ones that describe or explain the choices that an individual makes when deciding upon a career or some aspect of a career. In contrast, prescriptive decision-making theories focus upon an ideal approach to decision making. (p. 302)

Although both descriptive and prescriptive career decision-making theories are presented in the professional literature, the former are far more common, primarily because they are more in concert with the "realities" of counseling. Therefore, only descriptive theories are presented here.

Herr (1986) noted that three major personal factors are relative to an individual's decision-making behaviors. The first is **risk-taking style**: the degree to which an individual is willing to live with ambiguity and uncertainty of outcomes. The second is **investment**: the monetary and/or psychosocial "capital" the person uses to either create a choice or enhance the probability of the success of a choice. The third is **personal values**: the things, ideas, and perspectives the individual identifies as having personal worth. Each of these factors needs to be considered individually and collectively in order for individuals to make work-related decisions effectively (Herr & Cramer, 1988).

Two major theoretical perspectives underlay decision approaches. The first is **expectancy theory**, which has as its basic premise that "motivational force" is a product of expectancy multiplied by value. Any specific decision-making event involves consideration of a combination of the individual's perception of personal capability to achieve the potential outcome and the value the individual attributes to the outcome. Thus, expectancy theory holds that a person makes a decision toward an outcome the person believes can be achieved and which the person values. Career counseling based on this theory therefore incorporates, in part, clarification of the client's (typically self-perceived) capabilities and values.

The second major perspective is **self-efficacy theory.** Bandura (1977) proposed that an individual makes decisions primarily on the basis of the belief that a specific behavior can be performed; that is, that the individual can be self-efficacious. The level and strength of the person's belief determine whether a specific behavior will be initiated as well as the amount and duration of effort that will be expended in the behavior. Expectations about behavioral self-efficacy are derived from four sources: personal accomplishments, vicarious experiences, emotional arousal, and verbal persuasion. Thus, many career counseling approaches use this theory to incorporate examination of the client's previous experiences and feelings about various aspects of work, and "persuade" the client to consider various alternatives.

A considerable number of "decision-making paradigms" presented for use in the context of career counseling have been developed from these two theoretical perspectives, and most of them approximate conceptualizations of "scientific analysis." For example, Bergland (1974) stated that career-related decision making involves (1) defining the problem, (2) generating alternatives, (3) gathering information, (4) processing information, (5) identifying goals and making plans, and (6) implementing and evaluating activities. Relatedly, Pitz and Harren (1980) stated that any decision problem can be examined in terms of four sets of elements: *objectives* sought, available *choices*, possible *outcomes*, and *attributes* of the outcomes. More recently, Peterson, Sampson, and Reardon (1991) related an information processing paradigm to career decision-making, including the following components:

1. Information is received which signals that a problem exists. One then queries oneself and the world to locate the gap [i.e., difference between existing and ideal states of affairs] that is the problem. (*communication*)

2. The causes of the problem are identified and the relationships among them are placed in a conceptual framework. (*analysis*)

3. Possible courses of action are formulated. (*synthesis*)

4. Each course of action is prioritized according to its likelihood of success or failure and its probable impact on self or others. (*valuing*)

5. Once a course of action has been selected, a strategy is formulated to carry it out. (*execution*) (p. 28)

The CASVE model, as well as others, synthesizes the components of decision-making into an "action" plan for career counseling.

Gelatt (1962, 1989) proposed a decision-making paradigm for career counseling which contains three major components: prediction system, value system, and decision system. Accurate and timely information is essential for Gelatt's approach (Osipow, 1983). For example, the **prediction system** requires information about choice alternatives, possible outcomes, and their associated probabilities; the **valuing system** requires information about relative strengths of preferences; and the **decision system** requires information about rules used in decision-making processes. An interesting formulation within Gelatt's (1962) approach was that decisions made could be viewed (by the client) as either final (i.e., terminal) or investigatory (i.e., allowing for decisions to be made so that additional information can be obtained upon which to make subsequent and presumably final decisions). More recently, Gelatt (1989) adopted the term *positive uncertainty* to characterize this tentativeness. Thus, a key feature of Gelatt's model is allowance for uniquely human idiosyncracies in decision making. Gelatt's paradigm represents a cognitive approach because of the focus on cognitive information. However, the approach allows for, and in fact typically includes, the use of both objective and subjective information.

Krumboltz, Mitchell, and Jones (1978) and Mitchell and Krumboltz (1990) presented an approach to career counseling based on social learning theory. They suggested that four sets of factors are most influential in work-related decision-making: (1) *genetic endowment and special abilities*, including gender, ethnicity, physical limitations, intelligence, and specific aptitudes; (2) *environmental conditions and events,* including job and training opportunities, social policies, labor market conditions, and technological events; (3) *learning experiences*, including instrumental learning (e.g., experiential learning or participation in formal educational experiences) and associative learning (e.g., observational or vicarious learning); and (4) *task-approach skills*, including work habits, mental sets, perceptual and cognitive processes, and personal performance standards and values. They also suggested that three categories of outcomes are possible from the interaction(s) of the four types of influencing factors: (1) *self-observation generalizations*, including evaluation of similarities and differences between self and others; (2) *world-view generalizations*, including projections of self in different psychological, social, and physical environments; (3) *task-approach skills*, including cognitive and performance abilities and predispositions for coping with future environments and conditions. Career counseling under this theory is comprehensive because it includes wide-spread information gathering (vis-a-vis direct and vicarious learning), extensive analysis of information obtained, and projections of outcomes.

Although some authors (e.g., Herr & Cramer, 1988) classify Tiedeman and O'Hara's (1963) career counseling model as a developmental approach, most authors view it as decision-making paradigm. Tiedeman and O'Hara's approach focuses upon the intersection of processes for the anticipation of occupational choices and adjusting to a choice. The anticipation process includes the *exploration, crystallization, choice,* and *clarification phases,* wherein occupational alternatives are identified and explored. The adjusting to a choice process includes *induction, reformation,* and *integration phases,* wherein the individual develops an understanding of the occupation chosen within both personal and social contexts. Although the anticipation and adjusting processes are sequential, the respective phases within them are not always sequential; thus the focus is on decision-making rather than stage progression (Sharf, 1992).

Tiedeman and O'Hara (1963) also proposed that career development is a continuing process of differentiating ego identity, and used Erikson's (1963) model of psychosocial crises at seven developmental stages as a means to explain differences in career development. They also stressed the interaction of the self-concept with the concept of career as both develop over time. Later, Peatling and Tiedeman (1977) emphasized the individual's *competence, autonomy,* and *agency* as major factors in the career development process. In brief, this approach holds that career development "... grows out of a continuously differentiating and reintegrating ego identity as it forms and reforms from experience as a self-organizing system" (Miller-Tiedeman & Tiedeman, 1990).

In recent years, Miller-Tiedeman and Tiedeman (1990) have reformulated Tiedeman and O'Hara's (1963) conceptualizations into what they refer to as the *individualistic perspective* (Sharf, 1992). While retaining most of Tiedeman and O'Hara's original premises and constructs, their individualistic perspective incorporates greater attention to ego development and valuing in the career development process (Sharf, 1992). Miller-Tiedeman and Tiedeman (1990) noted:

> Our approach to career decision making is a response to the need we perceive to expand the horizons of previously

mapped dimensions of career development. In past years, career theorists have presented theories of how individuals end up in particular occupations, jobs, or careers. But career theorists have often neglected the essence of the individual's life processes in career development, particularly those of growth, choice, willingness and capacity to adapt and change, and continued self-exploration and self-renewal. (p. 308)

Thus, Miller-Tiedeman and Tiedeman's individualistic perspective at least philosophically purports to address a wide variety of human characteristics to explain career development.

Peterson, Sampson, and Reardon (1991) presented a *cognitive information processing* (CIP) approach to career development based on the CASVE process described previously. They listed 10 assumptions underlying the CIP paradigm:

1. Career choice results from an interaction of cognitive and affective processes.
2. Making career choices is a problem-solving activity.
3. The capabilities of career problem solvers depend on the availability of cognitive operations as well as knowledge.
4. Career problem solving is a high-memory-load task.
5. Motivation (must be present for career development).
6. Career development involves continual growth and change in knowledge structures.
7. Career identity depends on self-knowledge.
8. Career maturity depends on one's ability to solve career problems.
9. The ultimate goal of career counseling is achieved by facilitating the growth of information processing skills.
10. The ultimate aim of career counseling is to enhance the client's capabilities as a career problem solver and decision maker. (pp. 8-9)

The CIP model incorporates many constructs and concepts from other career development theories but couches them in an information processing perspective. Thus the CIP model is in essence a reframing of established career development ideas into a newer paradigm. The advantage of the CIP model is that it is consistent with much of what counselors do in many other types of counseling; to wit, help clients think about things in new, presumably more effective, ways.

Sociological/Economic Approaches

Sociological, sometimes called situational, approaches to career development and counseling evolved from the belief that other, primarily psychological, approaches placed too little emphasis on the context in which career development takes place. Herr (1986) stated:

> Situational or sociological approaches to career development accentuate the reality that one's environment both provides the kinds of choices from which one can choose and also shapes the likelihood that persons holding membership in different groups are likely to make certain choices and not others. A sociological or situational view of career development suggests that the narrowness or the breadth of the individual's cultural or social class boundaries has much to do with the choices the person is likely to consider, make, or implement. (p. 182)

Relatedly, Osipow (1983) observed:

> The sociological approach is fundamentally based on the notion that elements beyond the individual's control exert a major influence on the course of life, including educational and vocational decisions. Supporters of this view suggest that the degree of freedom of occupational choice a person has is far less than might at first be assumed and that one's self-expectations are not independent of the society's expectations. (p. 225)

In general, psychological career-development models presume that individuals have considerable control over their own lives, particularly in regard to impacting their own career developments. Comparatively, sociological/economic career-development models presume that life circumstances have much impact on individuals' lives and, therefore, individuals can control directions of their lives only to certain extents.

Given that sociological/economic factors influence individuals' career developments, the question becomes which factors are most important and therefore merit the most attention? Unfortunately, a simple answer to this question is unavailable, and, in fact, a multitude of factors have been suggested as being important. However, only a few of them can be briefly discussed here.

Culture and social class boundaries have been identified as major, usually restricting, factors in career development (Fredrickson, 1982). In general, although career progression is generally viewed as a primary means to "rise above one's station in life," such progression is not always easily achieved, particularly for those in lower socioeconomic strata (Sharf, 1992). The extant conditions in those strata often inhibit and obstruct career upward mobility because of limited economic and other resources, de-emphasis on education and training, conflicting values, and lack of role models.

Chance is viewed as a significant factor in career development within sociological/economic perspectives on career development (but not in traditional psychological perspectives). Bandura (1982) described two major classifications of chance encounters affecting career development. The first is an individual's chance encounters with people who directly or indirectly exert strong subsequent influence on the individual's career-related decisions. The second is chance encounters with events: those happenings to which an individual is "accidently" exposed which subsequently influence the individual's career-related decisions. Chance encounters are viewed as significant components of career development because of the roles they may play in changing, either positively or negatively, an individual's career motivations and aspirations (Bandura, 1982). Cabral and Salamone (1990) noted that the individual's level of self-concept and sense of internal locus of control are important determinants of how an individual copes with chance encounters relevant to career development.

Social structures are an important factor in career development, primarily because of the influences they exert on individuals' personality development. Because humans tend to be adaptive, they are responsive to the social structures in which they are enmeshed. When their social structures change, their personalities attempt to adapt to the changes. Regardless of the outcome of the attempt at adaptation, the change itself affects the individual's personality and, therefore, affects the individual's existing career-development pattern.

Only three sociological/economic theories of career development have received much attention in the counseling literature (Sharf, 1992). ***Accident theory*** holds that much of career development is the result of either positive or negative "accidents" (i.e., chance encounters). For example, an adolescent's career development might be changed significantly, either positively or negatively, by an "accidental" encounter with a particular secondary school teacher or counselor. ***Status attainment theory*** takes into account the roles of social status and achievement in explanation of an individual's career development. For example, an child's current family social status is a good predictor of a child's eventual social status (including a status-appropriate career), unless the child has status-inappropriate higher or lower achievement motivation. ***Human capital theory*** holds that individuals invest in their own education and training so that they can achieve the highest possible lifetime earnings.

Sociological or situational approaches to career development are significant because they identify many factors not usually considered in "narrower" (i.e., psychological) approaches. However, because of the complexities and expansiveness of the concepts and factors involved in sociological/economic approaches, career counseling based on such approaches are much less defined or distinct. Typically, professional counselors incorporate sociological/economic considerations into other career development and counseling approaches.

Personality Approaches

Approaches to career counseling and development in this category are distinctive in that they focus almost exclusively on an individual's personal characteristics and give little attention to external factors such as job characteristics or sociological/ economic conditions. Moreover, whereas the trait-and-factor approaches tends to focus on relatively easily-identifiable traits and abilities, personality approaches often involve "inferred" characteristics. Thus, personality approaches to career development and counseling are closely aligned with (aspects of) theories of personality and attempt to relate those theories to occupational and career development behavior.

Freud's psychoanalytic theory has served as the basis for some approaches. Osipow (1983) stated that "The most ambitious scheme for defining the process of career development within the psychoanalytic framework and with the appropriate language was proposed by Bordin, Nachmann, and Segal (1963)" (p. 42). They constructed a theoretical framework for career development based on a set of eight propositions:

1. Human development is continuous; early (i.e., in infancy) psychological and physiological activities are associated with those in adult life.

2. Sources of gratification are the same for children and adults; only the form of gratification differs.

3. The individual's pattern of needs develops early in life, usually during the first six years.

4. The occupation sought is related to the individual's needs.

5. The theory applies to all types of people and work, except where external (e.g., cultural or financial) factors preclude its application.

6. Work may be conceived of as the sublimation of infantile impulses into socially acceptable forms.

7. Either emotional blocking or a severe lack of information can inhibit fulfillment of occupational expectations.

8. A number of psychic dimensions and/or body zones can be gratified in any job.

According to Bordin et al., the eighth proposition covers the following psychoanalytic dimensions: (1) **nurturant,** including feeling and fostering; (2) **oral aggressive,** including cutting, biting, and devouring; (3) **manipulative,** including physical and psychological control; (4) **sensual,** including sight, sound, and touch; (5) **anal,** including acquiring and time-ordering; (6) **genital,** including erection, penetration, impregnation, and producing; (7) **exploration;** (8) **flowing and quenching;** (9) **exhibiting;** and (10) **rhythmic movement.**

More recently, Bordin (1990) updated his conceptualizations, including acknowledgement of the importance of play in people's lives in general and their career developments in particular. Bordin also presented seven newer propositions underlying his theory:

1. This sense of wholeness [achieved through play], this experience of joy, is sought by all persons, preferably in all aspects of life, including work.

2. The degree of fusion of work and play is a function of an individual's developmental history regarding compulsion and effort.

3. A person's life can be seen as a string of career decisions reflecting an individual's groping for an ideal fit between self and work.

4. The most useful system of mapping occupations for intrinsic motives will be one that captures life-styles or character styles and simulates or is receptive to developmental conceptions.

5. The roots of the personal aspects of career development are to be found throughout the early development of the individual, sometimes in the earliest years.

6. Each individual seeks to build a personal identity that incorporates aspects of father and mother yet retains elements unique to the self.

7. One source of perplexity and paralysis at career decision points will be found in doubts in and dissatisfactions with current resolutions of self. (p. 105 ff)

Bordin and others have presented some research to support the notion that these propositions can be used to explain career behavior. However, the psychoanalytic approach to career development has not been employed extensively for several reasons. First, psychoanalytic personality theory has not been widely used in the counseling profession, and it follows that a career counseling approach based on it also would not be widely used. Second, this approach implies use of psychoanalytic interviewing techniques, which are typically too time consuming for effective use by most professional counselors. Finally, the measurement of important constructs and dynamics in the approach is at best difficult and therefore not suited to the circumstances of most professional counselors.

A more popular personality approach to career development is the one developed by Roe (1956). Her approach involves a synthesis of several perspectives on personality. One of the primary ones involved is Maslow's (1954) theory of prepotent needs. Maslow proposed that human needs may be arranged in a hierarchy of low-order to high-order needs:

1. Physiological.
2. Safety.
3. Belongingness and love.
4. Self-esteem, respect, and independence.
5. Information.
6. Understanding.
7. Beauty.
8. Self-actualization.

According to Maslow, people must fulfill lower-order needs (e.g., physiological or safety) before they can strive to fulfill higher-order needs (e.g., self-actualization). Roe used Maslow's conceptualizations to suggest that, in general, vocational behavior is the individual's attempt to fulfill certain needs and that the particular level of needs for which gratification is sought, in part, determines the nature of the behaviors used.

Roe emphasized the importance of using the child-rearing practices to which the individual had been exposed to help explain the individual's vocational behaviors. She described three general types of child-rearing practices. The first, *emotional concentration on the child*, includes the extremes of overprotection and overdemand on the child. Children reared under these conditions tend to have their lower-order physiological and safety needs met relatively quickly but not their higher-order needs such as those for belongingness, love, and self-esteem. Therefore, the prediction would be that they would seek fulfillment of these needs through their occupations. The second type is *avoidance of the child.* The supposition in this condition is that neither the physiological nor emotional needs of children raised under these conditions are fulfilled, and therefore individuals seek "things" and limited contact with other persons in their occupation. The third type, *acceptance of the child,* involves the child being accepted as an integral part of a "democratic" family unit, wherein many of the child's needs are met. Therefore, an individual raised in this condition would seek fulfillment of the highest needs in an occupation.

A third major component in Roe's approach is attention to *genetic endowments.* In general, Roe suggested that genetic endowments, such as intelligence or physical ability, are mitigating factors in the manifestations of previous child-rearing practices and need fulfillment behaviors. That is, the specific vocational behaviors exhibited by an individual are influenced by the individual's genetic endowments. Roe noted that sociological/economic factors, interests, and attitudes influenced career-related decisions, but that genetic endowment could be used to overcome these factors (Sharf, 1992).

Roe (1956) developed a "fields and levels" occupational classification scheme to facilitate understanding of her approach. In her schema, the *fields* are classified by interest and the primary focus of the occupations while the *levels* are classified by degrees of responsibility, capacity, and skill. The fields identified by Roe are (I) Service, (II) Business Contact, (III) Organizations, (IV) Technology, (V) Outdoor, (VI) Science, (VII) General Culture, and (VIII) Arts and Entertainment. The levels identified are (1) Professional and Managerial, higher, (2) Professional and Managerial, regular, (3) Semiprofessional and Small Business, (4) Skilled, (5) Semiskilled, and (6) Unskilled. When these fields and levels are configured as a eight-by-six matrix, any occupation (theoretically) can be placed in a cell representing the appropriate combination. More commonly, however, Roe's career development conceptualization is presented as a set of concentric circles where sectors represent the fields and the "rings" represent the levels.

Osipow (1983), in reviewing Roe's approach, commented that "The theory attends to every important aspect of vocational selection" (p. 19). Yet while the theoretical base of her approach is well-developed, career counseling methods derived from it are not widely used by counselors. This is perhaps because of the difficulties in gathering some of the needed information (e.g., that pertaining to early child-rearing practices and their effects) but more likely because Holland's approach has become so popular among counselors that all other personality approaches have been overshadowed.

The basic premise of Holland's (1966, 1973, 1985) approach to career development and counseling is that an individual is the product of heredity and environment; thus, career choice and adjustment are an extension of personality (Sharf, 1992). In general, early genetic endowments develop under the influences of various environmental factors such that an individual develops preferred modes and methods for coping and dealing with social and environmental tasks. The most typical way a person responds to his or her environment is known as the person's **modal personal orientation.** Holland proposed six general classifications of modal personal orientations (i.e., personality types): **realistic, investigative, artistic, social, enterprising,** and **conventional.** Holland further proposed that these same six classifications are appropriate for characterizing work environments. In Holland's view, people search for those work environments that allow them to use their skills and abilities and to express their attitudes and values, and that contain agreeable tasks and problems—in other words, that "match" their personality types. Accordingly, vocational behavior is a result of the interaction between the personality and environmental characteristics, and "effective" career development is the result of an effective matching of personality and environmental characteristics. Because Holland described personality characteristics and work environments in the same terms, he emphasized a perspective that has a long history in society in general and in the counseling profession in particular: specifically, that "work is a way of life."

Because of the centrality of the personal orientation/work environment classification system in Holland's theory, the categories are summarized here.

Realistic—activities that require explicit, ordered, or systematic manipulation of objects, tools, machines, or animals, and that reflect aversion to education or therapy.

Investigative—activities that involve observational, symbolic, systematic, and creative investigation of biological, physical, and cultural phenomena toward the goal of understanding and control, and that reflect an aversion to socializing, repetitiveness, or persuasion.

Artistic—activities that are ambiguous, imaginative, free, and unsystematic toward the manipulation of physical, verbal, or human material to create art forms and products and that reflect an aversion to explicit, systematic, and organized experiences.

Social—activities that involve manipulation of others to inform, train, develop, cure, or enlighten and that reflect an aversion to ordered and systematic use of machines, tools, or materials.

Enterprising—activities that require manipulation of others to achieve monetary gain or organizational goals and that reflect an aversion to observational, symbolic, or systematic experiences.

Conventional—activities that involve systematic, ordered, and explicit manipulation of data and that reflect an aversion to ambiguous, exploratory, or unsystematic experiences.

These personality/environment types are usually referred to by the first letter of each word; hence, the "RIASEC" model. This model is usually configured as a hexagon, as shown in Figure 13.1. Adjacent types are presumed to have more in common than diagonally opposite types. That is, the Realistic type is more similar to either the Investigative or Conventional types than it is to the Social, Enterprising, or Artistic types. Further, because people rarely fit within a single type, they are usually assigned a three-letter code. For example, a person assigned the code SEC would be presumed to be most like the Social type, next most like the Enterprising type, and next most like the Conventional type.

Holland's approach has found great favor among counseling researchers and practitioners. For example, over 400 research

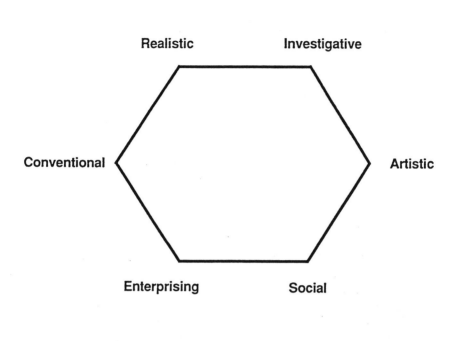

       Realistic   Investigative

Conventional   Artistic

     Enterprising   Social

Figure 13.1.   Holland's Hexagonal Model.

studies have been completed on various aspects of Holland's theory (Holland, 1985). Relatedly, numerous assessment instruments and approaches have been developed in the context of Holland's theoretical propositions and more recently, other existing instruments have been modified so that their results can be interpreted within the context of those propositions. One reason for the extensiveness of these efforts is that, in the context of Holland's theory, a vocational interest inventory is also a personality inventory, a situation which expands the potential interpretations of any research effort. However, also acknowledged is that Holland and his associates have done much to spur interest. For example, Holland developed the *Vocational Preference Inventory* and the *Self-Directed Search*, two widely used vocational interest inventories, based on his theory. He and his associates also have developed a set of three-letter codes, based on the RIASEC model, for over 12,000 occupations (Gottfredson & Holland, 1989). This latter effort in particular has made his approach popular because of the ease with which the system can be used by both counselors and clients.

Although Holland's approach is popular, it is not without criticism. For example, Osipow (1983) stated that, "Holland's theory possesses some general utility for counselors in their conceptualization of occupational selection for their clientele, but it offers little specific advice in the way of suggestions about procedures and techniques that the counselors may use in their face-to-face work with their clients" (p. 110). None the less, Holland's approach remains commonly used, probably because people other than Holland have devised numerous counseling techniques based on the theory.

Developmental Approaches

Developmental approaches differ from the previous ones in that they view occupational choice as much more an ongoing process than as isolated acts. Occupational choice in this context also is not restricted to a certain period in life but rather is a set of recurring events throughout the life cycle. Thus, career development may be viewed as an evolutionary process which is flexible and in which individuals adapt their occupational choices to changing conditions in their lives.

Ginzberg, Ginsburg, Axelrod, and Herma, (1951) indicated that the developmental process of occupational decision-making "is not a single decision but a series of decisions made over a period of years" (p. 185). They proposed that this process is divided into a set of phases. The first, from birth to approximately age 11, is called the *Fantasy* stage. In it, individuals have "idealistic" and typically unrealistic conceptualizations of the jobs they would like to assume. The second phase, *Tentative,* lasts from approximately ages 11 to 17, and contains the subperiods of interest, capacity, value, and transition. Individuals gather information about various occupations and make extremely tentative occupational decisions during this phase. The last phase, *Realistic,* lasts from approximately ages 17 to 21, and contains the subperiods of exploration and crystallization. Individuals engage in initial work activities and make "final" occupational decisions during this phase.

In the early formulations, Ginzberg and his associates postulated that occupational choices are a series of "compromises" among various influencing factors and that choices are relatively final after individuals reach their early twenties. However, Ginzberg (1972) later revised these propositions, and then used the term *optimization*, rather than compromise, to imply that occupational choice is the result of the individual's attempt to maximize the benefits of any occupational decision. He also suggested that occupational decision-making continues throughout life rather than being finalized in young adulthood.

The efforts of Ginzberg and his associates (1951) and later those of Ginzberg (1972) alone were significant; at the time of their initial presentation, they represented a very different view of career development. However, although Ginzberg spurred interest in developmental approaches to career development and counseling, his work was overshadowed by that of other developmental theorists. Thus, Ginzberg's work is given little recognition today, and few counselors use career counseling based directly on it.

Super's work on a theory of career development began shortly after Ginzberg's and, in part, was a reaction to what he perceived as deficiencies in Ginzberg's approach. Briefly, Super believed that Ginzberg failed to provide an effective definition of occupational "choice" and that the distinction between choice and "adjustment" was not as sharp as Ginzberg proposed (Herr & Cramer, 1988). Super's theory is multifaceted and borrows from a number of areas of psychology (Super, 1990). He described it as a differential-developmental-social-phenomenological psychology (Super, 1969). Perhaps more appropriately, Osipow (1983) referred to Super's work as a developmental self-concept theory. Four components of Super's work have received the most attention; life stages and their associated developmental tasks, self-concept as related to occupational choice, career maturity, and life roles.

Life Stages. Super (1957, 1977) proposed that five major life stages are present, each incorporating different developmental tasks that can be used to understand career development. The first stage, *Growth*, lasts from birth to approximately age 14. It includes the substages of fantasy (ages 4 to 10), interest (ages 11 to 12), and capacity (ages 13 to 14). The important developmental tasks in this stage are developing a self-concept and establishing an orientation toward the world of work. *Exploration*, the second stage, covers approximately ages 14 to 24, with the substage, tentative, existing approximately from ages 15 to 17. The primary developmental tasks in the Exploration stage are crystallizing a vocational preference, specifying the preference, and implementing the preference. The third stage, *Establishment*, lasts from approximately ages 24 to 44 and includes the substages of stabilization (ages 25 to 30) and advancement (ages 30 to 44). The major developmental tasks in this stage are stabilizing the vocational preference and advancing in occupations. *Maintenance*, the fourth stage, lasts from approximately ages 44 to 64. The major developmental task in this stage is preserving achieved status and gains. In the final stage, *Decline*, lasting from approximately age 64 on, there are two substages: deceleration (ages 64 to 70) and retirement (age 70 on). The major developmental tasks in this stage are decelerating occupational activities, and disengaging and retiring from occupational activities. More recently, Super (1990) has maintained the applicability of the sequential stages but blurred the age boundaries for them, ˙perhaps in reaction to increasing longevity.

Vocational Self-concept. The second major component in Super's approach is the development and implementation of the "vocational self-concept." A person's vocational self-concept is presumed to be a substantial and integral part of his/her total self-concept. Zunker (1986) stated that "the research has indicated that the vocational self-concept develops through physical and mental growth, observations of work, identification with working adults, general environment, and general experiences" (p. 11). The theory assumes that individuals choose occupations that are consistent with and allow expression of their vocational self-concepts. Thus, an individual's vocational self-concept is a major determinant of what work (i.e., occupations) will be appropriate for the individual. Commenting on the role of self-concept in career counseling, Herr (1986) noted:

> Thus, career . . . counseling must attend to the individual's need for in-depth and accurate information about vocational alternatives, but at least as importantly, the individual needs to be assisted to avoid unrealistic estimates of ability and vague understandings of personal values and preferences. (pp. 190-191)

Career Maturity. The concept of career maturity (sometimes referred to as vocational maturity) plays an important role in Super's approach. Super (1990) indicated:

> Career maturity is defined as the individual's readiness to cope with the developmental tasks with which he or she is confronted because of his or her biological and social developments and because of society's expectations of people who have reached that stage of development. (p. 213)

Thus, the concept implies that specific behaviors are indicative of an individual's mastery of various developmental tasks. Different authors have proposed different components of career maturity, such as career exploration ability, decision-making ability, career planning ability, knowledge of the world of work, and knowledge of preferred occupations. In addition, Super, Thompson, Lindeman, Jordaan, and Myers (1979) proposed career development skills while Crites (1973) proposed that attitudes toward involvement in the choice process, orientation toward work, independence in decision making, preference for choice factors, and conceptions of the choice process are important components of career maturity.

A basic assumption in Super's developmental stage approach is that the individual must master the tasks at one career development stage before the individual can move to the next stage. Therefore, measurement of career maturity is important because it allows inference about an individual's career development stage. Relatedly, conceptualizations of desired levels of career maturity at various career development stages are frequently used as the bases for establishing goals and objectives for various career guidance, education, and counseling activities.

Life Roles. Super (1990) now refers to his theory as the "life-span, life-space" approach to career development. Central to this perspective are six life roles that people have over the course of their life spans: (1) child, (2) student, (3) leisurite, (4) citizen, (5) worker, and (6) homemaker. Although individuals have more or less involvement in each of these roles throughout their lives, in combination they constitute "life career." Super uses the term *role salience* to indicate the relative importance of each life role at any point in a person's life. He created the "Life-Career Rainbow" to depict approximations of role salience across the life span. The Life-Career Rainbow is a set of concentric semicircles in which the bands represent the life roles and career development stages are indicated on the outer semicircle. Relative degrees of role salience are indicated by differentially shaded sections of the bands. The Life-Career Rainbow therefore is the most recent depiction of the major elements of Super's theory of career development.

The work of Super, his associates, and others who have based their work on his, has been widely accepted within the counseling profession. In fact, Holland's and Super's approaches are preeminent to the extent that the vast majority of current career development and counseling activities can be traced directly to one of these two approaches.

CAREER GUIDANCE, EDUCATION, AND COUNSELING

Hoyt (1972) presented a definition of career education that is still frequently used and quoted today:

> Career education is the total effort of public education and the community aimed at helping all individuals to become familiar with the values of a work-oriented society, to integrate those values into their personal value systems, and to integrate those values into their lives . . . . (p. 1)

In general, career education involves communication of information about jobs, the world of work, and career development concepts and approaches in the environments in which people exist. Two basic premises underlay career education. The first is that left to their own devices, people will not have sufficient opportunities or resources to obtain comprehensive information about a variety of jobs and careers. The second is that such comprehensive information is essential for effective occupational and career decision making, and therefore career development. Traditionally, career-education activities have taken place primarily within educational systems and institutions. However, they have recently been extended into other situations such as business and industry, government, and the military.

Approximately two decades ago, Hoyt (1974) presented a summary of conditions formulated by the United States Office of Education (USOE) that serve as the basis of the need for career education. These include the following situations: (1) too many students leaving educational systems are deficient in basic academic skills necessary for effective adjustment in society and the world of work, (2) too few students are able to relate what they learn in school to the world of work, (3) the American educational system is considerably less pertinent to non-collegebound students than it is to college bound students, (4) the American educational system does not adequately serve the vocational needs of ethnic minorities, women, or the disadvantaged, and (5) too many students leaving educational systems are deficient in vocational skills, self-understanding and career decision-making skills, and work attitudes necessary for successful transition from school to work. In sum, educational systems were viewed as not doing as much as they should or could do to prepare people for the world of work. This situation prompted a national impetus for career education in the 1970s. Unfortunately, these same conditions seem to exist in the 1990s.

The USOE's attention to career education in the 1970s resulted in the development of four national models for career education. The first is the *school-based* or *comprehensive* career-education model. This model was originally proposed as a method for revitalizing schools from within by infusing ideas, experiences, and skills (related to work and careers) not typically found in them. The general goals for this model included students' developments of career awareness, self-awareness, positive appreciations and attitudes toward work, decision-making skills, economic awareness, skill awareness and beginning competence, educational awareness, and educational identities. However, over 1000 other specific goals were developed in the construction of activities designed to implement these general goals (Herr & Cramer, 1988).

The second model, *employer-based* or *experienced-based*, was designed to meet the needs of students who did not do well in traditional learning environments. This model has goals similar to those for the first model, but the natures of the learning experiences involved are quite different. In this model, a significant portion of "education" occurs through direct involvement in ongoing work activities. Thus, under this model, students "learn by doing" through placements at actual employer sites in the community.

The third model is called the *home/community-based* model. This model was developed to be useful to adults and has goals such as the development of educational delivery systems in the home and community, new placement systems, new career education programs (specifically for adults), and more competent workers. The model makes extensive use of television and other mass media, referral sources, and community resources to facilitate learning among out-of-school adults.

Rural/residential, the fourth model, was developed to help entire disadvantaged, rural families improve their economic and social situations through intensive programs at residential centers. This model was implemented on a very limited basis, but the results of those efforts were generally favorable.

Because the conveyance of information is a primary (but certainly not the only) purpose of career education, a considerable number of resources about the world of work have been developed. Relatedly, a multitude of sources exists from which counselors can obtain such information for use in their respective settings and with their respective clients. Therefore, because of the large numbers involved, only a few representative examples can be presented here.

Until relatively recently, almost all occupational and career resources were in the form of printed material. These materials ranged from "occupational briefs" to the far more complete

Dictionary of Occupational Titles and the *Occupational Outlook Handbook*, from biographies of workers to stories in magazine form, and from brochures to newspapers. In fact, so many printed materials are available that counselors may become mind-boggled by the choices confronting them! Relatedly, public, private, governmental, and religious agencies as well as companies, corporations, and not-for-profit organizations all offer many different types of materials that are potentially suitable for an equally diverse array of audiences. Thus, counselors have the wide-ranging flexibility to either purchase a "complete career information system" or to develop a "home grown" system. That's the "good news." The bad news is that such systems require considerable storage space, frequently require sophisticated filing systems, and rapidly go out-of-date in regard to the information presented.

More recently, a variety of visual media have become available. These resources include filmstrips, multimedia presentation packages, films, and videotapes. These media have the advantage of a presentation format that is "more interesting" than those of printed materials, but many of the disadvantages of printed materials are also applicable to visual media.

One form of information conveyance that has found favor with many counselors is the "direct contact" approach. Generally, four types of activities are subsumed under this heading. The first is *simulations*, typically in the form of role-playing, in which clients "interact" with persons who have particular types of work and/or career knowledge. The second is *interviews*, in which clients interact with persons actually occupying particular jobs and/or involved in careers in which clients are potentially interested. The third type is *field trips*, wherein clients visit a particular employment setting for a limited time period to observe the work being done and talk with various employees. The final type is *apprenticeships*, which involve clients working in particular jobs, usually for pay, for reasonable time periods so that they can gain an understanding of the work involved in the occupation. While these activities are "popular" with clients, they necessitate considerable time investments by counselors to arrange and coordinate them.

McDaniels and Gysbers (1992), in discussing improvements in career information delivery systems, noted:

> The trend toward more effective career information resources received a boost in 1976, when congress authorized the National Occupational Information Coordinating Committee (NOICC) as a federal interagency committee that promotes the development and use of educational, occupational, labor market information. NOICC's primary mission is to improve coordination and communication among developers and users of career information and to help states meet the occupational information needs of various groups and individuals. (p. 240)

Congress also created State Occupational Information Coordinating Committees (SOICCs) in 1976 so that there would be an extensive, coordinated network of occupational information dissemination. Thus, governmental and private organizations work together through the NOICC and SOICC systems so that current career information is readily available both to counselors engaged in career counseling and their clients.

The most recent advancement in occupational and career information systems is the use of computers (particularly microcomputers) and computer technology. Among the most widely known systems available specifically for stand-alone use are the *System of Interactive Guidance and Information* (SIGI PLUS), *Career Information System* (CIS), *Coordinate Occupational Information Network* (COIN), *DISCOVER*, *Guidance Information System* (GIS), and *CHOICES* (McDaniels & Gysbers, 1992). Some of these systems allow integration of career information provided through the NOICC and SOICC systems. Each of these systems, and others like them, allow the client to "interact" with the computer both to gain information and to explore occupational and career possibilities. The advent of microcomputer versions of some of these systems has made them particularly attractive for career education because of reduced costs and the opportunity for clients to use them without substantial investments of the professional counselors' time. However, Sampson and Pyle (1983) and Peterson, Sampson, and Reardon (1991) have noted that such systems should never be used to "replace" career education or counseling by a professional counselor because of the limitations of such systems as well as ethical considerations. In addition, use of systems such as SIGI PLUS, DISCOVER, CHOICES, and the like merely for career education purposes is under utilization of their respective capabilities. That is, while these systems do in fact present much valuable career information, they are designed for use in *Computer-Assisted Career Guidance* (CACG) activities that involve much more than communication of information.

Career education is one of the major components under the broad rubric of career guidance; career counseling is the other. Career counseling quite obviously focuses on the facilitation of clients' decision-making and career development activities and is similar to other types of counseling in that it may be conducted individually or in groups. Brammer and Shostrom (1960) identified three types of goals for career counseling, including helping clients to (1) confirm choices already made, (2) clarify career objectives, or (3) discover facts about themselves and the world of work and then to use the information in decision-making. In both individual and group career counseling, the counseling process begins with the establishment of rapport between the professional counselor and the client(s). In the next step, the professional counselor, typically in collaboration with clients, determines if career counseling is merited or if the client(s) need(s) some other type of counseling. If career counseling is indicated, the professional counselor proceeds to implement strategies consistent with a theoretical orientation.

Herr and Cramer (1988) identified eight assumptions underlying career counseling intervention strategies: (1) many factors beyond control of the client will influence the client's decision-making, (2) clients are not able to obtain or process all information relevant to decision-making, (3) during counseling, clients are only able to make decisions that will allow them to achieve some of their objectives, (4) clients' decisions are typically evaluated in terms of the process used to reach them rather than on the basis of outcomes, (5) clients can be taught how to make decisions, (6) sometimes factors unknown to either the counselor or the client defeat the purposes of career counseling, (7) the importance of various factors in clients' decision-making varies across clients and the reasons for the variations are often unknown, and (8) career counseling presumes client motivation, but appropriate client motivation is not always present in the career counseling process. Although these assumptions may seem negative, they are not intended to be. Rather, they describe some of the obstacles with which career counselors must contend and they therefore provide a realistic perspective on the conditions under which career counseling is usually conducted.

One of the ways to maintain positive perspectives within career counseling is to do it in the context of empirical counseling as presented here. The individual and group counseling and assessment approaches presented are particularly noteworthy in this regard because they are readily adapted to the purposes of career counseling. Used in conjunction with any of the variety of available occupational information systems (e.g., within the context of CACG), the techniques presented in those chapters enable professional counselors, in collaboration with their clients, to develop appropriate goals, use effective strategies, and achieve desirable and measurable outcomes.

SUMMARY

Today, career education and career counseling are infrequently conducted as distinct activities; more typically they are included as parts of comprehensive career guidance programs (Herr & Cramer, 1988). Historically, such programs usually have been conducted in educational systems such as elementary, middle/junior high, or secondary schools, and colleges and universities, primarily because they were initiated by professional counselors and/or educators affiliated with those systems. More recently, career guidance programs have been started in business, industry, and other noneducational settings. For example, many "Employee Assistance Programs" incorporate career guidance components, activities, and services. In general, career guidance programs are now available to a large majority of people in society, and the number of programs continues to increase.

The broad goal of career guidance programming is the facilitation of individuals' career development through the provision of services and activities that can be responsive to any of the variety of career development needs of the individuals for whom the programs were established. This is indeed a lofty goal. However, effectively planned and implemented comprehensive career-guidance programs, and effective career education and career counseling within them, are able to achieve it.

Chapter **14**

ASSESSMENT AND MEASUREMENT

The essential goal of assessment is to quantify a client's behavior and characteristics for the purpose of enabling the professional counselor to understand and help the client. Professional counselors, however, have given much less attention to assessment than they have to other professional issues in counseling. Yet, data obtained through assessment is important in helping a professional counselor make calculated decisions. For this important reason, an understanding of assessment is necessary for effective counseling.

A starting point for an introductory discussion of assessment is terminology. Accordingly, definitions of often used terms as provided by Shertzer and Linden (1978) are presented below.

Assessment: the methods and processes used in gathering data about, or evidence of, human behavior. This term is frequently employed when a professional counselor wishes to emphasize the distinction between the medical use of diagnosis with its connotation of abnormality and the collection of information concerning the current state of human behavior.

Measurement: the act of identifying the amount or dimension of an attribute or distinguishing characteristic; an estimation of how much of a trait an individual displays or possesses.

Evaluation: the process of comparing measurements or relating them to other variables. For example, evaluation enables a professional counselor to form an opinion or to judge the adequacy or inadequacy of an attribute, trait, or object.

Appraisal: a term used synonymously with evaluation.

Interpretation: the act of interpreting the meaning or usefulness of behavioral data.

The goal of assessment in counseling is rather simple (i.e., to help the counselor and client). However, this goal becomes tremendously difficult to obtain if the data gathered are misused or misinterpreted. Incorrect interpretation or inappropriately used data result in wrong decisions, adversely affecting clients and limiting their opportunities. Further, many counselors-in-training mistakenly view assessment merely as "paper-and-pencil testing," but assessment in counseling is a multidimensional process of which paper and pencil testing is only one component. A professional counselor needs to be interested in the results of a client's performance in a given situation in relation to the client's total functioning. Therefore, effective assessment procedures take into consideration not only the client's performance but also the client's history, behavior, and environment. Because of this, assessment can be undertaken apart from the formal counseling process (e.g., through observations made by parents, loved ones, teachers, and/or employer).

Because good assessment is multidimensional, many areas within the process overlap. Yet, a dichotomy of functions exists: those that are involved within conventional assessment and those that are part of the **assessment process** which we shall refer to as **empirical counseling.** The discussion that follows is presented according to this dichotomy.

TRADITIONAL ASSESSMENT IN COUNSELING

The process of conventional assessment, which is based on the medical model, is diagnostic and evaluative in nature. The purposes of conventional assessment include diagnosis of traits and factors, assessment of strengths and weaknesses, classification, and selection for placement.

The outcome of conventional assessment leads to prescription which unfortunately tends to have as its focus the determination of what is "wrong" with a client. Its use in counseling dates back to the late 1930s, when the conventional-assessment model being used by psychologists was adopted with modifications by professional counselors (Williamson, 1939). The resulting model is referred to, in this text, as traditional assessment in counseling. In traditional assessment, the professional counselor assesses individual functioning and focuses on classifying or selecting people for training, educational, or vocational placement. Clients are expected to participate in assessment by reacting to the test results and the professional counselor's appraisal of their characteristics. However, a very highly skilled professional is needed to enable a client to be an active participant in the assessment process. Thus, a common concern with this model is that it often leads to prescription only, as mentioned earlier. The process of conventional assessment too often provides answers, solutions, and advice rather than encouraging clients to take charge of their lives. When properly utilized, the traditional assessment model is an important element in professional counseling. Therefore, the essential components of this assessment process and their use are presented in the following material.

Purposes

In the traditional assessment model, tests are administered by professional counselors for a variety of purposes, but primarily because they provide information to assist the counselor and client in making decisions. The specific reasons for giving tests vary, depending on the setting in which the professional counselor is working. Four reasons have been described by Cronbach (1970) and are presented below.

Prediction or Planning. Tests are often given for the purpose of assisting professional counselors, clients, or administrators with decisions concerning future performance (e.g., the planning of an educational program for an individual or a group in business, industry, or school). Tests designed for this purpose provide measures of ability, achievement, or other human characteristics and are used for making decisions.

Selection or Screening. A familiar use of tests involves the selection process employed by colleges and universities whereby individuals are accepted or rejected by an institution based, in part, on their performance on a standardized test. Tests are used by many employers as a means of selecting individuals to fill vacancies in their work force. In a school setting, tests often are administered for the purpose of screening students with superior academic abilities, social problems, or academic difficulties.

Classification or Placement. Most states have laws which specify a criteria for certain educational programs. For example, standardized tests provide measures to be used for placing students in programs such as those for the academically gifted or learning disabled student. Also, tests are frequently used by the military or government for selecting individuals to participate or to become eligible for benefits. In addition, tests can be used to classify students for individual or group counseling.

Many problems are apparent in the use of tests for the purpose of classification or placement decisions including problems with validity and reliability. Yet, most governmental regulations concerning people in public schools, the military, or agencies require that classification and placement decisions be based on test results.

Program Evaluation. In traditional assessment, a program, method, or treatment, rather than an individual, is being assessed. Suppose, for example, that High Point Hall, a drug rehabilitation center, decides to try an experimental aerobics program to help recovering substance abusers. Data would be needed concerning the effect(s) the experimental program might have upon the center's clients. The traditional treatment program would have to be evaluated, followed by the implementation and evaluation of the experimental aerobics program. Typically, tests would be administered to each client before and after the traditional treatment program, and the same pre-post testing procedure would be used during the experimental program. Clients' progress during the traditional program could then be compared with their progress during the experimental program for the purpose of evaluating the relative effectiveness of each.

Assessment of Individual Progress. An important use of tests not mentioned by Cronbach (1970) is the examination of client (or student) change or progress. Professional counselors' and clients' conclusions that progress is being made can sometimes be verified by the administration of standardized tests.

Standardized Tests

Professional counselors are required to administer, score, and interpret a multitude of standardized tests throughout their career. Because they also receive test information from colleagues and from a variety of other professionals outside the field of counseling, professional counselors need to have a working knowledge of standardized tests.

No one basic standardized test exists for counselors to use in assessment. Instead, they rely on a potpourri of instruments that can be classified into three categories of measurement: aptitude or general ability; achievement; and personality, vocational-interest, vocational-maturity, and attitude inventories. Also, certain types of tests are used more extensively by professional counselors in given settings. For example, tests purporting to yield information about vocational interest and maturity, personality, and attitude are more frequently used by the professional counselor who works with adolescents and adults.

The common characteristic of standardized tests is that they expose a person to a particular set of questions or tasks in order to obtain a performance that can be compared with that of individuals in a normative population. Another characteristic is their major strength of permitting tasks and questions to be presented in the same way to each person tested. Further, responses are scored in a predetermined and consistent manner, thus permitting the performances of several individual test takers to be compared.

The actual scores achieved on a test are referred to as *quantitative data,* (e.g., scoring at the 84th percentile on the verbal section of the Graduate Record Exam or earning an IQ score of 125). In addition to quantitative data, *qualitative information* can be derived from a standardized test. This information consists of nonsystematic observations made while a client is taking a test and/or while the counselor is discussing the results of the test with the client.

Standardized tests used in traditional assessment can be classified into two principal categories: those assessing the cognitive domain and those assessing the affective domain. The major testing subcategories of the cognitive domain will be presented first.

Assessing the Cognitive Domain

The presentation of cognitive-domain assessment is divided into subcategories according to general ability measures, tests of general intelligence, aptitude tests, and standardized achievement tests.

General Ability Measures. Dictionary definitions of intelligence include the ability to learn and understand or the ability to cope with new situations. Mehrens and Lehmann (1984) reported that definitions of intelligence include the capacity to learn, think abstractly, integrate new experiences, and adapt to new situations. Intelligence often has been used interchangeably with aptitude. Some test specialists, however, suggest that subtle shades of meaning distinguish these two terms. They consider intelligence to be a general mental ability and aptitude to be a specific ability factor. To illustrate this difference, the *Stanford-Binet Intelligence Test* would be considered a general measure of intelligence, whereas the *Seashore Musical Aptitude Test* would be viewed as a specific measure of aptitude. Historically, intelligence tests were assumed to measure innate characteristics that are not subject to change. As Mehrens and Lehmann reported, this assumption is invalid, and many test authors, in an attempt to avoid the implication of innateness, have instead adopted the term aptitude.

A helpful scheme for understanding aptitude tests is to categorize them as (1) individually administered instruments that provide a general measure of intelligence; (2) group administered tests that provide a general measure of intelligence; (3) group-administered, multifactor aptitude tests that provide multiple measures; and (4) group-administered aptitude instruments that provide a specific measure.

Individual Tests of General Intelligence. Although most schools, colleges, businesses, and industries use the traditional data obtained from group tests of intelligence, in some situations clinical information that can be gained most effectively through the administration of individual intelligence tests can be helpful. For example, clinically meaningful information can be obtained by having an opportunity for the examiner to observe the test taker's approach to problem solving, the amount of stress exhibited by the client during the test administration, and the client's test-taking behaviors.

The individual intelligence test has been considered the psychologist's basic tool (Bardon & Bennett, 1974). When correctly administered, individual intelligence tests provide a more reliable measure and a better understanding of the test-taker's behavior than do group intelligence tests. Correct administration, an important factor in obtaining a reliable measure, requires considerable training. In fact, many states mandate certain licensure, usually that of a psychologist, in order to use individual intelligence scores in any way that may affect a person's future. Instruments that require special qualifications to administer are referred to as *restricted,* such as the Stanford-Binet and the various Wechsler tests (*Wechsler Intelligence Scale for Children Revised,* [WISC-R], ages 6 through 16; *Wechsler Pre-school and Primary Scale of Intelligence,* [WPPSI], ages 4 through 6 1/2; and the *Wechsler Adult Intelligence Scale-Revised,* [WAIS-R]).

Group Tests of General Intelligence. As graduates of American schools and colleges know, group intelligence tests are very much a part of an individual's educational life. For example, two tests widely used in predicting college success are the *College Entrance Examination Board Scholastic Aptitude Test* (SAT) and the *American College Testing Program* (ACT). At the graduate school level, widely used tests are the *Graduate Record Examination* (GRE) and the *Miller Analogies Test* (MAT). Can you recall those times when you carefully and completely filled appropriate "bubbles" on an answer sheet with a heavy dark mark using a soft-lead pencil, for one of these tests?

Group intelligence tests are used much more frequently in educational settings than are individually administered tests, perhaps by a ratio as large as 20 to 1. Group intelligence tests are less expensive to administer because they can be given to a large number of individuals at one time. Also, they are not restricted tests and, therefore, are designed to be administered by non-licensed individuals. Their value and wide use, however, result generally from the fact that the data derived from them are comparable to those derived from the more time-consuming individual tests. Many group tests of general intelligence report two sub-scores such as verbal and quantitative ability.

Although most group tests can be scored by hand, more often they are scored by a machine that produces **raw scores, scaled scores,** and **percentile ranks.** Group intelligence tests, if properly used, can be extremely informative to the professional counselor, particularly when assessing a client's overall functioning. But the results of group testing always should be used with caution. A case in point concerns the cultural fairness of intelligence tests. People of different national origins and people in various diverse groups in America place different values upon verbal fluency and speed, factors which are important for performing well on intelligence tests. Also, educationally disadvantaged persons typically will be handicapped when intelligence tests are used to describe their functioning. No one intelligence test is best for all uses; care must be taken to select the correct test for a particular situation and population.

Multifactor Aptitude Tests. As mentioned earlier, differences of opinion are found on the value of multifactor aptitude tests in comparison to general intelligence measures. Supporters of multifactor aptitude tests believe that intelligence is composed of many specific abilities. Therefore, some professional counselors use multifactor aptitude tests for the practical reason that they facilitate vocational and educational counseling. They believe that differential descriptions of test results are helpful when discussing strengths and weaknesses with respective clients although, as Mehrens and Lehmann (1984) indicated, little data exist that support differential predictive validity.

Group Administered (Specific) Aptitude Tests. Specific aptitude tests usually measure the capacity to acquire proficiency in a specified activity. This type of test is typically used by professional counselors to help clients make vocational and educational selection decisions and by institutions for placement decisions.

Standardized Achievement Measures. Professional counselors working in school settings are frequently involved with school-wide achievement-testing programs. They make arrangements for teacher administration and computer scoring, and they are often requested by other school personnel to assist with selecting tests. The latter function usually involves a decision made by a committee comprised of teachers, administrators, school psychologists, and professional counselors. The professional counselor who is involved with any test selection process should make certain that the instruments selected are valid for their respective purposes and possess other necessary psychometric properties.

Achievement tests are designed to measure an individual's progress or current knowledge as a result of education or training. How well does Mary read? Does Burt know the definitions for a list of words? After reading a paragraph, is Nancy able to recall its content? These are examples of questions that can be answered using data derived from achievement tests. Standardized achievement tests are seldom used by professional counselors working in non-educational settings with the exception of using achievement tests for purposes of screening or placement (e.g., typing, shorthand, computer proficiency, and similar knowledge or skill-based tests).

Assessing an individual's achievement level is useful because it enables the professional counselor to help plan successful experiences for others in learning and/or training. This is particularly important with students and clients concerned with career and educational planning. A professional counselor can assist these individuals with identifying their cumulative achievement, determining their strengths and weaknesses in academic performance areas, and comparing their achievement level with their ability or intelligence level.

Many standardized achievement tests are available ranging from assessments of general information (i.e., survey achievement tests) to assessments of a specific knowledge area (i.e., diagnostic tests). However, the current trend in educational settings is less emphasis on survey achievement tests and greater emphasis on those that assess specific kinds of functioning related to school achievement.

Survey Achievement Tests. Survey achievement test batteries consist of a group of tests, each assessing performance in a different content area. All tests in a survey battery are standardized on the same population, thus permitting meaningful comparisons of the results in the various content areas.

A general survey achievement battery (e.g., *Stanford Achievement Tests* or *Iowa Tests of Basic Skills*) is used when school personnel are interested in a student's academic progress in all subject areas because comparative information will be available (e.g., whether the student is better in arithmetic, spelling, or reading). However, if school personnel are interested in a student's specific strengths or weaknesses are in a single-subject area, then a diagnostic test would be used.

Diagnostic Tests. This type of standardized achievement test is designed to identify a student's specific strengths and weaknesses in a particular academic area. Examples of standardized diagnostic tests are the *Stanford Diagnostic Reading Test* (SDRT), *Diagnostic Tests and Self-Helps in Arithmetic,*

Metropolitan Readiness Tests, and *Gates-MacGinitie Reading Test.* The belief is that specific data enable teachers, principals, professional counselors, and school psychologists to decide what kinds of classroom activities will be most effective in helping a student learn, and to plan and organize future learning tasks that are appropriate for a student's developmental level.

In general, the age of the test taker and the kind of information desired determine the achievement test to be used.

Assessing the Affective Domain

This section is concerned with standardized noncognitive group inventories. The discussion will address tests that are concerned with individuals' interests, personality, and attitudes: an assessment of the affective domain.

The primary characteristics of standardized noncognitive tests are uniform administration and objective scoring. Most of the tests have normative information that enables a professional counselor to make comparisons between a client and other individuals. With standardized noncognitive group tests, professional counselors can help answer questions such as, "What are Bill's interests?", "How does Ruth compare with other women concerning her interest in engineering?", "Is Tom abnormally aggressive?", and "Is Alice's concern about others atypical?"

Many children and adults have difficulty with age-appropriate behaviors because emotional, interest, or attitude factors interfere with their cognitive functioning. In this regard, standardized noncognitive tests can help ascertain important information that can be of value during counseling. In addition, professional counselors occasionally use standardized noncognitive tests for identifying clients for group counseling (e.g., establishing group counseling for clients who show similar characteristics of high anxiety).

A number of standardized noncognitive instruments are available, making it possible for the professional counselor to assess noncognitive functioning in a variety of ways. However, disadvantages do exist in using group tests in this domain. In comparison to cognitive measures, noncognitive instruments are not well documented concerning their predictive validity (i.e., the ability to foretell what a person's behaviors will be in the future). Also, a client's responses can be affected by the influence of social desirability. Professional counselors need to be sensitive to the fact that most people are unwilling to provide, on paper-and-pencil tests, responses which are presumed to be different from the norm.

Another problem associated with all standardized noncognitive group tests is their susceptibility to *client response set* (i.e., the tendency to reply in a particular direction, almost independent of the questions asked). For example, clients may be predisposed to remain in the "middle of the road" if a five-point, agree-disagree continuum is used or they may have the tendency to select true for true-false items. Other problems with this type of test include (1) a reading level that may be above the client's reading achievement level, making the test beyond his/her ability; (2) a tendency for clients to guess in order to provide a response; and (3) the sacrifice of speed for accuracy, or vice versa.

As imprecise as standardized noncognitive group tests are, they do provide professional counselors with valuable information to use in helping clients. A point must be remembered, however: Although this information is helpful, it certainly is not definitive. In addition, most standardized noncognitive group tests can be used with an individual. In fact, noncognitive tests are frequently administered to groups but interpreted on an individual basis.

In summary, knowledge about a client's interests, personality, and attitudes is important in helping a professional counselor to communicate effectively during counseling and with other professionals. However, the use of these tests is not without limitations.

Personality Assessment. Personality assessment can be either a structured or unstructured self-report. *Structured personality tests* consist of questions that can be interpreted in relatively the same way by all clients. **Unstructured personality tests,** referred to as projective tests (e.g., *Rorschach Inkblots Test*), consist of ambiguous pictures or items to which clients respond according to their interpretation of the stimulus.

A variety of structured, self-report personality tests are widely used by professional counselors in numerous ways; the counselor is usually not dependent upon a single personality test. The vast majority of these tests are intended for use with adults. However, some can be administered to elementary or secondary school age students if the students' reading ability is adequate. The general public appears opposed to the general use of personality tests in schools and therefore they are rarely used in school settings with groups of students. However, in some instances, they may be used with a few select students with whom the professional counselor is doing individual counseling. Perhaps the kinds most widely used across age levels are problem checklists and adjustment tests.

Attitude Assessment. Individual behavior is influenced by numerous confounding variables, many of which are extraneous to the person but which affect attitude. As research has demonstrated, individuals' attitudes are related to their behavior; they influence an individual's behavior concerning other people, activities, and objects. For example, if a group of students has an unfavorable attitude toward education, little learning will take place in the classroom. Accordingly, in order to know why Jim is behind in his college assignments and what can be done to help him improve his performance, or to know whether Jim is prejudiced, the professional counselor must develop an understanding of Jim's attitudes.

An important concern is that professional counselors understand that attitudes, which are not directly observable, are inferred from a person's verbal and nonverbal behaviors. To illustrate, prejudice cannot be seen as an object, but it can be observed, over a period of time, in the behavior of someone who is prejudiced.

Attitudes, which are learned, result from socialization and tend to be changeable, particularly with young people. The key to changing an attitude is to have knowledge of its status. This needed information can be gained through assessment using an attitude test or scale. As with all tests, the usefulness of any attitude scale depends upon its reliability, validity, and norms; the ease with which it can be administered and scored; and the meanings that can be derived from the data. However, perhaps more so than any other noncognitive assessment instrument, attitude scales have problems with psychometric properties. Typically, research correlations obtained between scores obtained using an attitude scale and observed behaviors are low. None the less, the information that a professional counselor and client can acquire from the client's performance on attitude tests makes them useful during counseling.

ASSESSMENT WITHIN EMPIRICAL COUNSELING

Empirical counseling, as used in this book, connotes the use of assessment for the purpose of determining goals, strategies, and effectiveness during the counseling process. For professional counselors to make decisions about a client's progress or services is becoming increasingly unpopular unless objective, systematically collected data can be amassed that bear directly upon those decisions. Collecting data at regular intervals during the counseling process provides direct information about the client's progress which is the essence of assessment in empirical counseling. The following discussion presents the goals of assessment in empirical counseling (i.e., improvement of counseling and accountability).

Improvement of Counseling. Through assessment, the professional can determine whether the counseling procedures being used are producing desired results and can facilitate the revision of unproductive counseling procedures. Accordingly, professional counselors can determine whether they are wasting a client's or their own time on ineffective counseling procedures. If counseling is producing desired results, the professional counselor can continue the counseling process with confidence.

Accountability. The second reason for professional counselors collecting quantified measures of their clients' progress is to respond to requirements for accountability. Within a school setting, for example, the professional counselor may have to demonstrate to the pupil-personnel director, principal, and/or board of education that counseling processes are actually helping students. In student development in higher education, a similar situation exists with the professional counselor needing accountability data for his or her supervisor or the institution's vice-president for student affairs. Or, a business or industry may want to compare several methods of communication-skill training workshops if it is concerned about which method will do the best job. Accountability data for the professional counselor in community or agency settings are needed for insurance companies and third-party payers as well as for supervisors. For example, counselors who want to receive payments from a health organization or insurance company may be required to submit a report after 8, 24, 40, and 60 sessions. The report asks for information about the client's problem, the provider's goals and planned interventions, and an estimate of progress. The latter is related to the specific treatment goals and typically derived from assessment data.

The *Diagnostic and Statistical Manual of Mental Disorders* (APA, 1987), which is most commonly referred to as the DSM-III-R, is employed by counselors for purposes of psychodiagnosis and treatment planning, insurance reimbursement, and communication with other helping professionals. Published by the American Psychiatric Association, this manual provides a "common denominator" among professionals from a variety of disciplines. The DSM-III-R includes 18 diagnostic categories that conceptualize behaviors as a pattern or syndrome associated with present distress (i.e., symptom), disability (i.e., impairment in one or more areas of functioning), or with significantly increased risk of suffering. The DSM-III-R contains specific diagnostic criteria, a clinical sketch of each disorder, diagnostic considerations, information about the onset and nature of a problem, and any predisposing factors. Behaviors classified using the DSM-III-R are viewed as "mental disorders" rather than expected responses to particular events. The language and "tone" of the DSM-III-R is reflective of the medical profession's view of human behavior as being either "free from" symptoms or free from illness (in a medical sense).

Professional counselors always have had to justify their existence. However, the necessity of establishing indices of progress for insurance companies requires knowledge of the DSM-III-R as a means of being accountable.

Assessment Process

The process of assessment during counseling helps the professional counselor know *what* the target problem is, *who* defines it as a problem, *when* and *where* its occurrence is visible and perceived as a problem, and *how well* counseling is progressing.

A self-coaching model for assessment in empirical counseling is presented in Figure 14.1. The components of the model are discussed separately here.

Step 1: Determine the Focus of Counseling. At the beginning of the counseling process, the professional counselor needs to establish a cooperative and mutually respectful relationship with the client. First, the professional counselor verbally and behaviorally conveys that he or she wants to help the client and values the relationship with the client. Next, the professional counselor makes an inventory of the spectrum of concerns as seen by the client, and perhaps by others if the client is seeking help as a result of a referral. However, much of today's counseling will be through self-choice rather than through the medical model of finding the problem and making a referral to a specialist.

Completion of this phase varies depending on the setting in which the professional counselor is working. For example, if the counselor is in private practice and a physician makes a referral (medical model), the referral will probably describe a specific concern the physician has about the client. The physician has most likely spent time with the client (e.g., perhaps a series of visits over several months), and the client has agreed that assistance is needed. However, the information conveyed by the physician to the professional counselor (i.e., the reason for referral) may not include the particular information necessary for the counselor to be of help to the client. Therefore, the professional counselor, by carefully

> **STEP 1**

DETERMINE THE FOCUS OF COUNSELING—Establish a relationship with the client and identify issues and concerns to be addressed during counseling.

> Establish relationship
> Identify spectrum of issues and concerns

> **STEP 2**

CLARIFY THE SITUATION—In cooperation with the client, clarify the priority of issues and concerns for counseling and the target attributes or specific behaviors needling intervention. This step includes identifying the conditions and circumstances of the target issues and concerns.

> Narrow list of target issues and concerns
> Determine expected attainment from counseling (goals)
> Gather data on specific issue and concern behaviors

> **STEP 3**

IDENTIFY COUNSELING ACTIVITIES—Determine concrete, detailed information on what will be done, how and when it will be done, and duration of intervention(s). Within this step, plans are made for measuring the client's target behavior(s) several times during the counseling process.

> Determine procedures for counseling
> Determine procedures for assessment

> **STEP 4**

INITIATE PLAN—Implement Step 3 and derive meaning by analyzing and interpreting data from the assessment. Utilize the results from the data analysis and, if necessary, make revisions in the counseling process.

Figure 14.1. Self-coaching model of preliminary assessment for empirical counseling.

interviewing and/or assessing the client, can acquire accurate information on the nature of the client's problem.

If the professional counselor is in a school setting, the referral may be a teacher's request for assistance. For example, the teacher might ask the counselor "to help Tammy adjust to the classroom because she's disrupting the other students." Of course, many reasons are possible for Tammy's behavior. The professional counselor's task, in this situation, is to help Tammy, while at the same time, assisting Tammy's teacher. Again, the professional counselor must first identify the spectrum of issues.

In contrast to the example of the physician's referral, Tammy's teacher has more than likely spent considerable time with the class and is likely to know much about Tammy and the other students. The teacher, however, may not be able to convey to the professional counselor the type of information necessary for helping Tammy. The counselor may need to obtain additional information by carefully interviewing the teacher and exacting specific data concerning Tammy's behaviors.

Step 2: Clarify the Situation. Usually the professional counselor's second step in individual assessment is to focus upon the primary concern(s) of the client. For a professional counselor to be presented with a spectrum of issues and concerns (e.g., inadequate social skills, marital difficulties, and uncertain vocational goals) is not infrequent. At times, establishing multiple goals for counseling is feasible, and measurement of each is necessary. On other occasions, and when possible, several different issues can be rank ordered when they are not of comparable importance to the client. In most situations, the professional counselor likely has identified several, if not a host of, target behaviors. Therefore, the counselor may have difficulty determining the priority of help needed and the associated specific, operational goals. This requires determining the priority of target concerns for counseling. Sundel and Sundel (1975) suggested the following general principles as a guide for the professional counselor (and, if possible, the client) when selecting a priority concern.

1. Select the concern with which the client or significant other is immediately concerned.

2. Select the concern which if continued will have the most aversive consequences for the client, significant others, or society thus minimizing the amount of pain inflicted on the client or others.

3. Select the concern with which the client would have immediate success thus providing the client with increased motivation and trust in the professional counselor and the counseling process.

4. Select the concern that needs attention before any other problem can be resolved.

During the clarifying stage of the assessment model, the professional counselor, in cooperation with the client, determines goals and objectives for counseling by gathering information about specific behaviors that the client considers important to the counseling outcome. These behaviors might be to speak-up more frequently in class or to reach a decision about the behavior of one's spouse.

The professional counselor identifies the focus of counseling within the larger situational context of its occurrence. To return to Tammy, the professional counselor would specify other elements related to her target concern(s). This might involve, but not be limited to, spending a period of time in Tammy's classroom to observe her reactions to the academic material, the teacher, and other children; her behavior when assignments are made; and her responses and/or reactions when called upon. Also, the counselor wants to obtain detailed information on the methods that have been tried by the teacher to help Tammy adjust to the classroom. In addition, the counselor may decide that more information is necessary from other significant people in Tammy's life, such as the school nurse, personnel director, and parents. Again, the professional counselor, through careful interviewing, can provide information, in exact detail, regarding which of Tammy's behaviors are of concern and what has taken place. The professional counselor is interested in the *who* and *where* of the target concern.

Finally in Step 2, the professional counselor gathers data about specific behaviors. In all cases, specific and concrete information needs to be obtained.

Step 3: Identify Counseling Activities. In Step 3 of the self-coaching model, the professional counselor describes in some detail the procedures to be used when working with a client (i.e., develops a counseling plan). Needed is information on *what* is to be done, *how* it will be done, and *when* it will be done (i.e., timing and duration). Basically, the components of the counseling process that the counselor has reason to believe are important to the counseling outcome need to be determined. Only when counseling procedures are planned are they modified or adapted to a new situation. Identifying counseling activities is necessary and important if the counselor is to improve counseling procedures and to help others.

Step 4: Initiate Plan. The professional counselor next begins to implement the activities in Step 3. Through an analysis of data, meaning is derived for the purposes of evaluating the client's progress and, if necessary, making revisions in the counseling process.

By being able to collect data early in the counseling process, the professional counselor is able to develop a substantial baseline for viewing progress. Baseline refers to measures of the specific behavior prior to, or at the beginning of, counseling. An attempt should be made, initially, to collect data on as large a number of measures of a client's behavior(s) as possible. As counseling proceeds, non-important or unhelpful measures can be abandoned and helpful measures retained.

SUMMARY

This chapter focused on the purpose and use of assessment with an emphasis on the counseling process. Understanding the need for assessment in effective counseling was stressed. Discussed were standardized tests, inventories, informal assessments, traditional assessment, assessment with empirical counseling, and a model for the counselor to employ when assessing clients.

Chapter **15**

RESEARCH IN PROFESSIONAL COUNSELING

For new problems to develop as a professional field grows and matures is not an uncommon event. Of concern, however, are old problems that continue to exist. In professional counseling, the old problem of determining the role of research for professional counselors and trainees has become particularly acute during the past ten years. An influential factor has been the requirement of additional research resulting from forces outside as well as within the profession. These forces include the profession's increasing involvement with standards of practice, accountability, litigation, and the public's increasing use of counseling services.

The professional counselor is primarily a practitioner of applied behavioral sciences whose work is to help others solve problems. The need for a counselor's time to be devoted to the direct service of helping others is usually viewed as urgent by supervisors, administrators, managers, clients, colleagues, and sometimes by counselors themselves. In contrast, conducting research is rarely viewed as urgent. Thus, professional counselors are often dismayed to find that many of their colleagues and clients fail to share the value they place on research. In fact, in some work settings research is viewed with suspicion and disdain. Such behavior can be attributed partially to the problem that many counseling service settings are beset by so many pressures and problems that they focus only on addressing the immediate *counseling* concerns with which they are confronted. In such settings, research is not viewed as an integral part of good practice but rather as a luxury to be conducted only if time is available for it. The appropriate situation is somewhere between these extremes. Professional counselors *should* devote most of their time to counseling activities, but research is an appropriate, small proportion of their time *and* an important part of good professional counseling practice.

Of all the personnel employed in places where counselors work, the professional counselor in many situations will have had the most training in formal scientific inquiry. Therefore, counselors often spend time discussing the nature of research in counseling. What is perplexing is why the topic of research has generated such differences of opinion. Perhaps the term appears to be pretentious, implying that it "guarantees" new insights. Or perhaps it conjures images of the professional counselor using clients and other personnel as mere subjects in some type of laboratory experiment that is not "helping oriented." Neither of these points of view is correct. Scientific inquiry, or research, is required if professional counselors are to draw valid conclusions about, or to evaluate effectively, counseling.

Inherent in the viewpoint that research and scientific inquiry are synonymous with drawing valid conclusions and making decisions is the need to perceive research from a much broader perspective than has been true among other professional groups. The core of this view is that professional counselors must habitually inquire and maintain a critical attitude about their professional work. Respect for objectivity and unbiased conclusions is integral to the professional counselor's training. Thus, *research is equated with inquiry* and not just with traditional methods of data gathering and analyses.

Professional counselors are continually engaged in careful, scientific reviews of all their activities, although some of that research may not be structurally well designed. In many work places, the procedures of rigorous, carefully controlled research studies admittedly are difficult, if not sometimes impossible, to carry out. Also, counselors do not ordinarily initiate studies which are removed from their work and clients. Most of their research is directed toward immediate concerns and not toward general problems in the field of counseling. The former can be described as research that addresses immediate concerns of a counseling situation (i.e., answering questions such as, "What progress is being made during counseling?" and "What techniques are most effective with the client?"). The latter form of research addresses issues that are more theoretical and general such as the "why" and "how" of counseling. Although the distinction between these different forms of research is forced, the distinction illustrates that research on what happens during counseling sessions focuses upon specific client situations where progress is of immediate concern to the counselor; it concentrates on information for helping the client. Research about the why and how of counseling, however, is more general and is concerned with inferences of basic issues about the process of counseling and other interventions; it is not necessarily specific to an individual client or group of clients. Researching the effect counseling is having on a client not only affects that client but affects all other clients as well. For example, if a professional counselor answers questions about Kate's progress in counseling, the resulting information can be used to alter what happens with other clients. The likelihood of professional counselors systematically researching a client's progress is considerably greater than the likelihood of conducting research on "why" or "how" clients change because the former directly affects the agency, school, business, or practice.

Research as an aspect of professionalism in counseling has been discussed in Chapter 3. The present discussion focuses on the nature of research practices by professional counselors. Research in counseling is often perceived as complex because of the terminology used. Therefore, the following discussion presents some of the important terms, concepts, and methods used with scientific inquiry.

Scientific inquiry or research is essentially a systematic and controlled extension of common sense (Kerlinger, 1986). Built into this extension is the development of theoretical structures and concepts that are continuously being tested and evaluated. Central to scientific inquiry is the research process with its basic components of reasoning and logic. The former can be delineated into deductive and inductive reasoning. In *deductive reasoning,* the logical progression is from the general to the specific (i.e., if a general idea or theory is true, then a specific behavior should be observable). *Inductive reasoning,* however, is inferential and progresses from the specific to the general; if a specific behavior is (consistently) observable, then a general idea or theory is true. In inductive reasoning, data are gathered and analyzed, and, depending upon the outcomes of the research, generalizations or inferences are made that relate back to theoretical structures and concepts.

SELECTING VARIABLES

An essential consideration in any research is selecting the variables to be measured, generally referred to as dependent and independent variables.

The *dependent variable* (i.e., that which is being measured) must logically relate to the behavior being studied. In addition, it needs to be observable, specific, and sensitive to performance differences. Because measurement of this variable provides an indication of a subject's actual level of performance, the most sensitive measure available should be used in order to assure precision of results.

The *independent variable* (i.e., the variable being manipulated and studied) is also referred to as the treatment. An independent variable can consist of more than one level. For example, if three methods of counseling were being compared, the dependent variable might be counseling effectiveness and the independent variable (i.e., counseling methods) would be divided into three levels, each representing one of the counseling methods.

RESEARCH DESIGNS AND PLANS

Effective research involves structured and carefully developed methods referred to as *research designs or plans*. The type of design used by professional counselors may involve a *continuous-measurement time-series experiment* or a traditional *pre-post experiment*. Both forms of research are effective in measuring selected behaviors in counseling, and both involve the element of experimental control. They differ by number of subjects, types of data generated, and types of questions studied.

Continuous-measurement Time-series Designs

Continuous-measurement designs are particularly useful with single-subject (one client) research or studies involving small number of subjects (clients). This type of research is most often used to address questions of difference (e.g., Is there a difference due to treatment?). Several sets of observations are undertaken through continuous (i.e., repeated) measurements during a given time period. Included in the data-gathering process are baseline (i.e., before counseling or intervention commences) information, continuous measurement during intervention, and post-intervention measurement. A client's behavioral characteristics are studied as well as the results of intervention.

With continuous measurement, the process is as important as the product or outcome, as is exemplified with the recording of baseline behavior and continuous performance data that are dependent upon intervention. Behavioral changes that occur as a result of intervention are attributed to the new condition since all other factors are (theoretically) held constant. Continuous measurement designs vary by treatment (i.e., intervention) format with the most common being the A-B, A-B-A-B, and multiple-baseline designs. A brief explanation of each follows.

A-B Design. Two phases constitute this design: *baseline* (A) followed by *intervention* (B). The latter is initiated after the baseline behavior achieves a level of stability that provides a satisfactory estimate of pretreatment performance. The criterion for satisfactory stability is defined by the counselor.

With this design, the assumption is made that any change in behavior is a (direct) result of intervention. However, with only two phases, it is difficult to be certain that this assumption is accurate and/or valid. Extraneous factors occurring simultaneously with the commencement of intervention also could influence outcomes. A means of circumventing this possibility is to replicate the two phases as in an A-B-A-B design.

A-B-A-B Design. This design extends the A-B format to include a sequential replication of the two phases (i.e., A and B). If the pattern of behavior observed during the first two phases is replicated during the last two phases (i.e., the pretreatment baseline contingencies are reestablished during the third phase and the intervention contingencies of phase two are reestablished during phase four), it can be assumed that the changes in behavior are accounted for by the intervention.

Although this design eliminates the problem of uncertainty of effect encountered with the A-B design, in many situations in counseling the A-B-A-B format would be detrimental to the client. For example, if an intervention technique introduced during the second phase was found to be effective in helping a client with acting-out aggressions toward his or her peers, a reversal to the baseline to reestablish aggressive behaviors would not be desirable. In situations of this nature, a multiple-baseline design is an effective alternative.

Multiple-baseline Design. In this design, multiple target behaviors are recorded simultaneously, and the respective baselines for the different behaviors are staggered. The assumption is made that subsequent behaviors serve as a means of control for the preceding behavior. Although deliberately oversimplified, the following illustration demonstrates the use of a multiple-baseline design in counseling. The Jacksons, who worked for different accounting firms, had been married for seven years and sought the help of a professional counselor because of marital problems which focused primarily on communication with each other. They worked with the professional counselor over a period of five weeks for three communication problem areas: use of obscenities, shouting, and negative statements. Using a multiple-baseline design to examine counseling effectiveness, the professional counselor divided the measurement of effectiveness into five phases, each of which lasted one week. During each phase, data were collected by recording the frequency with which each of the communication problems occurred. The data gathered during phase one became the baseline data against which the frequency counts for the remaining phases were compared. During phase two (second week), the Jacksons went to separate rooms whenever either individual used an obscenity. During phase three (third week), the Jacksons continued with the procedure introduced during phase two but also went to different rooms whenever there was shouting. With phase four (fourth week), the Jacksons focused on negative statements, again going to separate rooms when this behavior occurred. They also continued largely on their own with the procedures introduced in phases two and three. The three procedures used in phase four were continued in phase five (fifth week) for purposes of follow-up data collection.

To recap the illustration using the Jacksons, after baseline conditions have been established for three behaviors, phase two is introduced; it consists of initiating intervention for the first behavior and continuing with the baseline conditions for the remaining two behaviors. In changing to the third phase, intervention is introduced for the second behavior and the baseline condition is continued for the third behavior only. Finally, during the fourth phase, the intervention is used with all behaviors. A change in performance for all behaviors upon initiation of the intervention confirms that the results are due to the treatment effect only. Thus, multiple-baseline designs are considered the most powerful of the time-series experiments. However, in many counseling situations, the most rigorous procedure that a professional counselor can reasonably use is the A-B design.

Traditional Experimental Designs

Characteristic of traditional experimental research is a focus upon the product or outcomes due to intervention.

Questions studied in this form of research address relationships or correlations as well as differences. Unlike continuous-measurement designs, differences in traditional experimental designs essentially involve comparisons between groups of subjects or measurements within a group following intervention. Typically, less observations are made in traditional experimental research, with the outcomes often derived from a single performance measure on a group of subjects following intervention. Designs for this type of research vary but are based upon three main formats: independent group comparisons, repeated-measures comparisons, and mixed-group comparisons. These three formats and correlational studies are briefly summarized below.

Independent Group Comparisons. Studies employing this format involve different groups, each of which is independent of the others (i.e., the performance of one group does not influence the performance of the other groups being studied). In addition to the criterion of independence, the assumption is (and must be) that the groups were "equivalent" before the administration of intervention.

Studies that investigate only one experimental variable are referred to as single-factor designs. Two-factor designs involve the investigation of two experimental variables in the same study. The number of levels in each factor may vary. A study with two factors, each of which contains two levels, is referred to as a two-by-two design which is denoted as 2 X 2, indicating that two factors are used and each has two levels. If the two factors vary in number of levels, the notation changes accordingly (e.g., 2 X 3, 3 X 2, or 3 x 4). For example, in a business or industrial setting, the counselor might assign a section of employees (group 1) to a wellness-workshop training program, while a second section (i.e., a control group) would not receive wellness training. The professional counselor then divides the participants in each group into level-A and level-B personality types. Thus, the counselor has formulated a 2 X 2 study that consists of two groups (group 1 and the control group) and two levels within each group (A and B personality types).

Repeated-measures Comparisons. When the groups being studied are not independent of each other, or the same group of subjects are studied under two or more different conditions, a repeated-measures design can be employed. Studies of this nature may involve a pre-post design to compare differences due to treatment intervention (i.e., a pretest is administered, the intervention is employed, and a posttest is administered). As an example, repeated measures comparisons can be used by professional counselors to evaluate a group's progress. If a group of adult substance abusers is being studied for the purpose of examining their progress as a result of group counseling, Julie, their counselor, can gather data on (1) the incidence of substance abuse, (2) interpersonal relationship, and (3) absenteeism at work prior to group counseling and again after counseling is completed. Of note, however, is that with this form of data gathering, Julie needs to use a number of pretest and posttest measurements to assure that she acquires an accurate indication of progress.

Mixed-group Designs. Repeated measures can be employed with independent groups using a mixed-group design. This format is extremely flexible, allowing for variation in the number of repeated and independent variables. For example, the three conditions involved in a study may include one repeated and two independent, or two repeated and one independent variables. Mixed-group designs can become rather complex and, therefore, their results are more difficult to interpret.

Correlational Studies. In addition to differences between or within groups, traditional-experimental research often involves studies of a sample of subjects to determine the degree to which two or more variables correlate, or vary together. Using a minimum of two measures on each subject, a correlation coefficient is computed to determine an estimate of the relationship between given variables or to predict outcomes. For example, William, a professional counselor, is interested in answering the question, "How helpful are job-placement seminars for the future income of discharged employees?" To address this question, William could examine the relationship between income level and the frequency of the respective individual's attendance at the seminars.

FACTORS AFFECTING OUTCOMES

With the determination of an appropriate experimental design, consideration needs to be given to factors that can affect the outcome(s) of a research study (i.e., threats to internal and external validity).

Internal Validity

Internal validity is the basic minimum with which the results of an experiment are interpretable (Campbell & Stanley, 1963). Stated in a simplified manner, all systematic differences between the groups being studied are eliminated except the variable of concern; the research should be free of extraneous variables that may affect outcomes. When it is impossible to circumvent all threats to internal validity, those remaining need to be addressed in the interpretation of results. Drew (1976) reported eight threats to internal validity. They are briefly summarized in the paragraphs that follow.

One problem of internal validity that is difficult to control is *history* (i.e., specific incidents that can intervene during a study because the researcher may be unaware of them or unable to prevent their occurrence). An example is the effect which an airplane crash that was coincident with the research had upon a client with a fear of flying. The counselor working with this client was pleased with the progress being made. However, when the client learned of the reported airline accident, the progressive trend suddenly reversed.

When studies involve a long period of time, *maturation* may become a threat to the internal validity of a study. For example, a subject's performance may be affected by his or her hunger or fatigue or by aging if a longitudinal study is involved.

A third threat to internal validity is *testing* or *test practice.* Consideration needs to be given to whether change from pretest to posttest is due to treatment only or is due to test practice. Scores on a second, or post, test may be influenced simply by the experience of taking a pretest.

In addition to the subject's experience in test taking, consideration needs to be given to the effect that *instrumentation* may have upon the results of a study. Campbell and Stanley (1963) referred to this problem as "changes in the calibration of a measurement instrument or changes in the observers" (p. 175). Any changes made in the recording or scoring of a subject's responses during a study will subsequently affect the results of a study and therefore threaten internal validity.

Assigning subjects to particular groups on the basis of typical (usually extreme) scores poses another threat to internal validity because of *statistical regression.* When typical scores are used, the risk is always present that during the study subjects may regress toward their average performance, resulting in groups that may be more equivalent than different.

Another factor that may affect study performance and threaten internal validity is the *Hawthorne effect.* It occurs when a subject's performance is affected merely as a function of being in a study and feeling "special" about it.

A seventh threat to internal validity is *bias in group composition.* This is of particular concern with *quasi-experimental designs,* which differ from experimental designs by the manner in which subject groups are formed. In experimental designs, groups are formed by sampling a single-subject pool in a systematic manner (e.g., random sampling). These groups are similar until treatment begins. However, in *quasi-experimental designs,* the groups may not be similar and are not necessarily derived from the same subject pool because controlling for systematic differences that may exist between groups before the research begins is hard to do.

A final threat to internal validity is *experimental mortality,* or the loss of subjects. General loss of subjects is to be expected in research and often extra subjects are selected for the purpose of having a back-up or replacement pool. Experimental mortality, however, threatens internal validity when it results in significantly unequal numbers in comparison groups.

External Validity

External validity is concerned with generalizability (e.g., Are the results representative of or applicable to the population studied?). To facilitate external validity, a study uses subjects, settings, treatment variables, and measurement variables selected to be representative of another, usually larger, context to which the results are to be generalized. Threats to external validity that need to be circumvented (i.e., nonrepresentative experimental setting, population-sample differences, pretest influence, and multiple treatment interference) are discussed in the following paragraphs.

The *experimental setting* needs to be arranged, as much as possible, like the setting to which the results will be generalized. Significant deviations from the nonexperimental setting may affect subjects' performances, resulting in a sample that is not representative of the intended original population.

Population-sample differences, or using a nonrepresentative sample from a given population, poses a great threat to external validity. The interpretation of experimental results must be generalizable to the population represented by the subjects, but this is not possible if significant characteristic differences exist between the subjects and members of the larger population. Therefore, care needs to be taken to use a correct procedure for selecting representative subjects.

Pretest procedures can sometimes create a *pretest influence.* In general, a researcher wants to be assured that performance will be due to subject-task interaction rather than the subject's ability to learn to perform a particular behavior. However, such procedures, if given to one set of subjects in the study and not another, can threaten external validity if the pretested subjects' sensitivity to the experimental variable being studied is decreased or increased.

When multiple treatments are administered to the same subjects, a cumulative effect referred to as *multiple-treatment interference* may influence their performance and the generalizability of results then becomes questionable. This will most often be true in counseling research when the effects of prior treatments have not dissipated before the next treatment is introduced, resulting in increased or depressed sensitivity to the experimental task.

SELECTING SUBJECTS

Three related factors need to be considered in the subject-selection process: appropriateness, representativeness, and number of subjects.

Appropriateness

The subjects in a study need to fit the definition for the given population. As Kerlinger (1986) indicated, a population consists of all elements of any well-defined class of people, events, or objects being investigated. Consideration needs to be given to units or restrictions in the population as they relate to the topic being studied. This may result in selective inclusion or exclusion of particular potential subjects.

Representativeness

The subjects selected for a study need to be representative of the population if the research results are to be generalizable to the given set of individuals, events, or objects. Several different sampling procedures exist: simple random, stratified random, proportional, systematic, and cluster sampling.

Simple Random Sampling. This process assures that each individual, event, or object in a given population has an equal chance of being selected for the study. The assumption is made that the characteristics of the population are presented in the subjects selected (i.e., sample) to the same degree that the characteristics exist in the population. However, the more heterogeneous a population is, the greater is the chance that the members' diverse characteristics will not be appropriately represented in the sample selected.

A variety of techniques can be used to randomly select subjects from a given population (e.g., drawing names from a hat). However, probably the most effective technique is using a *table of random numbers.* Each potential subject is assigned a number and then a table of random numbers is used to identify the appropriate subjects.

Stratified Random Sample. This process is used when two or more groups of individuals, events, or objects that are distinctly different on an important variable in the study are being studied. Each of these different sets or subpopulations, referred to as *strata,* must have representative subjects selected from it. Therefore, after the strata are clearly defined, a random sample is drawn from each of the respective strata.

Proportional Sampling. Occasionally, a particular subgroup represents only a proportion of the population. To avoid misrepresentation, the selection of subjects in this case needs to be proportionate to that of the larger population. In this sampling technique, the lists of subpopulation individuals, events, or objects are developed using the same proportions that exist in the larger population, and subjects are then randomly drawn from each list in proportional representation.

Systematic Sampling. In this procedure subjects are systematically drawn from a population based on an appropriate arrangement of the list of individuals, events, or objects in the population. The names of individuals meeting the selection criteria are listed in a predetermined, unbiased manner, and the researcher randomly selects a starting point in the list and then selects every nth individual until the desired number of subjects is obtained. This technique is easily managed and therefore appealing to many researchers. However, caution is advised in that the list of potential subjects must be free of any influential trends in the ordering.

Cluster Sampling. Potential subjects for some studies may already be formed into predetermined groups or clusters. In these situations, clusters are initially selected and then the subjects are randomly selected from within the clusters. Consideration needs to be given to representative sampling of both the initially selected clusters and the actual subjects.

Sample Size

Because no set sample size is required under all conditions, the number of subjects "necessary" for a given study is unclear. One influential factor is the amount of variation in the population being studied. For example, smaller samples can be used with more homogeneous populations because less variation occurs. Likewise, populations containing a large amount of variation necessitate larger samples to better represent the variation. Because an adequate sample of behavior needs to be obtained, sample size must be judged according to the original population and its characteristics.

STATISTICAL ANALYSES

An important consideration in the process of developing a research study is the statistical procedures used to analyze the data collected. Decisions concerning data analyses are made when designing the study because the statistical tools used are dependent upon the purpose of the research undertaken and the type of data derived. Therefore, the selection of appropriate statistical analyses is important.

Type of Measurement Scale

The data to be analyzed vary by type of measurement scale used. The first type, *nominal data,* also referred to as classification or categorical data, consists of information in the form of mutually exclusive groups or categories. Each category is presumably distinct from the other categories, with the data serving only as labels of identification. Examples of nominal data include year in school, occupation, and yes or no responses to a question.

Ordinal data are characterized by rank-order measurements and an underlying continuum. The component of identity found with nominal data is extended to include the dimension of order and thus, a relative measure of "more than" or "less than." Measurements using *Likert-type scales* (e.g., a five-step continuum from "none of the time" to "all of the time") exemplify this data type.

The properties of identity and degree of difference found in ordinal data are extended to include magnitude of difference (i.e., the property of additivity) for *interval data.* As its name implies, interval data address known and constant magnitudinal differences between scores (i.e., interval distances). Also characteristic of this type of data is an arbitrary zero point. Examples of interval data include the Celsius and Fahrenheit temperature scales as well as calendar time.

The last type of data, *ratio data,* includes all the properties of interval data, except the zero point is not arbitrary. A score of zero represents total absence of the variable being measured. Examples of ratio data include response time, weight, and height.

Descriptive Statistics—Central Tendency

Descriptive statistics are used when the researcher only is interested in describing the group(s) being studied. This may be the only type of statistical analysis undertaken in a study or it can be followed with statistical analyses for inferential purposes, which will be discussed later.

Descriptive statistics can be divided into two general categories of measures: central tendency and dispersion or variance. The most common measures of central tendency are the mean, median, and mode.

Mean. Also referred to as the arithmetic average, the mean of a distribution of scores is derived by summing all the scores in a distribution and dividing the same by the number of scores in the set. Although this statistic is not used with nominal or ordinal data, it is the most frequently used measure of central tendency. It is more stable than the other measures of central tendency and is amenable to additional manipulation, making it useful in inferential statistics. However, the mean is affected by extreme, or outlying, scores. Therefore, if a distribution has a few extreme scores and accuracy of measurement is important, the median will be a more appropriate measure of central tendency.

Median. This measure of central tendency represents the middle point in a distribution of scores; the point above or below which half of the scores fall. The median is used with all types of data except nominal data.

Mode. The most frequently occurring score or interval in a distribution is referred to as the mode. This statistic is the only measure of central tendency to use with nominal data, but it also may be used with the other three types.

Descriptive Statistics—Dispersion Measures

The second category of descriptive statistic includes dispersion measures or the degree to which scores vary from a measure of central tendency. Statistics in this category are the range, semi-interquartile range, and standard deviation.

Range. The range, which provides a quick index of the amount of variability in a distribution, is determined by subtracting the lowest from the highest scores in the distribution, and adding 1. Therefore, the range, as a measure of dispersion, is limited in its usefulness because it is not representative of most of the data in the distribution.

Semi-interquartile Range. A distribution is divided into four equal parts separated by points referred to as quartiles. Thus, 50% of the scores in a distribution fall between the first quartile (Q1) and the third quartile (Q3). The difference between Q1 and Q3 divided by 2 represents the semi-interquartile range. Because this statistic uses more of the scores in a distribution than does the simple range, it provides a more stable measure of dispersion and a more representative picture of the distribution of scores.

Standard Deviation. Although this statistic is not as easy to calculate as the other measures of variability, it is used more often. The standard deviation, which provides a "standardized" measure of a score's deviation above or below the mean, is limited to interval and ratio data. The major advantages of this statistic are that it is used in many more complex statistics and it is considerably less affected by extreme scores.

Inferential Statistics

As implied, inferential statistics enable a counselor/researcher to make inferences that the treatment(s) in a study actually generated the observed performance(s). Implications can be drawn from the resulting data to variables not directly involved in the study because inferential statistics provide an indication of the degree to which the results are due to treatment or to chance.

Studies involving this form of statistical analysis involve questions of difference or relationship. Also, a variety of statistical tests of significance can be employed. The acceptable probability level that the results are due to treatment rather than chance is usually $p < .05$ or $p < .01$. If $p < .05$ or $p < .01$, the results obtained in a study would be due to chance only 5 or 1, respectively, or less times out of 100.

Tests of significance are applied to either parametric or nonparametric statistics, depending upon reasonable and supportable assumptions made concerning the population being studied. Generally, nonparametric statistics require fewer and less rigorous assumptions about population parameters (i.e., values such as mean and standard deviation) than do parametric statistics. Also, nonparametric statistics can be applied to all types of data, but parametric statistical analyses may be used only with interval and ratio data. Larger sample sizes also are required for parametric statistical analyses, but this type of statistics can be applied to a greater variety of research questions.

Statistical Analyses Addressing Relationships

The degree to which two or more phenomena are related or vary together are the focus of studies addressing relationship questions. The statistic that provides an estimate of the relationship between given variables is the *correlation coefficient.* This coefficient ranges from -1.00 to +1.00 with coefficients between zero and +1.00 indicating that the two variables tend to vary in the same direction (i.e., have a positive relationship). Negative correlations (i.e., coefficients falling between zero and -1.00) indicate an inverse relationship; the two variables vary in opposite directions. Correlation coefficients with higher numbers indicate stronger relationships whereas coefficients approaching zero are indicators of weak relationships. Likewise, a correlation coefficient of zero signifies a total lack of systematic variation between the two variables; they vary independently of one another.

The correlation technique employed depends on the type of data. When interval or ratio data are involved, the *Pearson product-moment correlation* is used. The *Spearman rank-order correlation* and *Kendall's tau* are typically used with ordinal data.

More than two variables can be compared using a **multiple correlation analysis.** This technique can be extended by a **multiple regression analysis** which provides a measure of the amount of variance in the dependent variable accounted for by each independent variable being studied. An alternative use of the multiple regression analysis is to predict the effectiveness of given treatments.

TRADITIONAL VERSUS SINGLE-SUBJECT RESEARCH

Although professional counselors apply scientific inquiry as the basis for helping others, they have done little to integrate science into counseling through traditional experimental research. Although this appears to be due to several reasons, the major problem, with few exceptions, is that traditional experimental designs have emphasized data collection using large groups of subjects, normative research, and analyses based on within-group or between-group treatments. Applying methodology of this nature to a counseling practitioner's problems poses immense practical difficulties (Gelso, 1985).

Traditional experimental designs require, among other things, a large number of relatively homogeneous clients at a given period of time. Consider for example a professional counselor who is interested in studying the effectiveness of two treatment approaches for adolescents who are concerned with their sexual behavior. Using the traditional approach, the counselor would need approximately 30 clients matched on relevant background variables (e.g., age, gender, severity of problem, and history of previous treatment), who ideally would need to receive counseling within approximately the same time frame. This in itself is a rather difficult task considering the type of clients and time allotment. Further, utilizing even a simple experimental design of a treatment group and no-treatment control group format to examine effects due to treatment would entail near-impossible demands for the professional counselor to meet. Of course, this illustration has deliberately been oversimplified. However, it does illustrate the problems encountered when conducting research using a traditional experimental design.

Another effect upon the professional counselor's use of traditional experimental research methodology is the ethical factors involved in selecting control groups by withholding treatment from clients. This, of course, should not be done without careful consideration of the risks involved for the untreated group. An interesting argument on this subject, advanced by Barlow, Hayes, and Nelson (1984), is as follows:

> . . . in most instances there is no evidence that the treatment works in the first place, which forms the basis for conducting research on its effectiveness. Therefore, one could argue that withholding an unproven treatment for a control group might be less of a risk than applying this treatment to the experimental group. (p.26)

The traditional research methodology of working with large groups and determining average results, with associated disregard for individual differences, has limited relevance in contributing to improvements for specific clients. Therefore, traditional research methodology has had little influence in affecting the professional counselor's practice or self-evaluation because it has not been relevant to applied settings.

The question of what can be done remains. Goldman (1977), in recognizing the lack of influence of traditional research, advised professional counselors ". . . to return to the conception of research as imaginative searching by intelligent and informed people who are aware of the important questions that we as a profession and society in general need to have answered" (p.366). Goldman probably would agree that, while traditional comparison-group research designs remain indispensable tools for professional counselors, they have specific limitations that render them dysfunctional in situations and settings where counselors typically work.

An alternative would be to use *single-subject designs* for measuring and demonstrating the effect(s) of counseling. This type of design adapts the traditional experimental research approach to fit the practice of counseling. Single-subject methods can be generalized across all settings and situations because the techniques can vary depending on the particular circumstances and goals of each client. Also, the methods are not dependent upon any particular theoretical orientation, but rather reflect "a way of thinking." The basic elements of single-subject research consist of measuring change, relating this change to a particular aspect of counseling, and basing future professional actions on the observations.

Will debates over what should be the nature of research conducted by counselors ever be fully resolved? Probably not. Therefore, Gelso's (1985) statements provide a reasonable alternative:

> Attempts to solve the problem of low relevance create other problems (i.e., those caused by low rigor). If we attack these other problems by doing more rigorous research, for example, this makes for research that is less relevant to practice. Our solutions to problems create other problems. In effect, there are no ready solutions.

> My personal and partial solution to this apparent dilemma is to conduct a wide range of research along what may be labeled a rigor-relevance continuum. I also think that this is the most fruitful way for the field of counseling to proceed. If the pendulum of beliefs in counseling research swings too far to one side or the other (on the rigor-relevance continuum), the field and the amount and quality of knowledge that it generates will suffer. (p. 552)

AN OBSERVATION

Most professional counselors, in addition to applying scientific inquiry as the basis of helping others, also continue to read the research literature in counseling and attend professional meetings where research papers are presented. Also, professional counselors, who do research at their work places, are careful not to give their clients or others the impression that research is more important than the direct practice of helping. Clients and other personnel can easily perceive themselves as mere subjects in some type of laboratory experiment being directed by the counselor. Professional counselors avoid these problems by carefully explaining the value of the research activity and how it may help the client and other personnel in return.

SUMMARY

Professional counselors should devote most of their time to counseling activities, but research is also appropriate and an important part of good professional counseling practice. Scientific research is required if professional counselors are to effectively evaluate counseling. Additionally, it fosters objectivity and an unbiased critical attitude toward the counselor's professional work.

Effective research involves structured methods referred to as research designs or plans. Two types of designs used by professional counselors are continuous-measurement time-series experiments, which include A-B, A-B-A-B, and multiple-baseline designs, and pre-post experiments or traditional experimental designs, which include independent group comparisons, repeated-measures comparisons, mixed-group designs, and correlation studies.

In all types of studies, the professional counselor needs to be concerned with factors which affect the outcome of a study. Internal validity is one of these factors and assumes that the research is free of extraneous variables that may affect outcomes. It says that all systematic differences between groups being studied are eliminated except the variable of concern, and when that is impossible the remaining are addressed in the interpretation of results. Threats to internal validity are history, maturation, test practice, instrumentation, statistical regression, Hawthorne effect, bias in group composition, and experimental mortality.

Another factor which the professional counselor needs to consider in the outcome of a study is external validity. External validity is concerned with how representative or applicable the results are to the population studied. Threats to external validity are experimental setting, population-sample differences, pretest influence, and multiple treatment interference.

Selecting variables to be measured and selecting subjects are essential considerations in any research. Selecting variables is concerned with choosing the dependent variable or that which is being measured and choosing the independent variable or that variable being manipulated and studied. In selecting subjects three factors must be considered: appropriateness, representativeness, and number of subjects. In attending to the representativeness of subjects, several different sampling procedures exist: simple random, stratified random, proportional, systematic, and cluster sampling.

Developing a research study also involves analyzing the data collected. A number of statistical tools are used in this analysis and include types of measurement scale, descriptive statistics, inferential statistics, and statistical analysis addressing relationships.

A final issue that confronts professional counselors with regard to scientific inquiry are the number of real prohibitions to doing traditional research. Applying the methodology required in traditional research poses immense practical and ethical difficulties to a counselor in practice. A suggested alternative for the counselor is to use single-subject designs for measuring and demonstrating the effect of counseling.

Research in counseling is a necessity for determining practice. This chapter discussed the scientific tradition of research in general, and counseling in particular. Emphasized was the value of systematically evaluating counseling practice through formal procedures. Various methodologies, including traditional, experimental, and single-subject designs were examined. Other issues presented included internal and external validity, selecting subjects, and statistical analyses.

APPENDIX I
ETHICAL STANDARDS OF THE AMERICAN COUNSELING ASSOCIATION

ETHICAL STANDARDS OF THE
AMERICAN COUNSELING ASSOCIATION

[formally the American Association for Counseling and Development]
(As Revised by AACD Governing Council, March 1988)

Preamble

The Association is an educational, scientific, and professional organization whose members are dedicated to the enhancement of the worth, dignity, potential, and uniqueness of each individual and thus to the service of society.

The Association recognizes that the role definitions and work settings of its members include a wide variety of academic disciplines, levels of academic preparation and agency services. This diversity reflects the breadth of the Association's interest and influence. It also poses challenging complexities in efforts to set standards for the performance of members, desired requisite preparation or practice, and supporting social, legal, and ethical controls.

The specification of ethical standards enables the Association to clarify to present and future members and to those served by members, the nature of ethical responsibilities held in common by its members.

The existence of such standards serves to stimulate greater concern by members for their own professional functioning and for the conduct of fellow professionals such as counselors, guidance and student personnel workers, and others in the helping professions. As the ethical code of the Association, this document establishes principles that define the ethical behavior of Association members. Additional ethical guidelines developed by the Association's Divisions for their specialty areas may further define a member's ethical behavior.

Section A: General

1. The member influences the development of the profession by continuous efforts to improve professional practices, teaching, services, and research. Professional growth is continuous throughout the member's career and is exemplified by the development of a philosophy that explains why and how a member functions in the helping relationship. Members must gather data on their effectiveness and be guided by the findings. Members recognize the need for continuing education to ensure competent service.

2. The member has a responsibility both to the individual who is served and to the institution within which the service is performed to maintain high standards of professional conduct. The member strives to maintain the highest levels of professional services offered to the individuals to be served. The member also strives to assist the agency, organization, or institution in providing the highest caliber of professional services. The acceptance of employment in an institution implies that the member is in agreement with the general policies and principles of the institution. Therefore the professional activities of the member are also in accord with the objectives of the institution. If, despite concerted efforts, the member cannot reach agreement with the employer as to acceptable standards of conduct that allow for changes in institutional policy conducive to the positive growth and development of clients, then terminating the affiliation should be seriously considered.

3. Ethical behavior among professional associates, both members and nonmembers, must be expected at all times. When information is possessed that raises doubt as to the ethical behavior of professional colleagues, whether Association members or not, the member must take action to attempt to rectify such a condition. Such action shall use the institution's channels first and then use procedures established by the Association.

4. The member neither claims nor implies professional qualifications exceeding those possessed and is responsible for correcting any misrepresentations of these qualifications by others.

5. In establishing fees for professional counseling services, members must consider the financial status of clients and locality. In the event that the established fee structure is inappropriate for a client, assistance must be provided in finding comparable services of acceptable cost.

6. When members provide information to the public or to subordinates, peers or supervisors, they have a responsibility to ensure that the content is general, unidentified client information that is accurate, unbiased, and consists of objective, factual data.

7. Members recognize their boundaries of competence and provide those services and use only those techniques for which they are qualified by training or experience. Members should only accept those positions for which they are professionally qualified.

8. In the counseling relationship the counselor is aware of the intimacy of the relationship and maintains respect for the client and avoids engaging

in activities that seek to meet the counselor's personal needs at the expense of that client.

9. Members do not condone or engage in sexual harassment which is defined as deliberate or repeated comments, gestures, or physical contacts of a sexual nature.

10. The member avoids bringing personal issues into the counseling relationship, especially if the potential for harm is present. Through awareness of the negative impact of both racial and sexual stereotyping and discrimination, the counselor guards the individual rights and personal dignity of the client in the counseling relationship.

11. Products or services provided by the member by means of classroom instruction, public lectures, demonstrations, written articles, radio or television programs, or other types of media must meet the criteria cited in these standards.

Section B: Counseling Relationship

This section refers to practices and procedures of individual and/or group counseling relationships.

The member must recognize the need for client freedom of choice. Under those circumstances where this is not possible, the member must apprise clients of restrictions that may limit their freedom of choice.

1. The member's primary obligation is to respect the integrity and promote the welfare of the client(s), whether the client(s) is (are) assisted individually or in a group relationship. In a group setting, the member is also responsible for taking reasonable precautions to protect individuals from physical and/ or psychological trauma resulting from interaction within the group.

2. Members make provisions for maintaining confidentiality in the storage and disposal of records and follow an established record retention and disposition policy. The counseling relationship and information resulting therefrom must be kept confidential, consistent with the obligations of the member as a professional person. In a group counseling setting, the counselor must set a norm of confidentiality regarding all group participants' disclosures.

3. If an individual is already in a counseling relationship with another professional person, the member does not enter into a counseling relationship without first contacting and receiving the approval of that other professional. If the member discovers that the client is in another counseling relationship

after the counseling relationship begins, the member must gain the consent of the other professional or terminate the relationship, unless the client elects to terminate the other relationship.

4. When the client's condition indicates that there is clear and imminent danger to the client or others, the member must take reasonable personal action or inform responsible authorities. Consultation with other professionals must be used where possible. The assumption of responsibility for the client(s) behavior must be taken only after careful deliberation. The client must be involved in the resumption of responsibility as quickly as possible.

5. Records of the counseling relationship, including interview notes, test data, correspondence, tape recordings, electronic data storage, and other documents, are to be considered professional information for use in counseling, and they should not be considered a part of the records of the institution or agency in which the counselor is employed unless specified by state statute or regulation. Revelation to others of counseling material must occur only upon the expressed consent of the client.

6. In view of the extensive data storage and processing capacities of the computer, the member must ensure that data maintained on a computer is: (a) limited to information that is appropriate and necessary for the services being provided; (b) destroyed after it is determined that the information is no longer of any value in providing services; and (c) restricted in terms of access to appropriate staff members involved in the provision of services by using the best computer security methods available.

7. Use of data derived from a counseling relationship for purposes of counselor training or research shall be confined to content that can be disguised to ensure full protection of the identity of the subject client.

8. The member must inform the client of the purposes, goals, techniques, rules of procedure and limitations that may affect the relationship at or before the time that the counseling relationship is entered. When working with minors or persons who are unable to give consent, the member protects these clients' best interest.

9. In view of common misconceptions related to the perceived inherent validity of computer-generated data and narrative reports, the member must ensure that the client is provided with information as part of the counseling relationship that adequately explains the limitations of computer technology.

10. The member must screen prospective group participants, especially when the emphasis is on self-understanding and growth through self-disclosure.

The member must maintain an awareness of the group participants' compatibility throughout the life of the group.

11. The member may choose to consult with any other professionally competent person about a client. In choosing a consultant, the member must avoid placing the consultant in a conflict of interest situation that would preclude the consultant's being a proper party to the member's efforts to help the client.

12. If the member determines an inability to be of professional assistance to the client, the member must either avoid initiating the counseling relationship or immediately terminate that relationship. In either event, the member must suggest appropriate alternatives. (The member must be knowledgeable about referral resources so that a satisfactory referral can be initiated). In the event the client declines the suggested referral, the member is not obligated to continue the relationship.

13. When the member has other relationships, particularly of an administrative, supervisory and/or evaluative nature with an individual seeking counseling services, the member must not serve as the counselor but should refer the individual to another professional. Only in instances where such an alternative is unavailable and where the individual's situation warrants counseling intervention should the member enter into and/or maintain a counseling relationship. Dual relationships with clients that might impair the member's objectivity and professional judgment (e.g., as with close friends or relatives) must be avoided and/or the counseling relationship terminated through referral to another competent professional.

14. The member will avoid any type of sexual intimacies with clients. Sexual relationships with clients are unethical.

15. All experimental methods of treatment must be clearly indicated to prospective recipients, and safety precautions are to be adhered to by the member.

16. When computer applications are used as a component of counseling services, the member must ensure that: (a) the client is intellectually, emotionally, and physically capable of using the computer application; (b) the computer application is appropriate for the needs of the client; (c) the client understands the purpose and operation of the computer application; and (d) a follow-up of client use of a computer application is provided to both correct possible problems (misconceptions or inappropriate use) and assess subsequent needs.

17. When the member is engaged in short-term group treatment/training programs (e.g., marathons and other encounter-type or growth groups), the member ensures that there is professional assistance available during and following the group experience.

18. Should the member be engaged in a work setting that calls for any variation from the above statements, the member is obligated to consult with other professionals whenever possible to consider justifiable alternatives.

19. The member must ensure that members of various ethnic, racial, religious, disability, and socioeconomic groups have equal access to computer applications used to support counseling services and that the content of available computer applications does not discriminate against the groups described above.

20. When computer applications are developed by the member for use by the general public as self-help/stand-alone computer software, the member must ensure that: (a) self-help computer applications are designed from the beginning to function in a stand-alone manner, as opposed to modifying software that was originally designed to require support from a counselor; (b) self-help computer applications will include within the program statements regarding intended user outcomes, suggestions for using the software, a description of the conditions under which self-help computer applications might not be appropriate, and a description of when and how counseling services might be beneficial; and (c) the manual for such applications will include the qualifications of the developer, the development process, validation data, and operating procedures.

Section C: Measurement and Evaluation

The primary purpose of educational and psychological testing is to provide descriptive measures that are objective and interpretable in either comparative or absolute terms. The member must recognize the need to interpret the statements that follow as applying to the whole range of appraisal techniques including test and non-test data. Test results constitute only one of a variety of pertinent sources of information for personnel, guidance, and counseling decisions.

1. The member must provide specific orientation or information to the examinee(s) prior to and following the test administration so that the results of testing may be placed in proper perspective with other relevant factors. In so doing, the member must recognize the effects of socioeconomic, ethnic

and cultural factors on test scores. It is the member's professional responsibility to use additional, unvalidated information carefully in modifying interpretation of test results.

2. In selecting tests for use in a given situation or with a particular client, the member must consider carefully the specific validity, reliability and appropriateness of the test(s). General validity, reliability, and related issues may be questioned legally as well as ethically when tests are used for vocational and education selection, placement, or counseling.

3. When making any statements to the public about tests and testing, the member must give accurate information and avoid false claims or misconceptions. Special efforts are often required to avoid unwarranted connotations of such terms as IQ and grade equivalent scores.

4. Different tests demand different levels of competence for administration, scoring, and interpretation. Members must recognize the limits of their competence and perform only those functions for which they are prepared. In particular, members using computer-based test interpretations must be trained in the construct being measured and the specific instrument being used prior to using this type of computer application.

5. In situations where a computer is used for test administration and scoring, the member is responsible for ensuring that administration and scoring programs function properly to provide clients with accurate test results.

6. Tests must be administered under the same conditions that were established in their standardization. When tests are not administered under standard conditions or when unusual behavior or irregularities occur during the testing session, those conditions must be noted and the results designated as invalid or of questionable validity. Unsupervised or inadequately supervised test-taking, such as the use of tests through the mail, is considered unethical. On the other hand, the use of instruments that are so designed or standardized to be self-administered and self-scored, such as interest inventories, is to be encouraged.

7. The meaningfulness of test results used in personnel, guidance, and counseling functions generally depends on the examinees' unfamiliarity with the specific items on the test. Any prior coaching or dissemination of the test materials can invalidate test results. Therefore, test security is one of the professional obligations of the member. Conditions that produce most favorable test results must be made known to the examinee.

8. The purpose of testing and the explicit use of the results must be made known to the examinee prior to testing. The counselor must ensure that instrument limitations are not exceeded and that periodic review and/or retesting are made to prevent client stereotyping.

9. The examinee's welfare and explicit, prior understanding must be the criteria for determining the recipients of the test results. The member must see that specific interpretation accompanies any release of individual or group test data. The interpretation of test data must be related to the examinee's particular concerns.

10. Members responsible for making decisions based on test results have an understanding of educational and psychological measurement, validation criteria, and test research.

11. The member must be cautious when interpreting the results of research instruments possessing insufficient technical data. The specific purposes for the use of such instruments must be stated explicitly to examinees.

12. The member must proceed with caution when attempting to evaluate and interpret the performance of minority group members or other persons who are not represented in the norm group on which the instrument was standardized.

13. When computer-based test interpretations are developed by the member to support the assessment process, the member must ensure that the validity of such interpretations is established prior to the commercial distribution of such a computer application.

14. The member recognizes that test results may become obsolete. The member will avoid and prevent the misuse of obsolete test results.

15. The member must guard against the appropriation, reproduction, or modification of the published tests or parts thereof without acknowledgment and permission from the previous publisher.

16. Regarding the preparation, publication and distribution of tests, reference should be made to:

a. "Standards for Educational and Psychological Testing," revised edition, 1985, published by the American Psychological Association on behalf of itself, the American Educational Research Association and the National Council on Measurement in Education.

b. "The Responsible Use of Tests: A Position Paper of AMEG, APGA, and NCME," *Measurement and Evaluation in Guidance,* 1972, 5, 385-388.

c. "Responsibilities of Users of Standardized Tests," APGA, *Guidepost,* October 5, 1978, pp.5-8.

Section D: Research and Publication

1. Guidelines on research with human subjects shall be adhered to, such as:

a. *Ethical Principles in the Conduct of Research with Human Participants,* Washington, D.C.: American Psychological Association, Inc., 1982.

b. *Code of Federal Regulations, Title 45, Subtitle A, Part 46,* as currently issued.

c. *Ethical Principles of Psychologists,* American Psychological Association, Principle #9: Research with Human Participants.

d. Family Educational Rights and Privacy Act (the Buckley Amendment).

e. Current federal regulations and various state rights privacy acts.

2. In planning any research activity dealing with human subjects, the member must be aware of and responsible to all pertinent ethical principles and ensure that the research problem, design, and execution are in full compliance with them.

3. Responsibility for ethical research practice lies with the principal researcher, while others involved in the research activities share ethical obligation and full responsibility for their own actions.

4. In research with human subjects, researchers are responsible for the subjects' welfare throughout the experiment and they must take all reasonable precautions to avoid causing injurious psychological, physical, or social effects on their subjects.

5. All research subjects must be informed of the purpose of the study except when withholding information or providing misinformation to them is essential to the investigation. In such research the member must be

responsible for corrective action as soon as possible following completion of the research.

6. Participation in research must be voluntary. Involuntary participation is appropriate only when it can be demonstrated that participation will have no harmful effects on subjects and is essential to the investigation.

7. When reporting research results, explicit mention must be made of all variables and conditions known to the investigator that might affect the outcome of the investigation or the interpretation of the data.

8. The member must be responsible for conducting and reporting investigations in a manner that minimizes the possibility that results will be misleading.

9. The member has an obligation to make available sufficient original research data to qualified others who may wish to replicate the study.

10. When supplying data, aiding in the research of another person, reporting research results, or making original data available, due care must be taken to disguise the identity of the subjects in the absence of specific authorization from such subjects to do otherwise.

11. When conducting and reporting research, the member must be familiar with, and give recognition to, previous work on the topic, as well as to observe all copyright laws and follow the principles of giving full credit to all to whom credit is due.

12. The member must give due credit through joint authorship, acknowledgment, footnote statements, or other appropriate means to those who have contributed significantly to the research and/or publication, in accordance with such contributions.

13. The member must communicate to other members the results of any research judged to be of professional or scientific value. Results reflecting unfavorably on institutions, programs, services, or vested interests must be withheld for such reasons.

14. If members agree to cooperate with another individual in research and/or publication, they incur an obligation to cooperate as promised in terms of punctuality of performance and with full regard to the completeness and accuracy of the information required.

15. Ethical practice requires that authors not submit the same manuscript, or one essentially similar in content, for simultaneous publication consideration by two or more journals. In addition, manuscripts published in whole or in substantial part in another journal or published work should not be submitted for publication without acknowledgment and permission from the previous publication.

Section E: Consulting

Consultation refers to a voluntary relationship between a professional helper and help-needing individual, group or social unit in which the consultant is providing help to the client(s) in defining and solving a work-related problem or potential problem with a client or client system.

1. The member acting as consultant must have a high degree of self-awareness of his/her own values, knowledge, skills, limitations, and needs in entering a helping relationship that involves human and/or organizational change and that the focus of the relationship be on the issues to be resolved and not on the person(s) presenting the problem.

2. There must be understanding and agreement between member and client for the problem definition, change goals, and predicated consequences of interventions selected.

3. The member must be reasonably certain that she/he or the organization represented has the necessary competencies and resources for giving the kind of help that is needed now or may be needed later and that appropriate referral resources are available to the consultant.

4. The consulting relationship must be one in which client adaptability and growth toward self-direction are encouraged and cultivated. The member must maintain this role consistently and not become a decision maker for the client or create a future dependency on the consultant.

5. When announcing consultant availability for services, the member conscientiously adheres to the Association's Ethical Standards.

6. The member must refuse a private fee or other remuneration for consultation with persons who are entitled to these services through the member's employing institution or agency. The policies of a particular agency may make explicit provisions for private practice with agency clients by members of its staff. In such instances, the clients must be apprised of other options open to them should they seek private counseling services.

Section F: Private Practice

1. The member should assist the profession by facilitating the availability of counseling services in private as well as public settings.

2. In advertising services as a private practitioner, the member must advertise the services in a manner that accurately informs the public as to services, expertise, and techniques of counseling available. A member who assumes an executive leadership role in the organization shall not permit his/her name to be used in professional notices during periods when he/she is not actively engaged in the private practice of counseling.

3. The member may list the following: highest relevant degree, type and level of certification and/or license, address, telephone number, office hours, type and/or description of services, and other relevant information. Such information must not contain false, inaccurate, misleading, partial, out-of-context, or deceptive material or statements.

4. Members do not present their affiliation with any organization in such a way that would imply inaccurate sponsorship or certification by that organization.

5. Members may join in partnership/corporation with other members and/or other professionals provided that each member of the partnership or corporation makes clear the separate specialties by name in compliance with the regulations of the locality.

6. A member has an obligation to withdraw from a counseling relationship if it is believed that employment will result in violation of the Ethical Standards. If the mental or physical condition of the member renders it difficult to carry out an effective professional relationship or if the member is discharged by the client because the counseling relationship is no longer productive for the client, then the member is obligated to terminate the counseling relationship.

7. A member must adhere to the regulations for private practice of the locality where the services are offered.

8. It is unethical to use one's institutional affiliation to recruit clients for one's private practice.

Section G: Personnel Administration

It is recognized that most members are employed in public or quasi-public institutions. The functioning of a member within an institution must contribute to the goals of the institution and vice versa if either is to accomplish their respective goals or objectives. It is therefore essential that the member and the institution function in ways to: (a) make the institution's goals specific, and public; (b) make the member's contribution to institutional goals specific; and (c) foster mutual accountability for goal achievement.

To accomplish these objectives, it is recognized that the member and the employer must share responsibilities in the formulation and implementation of personnel policies.

1. Members must define and describe the parameters and levels of their professional competency.

2. Members must establish interpersonal relations and working agreements with supervisors and subordinates regarding counseling or clinical relationships, confidentiality, distinction between public and private material, maintenance, and dissemination of recorded information, work load and accountability. Working agreements in each instance must be specified and made known to those concerned.

3. Members must alert their employers to conditions that may be potentially disruptive or damaging.

4. Members must inform employers of conditions that may limit their effectiveness.

5. Members must submit regularly to professional review and evaluation.

6. Members must be responsible for in-service development of self and/or staff.

7. Members must inform their staff of goals and programs.

8. Members must provide personnel practices that guarantee and enhance the rights and welfare of each recipient of their services.

9. Members must select competent persons and assign responsibilities compatible with their skills and experiences.

10. The member, at the onset of a counseling relationship, will inform the client of the member's intended use of supervisors regarding the disclosure of information concerning this case. The member will clearly inform the client of the limits of confidentiality in the relationship.

11. Members, as either employers or employees, do not engage in or condone practices that are inhumane, illegal, or unjustifiable (such as considerations based on sex, handicap, age, race) in hiring, promotion, or training.

Section H: Preparation Standards

Members who are responsible for training others must be guided by the preparation standards of the Association and relevant Division(s). The member who functions in the capacity of trainer assumes unique ethical responsibilities that frequently go beyond that of the member who does not function in a training capacity. These ethical responsibilities are outlined as follows:

1. Members must orient students to program expectations, basic skills development, and employment prospects prior to admission to the program.

2. Members in charge of learning experience must establish programs that integrate academic study and supervised practice.

3. Members must establish a program directed toward developing students' skills, knowledge, and self-understanding, stated whenever possible in competency or performance terms.

4. Members must identify the levels of competencies of their students in compliance with relevant Division standards. These competencies must accommodate the para-professional as well as the professional.

5. Members, through continual student evaluation and appraisal, must be aware of the personal limitations of the learner that might impede future performance. The instructor must not only assist the learner in securing remedial assistance but also screen from the program those individuals who are unable to provide competent services.

6. Members must provide a program that includes training in research commensurate with levels of role functioning. Paraprofessional and technician-level personnel must be trained as consumers of research. In addition, personnel must learn how to evaluate their own and their program's effectiveness. Graduate training, especially at the doctoral level, would include preparation for original research by the member.

7. Members must make students aware of the ethical responsibilities and standards of the profession.

8. Preparatory programs must encourage students to value the ideals of service to individuals and to society. In this regard, direct financial remuneration or lack thereof must not be allowed to overshadow professional and humanitarian needs.

9. Members responsible for educational programs must be skilled as teachers and practitioners.

10. Members must present thoroughly varied theoretical positions so that students may make comparisons and have the opportunity to select a position.

11. Members must develop clear policies within their educational institutions regarding field placement and the roles of the student and the instructor in such placements.

12. Members must ensure that forms of learning focusing on self-understanding or growth are voluntary, or if required as part of the education program, are made known to prospective students prior to entering the program. When the education program offers a growth experience with an emphasis on self-disclosure or other relatively intimate or personal involvement, the member must have no administrative, supervisory, or evaluating authority regarding the participant.

13. The member will at all times provide students with clear and equally acceptable alternatives for self-understanding or growth experiences. The member will assure students that they have a right to accept these alternatives without prejudice or penalty.

14. Members must conduct an educational program in keeping with the current relevant guidelines of the Association.

APPENDIX II

NATIONAL BOARD
FOR CERTIFIED COUNSELORS
CODE OF ETHICS

Reprinted with permission of the National Board for Certified Counselors.

NATIONAL BOARD FOR CERTIFIED COUNSELORS
CODE OF ETHICS

Preamble

The National Board for Certified Counselors (NBCC) is an educational, scientific, and professional organization dedicated to the enhancement of the worth, dignity, potential, and uniqueness of each individual and, thus, to the service of society. This code of ethics enables the NBCC to clarify the nature of ethical responsibilities for present and future certified counselors.

Section A: General

1. Certified counselors influence the development of the profession by continuous efforts to improve professional practices, services, and research. Professional growth is continuous throughout the certified counselor's career and is exemplified by the development of a philosophy that explains why and how a certified counselor functions in the helping relationship. Certified counselors must gather data on their effectiveness and be guided by their findings.

2. Certified counselors have a responsibility to the clients they are serving and to the institutions within which the services are being performed. Certified counselors also strive to assist the respective agency, organization, or institution in providing the highest caliber of professional services. The acceptance of employment in an institution implies that the certified counselor is in agreement with the general policies and principles of the institution. Therefore, the professional activities of the certified counselor are in accord with the objectives of the institution. If, despite concerted efforts, the certified counselor cannot reach agreement with the employer as to acceptable standards of conduct that allow for changes in institutional policy that are conducive to the positive growth and development of clients, then terminating the affiliation should be seriously considered.

3. Ethical behavior among professional associates (i.e., both certified and non-certified counselors) must be expected at all times. When accessible information raises doubt as to the ethical behavior of professional colleagues, whether certified counselors or not, the certified counselor must take action to attempt to rectify this condition. Such action uses the respective institution's channels first and then uses procedures established by the NBCC.

4. Certified counselors neither claim nor imply professional qualifications which exceed those possessed, and are responsible for correcting any misrepresentations of these qualifications by others.

5. Certified counselors must refuse a private fee or other remuneration for consultation or counseling with persons who are entitled to these services through the certified counselor's employing institution or agency. The policies of some agencies may make explicit provisions for staff members to engage in private practice with agency clients. However, should agency clients desire private counseling or consulting services, they must be apprised of other options available to them. Certified counselors must not divert to their private practices legitimate clients in their primary agencies or of the institutions with which they are affiliated.

6. In establishing fees for professional counseling services, certified counselors must consider the financial status of clients and the respective locality. In the event that the established fee status is inappropriate for a client, assistance must be provided in finding comparable services of acceptable cost.

7. Certified counselors seek only those positions in the delivery of professional services for which they are professionally qualified.

8. Certified counselors recognize their limitations and provide services or only use techniques for which they are qualified by training and/or experience. Certified counselors recognize the need, and seek continuing education, to assure competent services.

9. Certified counselors are aware of the intimacy in the counseling relationship, maintain respect for the client, and avoid engaging in activities that seek to meet their personal needs at the expense of the client.

10. Certified counselors do not condone or engage in sexual harassment which is defined as deliberate or repeated comments, gestures, or physical contacts of a sexual nature.

11. Certified counselors avoid bringing their personal or professional issues into the counseling relationship. Through an awareness of the impact of stereotyping and discrimination (i.e., biases based on age, disability, ethnicity, gender, race, religion, or sexual preference), certified counselors

guard the individual rights and personal dignity of the client in the counseling relationship.

12. Certified counselors are accountable at all times for their behavior. They must be aware that all actions and behaviors of the counselor reflect on professional integrity and, when inappropriate, can damage the public trust in the counseling profession. To protect public confidence in the counseling profession, certified counselors avoid public behavior that is clearly in violation of accepted moral and legal standards.

13. Certified counselors have a social responsibility because their recommendations and professional actions may alter the lives of others. Certified counselors remain fully cognizant of their impact and are alert to personal, social, organizational, financial, or political situations or pressures which might lead to misuse of their influence.

14. Products or services provided by certified counselors by means of classroom instruction, public lectures, demonstrations, written articles, radio or television programs or other types of media must meet the criteria cited in Sections A through F of these Standards.

Section B: Counseling Relationship

1. The primary obligation of certified counselors is to respect the integrity and promote the welfare of a client, regardless of whether the client is assisted individually or in a group relationship. In a group setting, the certified counselor is also responsible for taking reasonable precautions to protect individuals from physical and/or psychological trauma resulting from interaction within the group.

2. The counseling relationship and information resulting from it remains confidential, consistent with the legal obligations of the certified counselor. In a group counseling setting, the certified counselor sets a norm of confidentiality regarding all group participants' disclosures.

3. Certified counselors know and take into account the traditions and practices of other professional groups with whom they work and cooperate fully with such groups. If a person is receiving similar services from another professional, certified counselors do not offer their own services directly

to such a person. If a certified counselor is contacted by a person who is already receiving similar services from another professional, the certified counselor carefully considers that professional relationship as well as the client's welfare and proceeds with caution and sensitivity to the therapeutic issues. Certified counselors discuss these issues with clients so as to minimize the risk of confusion and conflict.

4. When a client's condition indicates that there is a clear and imminent danger to the client or others, the certified counselor must take reasonable personal action or inform responsible authorities. Consultation with other professionals must be used where possible. The assumption of responsibility for the client's behavior must be taken only after careful deliberation, and the client must be involved in the resumption of responsibility as quickly as possible.

5. Records of the counseling relationship, including interview notes, test data, correspondence, audio or visual tape recordings, electronic data storage, and other documents are to be considered professional information for use in counseling. They should not be considered a part of the records of the institution or agency in which the counselor is employed unless specified by state statute or regulation. Revelation to others of counseling material must occur only upon the expressed consent of the client; certified counselors must make provisions for maintaining confidentiality in the storage and disposal of records. Certified counselors providing information to the public or to subordinates, peers, or supervisors have a responsibility to ensure that the content is general; unidentified client information should be accurate and unbiased, and should consist of objective, factual data.

6. Certified counselors must ensure that data maintained in electronic storage are secure. By using the best computer security methods available, the data must be limited to information that is appropriate and necessary for the services being provided and accessible only to appropriate staff members involved in the provision of services. Certified counselors must also ensure that the electronically stored data are destroyed when the information is no longer of value in providing services.

7. Any data derived from a client relationship for use in counselor training or research shall be confined to content that can be disguised to ensure full protection of the identity of the subject/client and shall be obtained with informed consent.

8. Certified counselors must inform clients before or at the time the counseling relationship commences, of the purposes, goals, techniques, rules and procedures, and limitations that may affect the relationship.

9. All methods of treatment by certified counselors must be clearly indicated to prospective recipients and safety precautions must be taken in their use.

10. Certified counselors who have an administrative, supervisory and/ or evaluative relationship with individuals seeking counseling services must not serve as the counselor and should refer the individuals to other professionals. Exceptions are made only in instances where an individual's situation warrants counseling intervention and another alternative is unavailable. Dual relationships with clients that might impair the certified counselor's objectivity and professional judgment must be avoided and/or the counseling relationship terminated through referral to another competent professional.

11. When certified counselors determine an inability to be of professional assistance to a potential or existing client, they must, respectively, not initiate the counseling relationship or immediately terminate the relationship. In either event, the certified counselor must suggest appropriate alternatives. Certified counselors must be knowledgeable about referral resources so that a satisfactory referral can be initiated. In the event that the client declines a suggested referral, the certified counselor is not obligated to continue the relationship.

12. Certified counselors may choose to consult with any other professionally competent person about a client and must notify clients of this right. Certified counselors must avoid placing a consultant in a conflict-of-interest situation that would preclude the consultant's being a proper party to the certified counselor's efforts to help the client.

13. Certified counselors who counsel clients from cultures different from their own must gain knowledge, personal awareness, and sensitivity pertinent to the client populations served and must incorporate culturally relevant techniques into their practice.

14. When certified counselors are engaged in intensive, short-term therapy, they must ensure that professional counseling assistance is available to the client(s) during and following the counseling.

15. Certified counselors must screen prospective group counseling participants, especially when the emphasis is on self-understanding and growth through self-disclosure. Certified counselors must maintain an awareness of each group participant's welfare throughout the group process.

16. When electronic data and systems are used as a component of counseling services, certified counselors must ensure that the computer application, and any information it contains, is appropriate for the respective needs of clients and is non-discriminatory. Certified counselors must ensure that they themselves have acquired a facilitation level of knowledge with any system they use including hands-on application, search experience, and understanding of the uses of all aspects of the computer-based system. In selecting and/or maintaining computer-based systems that contain career information, counselors must ensure that the system provides current, accurate, and locally relevant information. Certified counselors must also ensure that clients are intellectually, emotionally, and physically compatible to using the computer application and understand its purpose and operation. Client use of a computer application must be evaluated to correct possible problems and assess subsequent needs.

17. Certified counselors who develop self-help/stand-alone computer software for use by the general public must first ensure that it is initially designed to function in a stand-alone manner, as opposed to modifying software that was originally designed to require support from a counselor. Secondly, the software must include program statements that provide the user with intended outcomes, suggestions for using the software, descriptions of inappropriately used applications, and descriptions of when and how counseling services might be beneficial. Finally, the manual must include the qualifications of the developer, the development process, validation data, and operating procedures.

Section C: Measurement and Evaluation

1. Certified counselors must provide specific orientation or information to an examinee prior to and following the administration of assessment instruments or techniques so that the results may be placed in proper perspective with other relevant factors. The purpose of testing and the implicit use of the results must be made known to an examinee prior to testing.

2. In selecting assessment instruments or techniques for use in a given situation or with a particular client, certified counselors must evaluate

carefully the instrument's specific theoretical bases and characteristics, validity, reliability and appropriateness. Certified counselors are professionally responsible for using invalidated information carefully.

3. When making statements to the public about assessment instruments or techniques, certified counselors must provide accurate information and avoid false claims or misconceptions concerning the meaning of psychometric terms. Special efforts are often required to avoid unwarranted connotations of terms such as IQ and grade-equivalent scores.

4. Because many types of assessment techniques exist, certified counselors must recognize the limits of their competence and perform only those functions for which they have received appropriate training.

5. Certified counselors must note when tests are not administered under standard conditions or when unusual behavior or irregularities occur during a testing session, and the results must be designated as invalid or of questionable validity. Unsupervised or inadequately supervised assessments, such as mail-in tests, are considered unethical. However, the use of standardized instruments that are designed to be self-administered and self-scored, such as some interest inventories, is appropriate.

6. Because prior coaching or dissemination of test materials can invalidate test results, certified counselors are professionally obligated to maintain test security. In addition, conditions that produce most favorable test results must be made known to an examinee (e.g., lack of penalty for guessing).

7. Certified counselors must consider psychometric limitations when selecting and using an instrument, and must be cognizant of the limitations when interpreting the results. When tests are used to classify clients, certified counselors must ensure that periodic review and/or retesting are made to prevent client stereotyping.

8. An examinee's welfare, explicit prior understanding, and agreement are the factors used when determining who receives the test results. Certified counselors must see that appropriate interpretation accompanies any release of individual or group test data (e.g., limitations of instrument and norms).

9. Certified counselors must ensure that computer-generated test administration and scoring programs function properly, thereby providing clients with accurate test results.

10. Certified counselors, who are responsible for making decisions based on assessment results, must have appropriate training and skills based on educational and psychological measurement, validation criteria, test research, and guidelines for test development and use.

11. Certified counselors must be cautious when interpreting the results of instruments that possess insufficient technical data, and must explicitly state to examinees the specific purposes for the use of such instruments.

12. Certified counselors must proceed with caution when attempting to evaluate and interpret performances of minority group members or other persons who are not represented in the norm group on which the instrument was standardized.

13. Certified counselors who develop computer-based test interpretations to support the assessment process must ensure that the validity of the interpretations is established prior to the commercial distribution of the computer application.

14. Certified counselors recognize that test results may become obsolete, and avoid the misuse of obsolete data.

15. Certified counselors must avoid the appropriation, reproduction, or modification of published tests or parts thereof without acknowledgement and permission from the publisher except as permitted by the 'fair educational use' provisions of the U.S. copyright law.

Section D: Research and Publication

1. Certified counselors will adhere to relevant guidelines on research with human subjects. These include the:

a. *Ethical Principles in the Conduct of Research with Human Participants*, Washington, D.C.: American Psychological Association Inc., 1982.

b. *Code of Federal Regulations, Title 45, Subtitle A, Part 46*, as currently issued.

c. *Ethical Principles of Psychologists*. American Psychological Association. Principle #9: Research with Human Participants.

d. Buckley Amendment.

e. Current federal regulations and various state rights privacy acts.

2. In planning research activities involving human subjects, certified counselors must be aware of and responsive to all pertinent ethical principles and ensure that the research problem, design, and execution are in full compliance with the principles.

3. The ultimate responsibility for ethical research lies with the principal researcher, though others involved in the research activities are ethically obligated and responsible for their own actions.

4. Certified counselors who conduct research with human subjects are responsible for the subjects' welfare throughout the experiment and must take all reasonable precautions to avoid causing injurious psychological, physical, or social effects on their subjects.

5. Certified counselors, who conduct research, must abide by the following basic elements of informed consent:

a. A fair explanation of the procedures to be followed, including an identification of those which are experimental.

b. A description of the attendant discomforts and risks.

c. A description of the benefits to be expected.

d. A disclosure of appropriate alternative procedures that would be advantageous for subjects.

e. An offer to answer any inquiries concerning the procedures.

f. An instruction that subjects are free to withdraw their consent and to discontinue participation in the project or activity at any time.

6. When reporting research results, explicit mention must be made of all the variables and conditions known to the investigator that may have affected the outcome of the study or the interpretation of the data.

7. Certified counselors who conduct and report research investigations must do so in a manner that minimizes the possibility that the results will be misleading.

8. Certified counselors are obligated to make available sufficient original research data to qualified others who may wish to replicate the study.

9. Certified counselors who supply data, aid in the research of another person, report research results, or make original data available, must take due care to disguise the identity of respective subjects in the absence of specific authorization from the subjects to do otherwise.

10. When conducting and reporting research, certified counselors must be familiar with, and give recognition to, previous work on the topic, must observe all copyright laws, and must follow the principles of giving full credit to those to whom credit is due.

11. Certified counselors must give due credit through joint authorship, acknowledgement, footnote statements, or other appropriate means to those who have contributed significantly to the research and/or publication, in accordance with such contributions.

12. Certified counselors should communicate to other counselors the results of any research judged to be of professional value. Results that reflect unfavorably on institutions, programs, services, or vested interests must be withheld.

13. Certified counselors who agree to cooperate with another individual in research and/or publication must incur an obligation to cooperate as promised in terms of punctuality of performance and with full regard to the completeness and accuracy of the information required.

14. Certified counselors must not submit the same manuscript, or one essentially similar in content, for simultaneous publication consideration by two or more journals. In addition, manuscripts that are published in whole or substantial part in another journal or published work should not be submitted for publication without acknowledgement and permission from the previous publication.

Section E: Consulting

Consultation refers to a voluntary relationship between a professional helper and help-needing individual, group, or social unit in which the consultant is providing help to the client(s) in defining and solving a work-related problem or potential work-related problem with a client or client system.

1. Certified counselors, acting as consultants, must have a high degree of self-awareness of their own values, knowledge, skills, limitations, and needs in entering a helping relationship that involves human and/or

organizational change. The focus of the consulting relationship must be on the issues to be resolved and not on the person(s) presenting the problem.

2. In the consulting relationship, the certified counselor and client must understand and agree upon the problem definition, subsequent goals, and predicted consequences of interventions selected.

3. Certified counselors must be reasonably certain that they, or the organization represented, have the necessary competencies and resources for giving the kind of help that is needed or that may develop later, and that appropriate referral resources are available to the consultant.

4. Certified counselors in a consulting relationship must encourage and cultivate client adaptability and growth toward self-direction. Certified counselors must maintain this role consistently and not become a decision maker for clients or create a future dependency on the consultant.

5. Certified counselors conscientiously adhere to the NBCC Code of Ethics when announcing consultant availability for services.

Section F: Private Practice

1. Certified counselors should assist the profession by facilitating the availability of counseling services in private as well as public settings.

2. In advertising services as a private practitioner, certified counselors must advertise in a manner that accurately informs the public of the professional services, expertise, and techniques of counseling available.

3. Certified counselors who assume an executive leadership role in a private practice organization do not permit their names to be used in professional notices during periods of time when they are not actively engaged in the private practice of counseling.

4. Certified counselors may list their highest relevant degree, type and level of certification and/or license, address, telephone number, office hours, type and/or description of services, and other relevant information. Listed information must not contain false, inaccurate, misleading, partial, out-of-context, or otherwise deceptive material or statements.

5. Certified counselors who are involved in a partnership/corporation with other certified counselors and/or other professionals, must clearly

specify the separate specialties of each member of the partnership or corporation, in compliance with the regulations of the locality.

6. Certified counselors have an obligation to withdraw from a private practice counseling relationship if it violates this Code of Ethics, or the mental or physical condition of the certified counselor renders it difficult to carry out an effective professional relationship, or the counseling relationship is no longer productive for the client.

Appendix: Certification Examination

1. Applicants for the National Counselor Examination must have fulfilled all current eligibility requirements, and are responsible for the accuracy and validity of all information and/or materials provided by themselves or by others for fulfillment of eligibility criteria.

2. Participation in the National Counselor Examination by any person under the auspices of eligibility ascribed to another person (i.e., applicant) is prohibited. Applicants are responsible for ensuring that no other person participates in the National Counselor Examination through use of the eligibility specifically assigned to the applicant.

3. Participants in the National Counselor Examination must refrain from the use of behaviors and/or materials which would afford them unfair advantage for performance on the Examination. These behaviors and/or materials include, but are not limited to, any form of copying of responses from another participant's answer sheet, use of unauthorized notes or other informational materials, or communication with other participants during the Examination.

4. Participants in the National Counselor Examination must, at the end of the regularly scheduled Examination period, return all Examination materials to the test administrator.

5. After completing the National Counselor Examination, participants must not disclose, in either verbal or written form, items which appeared on the Examination form.

Approved on July 1, 1982
Amended on February 21, 1987 and January 6, 1989

ACKNOWLEDGEMENT

Reference documents, statements, and sources for the development of the NBCC Code of Ethics were as follows:

Ethical Standards of the American Counseling Association, Responsible Uses of Standardized Tests (AMECD), *Codes of ethics for the American Psychological Association, National Academy of Certified Clinical Mental Health Counselors,* and the *National Career Development Association, Handbook of Standards for Computer-Based Career Information Systems and Guidelines for the Use of Computer-Based Career Information and Guidance Systems* (ACSCI).

APPENDIX III

ETHICAL STANDARDS
FOR SCHOOL COUNSELORS
AMERICAN SCHOOL COUNSELORS
ASSOCIATION

ETHICAL STANDARDS FOR SCHOOL COUNSELORS
AMERICAN SCHOOL COUNSELORS ASSOCIATION

PREAMBLE

The American School Counselor Association is a professional organization whose members have a unique and distinctive preparation, grounded in the behavioral sciences, with training in clinical skills adapted to the school setting. School counselors subscribe to the following basic tenets of the counseling process from which professional responsibilities are derived:

1. Each person has the right to respect and dignity as a human being and to counseling services without prejudice as to person, character, belief or practice.

2. Each person has the right to self-direction and self-development.

3. Each person has the right of choice and the responsibility for decisions reached.

4. The counselor assists in the growth and development of each individual and uses his/her highly specialized skills to insure that the rights of the counselee are properly protected within the structure of the school program.

5. The counselor-client relationship is private and thereby requires compliance with all laws, policies and ethical standards pertaining to confidentiality.

In this document, the American School Counselor Association has identified the standards of conduct necessary to maintain and regulate the high standards of integrity and leadership among its members. The Association recognizes the basic commitment of its members to the Ethical Standards of its parent organization, the American Association for Counseling and Development, and nothing in this document shall be construed to supplant that code. The Ethical standards for School Counselors was developed to complement the AACD standards by clarifying the nature of ethical responsibilities of counselors in the school setting. The purposes of this document are to:

1. Serve as a guide for the ethical practices of all school counselors regardless of level, area, or population served.

2. Provide benchmarks for both self-appraisal and peer evaluation regarding counselor responsibilities to pupils, parents, professional colleagues, school and community, self, and the counselor profession.

3. Inform those served by the school counselor of acceptable counselor practices and expected professional deportment.

A. RESPONSIBILITIES TO PUPILS

The school counselor:

1. Has a primary obligation and loyalty to the pupil, who is to be treated with respect as a unique individual.

2. Is concerned with the total needs of the pupil (educational, vocational, personal and social) and encourages the maximum growth and development of each counselee.

3. Informs the counselee of the purposes, goals, techniques, and rules of procedure under which she/he may receive counseling assistance at or before the time when the counseling relationship is entered. Prior notice includes the possible necessity for consulting with other professionals, privileged communication, and legal or authoritative restraints.

4. Refrains from consciously encouraging the counselee's acceptance of values, lifestyles, plans, decisions, and beliefs that represent only the counselor's personal orientation.

5. Is responsible for keeping abreast of laws relating to pupils and ensures that the rights of pupils are adequately provided for and protected.

6. Makes appropriate referrals when professional assistance can no longer be adequately provided to the counselee. Appropriate referral necessitates knowledge about available resources.

7. Protects the confidentiality of pupil records and releases personal data only according to prescribed laws and school policies. The counselor shall provide an accurate, objective, and appropriately detailed interpretation of pupil information.

8. Protects the confidentiality of information received in the counseling process as specified by law and ethical standards.

9. Informs the appropriate authorities when the counselee's condition indicates a clear and imminent danger to the counselee or others. This is to be done after careful deliberation and, where possible, after consultation with other professionals.

10. Provides explanations of the nature, purposes, and results of tests in language that is understandable to the client(s).

11. Adheres to relevant standards regarding selection, administration, and interpretation of assessment techniques.

B. RESPONSIBILITIES TO PARENTS

The school counselor:

1. Respects the inherent rights and responsibilities of parents for their children and endeavors to establish a cooperative relationship with parents to facilitate the maximum development of the counselee.

2. Informs parents of the counselor's role with emphasis on the confidential nature of the counseling relationship between the counselor and counselee.

3. Provides parents with accurate, comprehensive and relevant information in an objective and caring manner.

4. Treats information received from parents in a confidential and appropriate manner.

5. Shares information about a counselee only with those persons properly authorized to receive such information.

6. Follows local guidelines when assisting parents experiencing family difficulties which interfere with the counselee's effectiveness and welfare.

C. RESPONSIBILITIES TO COLLEAGUES AND PROFESSIONAL ASSOCIATES

The school counselor:

1. Establishes and maintains a cooperative relationship with faculty, staff, and administration to facilitate the provision of optimum guidance and counseling services.

2. Promotes awareness and adherence to appropriate guidelines regarding confidentiality, the distinction between public and private information, and staff consultation.

3. Treats colleagues with respect, courtesy, fairness, and good faith. The qualifications, views, and findings of colleagues are represented accurately and fairly to enhance the image of competent professionals.

4. Provides professional personnel with accurate, objective, concise and meaningful data necessary to adequately evaluate, counsel, and assist the counselee.

5. Is aware of and fully utilizes related professions and organizations to whom the counselee may be referred.

D. RESPONSIBILITIES TO THE SCHOOL AND COMMUNITY

The school counselor:

1. Supports and protects the educational program against any infringement not in the best interest of pupils.

2. Informs appropriate officials of conditions that may be potentially disruptive or damaging to the school's mission, personnel, and property.

3. Delineates and promotes the counselor's role and function in meeting the needs of those served. The counselor will notify appropriate school officials of conditions which may limit or curtail their effectiveness in providing services.

4. Assists in the development of (1) curricular and environmental conditions appropriate for the school and community, (2) educational procedures and programs to meet pupil needs, and (3) a systematic evaluation process for guidance and counseling programs, services, and personnel.

5. Works cooperatively with agencies, organizations, and individuals in the school and community in the best interest of counselees and without regard to personal reward or remuneration.

E. RESPONSIBILITIES TO SELF

The school counselor:

1. Functions within the boundaries of individual professional competence and accepts responsibility for the consequences of his/her actions.

2. Is aware of the potential effects of personal characteristics on services to clients.

3. Monitors personal functioning and effectiveness and refrains from any activity likely to lead to inadequate professional services or harm to a client.

4. Strives through personal initiative to maintain professional competence and keep abreast of innovations and trends in the profession.

F. RESPONSIBILITIES TO THE PROFESSION

The school counselor:

1. Conducts herself/himself in such a manner as to bring credit to self and the profession.

2. Conducts appropriate research and reports findings in a manner consistent with acceptable educational and psychological research practices.

3. Actively participates in local, state, and national associations which foster the development and improvement of school counseling.

4. Adheres to ethical standards of the profession, other official policy statements pertaining to counseling and relevant statutes established by federal, state, and local governments.

5. Clearly distinguishes between statements and actions made as a private individual and as a representative of the school counseling profession.

G. MAINTENANCE OF STANDARDS

Ethical behavior among professional school counselors is expected at all times. When there exists serious doubt as to the ethical behavior of colleagues, or if counselors are forced to work in situations or abide by policies which do not reflect the standards as outlined in these Ethical Standards for School Counselor or the AACD Ethical Standards, the counselor is obligated to take appropriate action to rectify the condition. The following procedure may serve as a guide:

1. The counselor shall utilize the channels established within the school and/or system. This may include both informal and formal procedures.

2. If the matter remains unresolved, referral for review and appropriate action should be made to the Ethics Committees in the following sequence:

—local counselor association
—state counselor association
—national counselor association

H. REFERENCES

School counselors are responsible for being aware of and acting in accord with the standards and positions of the counseling profession as represented in such official documents as those listed below. A more extensive bibliography is available from the ASCA Ethics Committee upon request.

Ethical Standards (1981). American Counseling Association, Alexandria, VA.

Ethical Guidelines for Group Leaders (1980). Association for Specialists in Group Work, Alexandria, VA.

Principles of Confidentiality (1974). ASCA Position Statement, American School Counselor Association, Alexandria, VA.

Standards for Educational and Psychological Tests and Manuals (1974). American Psychological Association, Washington, D.C.

Ethical Principles in the Conduct of Research with Human Participants (1973). American Psychological Association, Washington, D.C.

(Ethical Standards for School Counselors is an adaptation of the ASCA Code of Ethics [1972] and the California School Counselor Association Code of Ethics [revised, 1984]. Adopted by the ASCA Delegate Assembly March 19, 1984).

APPENDIX IV

CODE OF PROFESSIONAL ETHICS FOR REHABILITATION COUNSELORS

CODE OF PROFESSIONAL ETHICS
FOR REHABILITATION COUNSELORS

The Commission on Rehabilitation Counselor Certification has adopted the Code of Professional Ethics for Certified Rehabilitation Counselors; and the following professional organizations have adopted the Code for their memberships: American Rehabilitation Counseling Association, National Rehabilitation Counseling Association, and National Council on Rehabilitation Education.

PREAMBLE

Rehabilitation Counselors are committed to facilitating personal, social, and economic independence of individuals with disabilities. In fulfilling this commitment, Rehabilitation Counselors work with people, programs, institutions, and service delivery systems. Rehabilitation Counselors recognize that both action and inaction can be facilitating or debilitating. Rehabilitation Counselors may be called upon to provide counseling; vocational exploration; psychological and vocational assessment; evaluation of social, medical, vocational, and psychiatric information; job placement and job development services; and other rehabilitation services, and do so in a manner that is consistent with their education and experience. Moreover, Rehabilitation Counselors also must demonstrate adherence to ethical standards and must ensure that the standards are enforced vigorously. The Code of Professional Ethics, henceforth referred to as the Code, is designed to facilitate the accomplishment of these goals.

The primary obligation of Rehabilitation Counselors is to their clients, defined in this Code as people with disabilities who are receiving services from rehabilitation counselors. The basic objective of the Code is to promote the public welfare by specifying and enforcing ethical behavior expected of Rehabilitation Counselors. Accordingly, the Code consists of two kinds of standards, Canons and Rules of Professional Conduct.

The Canons are general standards of an aspirational and inspirational nature reflecting the fundamental spirit of caring and respect which professionals share. They are maxims which serve as models of exemplary professional conduct. The Canons also express general concepts and principles from which more specific Rules are derived. Unlike the Canons, the Rules are more exacting standards that provide guidance in specific circumstances.

Rehabilitation Counselors who violate the Code are subject to disciplinary action. A rule violation is interpreted as a violation of the applicable Canon and the general principles embodied thereof. Since the use of the Certified Rehabilitation Counselor (CRC) designation is a privilege granted by the Commission on Rehabilitation Counselor Certification (CRCC), the CRCC reserves unto itself the power to suspend or to revoke the privilege or to approve other penalties for a Rule violation. Disciplinary penalties are imposed as warranted by the severity of the offense and its attendant circumstances. All disciplinary actions are undertaken in accordance with published procedures and penalties designed to assure the proper enforcement of the Code within the framework of due process and equal protection of the laws.

When there is reason to question the ethical propriety of specific behaviors, persons are encouraged to refrain from engaging in such behaviors until the matter has been clarified. Certified Rehabilitation Counselors who need assistance in interpreting the Code should request in writing an advisory opinion from the Commission on Rehabilitation Counselor Certification. Rehabilitation Counselors who are not certified and require assistance in interpreting the Code should request in writing an advisory opinion from their appropriate professional organization.

CANON 1 — MORAL AND LEGAL STANDARDS

Rehabilitation Counselors shall behave in a legal, ethical, and moral manner in the conduct of their profession, maintaining the integrity of the Code and avoiding any behavior which would cause harm to others.

Rules of Professional Conduct

R1.1 Rehabilitation Counselors will obey the laws and statutes in the legal jurisdiction in which they practice and are subject to disciplinary action for any violation, to the extent that such violation suggests the likelihood of professional misconduct.

R1.2 Rehabilitation Counselors will be thoroughly familiar with, will observe, and will discuss with their clients the legal limitations of their services, or benefits offered to clients so as to facilitate honest and open communication and realistic expectations.

R1.3 Rehabilitation Counselors will be alert to legal parameters relevant to their practices and to disparities between legally mandated ethical and professional standards and the Code. Where such disparities exist, Rehabilitation Counselors will follow the legal mandates and will formally communicate any disparities to the appropriate committee on professional ethics. In the absence of legal guidelines, the Code is ethically binding.

R1.4 Rehabilitation Counselors will not engage in any act or omission of a dishonest, deceitful, or fraudulent nature in the conduct of their professional activities. They will not allow the pursuit of financial gain or other personal benefit to interfere with the exercise of sound professional judgment and skills, nor will Rehabilitation Counselors abuse their relationships with clients to promote personal or financial gain or the financial gain of their employing agencies.

R1.5 Rehabilitation Counselors will understand and abide by the Canons and Rules of Professional Conduct which are prescribed in the Code.

R1.6 Rehabilitation Counselors will not advocate, sanction, participate in, cause to be accomplished, otherwise carry out through another, or condone any act which Rehabilitation Counselors are prohibited from performing by the Code.

R1.7 Rehabilitation Counselors' moral and ethical standards of behavior are a personal matter to the same degree as they are for any other citizen, except as these may compromise the fulfillment of their professional responsibilities or reduce the public trust in Rehabilitation Counselors. To protect public confidence, Rehabilitation Counselors will avoid public behavior that clearly is in violation of accepted moral and ethical standards.

R1.8 Rehabilitation Counselors will respect the rights and reputation of any institution, organization, or firm with which they are associated when making oral or written statements. In those instances where they are critical of policies, they attempt to effect change by constructive action within the organization.

R1.9 Rehabilitation Counselors will refuse to participate in employment practices which are inconsistent with the moral or legal standards regarding the treatment of employees or the public. Rehabilitation Counselors will not condone practices which result in illegal or otherwise unjustifiable discrimination on any basis in hiring, promotion, or training.

CANON 2 — COUNSELOR-CLIENT RELATIONSHIP

Rehabilitation Counselors shall respect the integrity and protect the welfare of people and groups with whom they work. The primary obligation of Rehabilitation Counselors is to their clients, defined as people with disabilities who are receiving services from rehabilitation counselors. Rehabilitation counselors shall endeavor at all times to place their clients' interests above their own.

Rules of Professional Conduct

R2.1 Rehabilitation Counselors will make clear to clients the purposes, goals, and limitations that may affect the counseling relationship.

R2.2 Rehabilitation Counselors will not misrepresent their role or competence to clients. Rehabilitation Counselors will provide information about their credentials, if requested, and will refer clients to other specialists as the needs of clients dictate.

R2.3 Rehabilitation Counselors will be continually cognizant of their own needs, values, and of their potentially influential positions, vis-a-vis clients, students, and subordinates. They avoid exploiting the trust and dependency of such persons. Rehabilitation Counselors make every effort to avoid dual relationships that could impair their professional judgments or increase the risk of exploitation. Examples of dual relationships include, but are not limited to, research with and treatment of employees, students, supervisors, close friends, or relatives. Sexual intimacies with clients are unethical.

R2.4 Rehabilitation Counselors who provide services at the request of a third party will clarify the nature of their relationships to all involved parties. They will inform all parties of their ethical responsibilities and take appropriate action. Rehabilitation Counselors employed by third parties as case consultants or expert witnesses, where there is no pretense or intent to provide rehabilitation counseling services directly to clients beyond file review, initial interview and/or assessment, will clearly define, through written or oral means, the limits of their relationship, particularly in the area of informed consent and legally privileged communications, to involved individuals. As case consultants or expert witnesses, Rehabilitation Counselors have an obligation to provide unbiased, objective opinions.

R2.5 Rehabilitation Counselors will honor the right of clients to consent to participate in rehabilitation counseling services. Rehabilitation Counselors will inform clients or the clients' legal guardians of factors that may affect clients' decisions to participate in rehabilitation counseling services, and they will obtain written consent after clients or their legal guardians are fully informed of such factors. Rehabilitation Counselors who work with minors or other persons who are unable to give voluntary, informed consent will take special care to protect the best interests of clients.

R2.6 Rehabilitation Counselors will avoid initiating or continuing consulting or counseling relationships if it is expected that the relationship can be of no benefit to clients, in which case Rehabilitation Counselors will suggest to clients appropriate alternatives.

R2.7 Rehabilitation Counselors will recognize that families are usually an important factor in clients' rehabilitation and will strive to enlist family understanding and involvement as a positive resource in promoting rehabilitation. The permission of clients will be secured prior to family involvement.

R2.8 Rehabilitation Counselors and their clients will work jointly in devising an integrated, individualized rehabilitation plan which offers reasonable promise of success and is consistent with the abilities and circumstances of clients. Rehabilitation Counselors will persistently monitor rehabilitation plans to ensure their continued viability and effectiveness, remembering that clients have the right to make choices.

R2.9 Rehabilitation Counselors will work with their clients in considering employment for clients in only jobs and circumstances that are consistent with the clients' overall abilities, vocational limitations, physical restrictions, general temperament, interest and aptitude patterns, social skills, education, general qualifications, and other relevant characteristics and needs. Rehabilitation Counselors will neither place nor participate in placing clients in positions that will result in damaging the interest and welfare of either clients or employers.

CANON 3 — CLIENT ADVOCACY

Rehabilitation Counselors shall serve as advocates for persons with disabilities.

Rules of Professional Conduct

R3.1 Rehabilitation Counselors will be obligated at all times to promote access for persons with disabilities in programs, facilities, transportation, and communication so that clients will not be excluded from opportunities to participate fully in rehabilitation, education, and society.

R3.2 Rehabilitation Counselors will assure, prior to referring clients to programs, facilities, or employment settings, that they are appropriately accessible.

R3.3 Rehabilitation Counselors will strive to understand accessibility problems of persons with cognitive, hearing, mobility, visual and/or other disabilities and demonstrate such understanding in the practice of their profession.

R3.4 Rehabilitation Counselors will strive to eliminate attitudinal barriers, including stereotyping and discrimination, toward persons with disabilities and will enhance their own sensitivity and awareness toward persons with disabilities.

R3.5 Rehabilitation Counselors will remain aware of the actions taken by cooperating agencies on behalf of their clients and will act as advocates of clients to ensure effective service delivery.

CANON 4 — PROFESSIONAL RELATIONSHIPS

Rehabilitation Counselors shall act with integrity in their relationships with colleagues, other organizations, agencies, institutions, referral sources, and other professions so as to facilitate the contribution of all specialists toward achieving optimum benefit for clients.

Rules of Professional Conduct

R4.1 Rehabilitation Counselors will ensure that there is fair mutual understanding of the rehabilitation plan by all agencies cooperating in the rehabilitation of clients and that any rehabilitation plan is developed with such mutual understanding.

R4.2 Rehabilitation Counselors will abide by and help to implement "team" decisions in formulating rehabilitation plans and procedures, even when not personally agreeing with such decisions, unless these decisions breach the ethical Rules.

R4.3 Rehabilitation Counselors will not commit receiving counselors to any prescribed courses of action in relation to clients when transferring clients to other colleagues or agencies.

R4.4 Rehabilitation Counselors, as referring counselors, will promptly supply all information necessary for a cooperating agency or counselor to begin serving clients.

R4.5 Rehabilitation Counselors will not offer on-going professional counseling/case management services to clients receiving such services from other Rehabilitation Counselors without first notifying the other counselor. File review and second opinion services are not included in the concept of professional counseling/case management services.

R4.6 Rehabilitation Counselors will secure from other specialists appropriate reports and evaluations, when such reports are essential for rehabilitation planning and/or service delivery.

R4.7 Rehabilitation Counselors will not discuss in a disparaging way with clients the competency of other counselors or agencies, or the judgments made, the methods used, or the quality of rehabilitation plans.

R4.8 Rehabilitation Counselors will not exploit their professional relationships with supervisors, colleagues, students, or employees sexually or otherwise. Rehabilitation Counselors will not condone or engage in sexual harassment, defined as deliberate or repeated comments, gestures, or physical contacts of a sexual nature unwanted by recipients.

R4.9 Rehabilitation Counselors who know of an ethical violation by another Rehabilitation Counselor will informally attempt to resolve the issue with the counselor, when the misconduct is of a minor nature and/or appears to be due to lack of sensitivity, knowledge, or experience. If the violation does not seem amenable to an informal solution, or is of a more serious nature, Rehabilitation Counselors will bring it to the attention of the appropriate committee on professional ethics.

R4.10 Rehabilitation Counselors possessing information concerning an alleged violation of this Code, will, upon request, reveal such information to the Commission on Rehabilitation Counselor Certification or other authority empowered to investigate or act upon the alleged violation, unless the information is protected by law.

R4.11 Rehabilitation Counselors who employ or supervise other professionals or students will facilitate professional development of such individuals. They provide appropriate working conditions, timely evaluations, constructive consultation, and experience opportunities.

CANON 5 — PUBLIC STATEMENTS/FEES

Rehabilitation Counselors shall adhere to professional standards in establishing fees and promoting their services.

<u>Rules of Professional Conduct</u>

R5.1 Rehabilitation Counselors will consider carefully the value of their services and the ability of clients to meet the financial burden in establishing reasonable fees for professional services.

R5.2 Rehabilitation Counselors will not accept for professional work a fee or any other form of remuneration from clients who are entitled to their services through an institution or agency or other benefits structure, unless clients have been fully informed of the availability of services from other sources.

R5.3 Rehabilitation Counselors will neither give nor receive a commission or rebate or any other form of remuneration for referral of clients for professional services.

R5.4 Rehabilitation Counselors who describe rehabilitation counseling or the services of Rehabilitation Counselors to the general public will fairly and accurately present the material, avoiding misrepresentation through sensationalism, exaggeration, or superficiality. Rehabilitation Counselors are guided by the primary obligation to aid the public in developing informed judgments, opinions, and choices.

CANON 6 — CONFIDENTIALITY

Rehabilitation Counselors shall respect the confidentiality of information obtained from clients in the course of their work.

<u>Rules of Professional Conduct</u>

R6.1 Rehabilitation Counselors will inform clients at the onset of the counseling relationship of the limits of confidentiality.

R6.2 Rehabilitation Counselors will take reasonable personal action, or inform responsible authorities, or inform those persons at risk, when the conditions or actions of clients indicate that there is clear and imminent danger to clients or others after advising clients that this must be done.

Consultation with other professionals may be used where appropriate. The assumption of responsibility for clients must be taken only after careful deliberation and clients must be involved in the resumption of responsibility as quickly as possible.

R6.3 Rehabilitation Counselors will not forward to another person, agency, or potential employer any confidential information without the written permission of clients or their legal guardians.

R6.4 Rehabilitation Counselors will ensure that there are defined policies and practices in other agencies cooperatively serving rehabilitation clients which effectively protect information confidentiality.

R6.5 Rehabilitation Counselors will safeguard the maintenance, storage, and disposal of the records of clients so that unauthorized persons shall not have access to these records. All non-professional persons who must have access to these records will be thoroughly briefed concerning the confidential standards to be observed.

R6.6 Rehabilitation Counselors, in the preparation of written and oral reports, will present only germane data and will make every effort to avoid undue invasion of privacy.

R6.7 Rehabilitation Counselors will obtain written permission from clients or their legal guardians prior to taping or otherwise recording counseling sessions. Even with guardians' written consent, Rehabilitation Counselors will not record sessions against expressed wishes of clients.

R6.8 Rehabilitation Counselors will persist in claiming the privileged status of confidential information obtained from clients, where communications are privileged by statute for Rehabilitation Counselors.

R6.9 Rehabilitation Counselors will provide prospective employers with only job relevant information about clients and will secure the permission of clients or their legal guardians for the release of any information which might be considered confidential.

CANON 7 — ASSESSMENT

Rehabilitation Counselors shall promote the welfare of clients in the selection, utilization, and interpretation of assessment measures.

Rules of Professional Conduct

R7.1 Rehabilitation Counselors will recognize that different tests demand different levels of competence for administration, scoring, and interpretation, and will recognize the limits of their competence and perform only those functions for which they are trained.

R7.2 Rehabilitation Counselors will consider carefully the specific validity, reliability, and appropriateness of tests when selecting them for use in a given situation or with particular clients. Rehabilitation Counselors will proceed with caution when attempting to evaluate and interpret the performance of peoples with disabilities, minority group members, or other persons who are not represented in the standardized norm groups. Rehabilitation Counselors will recognize the effects of socioeconomic, ethnic, disability, and cultural factors on test scores.

R7.3 Rehabilitation Counselors will administer tests under the same conditions that were established in their standardization. When tests are not administered under standard conditions, as may be necessary to accommodate modifications for clients with disabilities or when unusual behavior or irregularities occur during the testing session, those conditions will be noted and taken into account at the time of interpretation.

R7.4 Rehabilitation Counselors will ensure that instrument limitations are not exceeded and that periodic reassessments are made to prevent stereotyping of clients.

R7.5 Rehabilitation Counselors will make known the purpose of testing and the explicit use of the results to clients prior to administration. Recognizing the right of clients to have test results, Rehabilitation Counselors will give explanations of test results in language clients can understand.

R7.6 Rehabilitation Counselors will ensure that specific interpretation accompanies any release of individual data. The welfare and explicit prior permission of clients will be the criteria for determining the recipients of the test results. The interpretation of assessment data will be related to the particular goals of evaluation.

R7.7 Rehabilitation Counselors will attempt to ensure when utilizing computerized assessment services that such services are based on appropriate research to establish the validity of the computer programs and procedures used in arriving at interpretations. Public offering of an automated test interpretation service will be considered as a professional-to-professional consultation. In this instance, the formal responsibility of the consultant is to the consultee, but the ultimate and overriding responsibility is to clients.

R7.8 Rehabilitation Counselors will recognize that assessment results may become obsolete. They make every effort to avoid and prevent the misuse of obsolete measures.

CANON 8 — RESEARCH ACTIVITIES

Rehabilitation Counselors shall assist in efforts to expand the knowledge needed to more effectively serve persons with disabilities.

Rules of Professional Conduct

R8.1 Rehabilitation Counselors will ensure that data for research meets rigid standards of validity, honesty, and protection of confidentiality.

R8.2 Rehabilitation Counselors will be aware of and responsive to all pertinent guidelines on research with human subjects. When planning any research activity dealing with human subjects, Rehabilitation Counselors will ensure that research problems, design, and execution are in full compliance with such guidelines.

R8.3 Rehabilitation Counselors presenting case studies in classes, professional meetings, or publications will confine the content to that which can be disguised to ensure full protection of the identity of clients.

R8.4 Rehabilitation Counselors will assign credit to those who have contributed to publications in proportion to their contribution.

R8.5 Rehabilitation Counselors recognize that honesty and openness are essential characteristics of the relationship between Rehabilitation Counselors and research participants. When methodological requirements of a study necessitate concealment or deception, Rehabilitation Counselors will ensure that participants understand the reasons for this action.

CANON 9 — COMPETENCE

Rehabilitation Counselors shall establish and maintain their professional competencies at such a level that their clients receive the benefit of the highest quality of services the profession is capable of offering.

R9.1 Rehabilitation Counselors will function within the limits of their defined role, training, and technical competency and will accept only those positions for which they are professionally qualified.

R9.2 Rehabilitation Counselors will continuously strive through reading, attending professional meetings, and taking courses of instruction to keep abreast of new developments, concepts, and practices that are essential to providing the highest quality of services to their clients.

R9.3 Rehabilitation Counselors, recognizing that personal problems and conflicts may interfere with their professional effectiveness, will refrain from undertaking any activity in which their personal problems are likely to lead to inadequate performance. If they are already engaged in such activity when they become aware of their personal problems, they will seek competent professional assistance to determine whether they should suspend, terminate, or limit the scope of their professional activities.

R9.4 Rehabilitation Counselors who are educators will perform their duties based on careful preparation so that their instruction is accurate, up-to-date, and scholarly.

R9.5 Rehabilitation Counselors who are educators will ensure that statements in catalogs and course outlines are accurate, particularly in terms of subject matter covered, bases for grading, and nature of classroom experiences.

R9.6 Rehabilitation Counselors who are educators will maintain high standards of knowledge and skill by presenting rehabilitation counseling information fully and accurately, and by giving appropriate recognition to alternative viewpoints.

CANON 10 — CRC CREDENTIAL

Rehabilitation Counselors holding the Certified Rehabilitation Counselor (CRC) designation shall honor the integrity and respect the limitations placed upon its use.

Rules of Professional Conduct

R10.1 Certified Rehabilitation Counselors will use the Certified Rehabilitation Counselor (CRC) designation only in accordance with the relevant Guidelines promulgated by the Commission on Rehabilitation Counselor Certification.

R10.2 Certified Rehabilitation Counselors will not attribute to the mere possession of the designation depth or scope of knowledge, skill, and professional capabilities greater than those demonstrated by achievement of the CRC designation.

R10.3 Certified Rehabilitation Counselors will not make unfair comparisons between a person who holds the Certified Rehabilitation Counselor (CRC) designation and one who does not.

R10.4 Certified Rehabilitation Counselors will not write, speak, nor act in ways that lead others to believe Certified Rehabilitation Counselors are officially representing the Commission on Rehabilitation Counselor Certification, unless such written permission has been granted by the said Commission.

R10.5 Certified Rehabilitation Counselors will make no claim to unique skills or devices not available to others in the profession unless the special efficacy of such unique skills or devices has been demonstrated by scientifically accepted evidence.

R10.6 Certified Rehabilitation Counselors will not initiate or support candidacy of an individual for certification by the Commission on Rehabilitation Counselor Certification if the individual is known to engage in professional practices which violate this Code.

APPENDIX V

ETHICAL CODE FOR THE INTERNATIONAL ASSOCIATION OF MARRIAGE AND FAMILY COUNSELORS

ETHICAL CODE FOR THE INTERNATIONAL ASSOCIATION OF MARRIAGE AND FAMILY COUNSELORS

PREAMBLE

The IAMFC (The International Association of Marriage and Family Counselors) is an organization dedicated to advancing the practice, training, and research of marriage and family counselors. Members may specialize in areas such as: premarital counseling, intergenerational counseling, separation and divorce counseling, relocation counseling, custody assessment and implementation, single parenting, stepfamilies, nontraditional family and marriage life-styles, healthy and dysfunctional family systems, multicultural marriage and family concerns, displaced and homeless families, interfaith and interracial families, and dual career couples. In conducting their professional activities, members commit themselves to protect and advocate for the healthy growth and development of the family as a whole, even as they conscientiously recognize the integrity and diversity of each family and family member's unique needs, situations, status, and member's unique needs, situations, status, and condition. The IAMFC member recognizes that the relationship between the provider and consumer of services is characterized as an egalitarian process emphasizing co-participation, co-equality, coauthority, co-responsibility, and client empowerment. This code of ethics promulgates a framework for ethical practice by IAMFC members and is divided into eight sections: client well-being, confidentiality, competence, assessment, private practice, research and publications, supervision, and media and public statements. The ideas presented within these eight areas are meant to supplement the ethical standards of the American Counseling Association (ACA), formerly the American Association for Counseling and Development (AACD), and all members should know and keep to the standards of our parent organization. Although an ethical code cannot anticipate every possible situation or dilemma, the IAMFC ethical guidelines can aid members in ensuring the welfare and dignity of the couples and families they have contact with, as well as assisting in the implementation of the Hippocratic mandate for healers: Do no harm.

SECTION 1: CLIENT WELL-BEING

A. Members demonstrate a caring, empathic, respectful, fair, and active concern for family well-being. They promote client safety, security, and place-of-belonging in family, community, and society. Due to the risk involved, members should not use intrusive interventions without a sound theoretical rationale and having thoroughly thought through the potential ramifications to the family and its members.

B. Members recognize that each family is unique. They respect the diversity of personal attributes and do not stereotype or force families into prescribed attitudes, roles, or behaviors.

C. Members respect the autonomy of the families that they work with. They do not make decisions that rightfully belong to family members.

D. Members respect cultural diversity. They do not discriminate on the basis of race, sex, disability, religion, age, sexual orientation, cultural background, national origin, marital status, or political affiliation.

E. Members strive for an egalitarian relationship with clients by openly and conscientiously sharing information, opinions, perceptions, processes of decision making, strategies of problem solving, and understanding of human behavior.

F. Members pursue a just relationship that acknowledges, respects, and informs clients of their rights, obligations, and expectations as a consumer of services, as well as the rights, obligations, and expectations of the provider(s) of service. Members inform clients (in writing if feasible) about the goals and purpose of the counseling, the qualifications of the counselor(s), the scope and limits of confidentiality, potential risks and benefits associated with the counseling process and with specific counseling techniques, reasonable expectations for the outcomes and duration of counseling, costs of services, and appropriate alternatives to counseling.

G. Members strive for a humanistic relationship that assists clients to develop a philosophy of meaning, purpose, and direction of life and living that promotes a positive regard of self, of family, of different and diverse others, and of the importance of humane concern for the community, nation, and the world at large.

H. Members promote primary prevention. They pursue the development of clients' cognitive, moral, social, emotional, spiritual, physical, educational, and career needs, as well as parenting, marriage, and family living skills, in order to prevent future problems.

I. Members have an obligation to determine and inform all persons involved who their primary client is — i.e., is the counselor's primary obligation to the individual, the family, a third party, or an institution? When there is a conflict of interest between the needs of the client and counselor's employing institution, the member works to clarify his or her commitment to all parties. Members recognize that the acceptance of employment implies that they are in agreement with the agency's policies and practices, and so monitor their place of employment to make sure that the environment is conducive to the positive growth and development of clients. If, after utilizing appropriate institutional channels for change, the member finds that the agency is not working toward the well-being of clients, the member has an obligation to terminate his or her institutional affiliation.

J. Members do not harass, exploit, coerce, engage in dual relationships, or have sexual contact with any current or former client or family member to whom they have provided professional services.

K. Members have an obligation to withdraw from a counseling relationship if the continuation of services is not in the best interest of the client or would result in a violation of ethical standards. If a client feels that the counseling relationship is no longer productive, the member has an obligation to assist in finding alternative services.

L. Members maintain accurate and up-to-date records. They make all file information available to clients unless the sharing of such information would be damaging to the status, goals, growth, or development of the client.

M. Members have the responsibility to confront unethical behavior conducted by other counselors. The first step should be to discuss the violation directly with the counselor. If the problem continues, the member should first use procedures established by the employing institution and then those of the IAMFC. Members may wish to also contact any appropriate licensure or certification board. Members may contact the IAMFC executive director, president, executive board members, or chair of the ethics committee at any time for consultation on remedying ethical violations.

SECTION II: CONFIDENTIALITY

A. Clients have the right to expect that information shared with the counselor will not be disclosed to others and, in the absence of any law to the contrary, the communications between clients and marriage and family counselors should be viewed as privileged. The fact that a contact was made with a counselor is to be considered just as confidential as the information shared during that contact. Information obtained from a client can only be disclosed to a third party under the following conditions:

1. The client consents to disclosure by a signed waiver. The client must fully understand the nature of the disclosure (i.e., give informed consent), and only information described in the waiver may be disclosed. If more than one person is receiving counseling, each individual who is legally competent to execute a waiver must sign.

2. The client has placed him- or herself or someone else in clear and imminent danger.

3. The law mandates disclosure.

4. The counselor is a defendant in a civil, criminal, or disciplinary action arising from professional activity.

5. The counselor needs to discuss a case for consultation or education purposes. These discussions should not reveal the identity of the client or any other unnecessary aspects of the case and should only be done with fellow counseling professionals who subscribe to the IAMFC ethical code. The consulting professional counselor has an obligation to keep all shared information confidential.

B. All clients must be informed of the nature and limitations of confidentiality. They must also be informed of who may have access to their counseling records, as well as any information that may be released to other agencies or professionals for insurance reimbursement. These disclosures should be made both orally and in writing, whenever feasible.

C. All client records should be stored in a way that ensures confidentiality. Written records should be kept in a locked drawer or cabinet and computerized record systems should use appropriate passwords and safeguards to prevent unauthorized entry.

D. Clients must be informed if sessions are to be recorded on audio- or videotape and sign a consent form for doing so. When more than one person is receiving counseling, all persons who are legally competent must give informed consent in writing for the recording.

E. Unless alternate arrangements have been agreed upon by all participants, statements made by a family member to the counselor during an individual counseling or consultation contact are to be treated as confidential and are not disclosed to other family members without the individual's permission. If a client's refusal to share information from individual contacts interferes with the agreed upon goals of counseling, the counselor may have to terminate treatment and refer the clients to another counselor.

SECTION III: COMPETENCE

A. Members have the responsibility to develop and maintain basic skills in marriage and family counseling through graduate work, supervision, and peer review. An outline of these skills is provided by the Council for Accreditation of Counseling and Related Educational Programs (CACREP) *Environmental and Specialty Standards for Marriage and Family Counseling/ Therapy.* The minimal level of training shall be considered master's degree in a helping profession.

B. Members recognize the need for keeping current with new developments in the field of marriage and family counseling. They pursue continuing education in forms such as books, journals, classes, workshops, conferences, and conventions.

C. Members accurately represent their education, areas of expertise, training, and experience.

D. Members do not attempt to diagnose or treat problems beyond the scope of their abilities and training.

E. Members do not undertake any professional activity in which their personal problems might adversely affect their performance. Instead, they focus their energies on obtaining appropriate professional assistance to help them resolve the problem.

F. Members do not engage in actions that violate the moral or legal standards of their community.

SECTION IV: ASSESSMENT

A. Members utilize assessment procedures to promote the best interests and well-being of the client in clarifying concerns, establishing treatment goals, evaluating therapeutic progress, and promoting objective decision making.

B. Clients have the right to know the results, interpretation, and conclusions drawn from assessment interviews and instruments, as well as how this information will be used.

C. Members utilize assessment methods that are reliable, valid, and germane to the goals of the client. When using computer-assisted scoring, members obtain empirical evidence for the reliability and validity of the methods and procedures used.

D. Members do not use inventories and tests that have outdated test items or normative data.

E. Members do not use assessment methods that are outside the scope of their qualifications, training, or statutory limitations. Members using tests or inventories have a thorough understanding of measurement concepts.

F. Members read the manual before using a published instrument. They become knowledgeable about the purpose of the instrument and relevant psychometric and normative data.

G. Members conducting custody evaluations recognize the potential impact that their reports can have on family members. As such, they are committed to a thorough assessment of both parents. Therefore, custody recommendations should not be made on the basis of information from only one parent. Members only use instruments that have demonstrated validity in custody evaluations and do not make recommendations based solely on test and inventory scores.

H. Members strive to maintain the guidelines in the *Standards for Educational and Psychological Testing*, written in collaboration by the American Educational Research Association, American Psychological Association, and National Council on Measurement in Evaluation, as well as the *Code of Fair Testing Practices*, published by the Joint Committee on Testing Practices.

SECTION V: PRIVATE PRACTICE

A. Members assist the profession and community by facilitating, whenever feasible, the availability of counseling services in private settings.

B. Due to the independent nature of their work, members in private practice recognize that they have a special obligation to act ethically and responsibly, keep their services at little or no cost as a service to the community. They also provide referral services for clients who will not be seen pro bono and who are unable to afford private services.

C. Members in private practice provide a portion of their services at little or no cost as a service to the community. They also provide referral service for clients who will not be seen pro bono and who are unable to afford private services.

D. Members only enter into partnerships in which each member adheres to the ethical standards of their profession.

E. Members should not charge a fee for offering or accepting referrals.

SECTION VI: RESEARCH AND PUBLICATIONS

A. Members shall be fully responsible for their choice of research topics and the methods used for investigation, analysis, and reporting. They must be particularly careful that findings do not appear misleading, that the research is planned to allow for the inclusion of alternative hypotheses, and that provision is made for discussion of the limitations of the study.

B. Members safeguard the privacy of their research participants. Data about an individual participant are not released unless the individual is informed about the exact nature of the information to be released and gives written permission for doing so.

C. Members safeguard the safety of their research participants. Members receive approval from and follow guidelines of, any institutional research committee. Prospective participants are informed, in writing, about any potential danger associated with a study and are notified that they can withdraw at any time.

D. Members make their original data available to other researchers.

E. Members only take credit for research in which they made a substantial contribution, and give credit to all such contributors. Authors are listed from greatest to least amount of contribution.

F. Members do not plagiarize. Ideas or data that did not originate with the author(s) and are not common knowledge are clearly credited to the original source.

G. Members are aware of their obligation to be a role model for graduate students and other future researchers and so act in accordance with the highest standards possible while engaged in research.

SECTION VII: SUPERVISION

A. Members who provide supervision acquire and maintain skills pertaining to the supervision process. They are able to demonstrate for supervisees the application of counseling theory and process to client issues. Supervisors are knowledgeable about different methods and conceptual approaches to supervision.

B. Members who provide supervision respect the inherent imbalance of power in the supervisory relationship. They do not use their potentially influential positions to exploit students, supervisees, or employees. Supervisors do not ask supervisees to engage in behaviors not directly related to the supervision process, and they clearly separate supervision and evaluation. Supervisors also avoid dual relationships that might impair their professional judgment or increase the possibility of exploitation. Sexual intimacy with students or supervisees is prohibited.

C. Members who provide supervision are responsible for both the promotion of supervisee learning and development and the advancement of marriage and family counseling. Supervisors recruit students into professional organizations, educate students about professional ethics and standards, provide service to professional organizations strive to educate new professionals, and work to improve professional practices.

D. Members who provide supervision have the responsibility to inform students of the specific expectations surrounding skill building, knowledge acquisition, and the development of competencies. Members also provide ongoing and timely feedback to their supervisees.

E. Members who provide supervision are responsible for protecting the rights and well-being of their supervisees' clients. They monitor their supervisees' counseling on an ongoing basis, and create procedures to protect the confidentiality of clients whose sessions have been electronically recorded.

F. Members who provide supervision strive to reach and maintain the guidelines provided in the *Standards for Counseling Supervisors* published by the ACA Governing Council (cf. *Journal of Counseling & Development*, 1990, Vol. 69, pp. 3-32).

G. Members who are counselor educators encourage their programs to reach and maintain the guidelines provided in the CACREP *Environmental and Specialty Standards for Marriage and Family Counseling/Therapy.*

SECTION VIII: MEDIA AND PUBLIC STATEMENTS

A. Members accurately and objectively represent their professional qualifications, skills, and functions to the public. Membership in a professional organization is not to be used to suggest competency.

B. Members have the responsibility to provide information to the public that enhances marriage and family life. Such statements should be based on sound, scientifically acceptable theories, techniques, and approaches. Due to the inability to complete a comprehensive assessment and provide follow-up, members should not give specific advice to an individual through the media.

C. The announcement or advertisement of professional services should focus on objective information that allows the client to make an informed decision. Providing information such as highest relevant academic degree earned, licenses or certifications, office hours, types of services offered, fee structure, and languages spoken can help clients decide whether the advertised services are appropriate for their needs. Members advertising a specialty within marriage and family counseling should provide evidence of training, education, and/or supervision in the area of specialization. Advertisements about workshops or seminars should contain a description of the audience for which the program is intended. Due to their subjective nature, statements either from clients or from the counselor about the uniqueness, effectiveness, or efficiency of services should be avoided. Announcements and advertisements should never contain false, misleading, or fraudulent statements.

D. Members promoting psychology tapes, books, or other products for commercial sale make every effort to ensure that announcements and advertisements are presented in a professional and factual manner.

APPENDIX VI

ETHICAL GUIDELINES FOR COUNSELING SUPERVISORS ASSOCIATION FOR COUNSELOR EDUCATION AND SUPERVISION

ETHICAL GUIDELINES FOR COUNSELING SUPERVISORS ASSOCIATION FOR COUNSELOR EDUCATION AND SUPERVISION

Adopted March 1993

Preamble

The Association for Counselor Education and Supervision (ACES) is composed of persons who are engaged in the professional preparation of counselors and people responsible for the ongoing supervision of counselors. ACES is a founding division of the American Counseling Association for (ACA) and as such adheres to ACA's current ethical standards (AACD, 1988) and to general codes of competence adopted throughout the mental health community.

ACES believes that counselor educators and counseling supervisors in universities and in applied counseling settings, including the range of education and mental health delivery systems, carry responsibilities unique to their job roles. Such responsibilities may include administrative supervision, clinical supervision, or both. Administrative supervision refers to those supervisory activities which increase the efficiency of the delivery of counseling services; whereas, clinical supervision includes the supportive and educative activities of the supervisor designed to improve the application of counseling theory and technique directly to clients.

Counselor educators and counseling supervisors encounter situations which challenge the help given by general ethical standards of the profession at large. These situations require more specific guidelines that provide appropriate guidance in everyday practice.

The Ethical Guidelines for Counseling Supervisors are intended to assist professionals by helping them:

1. observe ethical and legal protection of clients' and supervisee's rights;

2. meet the training and professional development needs of supervisees in ways consistent with clients' welfare and programmatic requirements; and

3. establish policies, procedures, and standards for implementing programs.

The specification of ethical guidelines enables ACES members to focus on and to clarify the ethical nature of responsibilities held in common. Such guidelines should be reviewed formally every five years, or more often if needed, to meet the needs of ACES members for guidance.

The Ethical Guidelines for Counselor Educators and Counseling Supervisors are meant to help ACES members in conducting supervision.

ACES is not currently in a position to hear complaints about alleged noncompliance with these guidelines. Any complaints about the ethical behavior of any ACA member should be measured against the ACA Ethical Standards and a complaint lodged with ACA in accordance with their procedures for doing so. One overriding assumption underlying this document is that supervision should be on-going throughout a counselor's career and not stop when a particular level of education, certification or membership in a professional organization is attained.

Definitions of Terms:

Applied Counseling Settings — Public or private organizations of counselors such as community mental health centers, hospitals, schools, and group or individual private practice settings.

Supervisees — Counselors-in-training in university programs at any level who work with clients in applied settings as part of their university training program, and counselors who have completed their formal education and are employed in an applied counseling setting.

Supervisors — Counselors who have been designated within their university or agency to directly oversee the professional clinical work of counselors. Supervisors also may be persons who offer supervision to counselors seeking state licensure and so provide supervision outside of the administrative aegis of an applied counseling setting.

1. Client Welfare and Rights

1.01 The primary obligation of supervisors is to train counselors so that they respect the integrity and promote the welfare of their clients. Supervisors should have supervisees inform clients that they are being supervised and that observation and/or recordings of the sessions may be reviewed by the supervisor.

1.02 Supervisors who are licensed counselors and are conducting supervision to aid a supervisee to become licensed should instruct the supervisee not to communicate or in any way convey to the supervisee's clients or to other parties that the supervisee is himself/herself licensed.

1.03 Supervisors should make supervisees aware of clients' rights, including protecting clients' right to privacy and confidentiality will not be violated by the supervisory relationship.

1.04 Records of the counseling relationship, including interview notes, test data, correspondence, the electronic storage of these documents, and audio and videotape recordings are considered to be confidential professional information. Supervisors should see that these materials are used in counseling, research, training and supervision of counselors with the full knowledge of the client, and that permission to use these materials is granted by the applied counseling setting offering service to the client. This professional information is to be used for the full protection of the client. Written consent from the client (or legal guardian, if a minor) should be secured prior to the use of such information for instructional, supervisory, and/or research purposes. Policies of the applied counseling setting regarding client records also should be followed.

1.05 Supervisors shall adhere to current professional and legal guidelines when conducting research with human participants such as Section D-1 of the ACA Ethical Standards.

1.06 Counseling supervisors are responsible for making every effort to monitor both the professional actions, and failures to take action, of their supervisees.

2. Supervisory Role

Inherent and integral to the role of supervisor are responsibilities for:

a. monitoring client welfare;

b. encouraging compliance with relevant legal, ethical, and professional standards for clinical practice;

c. monitoring clinical performance and professional development of supervisees; and

d. evaluating and certifying current performance and potential of supervisees for academic, screening, selection, placement, employment, and credentialing purposes.

2.01 Supervisors should have had training in supervision prior to initiating their role as supervisors.

2.02 Supervisors should pursue professional and personal continuing education activities such as advanced courses, seminars, and professional conferences on a regular and on-going basis. These activities should include both counseling and supervision topics and skills.

2.03 Supervisors should make their supervisees aware of professional and ethical standards and legal responsibilities of the counseling profession.

2.04 Supervisors of post-degree counselors who are seeking state licensure should encourage these counselors to adhere to the standards for practice established by the state licensure board of the state in which they practice.

2.05 Procedures for contacting the supervisor, or an alternative supervisors, to assist in handling crisis situations should be established and communicated to supervisees.

2.06 Actual work samples via audio and/or video tape or live observation in addition to case notes should be reviewed by the supervisor as a regular part of the ongoing supervisory process.

2.07 Supervisors of counselors should meet regularly in face-to-face sessions with their supervisees.

2.08 Supervisors should provide supervisees with ongoing feedback on their performance. This feedback should take a variety of forms, both formal and informal, and should include verbal and written evaluations. It should be formative during the supervisory experience and summative at the conclusions of the experience.

2.09 Supervisors who have multiple roles (e.g., teacher, clinical supervisor, administrative supervisor, etc.) with supervisees should minimize potential conflicts. Where possible, the roles should be divided among several supervisors. Where this is not possible, careful explanation should be conveyed to the supervisee as to the expectations and responsibilities associated with each supervisory role.

2.10 Supervisors should not participate in any form of sexual contact with supervisees. Supervisors should not engage in an form of social contact or interaction which would compromise the supervisor-supervisee relationship. Dual relationships with supervisees that might impair the supervisor's objectivity and professional judgment should be avoided and/or the supervisory relationship terminated.

2.11 Supervisors should not establish a psychotherapeutic relationship as a substitute for supervision. Personal issues should be addressed in supervision only in terms of the impact for these issues on clients and on professional functioning.

2.12 Supervisors, through ongoing supervisee assessment and evaluation, should be aware of any personal or professional limitations of supervisees which are likely to impede future professional performance. Supervisors have the responsibility of recommending remedial assistance to the supervisee and of screening from the training program, applied counseling setting, or state licensure those supervisees who are unable to provide competent professional services. These recommendations should be clearly and professionally explained in writing to the supervisees who are so evaluated.

2.13 Supervisors should not endorse a supervisee for certification, licensure, completion of an academic training program, or continued employment if the supervisor believes the supervisee is impaired in any way that would interfere with the performance of counseling duties. The presence of any such impairment should begin a process of feedback and remediation wherever possible so that the supervisee understands the nature of the impairment and has the opportunity to remedy the problem and continue with his/ her professional development.

2.14 Supervisors should incorporate the principles of informed consent and participation, clarity of requirements, expectations, roles and rules; due process and appeal into the establishment of policies and procedures of their institution, program, courses, and individual supervisory relationships. Mechanisms for due process appeal of individual supervisory actions should be established and made available to all supervisees.

3. Program Administration Role

3.01 Supervisors should ensure that the programs conducted and experiences provided are in keeping with current guidelines and standards of ACA and its divisions.

3.02 Supervisors should teach courses and/or supervise clinical work only in areas where they are fully competent and experienced.

3.03 To achieve the highest quality of training and supervision, supervisors should be active participants in peer review and peer supervision procedures.

3.04 Supervisors should provide experiences that integrate theoretical knowledge and practical application. Supervisors also should provide opportunities in which supervisees are able to apply the knowledge they have learned and understand the rationale for the skills they have acquired. The knowledge and skills conveyed should reflect current practice, research findings, and available resources.

3.05 Professional competencies, specific courses, and/or required experiences expected of supervisees should be communicated to them in writing prior to admission to the training program or placement/employment by the applied counseling setting, and, in the case of continued employment, in a timely manner.

3.06 Supervisors should accept only those persons as supervisees who meet identified entry level requirements for admission to a program of counselor training or for placement in an applied counseling setting. In the case of private supervision in search of state licensure, supervisees should have completed all necessary prerequisites as determined by the state licensure board.

3.07 Supervisors should inform supervisees of the goals, policies, theoretical orientations toward counseling, training, and supervision model or approach on which the supervision is based.

3.08 Supervisees should be encouraged and assisted to define their own theoretical orientation toward counseling, to establish supervision goals for themselves, and to monitor and evaluate their progress toward meeting these goals.

3.09 Supervisors should assess supervisees' skills and experience in order to establish standards for competent professional behaviors. Supervisors should restrict supervisees' activities to those that are commensurate with their current level of skills and experiences.

3.10 Supervisors should obtain practicum and fieldwork sites that meet minimum standards for preparing students to become effective counselors. No practicum of fieldwork setting should be approved unless it truly replicates a counseling work setting.

3.11 Practicum and fieldwork classes should be limited in size according to established professional standards to ensure that each student has ample opportunity for individual supervision and feedback. Supervisors in applied counseling settings should have a limited number of supervisees.

3.12 Supervisors in university settings should establish and communicate specific policies and procedures regarding field counselor, the university supervisor, and the field supervisor the policies should be clearly differentiated in areas such as evaluation, requirements, and confidentiality.

3.13 Supervision in training programs should communicate regularly with supervisors in agencies used as practicum and/or fieldwork sites regarding current professional practices, expectations of students, and preferred models and modalities of supervision.

3.14 Supervisors at the university should establish clear lines of communication among themselves, the field supervisors, and the student/supervisees.

3.15 Supervisors should establish and communicate to supervisees and to field supervisors specific procedures regarding consultation, performance review, and evaluation of supervisees.

3.16 Evaluations of supervisee performance in universities and in applied counseling settings should be available to supervisees in ways consistent with the Family Rights and Privacy Act and the Buckley Amendment.

3.17 Forms of training that focus primarily on self understanding and problem resolution (e.g., personal growth groups or individual counseling) should be voluntary. Those who conduct these forms of training should not serve simultaneously as supervisors of the supervisees involved in the training.

3.18 A supervisor may recommend participation in activities such as personal growth groups or personal counseling when it has been determined that a supervisee has deficits in the areas of self understanding and problem resolution which impede his/her professional functioning. The supervisor should not be the direct provider of these activities for the supervisee.

3.19 When a training program conducts a personal growth or counseling experience involving relatively intimate self disclosure, care should be taken to eliminate or minimize potential role conflicts for faculty and/or agency supervisors who may conduct these experiences and who also serve as teachers, group leaders, and clinical directors.

3.20 Supervisors should use the following prioritized sequence in resolving conflicts among the needs of the client, the needs of the supervisee, and the needs of the program or agency. Insofar as the client must be protected, it should be understood that client welfare is usually subsumed in federal and state laws such that these statutes should be the first point of reference. Where laws and ethical standards are not present or are unclear, the good judgment of the supervisor should be guided by the following list:

a. Relevant legal and ethical standards (e.g. duty to warn, state child abuse laws, etc.);

b. Client welfare;

c. Supervisee welfare;

d. Supervisor welfare; and

e. Program and/or agency service and administrative needs.

APPENDIX VII
CODE OF ETHICS
FOR MENTAL HEALTH COUNSELORS
AMERICAN MENTAL HEALTH
COUNSELORS ASSOCIATION

CODE OF ETHICS FOR MENTAL HEALTH COUNSELORS
AMERICAN MENTAL HEALTH COUNSELORS ASSOCIATION

Mental Health Counselors believe in the dignity and worth of the individual. They are committed to increasing knowledge of human behavior and understanding of themselves and others. While pursuing these endeavors, they make every reasonable effort to protect the welfare of those who seek their services or of any subject that may be the object of study. They use their skills only for purposes consistent with these values and do not knowingly permit their misuse by others. While demanding for themselves freedom of inquiry and community, mental health counselors accept the responsibility this freedom confers: competence, objectivity in the application of skills and concern for the best interests of clients, colleagues, and society in general. In the pursuit of these ideals, mental health counselors subscribe to the following principles:

PRINCIPLE 1. RESPONSIBILITY

In their commitment to the understanding of human behavior, mental health counselors value objectivity and integrity, and in providing services they maintain the highest standards. They accept responsibility for the consequences of their work and make every effort to insure that their services are used appropriately.

a. Mental health counselors accept ultimate responsibility for selecting appropriate areas for investigation and the methods relevant to minimize the possibility that their finding will be misleading. They provide thorough discussion of the limitations of their data and alternative hypotheses, especially where their work touches on social policy or might be misconstrued to the detriment of specific age, sex, ethnic, socioeconomic, or other social categories. In publishing reports of their work, they never discard observations that may modify the interpretation of results. Mental health counselors take credit only for the work they have actually done. In pursuing research, mental health counselors ascertain that their efforts will not lead to changes in individuals or organizations unless such changes are part of the agreement at the time of obtaining informal consent. Mental health counselors clarify in advance the expectations for sharing and utilizing research data. They avoid dual relationships which may limit objectivity, whether theoretical, political, or monetary, so that interference with data, subjects, and milieu is kept to a minimum.

b. As employees of an institution or agency, mental health counselors have the responsibility of remaining alert to institutional pressures which may distort reports of counseling findings or use them in ways counter to the promotion of human welfare.

c. When serving as members of governmental or other organizational bodies, mental health counselors remain accountable as individuals to the Code of Ethics of the American Mental Health Counselors Association (AMHCA).

d. As teachers, mental health counselors recognize their primary obligation to help others acquire knowledge and skill. They maintain high standards of scholarship and objectivity by presenting counseling information fully and accurately, and by giving appropriate recognition to alternative viewpoints.

e. As practitioners, mental health counselors know that they bear a heavy social responsibility because their recommendations and professional actions may alter the lives of others. They, therefore, remain fully cognizant of their impact and alert to personal, social, organizational, financial or political situations or pressures which might lead to misuse of their influence.

f. Mental health counselors provide reasonable and timely feedback to employees, trainees, supervisors, students, clients, and others whose work they may evaluate.

PRINCIPLE 2. COMPETENCE

The maintenance of high standards of professional competence is a responsibility shared by all mental health counselors in the interest of the public and the profession as a whole. Mental health counselors recognize the boundaries of their competence and the limitations of their techniques and only provide services, use techniques, or offer opinions as professionals that meet recognized standards. Throughout their careers, mental health counselors maintain knowledge of professional information related to the services they render.

a. Mental health counselors accurately represent their competence, education, training and experience.

b. As teachers, mental health counselors perform their duties based on careful preparation so that their instruction is accurate, up-to-date and scholarly.

c. Mental health counselors recognize the need for continuing training to prepare themselves to serve persons of all ages and cultural backgrounds.

They are open to new procedures and sensitive to differences between groups of people and changes in expectations and values over time.

d. Mental health counselors with the responsibility for decisions involving individuals or policies based on test results should know and understand literature relevant to the tests used and testing problems with which they deal.

e. Mental health counselors and practitioners recognize that their effectiveness depends in part upon their ability to maintain sound interpersonal relations, that temporary or more enduring aberrations on their part may interfere with their abilities or distort their appraisals of others. Therefore, they refrain from undertaking any activity in which their personal problems are likely to lead to inadequate professional services or harm to a client, or, if they are already engaged in such activity when they become aware of their personal problems, they would seek competent professional assistance to determine whether they should suspend or terminate services to one or all of their clients.

f. The mental health counselor has a responsibility both to the individual who is served and to the institution with which the service is performed to maintain high standards of professional conduct. The mental health counselor strives to maintain the highest levels of professional services offered to the individuals to be served. The mental health counselor also strives to assist the agency, organization or institution in providing the highest caliber of professional services. The acceptance of employment in an institution implies that the mental health counselors is in substantial agreement with the general policies and principles of the institution. If, despite concerted efforts, the member cannot reach agreement with the employer as to acceptable standards of conduct that allow for changes in institutional policy conducive to the positive growth and development of counselees, then terminating the affiliation should be seriously considered.

g. Ethical behavior among professional associates, mental health counselors and non-mental health counselors, is expected at all times. When information is possessed which raises serious doubt as to the ethical behavior of professional colleagues, whether Association members or not, the mental health counselor is obligated to take action to attempt to rectify such a condition. Such action shall utilize the institution's channels first and then utilize procedures established by the state, division, or Association.

h. The mental health counselor is aware of the intimacy of the counseling relationship and maintains a healthy respect for the personhood of the client and avoids engaging in activities that seek to meet the mental health counselor's personal needs at the expense of the client. Through awareness of the negative impact of both racial and sexual stereotyping and discrimination, the member strives to ensure the individual rights and personal dignity of the client in the counseling relationship.

PRINCIPLE 3. MORAL AND LEGAL STANDARDS

Mental health counselors moral, ethical and legal standards of behavior are a personal matter to the same degree as they are for any other citizen, except as these may compromise the fulfillment of their professional responsibilities, or reduce the trust in counseling or counselors held by the general public. Regarding their own behavior, mental health counselors should be aware of the prevailing community standards and of the possible impact upon the quality of professional services provided by their conformance to or deviation from these standards. Mental Health counselors should also be aware of the possible impact of their public behavior upon the ability of colleagues to perform their professional duties.

a. To protect public confidence in the profession of counseling, mental health counselors will avoid public behavior that is clearly in violation of accepted moral and legal standards.

b. To protect students, mental health counselors/teachers will be aware of the diverse backgrounds of students and, when dealing with topics that may give offense, will see that the material is treated objectively, that it is clearly relevant to the course, and that it is treated in a manner for which the student is prepared.

c. Providers of counseling services conform to the statutes relating to such services as established by their state and its regulating professional board(s).

d. As employees, mental health counselors refuse to participate in employer's practices which are inconsistent with the moral and legal standards established by federal or state legislation regarding the treatment of employees or of the public. In particular and for example, mental health counselors will not condone practices which result in illegal or otherwise unjustifiable discrimination on the basis of race, sex, religion or national origin in hiring, promotion or training.

e. In providing counseling services to clients mental health counselors avoid any action that will violate or diminish the legal and civil rights of clients or of others who may be affected by the action.

f. Sexual conduct, not limited to sexual intercourse, between mental health counselors and clients is specifically in violation of this code of ethics. This does not, however, prohibit the use of explicit instructional aids including films and video tapes. Such use is within accepted practices of trained and competent sex therapists.

PRINCIPLE 4. PUBLIC STATEMENTS

Mental health counselors in their professional roles may be expected or required to make public statements providing counseling information, professional opinions, or supply information about the availability of counseling products and services. In making such statement, mental health counselors take full account of the limits and uncertainties of present counseling knowledge and techniques. They represent, as objectively as possible, their professional qualifications, affiliations, and functions, as well as those of the institutions or organizations with which the statements may be associated. All public statements, announcements of services, and promotional activities should serve the purpose of providing sufficient information to aid the consumer public in making informed judgements and choices on matters that concern it.

a. When announcing professional counseling services, mental health counselors limit the information to: name, highest relevant degree conferred, certification or licensure, address, telephone number, office hours, cost of services, and a brief explanation of the other types of services offered but not evaluative as to their quality or uniqueness. They will not contain testimonials by implication. They will not claim uniqueness of skill or methods beyond those acceptable and public scientific evidence.

b. In announcing the availability of counseling services or products, mental health counselors will not display their affiliations with organizations or agencies in a manner that implies the sponsorship or certification of the organization or agency. They will not name their employer or professional associations unless the services are in fact to be provided by or under the responsible, direct supervision and continuing control of such organizations or agencies.

c. Mental health counselors associated with the development of promotion of counseling device, books, or other products offered for commercial sale will make every effort to insure that announcements and advertisements are presented in a professional and factually informative manner without unsupported claims of superiority and must be supported by scientifically acceptable evidence or by willingness to aid and encourage independent professional scrutiny or scientific test.

d. Mental health counselors engaged in radio, television or other public media activities will not participate in commercial announcements recommending to the general public the purchase or use of any proprietary or single-source product or service.

e. Mental health counselors who describe counseling or the services of professional counselors to the general public accept the obligation to present the material fairly and accurately, avoiding misrepresentation through sensationalism, exaggeration or superficiality. Mental health counselors will be guided by the primary obligation to aid the public in forming their own informed judgements, opinions and choices.

f. As teachers, mental health counselors ensure their statements in catalogs and course outlines are accurate, particularly in terms of subject matter to be covered, bases for grading, and nature of classroom experiences.

g. Mental health counselors accept the obligation to correct others who may represent their professional qualifications or associations with products or services in a manner incompatible with these guidelines.

h. Mental health counselors providing consultation, workshops, training, and other technical services may refer to previous satisfied clients in their advertising, provided there is no implication that such advertising refers to counseling services.

PRINCIPLE 5. CONFIDENTIALITY

Mental health counselors have a primary obligation to safeguard information about individuals obtained in the course of teaching, practice, or research. Personal information if communicated to others only with the person's written consent or in those circumstances where there is clear and imminent danger to the client, to others or to society. Disclosures of counseling information are restricted to what is necessary, relevant, and verifiable.

a. All materials in the official record shall be shared with the client who shall have the right to decide what information may be shared with anyone beyond the immediate provider of service and to be informed of the implications of the materials to be shared.

b. The anonymity of clients served in public and other agencies is preserved, if at all possible, by withholding names and personal identifying data. If external conditions require reporting such information, the client shall be so informed.

c. Information received in confidence by one agency or person shall not be forwarded to another person or agency without the client's written permission.

d. Service providers have a responsibility to insure the accuracy and to indicate the validity of data shared with their parties.

e. Case reports presented in classes, professional meetings, or in publications shall be so disguised that no identification is possible unless the client or responsible authority has read the report and agreed in writing to its presentation or publication.

f. Counseling reports and records are maintained under conditions of security and provisions are made for their destruction when they have outlived their usefulness. Mental health counselors insure that privacy and confidentiality are maintained by all persons in the employ or volunteers, and community aides.

g. Mental health counselors who ask that an individual reveal personal information in the course of interviewing, testing or evaluation, or who allow such information to be divulged, do so only after making certain that the person or authorized representative is fully aware of the purposes of the interview, testing or evaluation and of the ways in which the information will be used.

h. Sessions with clients are taped or otherwise recorded only with their written permission or the written permission of a responsible guardian. Even with guardian written consent one should not record a session against the expressed wishes of a client.

i. Where a child or adolescent is the primary client, the interests of the minor shall be paramount.

j. In work with families, the rights of each family member should be safe guarded. The provider of service also has the responsibility to discuss the contents of the record with the parent and/or child, as appropriate, and to keep separate those parts which should remain the property of each family member.

PRINCIPLE 6. WELFARE OF THE CONSUMER

Mental health counselors respect the integrity and protect the welfare of the people and groups with whom they work. When there is a conflict of interest between the client and the mental health counselor employing institution, the mental health counselors clarify the nature and direction of their loyalties and responsibilities and keep all parties informed of their commitments. Mental health counselors fully inform consumers as to the purpose and nature of any evaluative, treatment, educational or training procedure, and they freely acknowledge that clients, students, or subjects have freedom of choice with regard to participation.

a. Mental health counselors are continually cognizant both of their own needs and of their inherently powerful position "vis-a-vis" clients, in order to avoid exploiting the client's trust and dependency. Mental health counselors make every effort to avoid dual relationships with clients and/or relationships which might impair their professional judgement or increase the risk of client exploitation. Examples of such dual relationships include treating an employee or supervisor, treating a close friend or family relative and sexual relationships with clients.

b. Where mental health counselors work with members of an organization goes beyond reasonable conditions of employment, mental health counselors recognize possible conflicts of interest that may arise. When such conflicts occur, mental health counselors clarify the nature of the conflict and inform all parties of the nature and directions of the loyalties and responsibilities involved.

c. When acting as supervisors, trainers, or employers, mental health counselors accord recipients informed choice, confidentiality, and protection from physical and mental harm.

d. Financial arrangements in professional practice are in accord with professional standards that safeguard the best interests of the client and that are clearly understood by the client in advance of billing. This may best be done by the use of a contract. Mental health counselors are responsible for assisting clients in finding needed services in those instances where payment of the usual fee would be a hardship. No commission or rebate or other form of remuneration may be given or received for referral of clients for professional services, whether by an individual or by an agency.

e. Mental health counselors are responsible for making their services readily accessible to clients in a manner that facilitates the client's ability to make an informed choice when selecting a service provider. This responsibility includes a clear description of what the client may expect in the way of tests, reports, billing, therapeutic regime and schedules and the use of the mental health counselor's Statement of Professional Disclosure.

f. Mental health counselors who find that their services are not beneficial to the client have the responsibility to make this known to the responsible persons.

g. Mental health counselors are accountable to the parties who refer and support counseling services and to the general public and are cognizant of the indirect or long-range effects of their intervention.

h. The mental health counselor attempts to terminate a private service or consulting relationship when it is reasonably clear to the mental health counselor that the consumer is not benefitting from it. If a consumer is receiving services from another mental health professional, mental health counselors do not offer their services directly to the consumer without informing the professional persons already involved in order to avoid confusion and conflict for the consumer.

i. The mental health counselor has the responsibility to screen prospective group participants, especially when the emphasis is on self-understanding and growth through self-disclosure. The member should maintain an awareness of the group participants' compatibility throughout the life of the group.

j. The mental health counselor may choose to consult with any other professionally competent person about a client. In choosing a consultant, the mental health counselor should avoid placing the consultant in a conflict of interest situation that would preclude the consultant's being a proper party to the mental health counselors' efforts to help the clients.

k. If the mental health counselor is unable to be of professional assistance to the client, the mental health counselor should avoid initiating the counseling relationship or the mental health counselors terminates the relationship. In either event, the member is obligated to suggest appropriate alternatives. (It is incumbent upon the mental health counselors to be knowledgeable about referral resources so that a satisfactory referral can be initiated.) In the event the client declines the suggested referral, the mental health counselor is not obligated to continue the relationship.

l. When the mental health counselor has other relationships, particularly of an administrative, supervisory, and/or evaluative nature, with an individual seeking counseling services, the mental health counselor should not serve as the counselor but should refer the individual to another professional. Only in instances where such an alternative is unavailable and where the individual's situation definitely warrants counseling intervention should the mental health counselor enter into and/or maintain a counseling relationship. Dual relationships with clients which might impair the member's objectivity and professional judgement (such as with close friends or relatives, sexual intimacies with any client, etc.) must be avoided and/or the counseling relationship terminated through referral to another competent professional.

m. All experimental methods of treatment must be clearly indicated to prospective recipients, and safety precautions are to be adhered to by the mental health counselor instituting treatment.

n. When the member is engaged in short-term group treatment/training programs, e.g., marathons and other encounter-type or growth groups, the member ensures that there is professional assistance available during and following the group experience.

PRINCIPLE 7. PROFESSIONAL RELATIONSHIP

Mental health counselors act with due regard to the needs and feelings of their colleagues in counseling and other professions. Mental health counselors respect the prerogatives and obligations of the institutions or organizations with which they are associated.

a. Mental health counselors understand the areas of competence of related professions and make full use of other professional, technical, and administrative resources which best serve the interests of consumers. The absence of formal relationships with other professional workers does not relieve mental health counselors from the responsibility of securing for their clients the best possible professional service; indeed, this circumstance presents a challenge to the professional competence of mental health counselors, requiring special sensitivity to problems outside their areas of training, and foresight, diligence, and tact in obtaining the professional assistance needed by clients.

b. Mental health counselors know and take into account the traditions and practices of other professional groups with which they work and cooperate fully with members of such groups when research, services, and other functions are shared or in working for the benefit of public welfare.

c. Mental health counselors strive to provide positive conditions for those they employ and they spell out clearly the conditions of such employment.

They encourage their employees to engage in activities that facilitate their further professional development.

d. Mental health counselors respect the viability, reputation, and the proprietary right of organizations which they serve. Mental health counselors show due regard for the interest of their present or prospective employers. In those instances where they are critical of policies, they attempt to effect change by constructive action within the organization.

e. In the pursuit of research, mental health counselors give sponsoring agencies, host institutions, and publication channels the same respect and opportunity for giving informed consent that they accord to individual research participants. They are aware of their obligation to future research workers and insure that host institutions are given feedback information and proper acknowledgment.

f. Credit is assigned to those who have contributed to a publication, in proportion to their contribution.

g. When a mental health counselor violates ethical standards, mental health counselors who know first-hand of such activities should, if possible, attempt to rectify the situation. Failing an informal solution, mental health counselors should bring such unethical activities to the attention of the appropriate state, and/or national committee on ethics and professional conduct. Only after all professional alternatives have been utilized will a mental health counselor begin legal action for resolution.

PRINCIPLE 8. UTILIZATION OF ASSESSMENT TECHNIQUES

In the development, publication, and utilization of counseling assessment techniques, mental health counselors follow relevant standards. Individuals examined, or their legal guardians, have the right to know the results, the interpretations made, and where appropriate, the particulars on which final judgement was based. Test users should take precautions to protect test security but not at the expense of an individual's right to understand the basis for decisions that adversely affect that individual or that individual's dependents.

a. The client has the right to have and the provider has the responsibility to give explanations of test results in language the client can understand.

b. When a test is published or otherwise made available for operational use, it should be accompanied by a manual (or other published or readily available information) that makes every reasonable effort to describe fully the development of the test, the rationale, specifications followed in writing items analysis or other research. The test, the manual, the record forms and other accompanying material should help users make correct interpretations of the test results and should warn against common misuses. The test manual should state explicitly the purposes and applications for which the test is recommended and identify any special qualifications required to administer the test and to interpret it properly. Evidence of validity and reliability, along with other relevant research data, should be presented in support of any claims made.

c. Norms presented in test manuals should refer to defined and clearly described populations. These populations should be the groups with whom users of the test will ordinarily wish to compare the persons tested. Test users should consider the possibility of bias in tests or in test items. When indicated, there should be an investigation of possible differences in validity for ethnic, sex, or other subsamples that can be identified when the test is given.

d. Mental health counselors who have the responsibility for decisions about individuals or policies that are based on test results should have a thorough understanding of counseling or educational measurement and of validation and other test research.

e. Mental health counselors should develop procedures for systematically eliminating from data files test score information that has, because of the lapse of time, become obsolete.

f. Any individual or organization offering test scoring and interpretation services must be able to demonstrate that their programs are based on appropriate research to establish the validity of the programs and procedures used in arriving at interpretations. The public offering of an automated test interpretation service will be considered as a professional-to-professional consultation. In this the formal responsibility of the consultant is to the consultee but his/her ultimate and overriding responsibility is to the client.

g. Counseling services for the purpose of diagnosis, treatment, or personalized advice are provided only in the context of a professional relationship, and are not given by means of public lectures or demonstrations, newspapers or magazine articles, radio or television programs, mail, or similar media. The preparation of personnel reports and recommendations based on test data secured solely by mail is unethical unless such appraisals are an integral part of a continuing client relationship with a company, as a result of which the consulting clinical mental health counselor has intimate knowledge of the client's personal situation and can be assured thereby that his written appraisals will be adequate to the purpose and will be properly interpreted by the client. These reports must not be embellished with such detailed analyses of the subject's personality traits as would be appropriate only for intensive interviews with the subjects.

PRINCIPLE 9. PURSUIT OF RESEARCH ACTIVITIES

The decision to undertake research should rest upon a considered judgment by the individual mental health counselor about how best to contribute to counseling and to human welfare. Mental health counselors carry out their investigations with respect for the people who participate and with concern for their dignity and welfare.

a. In planning a study the investigator has the personal responsibility to make a careful evaluation of its ethical acceptability, taking into account the following principles for research with human beings. To the extent that this appraisal, weighing scientific and humane values, suggests a deviation from any principle, the investigator incurs an increasingly serious obligation to seek ethical advice and to observe more stringent safeguards to protect the rights of the human research participants.

b. Mental health counselors know and take into account the traditions and practices of other professional groups with members of such groups when research, services, and other functions are shared or in working for the benefit of public welfare.

c. Ethical practice requires the investigator to inform the participant of all features of the research that reasonable might be expected to influence willingness to participate, and to explain all other aspects of the research about which the participant inquires. Failure to make full disclosure gives added emphasis to the investigators abiding responsibility to protect the welfare and dignity of the research participant.

d. Openness and honesty are essential characteristics of the relationship between investigator and research participant. When the methodological requirements of a study necessitate concealment or deception, the investigator is required to insure as soon as possible the participant's understanding of the reasons for this action and to restore the quality of the relationship with the investigator.

e. In the pursuit of research, mental health counselors give sponsoring agencies, host institutions, and publication channels the same respect and opportunity for giving informed consent that they accord to individual research participants. They are aware of their obligation to future research workers and insure that host institutions are given feedback information and proper acknowledgment.

f. Credit is assigned to those who have contributed to a publication, in proportion to their contribution.

g. The ethical investigator protects participants from physical and mental discomfort, harm and danger. If the risk of such consequences exists, the investigator is required to inform the participant of that fact, secure consent before proceeding, and take all possible measures to minimize distress. A research procedure may not be used if it is likely to cause serious and lasting harm to participants.

h. After the data are collected, ethical practice requires the investigator to provide the participant with a full clarification of the nature of the study and to remove any misconceptions that may have arisen. Where scientific or humane values justify delaying or withholding information the investigator acquires a special responsibility to assure that there are no damaging consequences for the participants.

i. Where research procedure may result in undesirable consequences for the participant, the investigator has the responsibility to detect and remove or correct these consequences, including, where relevant, long-term after effects.

j. Information obtained about the research participants during the course of an investigation is confidential. When the possibility exists that others may obtain access to such information, ethical research practice requires that the possibility, together with the plans for protecting confidentiality be explained to the participants as a part of the procedure for obtaining informed consent.

PRINCIPLE 10. PRIVATE PRACTICE

a. A mental health counselor should assist where permitted by legislation or judicial decision the profession in fulfilling its duty to make counseling services available in private settings.

b. In advertising services as a private practitioner the mental health counselor should advertise the services in such a manner so as to accurately inform the public as to services, expertise, profession, techniques of counseling in a professional manner. A mental health counselor who assumes an executive leadership role in the organization shall not permit his/her name to be used in professional notices during periods when not actively engaged in the private practice of counseling. The mental health counselor may list the following: Highest relevant degree, type and level of certification or license, type and/or description of services and other relevant information. Such information should not contain false, inaccurate, misleading, partial, out-of-context or deceptive material or statements.

c. The mental health counselors may join in partnership/corporation with other mental health counselors and/or other professionals provided that each mental health counselor of the partnership or corporation makes clear the separate specialties by name in compliance with the regulations of the locality.

d. A mental health counselor has an obligation to withdraw from a counseling relationship if it is believed that employment will result in violation of the code of ethics, if their mental capacity or physical condition renders it difficult to carry out an effective professional relationship, or if the mental health counselor is discharged by the client because the counseling relationship is no longer productive for the client.

e. A mental health counselor should adhere to and support the regulations for private practice of the locality where the services are offered.

f. Mental health counselors are discouraged from deliberate attempts to utilize one's institutional affiliation to recruit clients for one's private practice. Mental health counselors are to refrain from offering their services in the private sector, when they are employed by an institution in which this is prohibited by stated policies reflecting conditions for employment.

g. In establishing fees for professional counseling services, mental health counselors should consider the financial status of clients and locality. In the event that the established fee structure is inappropriate for a client, assistance should be provided in finding services of acceptable cost.

PRINCIPLE 11. CONSULTING

a. The mental health counselor acting as consultant must have a high degree of self-awareness of his/her own values, knowledge, skills and needs in entering a helping relationship which involves human and/or organizational change and that the focus of the relationship be on the issues to be resolved and not on the person(s) presenting the problem.

b. There should be understanding and agreement between the mental health counselor and client for the problem definition, change goals and predicted consequences of intentions selected.

c. The mental health counselor must be reasonably certain that she/he or the organization represented have the necessary competencies and resources for giving the kind of help which is needed now or may develop later and that appropriate referral resources are available to the consultant, if needed later.

d. The mental health counselor relationship must be one in which client adaptability and growth toward self-direction are encouraged and cultivated. The mental health counselor must maintain this role consistently and not become a decision maker or substitute for the client.

e. When announcing consultant availability for services, the mental health counselor conscientiously adheres to professional standards.

f. The mental health counselors is expected to refuse a private fee or other remuneration for consultation with persons who are entitled to these services through the members' employing institution or agency. The policies of a particular agency may make explicit provisions for private practice with agency counselees by members of its staff. In such instances, the counselees must be apprised of other options open to them should they seek private counseling services.

PRINCIPLE 12. CLIENT'S RIGHTS

The following apply to all consumers of mental health services, including both in- and out-patients in all state, county, local, and private care mental health facilities, as well as patients/clients of mental health practitioners in private practice.

The client has the right:

a. to be treated with consideration and respect;

b. to expect quality service provided by concerned, competent staff;

c. to a clear statement of the purposes, goals, techniques, rules of procedure, and limitations as well as potential dangers of the services to be performed and all other information related to or likely to affect the on-going counseling relationship;

d. to obtain information about their case record and to have this information explained clearly and directly;

e. to full, knowledgeable, and responsible participation in the ongoing treatment plan, to the maximum feasible extent;

f. to expect complete confidentiality and that no information will be released without written consent;

g. to see and discuss their charges and payment records;

h. to refuse any recommended services and be advised of the consequences of this action.

APPENDIX VIII

NATIONAL ASSOCIATION OF CERTIFIED CLINICAL MENTAL HEALTH COUNSELORS CODE OF ETHICS

NATIONAL ASSOCIATION OF CERTIFIED CLINICAL MENTAL HEALTH COUNSELORS CODE OF ETHICS

Preamble

Certified Clinical Mental Health Counselors believe in the dignity and worth of the individual. They are committed to increasing knowledge of human behavior and understanding of themselves and others. While pursuing these endeavors, they make every reasonable effort to protect the welfare of those who seek their services or of any subject that may be the object of study. They use their skills only for purposes consistent with these values and do not knowingly permit their misuse by others. While demanding for themselves freedom of inquiry and communication, Certified Clinical Mental Health counselors accept the responsibility this freedom confers: competence, objectivity in the application of skills, and concern for the best interests of clients, colleagues, and society in general. In the pursuit of these ideals, clinical mental health counselors subscribe to the principles below.

When a certificant is found to be in violation of the Code of Ethics, the Board of Directors of the National Academy may publish the results of any disciplinary action taken.

Principle 1. Responsibility

In their commitment to the understanding of human behavior, clinical mental health counselors value objectivity and integrity, and in providing services they maintain the highest standards. They accept responsibility for the consequences of their work and make every effort to insure that their services are used appropriately.

a. Clinical mental health counselors accept ultimate responsibility for selecting appropriate areas for investigation and the methods relevant to minimize the possibility that their findings will be misleading. They provide thorough discussion of the limitations of their data and alternative hypotheses, especially where their work touches on social policy or might be misconstrued to the detriment of specific age, sex, ethnic, socio-economic, or other social categories. In publishing reports of their work, they never discard observations that may modify the interpretation of results. Clinical mental health counselors take credit only for the work they have actually done. In pursuing research, clinical mental health counselors ascertain that their efforts will not lead to changes in individuals or organizations unless such changes are part of the agreement at the time of obtaining informed consent. Clinical mental health counselors clarify in advance the expectations for sharing and utilizing research data. They avoid dual relationships which may limit objectivity, whether theoretical, political, or monetary, so that interference with data, subjects, and milieu is kept to a minimum.

b. As employees of an institution or agency, clinical mental health counselors have the responsibility of remaining alert to institutional pressures which may distort reports of counseling findings or use them in ways counter to the promotion of human welfare.

c. When serving as members of governmental or other organizational bodies, clinical mental health counselors remain accountable as individuals to the Code of Ethics of the National Academy of Certified Mental Health Counselors.

d. As teachers, clinical mental health counselors recognize their primary obligation to help others acquire knowledge and skill. They maintain high standards of scholarship and objectivity by presenting counseling information fully and accurately, and by giving appropriate recognition to alternative viewpoints.

e. As practitioners, clinical mental health counselors know that they bear a heavy social responsibility because their recommendations and professional actions may alter the lives of others. They therefore, remain fully cognizant of their impact and alert to personal, social, organizational, financial or political situations or pressures which might lead to misuse of their influence.

f. Clinical mental health counselors provide reasonable and timely feedback to employees, trainees, supervisors, students, and others whose work they may evaluate.

Principle 2. Competence

The maintenance of high standards of professional competence is a responsibility shared by all clinical mental health counselors in the interest of the public and the profession as a whole. Clinical mental health counselors recognize the boundaries of their competence and the limitations of their techniques and only provide services, use techniques, or offer opinions as professionals that meet recognized standards. Throughout their careers, clinical mental health counselors maintain knowledge of professional information related to the services they render.

a. Clinical mental health counselors accurately represent their competence, education, training and experience.

b. As teachers, clinical mental health counselors perform their duties based on careful preparation so that their instruction is accurate, up-to-date and scholarly.

c. Clinical mental health counselors recognize the need for continuing training to prepare themselves to serve persons of all ages and cultural backgrounds. They are open to new procedures and sensitive to differences between groups of people and changes in expectations and values over time.

d. Clinical mental health counselors with the responsibility for decisions involving individuals or policies based on test results should know and understand literature relevant to the tests used and testing problems with which they deal.

e. Clinical mental health counselors/practitioners recognize that their effectiveness depends in part upon their ability to maintain sound interpersonal relations, that temporary or more enduring aberrations on their part may interfere with their abilities or distort their appraisals of others. Therefore, they refrain from undertaking any activity in which their personal problems are likely to lead to inadequate professional services or harm to a client, or, if they are already engaged in such activity when they become aware of their personal problems, they would seek competent professional assistance to determine whether they should suspend or terminate services to one or all of their clients.

Principle 3. Moral and Legal Standards

Clinical mental health counselors' moral, ethical and legal standards of behavior are a personal matter to the same degree as they are for any other citizen, except as these may compromise the fulfillment of their professional responsibilities, or reduce the trust in counseling or counselors, held by the general public. Regarding their own behavior, clinical mental health counselors should be aware of the prevailing community standards and of the possible impact upon the quality of professional services provided by their conformance to or deviation from these standards. Clinical mental health counselors should also be aware of the possible impact of their public behavior upon the ability of colleagues to perform their professional duties.

a. To protect public confidence in the profession of counseling, clinical mental health counselors will avoid public behavior that is clearly in violation of accepted moral and legal standards.

b. To protect students counselors/teachers will be aware of the diverse backgrounds of students and, when dealing with topics that may give offense, will see that the material is treated objectively, that it is clearly relevant to the course, and that it is treated in a manner for which the student is prepared.

c. Providers of counseling services conform to the statutes relating to such services as established by their state and its regulating professional board(s).

d. As employees, clinical mental health counselors refuse to participate in employer's practices which are inconsistent with the moral and legal standards established by federal or state legislation regarding the treatment of employees or of the public. In particular and for example, clinical mental health counselors will not condone practices which result in illegal or otherwise unjustifiable discrimination on the basis of race, sex, religion or national origin in hiring, promotion or training.

e. In providing counseling services to clients, clinical mental health counselors avoid any action that will violate or diminish the legal and civil rights of clients or of others who may be affected by the action.

f. Sexual conduct, not limited to sexual intercourse, between clinical mental health counselors and clients is specifically in violation of this code of ethics. This does not, however, prohibit the use of explicit instructional aids including films and video tapes. Such use is within accepted practices of trained and competent sex therapists.

Principle 4. Public Statements

Clinical mental health counselors in their professional roles may be expected or required to make public statements providing counseling information, professional opinions, or supply information about the availability of counseling products and services. In making such statements, clinical mental health counselors take full account of the limits and uncertainties of present counseling knowledge and techniques. They represent, as objectively as possible, their professional qualifications, affiliations, and functions, as well as those of the institutions or organizations with which the statements may be associated. All public statements, announcements of services, and promotional activities should serve the purpose of providing informed judgments and choices on matters that concern it.

a. When announcing professional services, clinical mental health counselors limit the information to: name, highest relevant degree conferred, certification or licensure, address, telephone number, office hours, cost of services, and a brief explanation of the types of services offered but not evaluative as to their quality of uniqueness. Such announcements will not contain testimonial by implication. They will not claim uniqueness of skill or methods beyond those available to others in the profession unless determined by acceptable and public scientific evidence.

b. In announcing the availability of counseling services or products, clinical mental health counselors will not display their affiliations with organizations or agencies in a manner that implies the sponsorship or certification of the organization or agency. They will not name their employer or professional associations unless the services are in fact to be provided by or under the responsible, direct supervision and continuing control of such organizations or agencies.

c. Clinical mental health counselors associated with the development or promotion of counseling devices, books, or other products offered for commercial sale will make every effort to insure that announcements and advertisements are presented in a professional and factually informative manner without unsupported claims of superiority. Any claims must be supported by scientifically acceptable evidence or by willingness to aid and encourage independent professional scrutiny or scientific test.

d. Clinical mental health counselors engaged in radio, television or other public media activities will not participate in commercial announcements recommending to the general public the purchase or use of any proprietary or single-source product or service.

e. Clinical mental health counselors who describe counseling or the services of professional counselors to the general public accept the obligation to present the material fairly and accurately, avoiding misrepresentation through sensationalism, exaggeration or superficiality. Clinical mental health counselors will be guided by the primary obligation to aid the public in forming their own informed judgments, opinions and choices.

f. As teachers, clinical mental health counselors ensure that statements in catalogs and course outlines are accurate, particularly in terms of subject matter to be covered, bases for grading, and nature of classroom experiences. As practitioners providing private services, Certified Clinical Mental Health Counselors (CCMHCs) avoid improper, direct solicitation of clients and the conflict of interest inherent therein.

g. Clinical mental health counselors accept the obligation to correct others who may represent their professional qualifications or associations with products or services in a manner incompatible with these guidelines.

Principle 5. Confidentiality

Clinical mental health counselors have a primary obligation to safeguard information about individuals obtained in the course of teaching, practice, or research. Personal information is communicated to others only with the person's written consent or in those circumstances where there is clear and imminent danger to the client, to others or to society. Disclosures of counseling information are restricted to what is necessary, relevant, and verifiable.

a. All materials in the official record shall be shared with the client, who shall have the right to decide what information may be shared with anyone beyond the immediate provider of service and to be informed of the implications of the materials to be shared.

b. The anonymity of clients served in public and other agencies is preserved, if at all possible, by withholding named and personal identifying data. If external conditions require reporting such information, the client shall be so informed.

c. Information received in confidence by one agency or person shall not be forwarded to another person or agency without the client's written permission.

d. Service providers have a responsibility to insure the accuracy and to indicate the validity of data shared with their parties.

e. Case reports presented in classes, professional meetings, or in publications shall be so disguised that no identification is possible, unless the client or responsible authority has read the report and agreed in writing to its presentation or publication.

f. Counseling reports and records are maintained under conditions of security, and provisions are made for their destruction when they have out-lived their usefulness. Clinical mental health counselors insure that privacy and confidentiality are maintained by all persons in the employ or volunteers and community aides.

g. Clinical mental health counselors who ask that an individual reveal personal information in the course of interviewing, testing or evaluation, or who allow such information to be divulged, do so only after making certain that the person or authorized representative is fully aware of the purposes of the interview, testing or evaluation and of the ways in which the information will be used.

h. Sessions with clients are taped or otherwise recorded only with their written permission or the written permission of a responsible guardian. Even with guardian written consent, one should not record a session against the expressed wishes of a client.

i. Where a child or adolescent is the primary client, the interests of the minor shall be paramount.

j. In work with families, the rights of each family member should be safeguarded. The provider of service also has the responsibility to discuss the contents of the record with the parent and/or child, as appropriate, and to keep separate those parts which should remain the property of each family member.

Principle 6. Welfare of the Consumer

Clinical mental health counselors respect the integrity and protect the welfare of the people and groups with whom they work. When there is a conflict of interest between the client and the clinical mental health counselor employing institution, clinical mental health counselors clarify the nature and direction of their loyalties and responsibilities and keep all parties informed of their commitments. Clinical mental health counselors fully inform consumers as to the purpose and nature of any evaluative treatment, educational or training procedure, and they freely acknowledge that clients, students, or subjects have freedom of choice with regard to participation.

a. Clinical mental health counselors are continually cognizant both of their own needs and of their inherently powerful position vis-a-vis clients, in order to avoid exploiting the client's trust and dependency. Clinical mental health counselors make every effort to avoid dual relationships with clients and/or relationships which might impair their professional judgment or increase the risk of client exploitation. Examples of such dual relationships include treating an employee or supervisor, treating a close friend or family relative and sexual relationships with clients.

b. Where clinical mental health counselors' work with members of an organization goes beyond reasonable conditions of employment, clinical mental health counselors recognize possible conflicts of interests that may arise. When such conflicts occur, clinical mental health counselors clarify the nature of the conflict and inform all parties of the nature and directions of the loyalties and responsibilities involved.

c. When acting as supervisors, trainers, or employers, clinical mental health counselors accord recipients informed choice, confidentiality, and protection from physical and mental harm.

d. Financial arrangements in professional practice are in accord with professional standards that safeguard the best interests of the client and that are clearly understood by the client in advance of billing. This may best be done by the use of a contract. Clinical mental health counselors are responsible for assisting clients in finding needed services in those instances where payment of the usual fee would be a hardship. No commission or rebate or other form of remuneration may be given or received for referral clients for professional services, whether by an individual or by an agency.

e. Clinical mental health counselors are responsible for making their services readily accessible to clients in a manner that facilitates the client's ability to make an informed choice when selecting a service provider. This responsibility includes a clear written description of what the client may expect in the way of tests, reports, billing, therapeutic regime and schedules.

f. Clinical mental health counselors who find that their services are not beneficial to the client have the responsibility to make this known to the responsible persons.

g. Clinical mental health counselors are accountable to the parties who refer and support counseling services and to the general public and are cognizant of the indirect or long-range effects of their intervention.

h. The clinical mental health counselor attempts to terminate a private service or consulting relationship when it is reasonably clear to the clinical mental health counselor that the consumer is not benefiting from it. If a consumer is receiving services from another mental health professional, clinical mental health counselors do not offer their services directly to the consumer without informing the professional persons already involved in order to avoid confusion and conflict for the consumer.

Principle 7: Professional Relationship

Clinical mental health counselors act with due regard to the needs and feelings of their colleagues in counseling and other professions. Clinical mental health counselors respect the prerogatives and obligations of the institutions or organizations with which they are associated.

a. Clinical mental health counselors understand the areas of competence of related professions and make full use of other professional, technical, and administrative resources which best serve the interests of consumers. The absence of formal relationships with other professional workers does not relieve clinical mental health counselors from the responsibility of securing for their clients the best possible professional service; indeed, this circumstance presents a challenge to the professional competence of clinical mental health counselors, requiring special sensitivity to problems outside their areas of training, and foresight, diligence, and tact in obtaining the professional assistance needed by clients.

b. Clinical mental health counselors know and take into account the traditions and practices of other professional groups with which they work and cooperate fully with members of such groups when research, services, and other functions are shared or in working for the benefit of public welfare.

c. Clinical mental health counselors strive to provide positive conditions for those they employ and that they spell out clearly the conditions of such employment. They encourage their employees to engage in activities that facilitate their further professional development.

d. Clinical mental health counselors respect the viability, reputation, and the proprietary right of organizations which they serve. Clinical mental health counselors show due regard for the interests of their present or prospective employers. In those instances where they are critical of policies, they attempt to effect change by constructive action within the organization.

e. In the pursuit of research, clinical mental health counselors give sponsoring agencies, host institutions, and publication channels the same respect and opportunity for giving informed consent that they accord to individual research participants. They are aware of their obligation to future research and insure that host institutions are given feedback information and proper acknowledgment.

f. Credit is assigned to those who have contributed to a publication, in proportion to their contribution.

g. When a clinical mental health counselor violates ethical standards, clinical mental health counselors who know first-hand of such activities should, if possible, attempt to rectify the situation. Failing an informal solution, clinical mental health counselors should bring such unethical activities to the National Academy of Certified Clinical Mental Health Counselors.

Principle 8: Utilization of Assessment Techniques

In the development, publication, and utilization of counseling assessment techniques, clinical mental health counselors follow relevant standards. Individuals examined, or their legal guardians, have the right to know the results, the interpretations made, and where appropriate, the particulars on which final judgment was based. Test users should take precautions to protect test security but not at the expense of an individual's right to understand the basis for decisions that adversely affect that individual or that individual's dependents.

a. The client has the right to have, and the provider has the responsibility to give, explanations of test results in language the client can understand.

b. When a test is published or otherwise made available for operational use, it should be accompanied by a manual (or other published or readily available information) that makes every reasonable effort to describe fully the development of the test, the rational, specifications followed in writing items analysis or other research. The test, the manual, the record forms, and other accompanying material should help users make correct interpretations of the test results and should warn against common misuses. The test manual should state explicitly the purposes and applications for which the test is recommended and identify any special qualifications required to administer the test and to interpret it properly. Evidence of validity and reliability, along with other relevant research data, should be presented in support of any claims made.

c. Norms presented in test manuals should refer to defined and clearly described populations. These populations should be the groups with whom users of the test will ordinarily wish to compare the persons tested. Test users should consider the possibility of bias in tests or in test items. When indicated, there should be an investigation of possible differences in validity for ethnic, sex, or other subsamples that can be identified when the test is given.

d. Clinical mental health counselors who have the responsibility for decisions about individuals or policies that are based on test results should have a thorough understanding of counseling or educational measurement and of validation and other test research.

e. Clinical mental health counselors should develop procedures for systematically eliminating from data files test score information that has, because of the lapse of time, become obsolete.

f. Any individual or organization offering test scoring and interpretation services must be able to demonstrate that their programs are based on appropriate research to establish the validity of the programs and procedures used in arriving at interpretations. The public offering of an automated test interpretation service will be considered as a professional-toprofessional consultation. In this the formal responsibility of the consultant is to the consultee but his/her ultimate and overriding responsibility is to the client.

g. Counseling services for the purpose of diagnosis, treatment, or personalized advice are provided only in the context of a professional relationship, and are not given by means of public lectures or demonstrations, newspapers or magazine articles, radio or television programs, mail or similar media. The preparation of personnel reports and recommendations based on test data secured solely by mail is unethical unless such appraisals are an integral part of a continuing client relationship with a company as a result of which the consulting clinical mental health counselor has intimate knowledge of the client's personal situation and can be assured thereby that his <her> written appraisals will be adequate to the purpose and will be properly interpreted by the client. These reports must not be embellished with such detailed analyses of the subject's personality traits as would be appropriate only for intensive interviews with the subjects.

Principle 9: Pursuit of Research Activities

The decision to undertake research should rest upon a considered judgment by the individual clinical mental health counselor about how best to contribute to counseling and to human welfare. Clinical mental health counselors carry out their investigations with respect for the people who participate and with concern for their dignity and welfare.

a. In planning a study the investigator has the personal responsibility to make a careful evaluation of its ethical acceptability, taking into account the following principles for research with human beings. To the extent that this appraisal, weighing scientific and humane values, suggests a deviation from any principle, the investigator incurs an increasingly serious obligation to seek ethical advice and to observe more stringent safeguards to protect the rights of the human research participants.

b. Clinical mental health counselors know and take into account the traditions and practices of other professional groups with members of such groups when research, services, and other functions are shared or in working for the benefit of public welfare.

c. Ethical practice requires the investigator to inform the participant of all features of the research that reasonably might be expected to influence willingness to participate, and to explain all other aspects of the research about which the participant inquires. Failure to make full disclosure gives added emphasis to the investigator's abiding responsibility to protect the welfare and dignity of the research participant.

d. Openness and honesty are essential characteristics of the relationship between investigator and research participant. When the methodological requirements of a study necessitate concealment or deception, the investigator is required to insure as soon as possible the participant's understanding of the reasons for this action and to restore the quality of the relationship with the investigator.

e. In the pursuit of research, clinical mental health counselors give sponsoring agencies, host institutions, and publication channels the same respect and opportunity for giving informed consent that they accord to individual research participants. They are aware of their obligation to future research workers and insure that host institutions are given feedback information and proper acknowledgment.

f. Credit is assigned to those who have contributed to a publication, in proportion to their contribution.

g. The ethical investigator protects participants from physical and mental discomfort, harm and danger. If the risk of such consequences exists, the investigator is required to inform the participant of that fact, secure consent before proceeding, and take all possible measures to minimize distress.

A research procedure may not be used if it is likely to cause serious and lasting harm to participants.

h. After the data are collected, ethical practice requires the investigator to provide the participant with a full clarification of the nature of the study and to remove any misconceptions that may have arisen. Where scientific or humane values justify delaying or withholding information, the investigator acquires a special responsibility to assure that there are no damaging consequences for the participants.

i. Where research procedures may result in undesirable consequences for the participant, the investigator has the responsibility to detect and remove or correct these consequences, including, where relevant, long-term after effects.

j. Information obtained about the research participants during the course of an investigation is confidential. When the possibility exists that others may obtain access to such information, ethical research practice requires that the possibility, together with the plans for protecting confidentiality, be explained to the participants as a part of the procedure for obtaining informed consent.

APPENDIX IX

ASSOCIATION FOR SPECIALISTS IN GROUP WORK ETHICAL GUIDELINES FOR GROUP LEADERS

ASSOCIATION FOR SPECIALISTS IN GROUP WORK
ETHICAL GUIDELINES FOR GROUP LEADERS

1. *Orientation and Providing Information:* Group counselors adequately prepare prospective or new group members by providing as much information about the existing or proposed group as necessary.

- · Minimally, information related to each of the following areas should be provided.

    (a) Entrance procedures, time parameters of the group experience, group participation expectations, methods of payment (where appropriate), and termination procedures are explained by the group counselor as appropriate to the level of maturity of group members and the nature and purpose(s) of the group.

    (b) Group counselors have available for distribution, a professional disclosure statement that includes information on the group counselor's qualifications and group services that can be provided, particularly as related to the nature and purpose(s) of the specific group.

    (c) Group counselors communicate the role expectations, rights, and responsibilities of group members and group counselor(s).

    (d) The group goals are stated as concisely as possible by the group counselor including "whose" goal it is (the group counselor's, the institution's, the parent's, the law's, society's, etc.) and the role of group members in influencing or determining the group's goal(s).

    (e) Group counselors explore with group members the risks of potential life changes that may occur because of the group experience and help members explore their readiness to face these possibilities.

    (f) Group members are informed by the group counselor of unusual or experimental procedures that might be expected in their group experience.

    (g) Group counselors explain, as realistically as possible, what services can and cannot be provided within the particular group structure offered.

    (h) Group counselors emphasize the need to promote full psychological functioning and presence among group members. They inquire from prospective group members whether they are using any kind of drug or medication that may affect functioning in the group. They do not permit any use of alcohol and/or illegal drugs during group sessions and they discourage the use of alcohol and/or drugs (legal or illegal) prior to group meetings which may affect the physical or emotional presence of the member or other group members.

(i) Group counselors inquire from prospective group members whether they have ever been a client in counseling or psychotherapy. If a prospective group member is already in a counseling relationship with another professional person, the group counselor advises the prospective group member to notify the other professional of their participation in the group.

(j) Group counselors clearly inform group members about the policies pertaining to the group counselor's willingness to consult with them between group sessions.

(k) In establishing fees for group counseling services, group counselors consider the financial status and the locality of prospective group members. Group members are not charged fees for group sessions where the group counselor is not present and the policy of charging for sessions missed by a group member is clearly communicated. Fees for participating as a group member are contracted between group counselor and group member for a specified period of time. Group counselors do not increase fees for group counseling services until the existing contracted fee structure has expired. In the event that the established fee structure is inappropriate for a prospective member, group counselors assist in finding comparable services of acceptable cost.

2. *Screening of Members:* The group counselor screens prospective group members (when appropriate to their theoretical orientation). Insofar as possible, the counselor selects group members whose needs and goals are compatible with the goals of the group, who will not impede the group process, and whose well-being will not be jeopardized by the group experience. An orientation to the group (i.e., ASGW Ethical Guideline #1) is included during the screening process.)

· Screening may be accomplished in one or more ways, such as the following:

(a) Individual interview

(b) Group interview of prospective group members

(c) Interview as part of a team staffing

(d) Completion of a written questionnaire by prospective group members.

3. *Confidentiality:* Group counselors protect members by defining clearly what confidentiality means, why it is important, and the difficulties involved in enforcement.

   (a) Group counselors take steps to protect members by defining confidentiality and the limits of confidentiality (i.e., when a group member's condition indicates that there is clear and imminent danger to the member, others, or physical property, the group counselor takes reasonable personal action and/or informs responsible authorities).

   (b) Group counselors stress the importance of confidentiality and set a norm of confidentiality regarding all group participants' disclosures. The importance of maintaining confidentiality is emphasized before the group begins and at various times in the group. The fact that confidentiality cannot be guaranteed is clearly stated.

   (c) Members are made aware of the difficulties involved in enforcing and ensuring confidentiality in a group setting. The counselor provides examples of how confidentiality can nonmaliciously be broken to increase members' awareness, and helps to lessen the likelihood that this breach of confidence will occur. Group counselors inform group members about the potential consequences of intentionally breaching confidentiality.

   (d) Group counselors can only ensure confidentiality on their part and not on the part of the members.

   (e) Group counselors video or audio tape a group session only with the prior consent and the members' knowledge of how the tape will be used.

   (f) When working with minors, the group counselor specifies the limits of confidentiality.

   (g) Participants in a mandatory group are made aware of any reporting procedures required of the group counselor.

   (h) Group counselors store or dispose of group member records (written, audio. video, etc.) in ways that maintain confidentiality.

(i) Instructors of group counseling courses maintain the anonymity of group members whenever discussing group counseling cases.

4. *Voluntary/Involuntary Participation:* Group counselors inform members whether participation is voluntary or involuntary.

   (a) Group counselors take steps to ensure informed consent procedures in both voluntary and involuntary groups.

   (b) When working with minors in a group, counselors are expected to follow the procedures specified by the institution in which they are practicing.

   (c) With involuntary groups, every attempt is made to enlist the cooperation of the members and their continuance in the group on a voluntary basis.

   (d) Group counselors do not certify that group treatment has been received by members who merely attend sessions but did not meet the defined group expectations. Group members are informed about the consequences for failing to participate in a group.

5. *Leaving a Group:* Provisions are made to assist a group member to terminate in an effective way.

   (a) Procedures to be followed for a group member who chooses to exit a group prematurely are discusses by the counselor with all group members either before the group begins, during a pre-screening interview, or during the initial group session.

   (b) In case of legally mandated group counseling, group counselors inform members of the possible consequences for premature self termination.

   (c) Ideally, both the group counselor and the member can work cooperatively to determine the degree to which a group experience is productive or counterproductive for that individual.

   (d) Members ultimately have a right to discontinue membership in the group, at a designated time, if the predetermined trial period proves to be unsatisfactory.

   (e) Members have the right to exit a group, but it is important that they be made aware of the importance of informing the counselor and the group members prior to deciding to leave. The counselor discusses the possible risks of leaving the group prematurely with a member who is considering this option.

(f) Before leaving a group, the group counselor encourages members (if appropriate) to discuss their reasons for wanting to discontinue membership in the group. Counselors intervene if other members use undue pressure to force a member to remain in the group.

6. *Coercion and Pressure:* Group counselors protect member rights against physical threats, intimidation, coercion, and undue peer pressure insofar as is reasonably possible.

(a) It is essential to differentiate between "therapeutic pressure" that is part of any group and "undue pressure," which is not therapeutic.

(b) The purpose of a group is to help participants find their own answers, not to pressure them into doing what the group thinks is appropriate.

(c) Counselors exert care not to coerce participants to change in directions which they clearly state they do not choose.

(d) Counselors have responsibility to intervene when others use undue pressure or attempt to persuade members against their will.

(e) Counselors intervene when any member attempts to act out aggression in a physical way that might harm another member or themselves.

(f) Counselors intervene when a member is verbally abusive or inappropriately confrontive to another member.

7. *Imposing Counselor Values:* Group counselors develop an awareness of their own values and needs and the potential impact they have on the interventions likely to be made.

(a) Although group counselors take care to avoid imposing their values on members, it is appropriate that they expose their own beliefs, decisions, needs, and values, when concealing them would create problems for the members.

(b) There are values implicit in any group, and these are made clear to potential members before they join the group. (Examples of certain values include: expressing feelings, being direct and honest, sharing personal material with others, learning how to trust, improving interpersonal communication, and deciding for oneself.)

(c) Personal and professional needs of group counselors are not met at the members' expense.

(d) Group counselors avoid using the group for their own therapy.

(e) Group counselors are aware of their own values and assumptions and how these apply in a multi-cultural context.

(f) Group counselors take steps to increase their awareness of ways that their personal reactions to members might inhibit the group process and they monitor their countertransference. Through an awareness of the impact of stereotyping and discrimination (i.e., biases based on age, disability, ethnicity, gender, race, religion, or sexual preference), group counselors guard the individual rights and personal dignity of all group members.

8. *Equitable Treatment:* Group counselors make every reasonable effort to treat each member individually and equally.

(a) Group counselors recognize and respect differences (e.g., cultural, racial, religious, lifestyle, age, disability, gender) among group members.

(b) Group counselors maintain an awareness of their behavior toward individual group members and are alert to the potential detrimental effects of favoritism or partiality toward any particular group member to the exclusion or detriment of any other member(s). It is likely that group counselors will favor some members over others, yet all group members deserve to be treated equally.

(c) Group counselors ensure equitable use of group time for each member by inviting silent members to become involved, acknowledging nonverbal attempts to communicate, and discouraging rambling and monopolizing of time by members.

(d) If a large group is planned, counselors consider enlisting another qualified professional to serve as a co-leader for the group sessions.

9. *Dual Relationships:* Group counselors avoid dual relationships with group members that might impair their objectivity and professional judgment, as well as those which are likely to compromise a group member's ability to participate fully in the group.

(a) Group counselors do not misuse their professional role and power as group leader to advance personal or social contacts with members throughout the duration of the group.

(b) Group counselors do not use their professional relationship with group members to further their own interest either during the group or after the termination of the group.

(c) Sexual intimacies between group counselors and members are unethical.

(d) Group counselors do not barter (exchange) professional services with group members for services.

(e) Group counselors do not admit their own family members, relatives, employees, or personal friends as members to their groups.

(f) Group counselors discuss with group members the potential detrimental effects of group members engaging in intimate inter-member relationships outside of the group.

(g) Students who participate in a group as a partial course requirement for a group course are not evaluated for an academic grade based upon their degree of participation as a member in a group. Instructors of group counseling courses take steps to minimize the possible negative impact on students when they participate in a group course by separating course grades from participation in the group and by allowing students to decide what issues to explore and when to stop.

(h) It is inappropriate to solicit members from a class (or institutional affiliation) for one's private counseling or therapeutic groups.

10. *Use of Techniques:* Group counselors do not attempt any technique unless trained in its use or under supervision by a counselor familiar with the intervention.

(a) Group counselors are able to articulate a theoretical orientation that guides their practice, and they are able to provide a rationale for their interventions.

(b) Depending upon the type of an intervention, group counselors have training commensurate with the potential impact of a technique.

(c) Group counselors are aware of the necessity to modify their techniques to fit the unique needs of various cultural and ethnic groups.

(d) Group counselors assist members in translating in-group learnings to daily life.

11. *Goal Development:* Group counselors make every effort to assist members in developing their personal goals.

    (a) Group counselors use their skills to assist members in making their goals specific so that others present in the group will understand the nature of the goals.

    (b) Throughout the course of a group, group counselors assist members in assessing the degree to which personal goals are being met, and assist in revising any goals when it is appropriate.

    (c) Group counselors help members clarify the degree to which the goals can be met within the context of a particular group.

12. *Consultation:* Group counselors develop and explain policies about between-session consultation to group members.

    (a) Group counselors take care to make certain that members do not use between-session consultations to avoid dealing with issues pertaining to the group that would be dealt with best in the group.

    (b) Group counselors urge members to bring the issues discussed during between-session consultations into the group if they pertain to the group.

    (c) Group counselors seek out consultation and/or supervision regarding ethical concerns or when encountering difficulties which interfere with their effective functioning as group leaders.

    (d) Group counselors seek appropriate professional assistance for their own personal problems or conflicts that are likely to impair their professional judgment and work performance.

    (e) Group counselors discuss their group cases only for professional consultation and educational purposes.

(f) Group counselors inform members about policies regarding whether consultations will be held confidential.

13. *Termination from the Group:* Depending upon the purpose of participation in the group, counselors promote termination of members from the group in the most efficient period of time.

    (a) Group counselors maintain a constant awareness of the progress made by each group member and periodically invite the group members to explore and reevaluate their experiences in the group. It is the responsibility of group counselors to help promote the independence of members from the group in a timely manner.

14. *Evaluation and Follow-up:* Group counselors make every attempt to engage in ongoing assessment and to design follow-up procedures for their groups.

    (a) Group counselors recognize the importance of ongoing assessment of a group, and they assist members in evaluating their own progress.

    (b) Group counselors conduct evaluation of the total group experience at the final meeting (or before termination), as well as ongoing evaluation.

    (c) Group counselors monitor their own behavior and become aware of what they are modeling in the group.

    (d) Follow-up procedures might take the form of personal contact, telephone contact, or written contact.

    (e) Follow-up meetings might be with individuals, groups, or both to determine the degree to which: (i) members have reached their goals, (ii) the group had a positive or negative effect on the participants, and (iii) members could profit from some type of referral. Information is requested for possible modification of future groups. If there is no follow-up meeting, provisions are made available for individual follow-up meetings to any member who needs or requests such a contact.

15. *Referrals:* If the needs of a particular member cannot be met within the type of group being offered, the group counselor suggests other appropriate professional referrals.

(a) Group counselors are knowledgeable of local community resources for assisting group members regarding professional referrals.

(b) Group counselors help members seek further professional assistance, if needed.

16. *Professional Development:* Group counselors recognize that professional growth is a continuous, ongoing, developmental process throughout their career.

(a) Group counselors maintain and upgrade their knowledge and skill competencies through educational activities, clinical experiences, and participation in professional development activities.

(b) Group counselors keep abreast of research findings and new developments as applied to groups.

SAFEGUARDING ETHICAL PRACTICE AND
PROCEDURES FOR REPORTING UNETHICAL BEHAVIOR

The preceding remarks have been advanced as guidelines which are generally representative of ethical and professional group practice. They have not been proposed as rigidly defined prescriptions. However, practitioners who are thought to be grossly unresponsive to the ethical concerns addressed in this document may be subject to a review of their practices by the AACD Ethics Committee and ASGW peers.

· For consultation and/or questions regarding these ASGW Ethical Guidelines or group ethical dilemmas, you may contact the Chairperson of the ASGW Ethics Committee. The name, address, and telephone number of the current ASGW Ethics Committee Chairperson may be acquired by telephoning the AACD office in Alexandria, Virginia at 703/823-9800.

· If a group counselor's behavior is suspected as being unethical, the following procedures are to be followed:

(a) Collect more information and investigate further to confirm the unethical practice as determined by the ASGW Ethical Guidelines.

(b) Confront the individual with the apparent violation of ethical guidelines for the purposes of protecting the safety of any clients and to help the group counselor correct any inappropriate behaviors. If satisfactory resolution is not reached through this contact then:

(c) A complaint should be made in writing, including the specific facts and dates of the alleged violation and all relevant supporting data. The complaint should be included in an envelope marked "CONFIDENTIAL" to ensure confidentiality for both the accuser(s) and the alleged violator(s) and forward to all of the following sources:

1. The name and address of the Chairperson of the state Counselor Licensure Board for the respective state, if in existence.

2. The Ethics Committee
   c/o The President
   American Association for Counseling and Development
   5999 Stevenson Avenue
   Alexandria, Virginia 22304

3. The name and address of all private credentialing agencies in which the alleged violator maintains credentials or holds professional membership. Some of these include the following:

National Board for Certified Counselors, Inc.
5999 Stevenson Avenue
Alexandria, Virginia 22304

National Council for Credentialing of Career Counselors
c/o NBCC
5999 Stevenson Avenue
Alexandria, Virginia 22304

National Academy for Certified Clinical Mental Health Counselors
5999 Stevenson Avenue
Alexandria, Virginia 22304

Commission on Rehabilitation Counselor Certification
162 North State Street
Suite 317
Chicago, Illinois 60601

American Association for Marriage and Family Therapy
1717 K Street, N.W., Suite 407
Washington, D.C . 20006

American Psychological Association
1200 Seventeenth Street, N.W.
Washington, D.C. 20036

American Group Psychotherapy Association, Inc.
25 East 21st Street, 6th Floor
New York, New York 10010

APPENDIX X

NATIONAL CAREER DEVELOPMENT
ASSOCIATION ETHICAL STANDARDS

NATIONAL CAREER DEVELOPMENT ASSOCIATION
ETHICAL STANDARDS

These ethical standards were developed by the National Board for Certified Counselors (NBCC), an independent, voluntary, not-for-profit organization incorporated in 1982. Titled "Code of Ethics" by NBCC and last amended in February 1987, the Ethical Standards were adopted by the National Career Development Association (NCDA) Board of Directors at its April 1987 meeting in New Orleans, LA. Only minor changes in wording (e.g., the addition of specific references to NCDA members) were made.

Preamble: *NCDA is an educational, scientific, and professional organization dedicated to the enhancement of the worth, dignity, potential, and uniqueness of each individual and, thus, to the service of the society. This code of ethics enables the NCDA to clarify the nature of ethical responsibilities for present and future professional career counselors.*

Section A: General

1. NCDA members influence the development of the profession by continuous efforts to improve professional practices, services, and research. Professional growth is continuous through the career counselor's career and is exemplified by the development of a philosophy that explains why and how a career counselor functions in the helping relationship. Career counselors must gather data on their effectiveness and be guided by their findings.

2. NCDA members have a responsibility to the clients they are serving and to the institutions within which the services are being performed. Career counselors also strive to assist the respective agency, organization, or institution in providing the highest caliber of professional services. The acceptance of employment in an institution implies that the career counselor is in agreement with the general policies and principles of the institution. Therefore, the professional activities of the career counselor are in accord with the objective of the institution. If, despite concerted efforts, the career counselor cannot reach agreement with the employer as to acceptable standards that allow for changes in institutional policy that are conducive to the positive growth and development of clients, then terminating the affiliation should be seriously considered.

3. Ethical behavior among professional associates (e.g., career counselors) must be expected at all times. When accessible information raises doubt

as to the ethical behavior of professional colleagues, the NCDA member must take action to attempt to rectify this condition. Such action uses the respective institution's channels first and then uses procedures established by the American Association for Counseling and Development, of which NCDA is a division.

4. NCDA members neither claim nor imply professional qualifications which exceed those possessed, and are responsible for correcting any misrepresentations of these qualifications by others.

5. NCDA members must refuse a private fee or other remuneration for consultation or counseling with persons who are entitles to their services through the career counselor's employing institution or agency. The policies of some agencies may make explicit provisions for staff members to engage in private practice with agency clients. However, should agency clients desire private counseling or consulting services, they must be apprised of other options available to them. Career counselors must not divert to their private practices, legitimate clients in their primary agencies or of the institutions with which they are affiliated.

6. In establishing fees for professional counseling services, NCDA members must consider the financial status of clients and the respective locality. In the event that the established fee status is inappropriate for a client, assistance must be provided in finding comparable services of acceptable cost.

7. NCDA members seek only those positions in the delivery of professional services for which they are professionally qualified.

8. NCDA members recognize their limitations and provide services or use only techniques for which they are qualified by training and/or experience. Career counselors recognize the need, and seek continuing education, to assure competent services.

9. NCDA members are aware of the intimacy of the counseling relationship, maintain respect for the client, and avoid engaging in activities that seek to meet their personal needs at the expense of the client.

10. NCDA members do not condone or engage in sexual harassment which is defined as deliberate or repeated comments, gestures, or physical contacts of a sexual nature.

11. NCDA members avoid bringing their personal or professional issues into the counseling relationship. Through an awareness of the impact of stereotyping and discrimination, (i.e., biases on age, disability, ethnicity, gender, race, religion, or sexual preference), career counselors guard the individual rights and personal dignity of the client in the counseling relationship.

12. NCDA members are accountable at all times for their behavior. They must be aware that all actions and behaviors of a counselor reflect on professional integrity and, when appropriate, can damage the public trust in the counseling profession. To protect public confidence in the counseling profession, career counselors avoid public behavior that is clearly in violation of accepted moral and legal standards.

13. NCDA members have a social responsibility because their recommendations and professional actions may alter the lives of others. Career counselors remain fully cognizant of their impact and are alert to personal, social, organizational, financial, or political situations or pressures which might lead to the misuse of their influence.

14. Products or services provided by NCDA members by means of classroom instruction, public lectures, demonstrations, written articles, radio or television programs, or other types of media must meet the criteria cited in sections A through F of these Ethical Standards.

Section B: Counseling Relationship

1. The primary obligation of NCDA members is to respect the integrity and promote the welfare of the client, regardless of whether the client is assisted individually or in a group relationship. In a group setting, the career counselor is also responsible for taking reasonable precautions to protect individuals from physical and/or psychological trauma resulting from interaction within the group.

2. The counseling relationship and information resulting from it remains confidential, consistent with the legal obligations of the NCDA member. In a group counseling setting, the career counselor sets a norm of confidentiality regarding all group participants' disclosures.

3. NCDA members know and take into account the traditions and practices of other professional groups with whom they work and they cooperate fully with such groups. If a person is receiving similar services from another professional, career counselors do not offer their services directly to such

a person. If a career counselor is contacted by a person who is already receiving similar services from another professional, the career counselor carefully considers that professional relationship and proceeds with caution and sensitivity to the therapeutic issues as well as the client's welfare. Career counselors discuss these issues with clients so as to minimize the risk of confusion and conflict.

4. When a client's condition indicates that there is a clear and imminent danger to the client or others, the NCDA member must take reasonable personal action or inform responsible authorities. Consultation with other professionals must be used where possible.

5. Records of the counseling relationship, including interview notes, test data, correspondence, audio or visual tape recordings, electronic data storage, and other documents are to be considered professional information for use in counseling. They should not be considered a part of the records of the institution or agency in which the NCDA member is employed unless specified by state statute or regulation. Revelation to others of counseling material must occur only upon the expressed consent of the client; career counselors must make provisions for maintaining confidentiality in the storage and disposal of records. Career counselors providing information to the public or to subordinates, peers, or supervisors have a responsibility to ensure that the content is general; unidentified client information should be accurate and unbiased, and should consist of objective, factual data.

6. NCDA members must ensure that data maintained in electronic storage are secure. The data must be limited to information that is appropriate and necessary for the services being provided and accessible only to appropriate staff members involved in the provision of services by using the best computer security methods available. Career counselors must also ensure that electronically stored data are destroyed when the information is no longer of value in providing services.

7. Data derived from a counseling relationship for use in counselor training or research shall be confined to content that can be disguised to ensure full protection of the identity of the subject/client and shall be obtained with informed consent.

8. NCDA members must inform clients before or at the time the counseling relationship commences, of the purposes, goals, techniques, rules and procedures, and limitations that may affect the relationship.

9. All methods of treatment by NCDA members must be clearly indicated to prospective recipients and safety precautions must be taken in their use.

10. NCDA members who have an administrative, supervisory, and/or evaluative relationship with individuals seeking counseling services must not serve as the counselor and should refer the individuals to other professionals. Exceptions are made only in instances where an individual's situation warrants counseling intervention and another alternative is unavailable. Dual relationship with clients that might impair the counselor's objectivity and professional judgement must be avoided and/or the counseling relationship terminated through referral to another competent professional.

11. When NCDA members determine an inability to be of professional assistance to a potential or existing client, they must, respectively, not initiate the counseling relationship or immediately terminate the relationship. In either event, the career counselor must suggest appropriate alternatives. Career counselors must be knowledgeable about referral sources so that a satisfactory referral can be initiated. In the event that the client declines a suggested referral, the career counselor is not obligated to continue the relationship.

12. NCDA members may choose to consult with any other professionally competent person about a client and must notify clients of this right. Career counselors must avoid placing a consultant in a conflict-of-interest situation that would preclude the consultant's being a proper party to the career counselor's efforts to help the client.

13. NCDA members who counsel clients from cultures different from their own must gain knowledge, personal awareness, and sensitivity pertinent to the client populations served and must incorporate culturally relevant techniques into their practice.

14. When NCDA members engage in intensive counseling with a client, the client's counseling needs should be assessed. When needs exist outside the counselor's expertise, appropriate referrals should be made.

15. NCDA members must screen prospective group counseling participants, especially when the emphasis is on self-understanding and growth through self-disclosure. Career counselors must maintain an awareness of each group participant's welfare throughout the group process.

16. When electronic data and systems are used as a component of counseling services, NCDA members must ensure that the computer application, and any information it contains, is appropriate for the needs of the client and is non-discriminatory. Career counselors must ensure that they themselves have acquired a facilitation level of knowledge with any system they use including hands-on application, search experience, and understanding of the uses of all aspects of the computer-based system. In selecting and/ or maintaining computer-based systems that contain career information, career counselors must ensure that the systems provide current, accurate, and locally relevant information. Career counselors must also ensure that clients are intellectually, emotionally, and physically compatible to using the computer application and understand its purpose and operation. Client use of computer application must be evaluated to correct possible problems and assess subsequent needs.

17. NCDA members who develop self-help, stand-alone computer software for use by the general public, must first ensure that it is designed to function in a stand-alone manner, as opposed to modifying software that was originally designed to require support from a counselor. Secondly, the software must include program statements that provide the user with intended outcomes, suggestions for using the software, descriptions of inappropriately used applications, and descriptions of when and how counseling services might be beneficial. Finally, the manual must include the qualifications of the developer, the development process, validation data, and operating procedures.

Section C: Measurement and Evaluation

1. NCDA members must provide specific orientation or information to an examinee prior to and following the administration of assessment instruments or techniques so that the results may be placed in proper perspective with other relevant factors. The purpose of testing and the explicit use of the results must be made known to an examinee prior to testing.

2. In selecting assessment instruments or techniques for use in a given situation or with a particular client, NCDA members must evaluate carefully the instrument's specific theoretical bases and characteristics, validity, reliability, and appropriateness. Career counselors are professionally responsible for using unvalidated information with special care.

3. When making statements to the public about assessment instruments or techniques, NCDA members must provide accurate information and avoid false claims or misconceptions concerning the meaning of psychometric

terms. Special efforts are often required to avoid unwarranted connotations of terms such as IQ and grade-equivalent scores.

4. Because many types of assessment techniques exist, NCDA members must recognize the limits of their competence and perform only those functions for which they have received appropriate training.

5. NCDA members must note when tests are not administered under standard conditions or when unusual behavior or irregularities occur during a testing session and the results must be designated as invalid or of questionable validity. Unsupervised or inadequately supervised assessments, such as mail-in tests, are considered unethical. However, the use of standardized instruments that are designed to be self-administered and self-scored, such as interest inventories, is appropriate.

6. Because prior coaching or dissemination of test materials can invalidate test results, NCDA members are professionally obligated to maintain test security. In addition, conditions that produce most favorable test results must be made known to an examinee (e.g., penalty for guessing).

7. NCDA members must consider psychometric limitations when selecting and using an instrument, and must be cognizant of the limitations when interpreting the results. When tests are used to classify clients, career counselors must ensure that periodic review and/or retesting are conducted to prevent client stereotyping.

8. An examinee's welfare, explicit prior understanding, and agreement are the factors used when determining who receives the test results. NCDA members must see that appropriate interpretation accompanies any release of individual or group test data (e.g., limitations of instrument and norms).

9. NCDA members must ensure that computer-generated test administration and scoring programs function properly thereby providing clients with accurate test results.

10. NCDA members who are responsible for making decisions based on assessment results, must have appropriate training and skills in educational and psychological measurement — including validation criteria, test research, and guidelines for test development and use.

11. NCDA members must be cautious when interpreting the results of instruments that possess insufficient technical data, and must explicitly state to examinees the specific purposes for the use of such instruments.

12. NCDA members must proceed with caution when attempting to evaluate and interpret performances of minority group members or other persons who are not represented in the norm group on which the instrument was standardized.

13. NCDA members who develop computer-based test interpretations to support the assessment process, must ensure that the validity of the interpretations is established prior to the commercial distribution of the computer application.

14. NCDA members recognize that test results may become obsolete, and avoid the use of obsolete data.

15. NCDA members must avoid the appropriation, reproduction, or modification for published tests or parts thereof without acknowledgement and permission from the publisher.

Section D: Research and Publication

1. NCDA members will adhere to relevant guidelines on research with human subjects. These include:

  a. *Code of Federal Regulations,* Title 45, Subtitle A, Part 46, as currently issued.

  b. American Psychological Association. (1982). *Ethical principles in the conduct of research with human participants.* Washington, DC: Author.

  c. American Psychological Association. (1981). Research with human participants. *American Psychologist,* 36, 633-638.

  d. Family Educational Rights and Privacy Act. (Buckley Amendment to P.L. 93-380 of the Laws of 1974).

  e. Current federal regulations and various state privacy acts.

2. In planning research activities involving human subjects, NCDA members must be aware of and responsive to all pertinent ethical principles and ensure that the research problem, design, and execution are in full compliance with the principles.

3. The ultimate responsibility for ethical research lies with the principal researcher, though others involved in the research activities are ethically obligated and responsible for their own actions.

4. NCDA members who conduct research with human subjects are responsible for the subjects' welfare throughout the experiment and must take all reasonable precautions to avoid causing injurious psychological, physical, or social effects on their subjects.

5. NCDA members, who conduct research must abide by the following basic elements of informed consent:

a. a fair explanation of the procedures to be followed, including an identification of those which are experimental

b. a description of the attendant discomforts and risks

c. a description of the benefits to be expected

d. a disclosure of appropriate alternative procedures that would be advantageous for subjects

e. an offer to answer any inquiries concerning the procedures

f. an instruction that the subjects are free to withdraw their consent and to discontinue their participation in the project or activity at any time

6. When reporting research results, explicit mention must be made of all the variables and conditions known to the NCDA member that may have affected the outcome of the study or the interpretation of the data.

7. NCDA members who conduct and report research investigations must do so in a manner that minimizes the possibility that the results will be misleading.

8. NCDA members are obligated to make available sufficient original research data to qualified others who may wish to replicate the study.

9. NCDA members who supply data, aid in the research of another person, report research results, or make original data available, must take due care to disguise the identity of respective subjects in the absence of specific authorization from the subject to do otherwise.

10. When conducting and reporting research, NCDA members must be familiar with, and give recognition to, previous work on the topic, must observe all copyright laws, and must follow the principles of giving full credit to those to whom credit is due.

11. NCDA members must give credit through joint authorship, acknowledgement, footnote statements, or other appropriate means to those who have contributed significantly to the research and/or publication, in accordance with such contributions.

12. NCDA members should communicate to others the results of any research judged to be of professional value. Results that reflect unfavorably on institutions, programs, services, or vested interests must not be withheld.

13. NCDA members who agree to cooperate with another individual in research and/or publication must incur an obligation to cooperate as promised in terms of punctuality of performance and with full regard to the completeness and accuracy of the information required.

14. NCDA members must not submit the same manuscript, or one essentially similar in content, for simultaneous consideration by two or more journals. In addition, manuscripts that are published in whole or substantial part in another journal or published work should not be submitted for publication without acknowledgement and permission from the previous publication.

Section E: Consulting

Consultation refers to a voluntary relationship between a professional helper and a help-needing individual, group, or social unit in which the consultant is providing help to the client(s) in defining and solving a work-related problem or potential workrelated problem with a client or client system.

1. NCDA members, acting as consultants, must have a high degree of self-awareness of their own values, knowledge, skills, limitations, and needs in entering a helping relationship that involves human or organizational

change. The focus of the consulting relationship must be on the issues to be resolved and not on the person(s) presenting the problem.

2. In the consulting relationship, the NCDA member and client must understand and agree upon the problem definition, subsequent goals, and predicted consequences of interventions selected.

3. NCDA members must be reasonably certain that they, or the organization represented, have the necessary competencies and resources for giving the kind of help that is needed or that may develop later, and that appropriate referral sources are available to the consultant.

4. NCDA members in a consulting relationship must encourage and cultivate client adaptability and growth toward self-direction. NCDA members must maintain the role consistently and not become a decision-maker for clients or create a future dependency on the consultant.

5. NCDA members conscientiously adhere to the NCDA Ethical Standards when announcing consultant availability for services.

Section F: Private Practice

1. NCDA members should assist the profession by facilitating the availability of counseling services in private as well as public settings.

2. In advertising services as private practitioners, NCDA members must advertise in a manner that accurately informs the public of the professional services, expertise, and counseling techniques available.

3. NCDA members who assume an executive leadership role in a private practice organization do not permit their names to be used in professional notices during periods of time when they are not actively engaged in the practice of counseling.

4. NCDA members may list their highest relevant degree, type, and level of certification and/or license, address, telephone number, office hours, type and/or description of services, and other relevant information. Listed information must not contain false, inaccurate, misleading, partial, out-of-context, or otherwise deceptive material or statements.

5. NCDA members who are involved in a partnership or corporation with other professionals must, in compliance with the regulations of the

locality, clearly specify the separate specialties of each member of the partnership or corporation.

6. NCDA members have an obligation to withdraw form a privatepractice counseling relationship if it violates the NCDA Ethical Standards, if the mental or physical condition of the NCDA member renders it difficult to carry out an effective professional relationship, or if the counseling relationship is no longer productive for the client.

Section G: Procedures for Processing Ethical Complaints

As a division of the American Association for Counseling and Development (AACD), the National Career Development Association (NCDA) adheres to the guidelines and procedures for processing ethical complaints and the disciplinary sanctions adopted by AACD. A complaint against an NCDA member may be filed by an individual or group of individuals ("complainant"), whether or not the complainant is a member of NCDA. (Action will not be taken on anonymous complaints).

For specifics on how to file ethical complaints and a description of the guidelines and procedures for processing complaints, contact:

AACD Ethics Committee
c/o Executive Director
American Association for Counseling and Development
5999 Stevenson Avenue
Alexandria, VA 22304

REFERENCES

AACD Ethics Committee. (1991). Report of the AACD ethics committee: 1989-1991. *Journal of Counseling and Development, 70*(2), 278-280.

ACA plans revision of ethical standards. (1992, Summer). *ACES Spectrum,* 18-19.

Adler, A. (1958). *What life should mean to you.* New York: Capricorn Books.

Adler, A. (1964). *Problems of neurosis.* New York: Harper & Row.

Adler, A. (1972). *The neurotic constitution.* Freeport, NY: Books for Libraries Press. (Originally published in 1926).

Allen, V. B., Sampson, J.P., Jr., & Herlihy, B. (1988). Details of the 1988 AACD ethical standards. *Journal of Counseling and Development, 67*(3), 157-158.

Ambrose, D. M., & Lennox, L. (1988). Strategic market positions for mental health services. *Journal of Mental Health Administration, 15*(1), 5-9.

American Counseling Association. (1988). *Ethical standards of the American Association for Counseling and Development.* Alexandria, VA: Author.

American Mental Health Counselors Association. *Code of ethics for mental health counselors.* Alexandria, VA: Author.

American Psychiatric Association. (1987). *Diagnostic & statistical manual of mental disorders* (3rd ed., rev.). Washington, DC: Author.

American School Counselors Association. *Ethical standards for school counselors.* Alexandria, VA: Author.

Association for Counselor Education and Supervision. (1993). *Ethical guidelines for counseling supervisors.* Alexandria, VA: Author.

Association for Specialists in Group Work. (1980). *Ethical guidelines for group leaders.* Alexandria, VA: Author.

Atkinson, D. R., Morten, G., & Sue, D. W. (1989). *Counseling American minorities: A cross-cultural perspective* (3rd ed.). Dubuque, IA: W. C. Brown.

Axelson, J. A. (1985). *Counseling and development in a multicultural society.* Monterey, CA: Brooks/Cole.

Bacon, C. L. (1990). *Celebrating diversity: A learning tool for working with people of different cultures.* Washington, DC: American Association of Retired Persons.

Bandura, A. (1977). Self-efficacy: Toward a unifying theory of behavior change. *Psychological Review, 84,* 191-215.

Bandura, A. (1982). The psychology of chance encounters and life paths. *The American Psychologist 37*(7), 747-755.

Bardon, J. I., & Bennett, V. C. (1974). *School psychology.* Englewood Cliffs, NJ: Prentice-Hall.

Barlow, D. H., Hayes, S. C., & Nelson, R. O. (1984). *The scientist practitioner.* New York: Pergamon.

Bartlett, W. E., Lee, J. E., & Doyle, R. E. (1985). Historical development of the Association for Religious and Values Issues in Counseling. *Journal of Counseling and Development, 63*(7), 448-451.

Baruth, L. G., & Manning, M. L. (1991). *Multicultural counseling and psychotherapy.* New York: Macmillan.

Belkin, G. S. (1984). *Introduction to counseling.* DuBuque, IA: W.C. Brown.

Bergland, B. W. (1974). Career planning: The use of the sequential evaluated experience. In E. L. Herr (Ed.), *Vocational guidance and human development* (pp. 350-380). Boston: Houghton Mifflin.

Bernard, J. M. (1987). Ethical and legal considerations for supervisors. In L. D. Borders & G. R. Leddick, *Handbook for counseling supervision* (pp. 52-57). Alexandria, VA: Association for Counselor Education and Supervision.

Bindman, A. J. (1964). The psychologist as a mental health consultant. *Journal of Psychiatric Nursing, 2,* 367-380.

Bishop, J. B. (1990). The university counseling center: An agenda for the 1990s. *Journal of Counseling and Development, 68*(4), 408-413.

Blake, R. R., & Mouton, S. S. (1983). *Consultation.* Reading, MA: Addison-Wesley.

Blocker, D. (1975). *Developmental counseling* (2nd ed.) New York: Ronald Press.

Bloland, P. A., & Edwards, P. B. (1981). Work & leisure: A counseling synthesis. *Vocational Guidance Quarterly, 30,* 101-108.

Borders, L. D., & Leddick, G. R. (1987). *Handbook in counseling supervision.* Alexandria, VA: Association for Counselor Education and Supervision.

Bordin, E. S. (1990). *Psychodynamic model of career choice and satisfaction.* In D. Brown, L. Brooks, and Associates (Eds.), Career choice and development (pp. 102-144). San Francisco, CA: Jossey-Bass.

Bordin, E. S., Nachmann, B., & Segal, S. J. (1963). An articulated framework for vocational development. *Journal of Counseling Psychology, 10,* 107-116.

Brammer, L. M., & Shostrom, E. L. (1960). *Therapeutic psychology.* Englewood Cliffs, NJ: Prentice-Hall.

Brooks, D. K., & Gerstein, L. H. (1990a). Counselor credentialing and inter-professional collaboration. *Journal of Counseling and Development, 68*(5), 477-484.

Brooks, D. K., & Gerstein, L. H. (1990b). Interprofessional collaboration: Or shooting yourself in the foot only feels good when you stop. *Journal of Counseling and Development, 68*(5), 509-510.

Brown, D., & Srebalus, D.J. (1988). *An introduction to the counseling profession.* Englewood Cliffs, NJ: Prentice-Hall.

Bumpass, L. L. (1990). What's happening to the family? Interactions between demographic and institutional change. *Demography, 27,* 483-498.

Bumpass, L. L., & Sweet, J. A. (1989). Children's experience in single-parent families: Implications of cohabitation and marital transitions. *Family Planning Perspectives, 21,*256-260.

Burn, D. (1992). Ethical issues in cross-cultural counseling and training. *Journal of Counseling and Development, 70*(5), 578-583.

Burns, C. F., & Consolvo, C. A. (1992). The development of a campus-based substance abuse prevention program. *Journal of Counseling and Development, 70*(5), 639-641.

Butler, R. N., & Lewis, M. I. (1982). *Aging and mental health,* (3rd ed.). St. Louis, MO: Mosby.

Cabral, A. C., & Salamone, P. R. (1990). Chance and careers: Normative versus contextual development. *Career Development Quarterly, 39*(1), 5-17.

Campbell, D. T., & Stanley, J. C. (1963). *Experimental and quasi-experimental designs for research.* Chicago: Rand McNally.

Caplan, G. (1970). *The theory and practice of mental health consultation.* New York: Basic Books.

Carkhuff, R. R. (1974). *The art of helping.* Amherst, MA: Human Resource Development Press.

Carroll, M. R., & Levo, L. (1985). The Association for Specialists in Group Work. *Journal of Counseling and Development, 63*(7), 452-454.

Castro Martin, T., & Bumpass, L. L. (1989). Recent trends in marital disruption. *Demography, 26,*37-51.

Chartrand, J. M. (1991). The evolution of trait-and-factor career counseling: A person x environment fit approach. *Journal of Counseling and Development, 69*(6), 518-524.

Chickering, A. (1987). *Education and identity.* San Francisco, CA: Jossey-Bass.

Cohen, E. D. (1990). Confidentiality, counseling, and clients who have AIDS: Ethical foundations of a model rule. *Journal of Counseling and Development, 68*(3), 282-286.

Coleman, E., & Schaefer, S. (1988). Boundaries of sex and intimacy between client and counselor. In W. C. Huey & T. P. Remley, Jr. (Eds.), *Ethical & legal issues in school counseling* (pp. 286-298). Alexandria, VA: American School Counselor Association.

Commission on Rehabilitation Counselor Certification. *Code of professional ethics for rehabilitation counselors.* Chicago, IL: Author.

Corey, G. (1981). *Theory and practice of group counseling.* Monterey, CA: Brooks/Cole.

Corey, G. (1990). *Theory and practice of group counseling.* (3rd Ed.) Monterey, CA: Brooks/Cole.

Corey, M. S., & Corey, G. (1987). *Groups: Process and practice.* Monterey, CA: Brooks/Cole.

Corey, G., Corey, M. S., & Callanan, P. (1988). *Issues and ethics in the helping professions* (3rd ed.). Pacific Grove, CA: Brooks/Cole.

Corey, G., Corey, M. S., & Callanan, P. (1988). *Group techniques* (rev. ed.). Monterey, CA: Brooks/Cole.

Corey, G., Corey, M. S., & Callanan, P. (1993). *Issues and ethics in the helping professions* (4th ed.). Pacific Grove, CA: Brooks/Cole.

Coven T. M. (1992, Winter). Freedom of choice, supervision andsigning off by mental health professionals. *FMHCA Newsletter*, pp. 1, 3-5.

Cox, W. E. (1985). Military Educators and Counselors Association. *Journal of Counseling and Development, 63*(7), 461-463.

Crites, J. O. (1973). *Career Maturity Inventory*. Monterey, CA: California Test Bureau/McGraw-Hill.

Cronbach, L. J. (1970). *Essentials of psychological testing* (3rd ed). New York: Harper & Row.

Davenport, D. (1992). Ethical and legal problems with clientcentered supervision. *Counselor Education and Supervision, 31*(4), 227-231.

DiMichael, S. G., & Thomas, K. R. (1985). ARCA's journey in professionalism: A commemorative review on the 25th anniversary. *Journal of Counseling and Development, 63*(7), 428-435.

Drew, C. J. (1976). *Designing research and evaluation*. St. Louis, MO: Mosby.

Dworkin, S. H., & Guiterrez, F. (1989). Introduction to special issue. Counselors be aware: Clients come in every size, shape, color, and sexual orientation. *Journal of Counseling and Development, 68*(1), 6-8.

Dye, H. A., & Borders, L. D. (1990). Counseling supervisors: Standards for preparation and practice. *Journal of Counseling and Development, 69*(1), 27-29.

Eddy, W., & Lubin, B. (1971). Laboratory training and encounter groups. *Personnel and Guidance Journal, 49*(8), 625-635.

Egan, G. (1986). *The skilled helper*. Monterey, CA: Brooks/Cole.

Ekstrom, R., & Johnson, C. (1984). Introduction and overview. *Journal of Counseling and Development, 63*(3), 63.

Emener, W. G., & Cottone, R. R. (1989). Professionalization, deprofessionalization, and reprofessionalization of rehabilitation counseling according to criteria of professions. *Journal of Counseling and Development,* 67(10), 576-581.

Engels, D. W., & Muro, J. J. (1986). Silver to gold: The alchemy, potential, and maturing of ACES and CES. *Counselor Education and Supervision,* 25(4), 289-305.

Engels, D., Wilborn, B. L., & Schneider, L. J. (1990). Ethics curricula for counselor preparation programs. In B. Herlihy & L. B. Golden (Eds.), *Ethical standards casebook* (4th ed.) (pp. 111126). Alexandria, VA: American Association for Counseling and Development.

Erickson, S. H. (1990). Counseling the irresponsible AIDS client: Guidelines for decision making. *Journal of Counseling and Development,* 68(4), 454-455.

Erikson, E.H. (1963). *Childhood and society* (2nd ed.). New York: Norton.

Erikson, E. H. (1968). *Identity and crisis.* New York: Norton and Company.

Everett, C. A. (1990a). The field of marital and family therapy. *Journal of Counseling and Development,* 68(5), 498-502.

Everett, C. A. (1990b). Where have all the "gypsies" gone? *Journal of Counseling and Development,* 68(5), 507-508.

Fischer, L., & Sorenson, G. P. (1985). *School law for counselors, psychologists, and social workers.* New York: Longman.

Fong-Beyette, M. L. (1988). Do counseling and marketing mix? *Counselor Education and Supervision,* 27(4), 315-319.

Forrest, D. V., & Affeman, M. (1986). The future of mental health counselors in health maintenance organizations. *American Mental Health Counselors Association Journal,* 8(2), 65-72.

Fosler, R. S., Alonso, W., Myer, J. A., & Kern, R. (1990). *Demographic change and the American future.* Pittsburgh, PA: University of Pittsburgh Press.

Fredrickson, R. H. (1982). *Career information.* Englewood Cliffs, NJ: Prentice-Hall.

Freud, S. (1911). Formulation regarding the two principles of mental functioning. *Standard Edition, 12,* 218-228.

Fujimara, L. E., Weis, D. M., & Cochran, J. R. (1985). Suicide: Dynamics and implications for counseling. *Journal of Counseling and Development, 63*(10), 612-615.

Fuqua, D. R., & Newman, J. L. (1989). Research issues in the study of professional ethics. *Counselor Education and Supervision, 29*(2), 84-93.

Galassi, J. P., Stoltz, R. F., Brooks, L., & Trexler, K. A. (1987). Improving research training in doctoral programs. *Journal of Counseling and Development, 66*(1), 40-44.

Gazda, G. M. (1978). *Group counseling: A developmental approach.* Boston, MA: Allyn & Bacon.

Gazda, G. M. (1989). *Group counseling: A developmental approach.* (4th ed.) Boston, MA: Allyn & Bacon.

Gelatt, H. B. (1962). Decision-making: A conceptual frame of reference for counseling. *Journal of Counseling Psychology, 9,* 240-245.

Gelatt, H. B. (1989). Positive uncertainty: A new decision making framework for counseling. *Journal of Counseling Psychology, 36*(2), 252-256.

Gelso, C. J. (1985). Rigor, relevance, and counseling research: On the need to maintain our course between Sycila and Charybdis. *Journal of Counseling and Development, 63*(9), 551-553.

George, R. L., & Dustin, D. (1988). *Group counseling: Theory and practice.* New York: Prentice Hall.

Gerstcin, L. H., & Bayer, G. A. (1988). Employee assistance programs: A systemic investigation of their use. *Journal of Counseling and Development, 66*(6), 294-297.

Gilbert, S. P. (1992). Ethical issues in treatment of severe psychopathology in university and college counseling centers. *Journal of Counseling and Development, 70*(6), 695-699.

Gilchrist, L. A., & Stringer, M. (1992). Marketing counseling: Guidelines for training and practice. *Counselor Education and Supervision, 31*(3), 154-162.

Ginzberg, E. (1972). Restatement of the theory of occupational choice. *Vocational Guidance Quarterly, 20*(3), 169-176.

Ginzberg, E., Ginsburg, S. W., Axelrad, S., & Herma, J. (1951). *Occupational choice: An approach to general theory.* New York: Columbia University Press.

Gladding, S. T. (1988). Counseling: *A comprehensive profession.* Columbus, OH: Merrill.

Gladding, S. T. (1991). *Group work: A counseling specialty.* New York: Macmillan.

Goldman, L. (1976). A revolution in counseling research. *Journal of Counseling Psychology, 23,* 543-552.

Goldman, L. (1977). Toward more meaningful research. *Personnel and Guidance Journal, 55,* 363-368.

Goldman, L. (Ed.). (1978). *Research methods for counselors.* New York: Wiley.

Gonzalez, E. (1989). Hispanics bring "corazon" and "sensibilidad." *Momentum, 20,* 10-13.

Gottfredson, G. D., & Holland, J. L. (1989). *Dictionary of Holland occupational codes.* Odessa, FL: Psychological Assessment Resources.

Gray, L., & Harding, A. K. (1988). Confidentiality limits with clients who have the AIDS virus. *Journal of Counseling and Development, 66*(5), 219-223.

Gross, D. R., & Robinson, S. E. (1987). Ethics, violence, and counseling: Hear no evil, see no evil, speak no evil? *Journal of Counseling and Development, 65*(7), 340-344.

Gross, S. J. (1980). The holistic health movement. *Personnel and Guidance Journal, 59*(2), 96-102.

Grunwald, B.B., & McAbee, H.V. (1985). *Guiding the family: Practical counseling techniques.* Muncie, IN: Accelerated Development.

Gysbers, N. C. (1984). Major trends in career development theory and practice. *Vocational Guidance Quarterly, 33*(1), 15-25.

Hanson, T., Warner, R., & Smith, E. (1980). *Group counseling: Theory and process.* Chicago: Rand McNally.

Harris, T. A. (1967). *I'm OK—You're OK.* New York: Avon

Harris-Bowlsbey, J. (1984). High touch and high technology: The marriage that must succeed. *Counselor Education and Supervision,* 24(1), 6-16.

Havinghurst, R. S. (1972). *Developmental tasks and education* (3rd ed.). New York: McKay.

Healy, C. C. (1982). *Career development: Counseling through the life stages.* Boston: Allyn and Bacon.

Herlihy, B., Healy, M., Cook, E. P., & Hudson, P. (1987). Ethical practices of licensed professional counselors: A survey of state licensing boards. *Counselor Education and Supervision,* 27(1), 69-76.

Herlihy, B., & Sheeley, V. L. (1987). Privileged communication in selected helping professions: A comparison among statutes. *Journal of Counseling and Development,* 65(9), 479-483.

Herlihy, B., & Sheeley, V. L. (1988). Counselor liability and the duty to warn: Selected cases, statutory trends, and implications for practice. In W. C. Huey & T. P. Remley, Jr. (Eds.), *Ethical & legal issues in school counseling* (pp. 137142). Alexandria, VA: American School Counselor Association.

Hernandez, H. (1989). *Multicultural education—A teacher's guide to content and practice.* Columbus, OH: Merrill.

Herr, E.L. (1985). AACD: An association committed to unity through diversity. *Journal of Counseling and Development,* 63(7), 395-404.

Herr, E.L. (1986). Life-style and career development. In M. D. Lewis, R. L. Hayes, & J. A. Lewis (Eds.), *An introduction to the counseling profession* (pp. 167-214). Itasca, IL: F.E. Peacock.

Herr, E. L. (1989). *Counseling in a dynamic society: Opportunities and challenges.* Alexandria, VA: American Association of Counseling and Development.

Herr, E. L., & Cramer, S. H. (1988). *Career guidance and counseling through the lifespan* (3rd ed.). Glenview, IL: Scott,Foresman/Little, Brown.

Hock, E. L., Ross, A. O., & Winder, C. L. (Eds.). (1966). *Professional preparation of clinical psychologists: Proceedings of the conference on the professional preparation of clinical psychologists meeting at the Center for Continuing Education, Chicago, Illinois August 17 - September 1, 1965.* Washington, DC: American Psychological Association.

Hohenshil, T. H., & Brown, M. B. (1991). School counselors and prekindergarten children. *Elementary School Guidance & Counseling, 26*(1), 3.

Holland, J. L. (1966). *The psychology of vocational choice.* Waltham, MA: Blaisdell.

Holland, J. L. (1973). *Making vocational choices: A theory of careers.* Englewood Cliffs, NJ: Prentice-Hall.

Holland, J. L. (1985). *Making vocational choices: A theory of vocational personalities and work environments* (2nd ed.). Needham Heights, MA: Allyn & Bacon.

Hollis, J. W., & Wantz, R. A. (1986). *Counselor preparation 1986-89: Programs, personnel, and trends, sixth edition.* Muncie, IN: Accelerated Development.

Hollis, J. W., & Wantz, R. A. (1990). *Counselor preparation 1990-92: Programs, personnel, and trends, seventh edition.* Muncie, IN: Accelerated Development.

Hollis, J. W., & Wantz, R. A. (1993). *Counselor preparation 1993-95: Volume I: programs and personnel, eighth edition.* Muncie, IN: Accelerated Development.

Holmes, Oliver Wendell, Jr. (1921). New York Trust & Company v Eisner. 256 U.S. 345,349.

Hopkins, B. R., & Anderson, B. S. (1990). *The counselor and the law* (3rd ed.). Alexandria, VA: American Association for Counseling and Development.

Hopson, B. (1982). Counseling and helping. In R. Holdsworth (Ed.), *Psychology for career counseling* (pp. 61-79). Great Britain: Macmillan Press.

Hotelling, K. (1988). Ethical, legal, and administrative options to address sexual relationships between counselor and client. *Journal of Counseling and Development, 67*(4), 233-237.

Hoyt, K. B. (1972). *Career education: What it is and how to do it.* Salt Lake City, UT: Olympus.

Hoyt, K. B. (1974). *An introduction to career education.* U.S. Office of Education Policy Paper. Washington, DC: Author.

Hummel, D. L., Talbutt, L. C., & Alexander, M. D. (1985). *Law and ethics in counseling.* New York, NY: Van Nostrand Reinhold.

Ibrahim, F. A., & Arreondo, P. (1990). Ethical issues in multicultural counseling. In B. Herlihy & L. B. Golden (Eds.), *Ethical standards casebook* (4th ed.) (pp. 137-145). Alexandria, VA: American Association for Counseling and Development.

International Association of Marriage and Family Counselors. *Ethical code.* Alexandria, VA: Author.

Ivey, A. (1971). *Microcounseling: Innovations in interviewing training.* Springfield, IL: Charles C. Thomas.

Jackson, G. G. (1985). Cross-cultural counseling with AfroAmericans. In P. Pedersen (Ed.), *Handbook of cross-cultural counseling and therapy.* Westport, CT: Greenwood Press.

Jacobs, E., Harvill, R., & Masson, R. (1988). *Group counseling: Strategies and skills.* Springfield, IL: Charles C. Thomas.

Jaeger, R. M., & Frye, A. W. (1988). An assessment of the job relevance of the National Board for Certified Counselors Examination. *Journal of Counseling and Development, 67*(1), 2226.

Johnson, C. S. (1985). The American College Personnel Association. *Journal of Counseling and Development, 63*(7), 405-410.

Johnson, D.W., & Johnson, F.P. (1987). *Joining together* (3rd ed.). Englewood Cliffs, NJ: Prentice-Hall.

Kagan, N., & Krathwohl, D.R. (1967). *Studies in human interaction: Interpersonal process recall stimulated by videotape.* East Lansing, MI: Educational Publication Services, College of Education, Michigan State University.

Kain, C. D. (1988). To breach or not to breach: Is that the question? A response to Gray and Harding. *Journal of Counseling and Development, 66*(5), 224-225.

Kemp, C.A. (1970). *Foundations of group counseling.* New York: McGraw-Hill.

Kerlinger, F. N. (1986). *Foundations of behavioral research* (3rd ed). New York: Holt, Rinehart and Winston.

King, P. M. (1978). William Perry's theory of intellectual and ethical development. In L. Knefelkamp, C. Widick, & C. A. Parker (Ed.), *Applying new developmental findings* (pp. 35-54. San Francisco, CA: Jossey-Bass.

Kirby, J. (1985). *Consultation: Practice and practitioner.* Muncie, IN: Accelerated Development.

Kitchener, K. S. (1986). Teaching applied ethics in counselor education: An integration of psychological processes and philosophical analysis. *Journal of Counseling and Development, 64*(5), 306-310.

Kitchener, K. S. (1988). Dual role relationships: What makes them so problematic? *Journal of Counseling and Development, 67*(4), 217-221.

Kitchener, K. S., & Harding, S. S. (1990). Dual role relationships. In B. Herlihy & L. B. Golden (Eds.), *Ethical standards casebook* (4th ed.) (pp. 146-154). Alexandria, VA: American Association for Copunseling and Development.

Kohlberg, L. (1966). Moral education in the schools: A developmental view. *The School Review, 74,* 1-30.

Kottman, Y. (1990). Counseling middle school students: Techniques that work. *Elementary School Guidance & Counseling, 25*(2), 138-145.

Krumboltz, J. D., with Mitchell, A. M., & Jones, B. G. (1978). A social learning theory of career selection. In J. M. Whiteley and A. Resnikoff (Eds.), *Career counseling* (pp. 100-127). Monterey, CA: Brooks/Cole.

Kurpius, D., Gibson, G, Lewis, J., & Corbet, M. (1991). Ethical issues in supervising counseling practitioners. *Counselor Education and Supervision, 31*(1), 48-57.

Lanning, W. (1990). An educator/practitioner model for counselor education doctoral programs. *Counselor Education and Supervision, 30*(2), 163-169.

Lapiri v. Sears, Roebuck, & Co., 497 F. Supp. 195D (Neb. 1980).

Lee, C. C., & Richardson, B. L. (1991). *Multicultural issues in counseling: New approaches to diversity.* Alexandria, VA: American Association for Counseling and Development.

Lewis, J. A., & Hayes, B. A. (1984). Options for counselors in business and industry. *Counseling and Human Development, 17*(4), 1-8.

Loesch, L. C. (1984). Professional credentialing in counseling-1984. *Counseling and Human Development, 17*(2), 1-11.

Loesch, L. C. (1988). Preparation for helping professionals working with diverse populations. In N. A. Vacc, J. Wittmer, & S. Devaney (Eds.), *Experiencing and counseling multicultural and diverse populations* (2nd ed.). Muncie, IN: Accelerated Development.

Loesch, L. C., & Vacc, N. A. (1988). Results and possible implications of the National Board for Certified Counselors Examination. *Journal of Counseling and Development, 67*(1), 1721.

Loesch, L. C., & Vacc, N. A. (1991). *Technical manual for the National Counselor Examination.* Alexandria, VA: National Board for Certified Counselors.

Loesch, L. C., & Vacc, N. A. (in press). Setting minimum criterion scores for the National Counselor Examination. *Journal of Counseling and Development.*

Loesch, L. C., & Wheeler, P. T. (1982). *Principles of leisure counseling.* Minneapolis, MN: Educational Media Corporation.

Mabe, A. R., & Rollin, S. A. (1986). The role of a code of ethical standards in counseling. *Journal of Counseling and Development, 64*(5), 294-297.

Martin, D., & Martin, M. (1989). Bridging the gap between research and practice. *Journal of Counseling and Development, 67*(8), 491-492.

Maslow, A.H. (1954). *Motivation and personality.* New York: Harper & Row.

McDaniels, C. (1984). The work/leisure connection. *Vocational Guidance Quarterly, 33*(1), 35-44.

McDaniels, C., & Gysbers, N. C. (1992). *Counseling for career development: Theories, resources, and practice.* San Francisco, CA: Jossey-Bass.

McDavis, R. J., & Parker, W. M. (1988). Counseling black people. In N. A. Vacc, J. Wittmer, & S. DeVaney (Eds.), *Experiencing and counseling multicultural and diverse populations* (2nd ed.). Muncie, IN: Accelerated Development.

McFadden, J., & Lispcomb, W. D. (1985). History of the Association for Non-White Concerns in Personnel and Guidance. *Journal of Counseling and Development, 63*(7), 444-447.

McGowan, S. (1991, October). Confidentiality: Breaking a sacred trust. *AACD Guidepost,* pp. 14, 22.

McMann, N., & Oliver, R. (1988). Problems in families with gifted children: Implications for counselors. *Journal of Counseling and Development, 66*(6), 275-278.

Mehrens, W. A. (1978). Rigor and reality in counseling research. *Measurement and Evaluation in Guidance, 11*(1), 8-13.

Mehrens, W. A., & Lehmann, I. J. (1984). *Measurement and evaluation in education and psychology* (3rd ed.). New York: Holt, Rinehart and Winston.

Meyer, D., Helwig, A., Gjernes, O., & Chickering, J. (1985). The National Employment Counselors Association. *Journal of Counseling and Development, 63*(7), 440-443.

Miller, G. M. (1988). Counselor functions in excellent schools: Elementary through secondary. *The School Counselor, 36*(2), 88-94.

Miller-Tiedeman, A., & Tiedeman, D. V. (1990). Career decision making: An individualistic perspective. In D. Brown, L. Brooks, and Associates (Eds.), *Career choice and development* (pp. 308337). San Francisco, CA: Jossey-Bass.

Milliken, R.L., & Kirchner, R. (1971). Counselor's understanding of student's communication as a function of the counselor's perceptual defense. *Journal of Counseling Psychology, 18*, 4-18.

Minkoff, H. B., & Terres, C. K. (1985). ASCA perspectives: Past, present, and future. *Journal of Counseling and Development, 63*(7), 424-427.

Mitchell, L. K, & Krumboltz, J. D. (1990). Social learning theory approaches to career decision making: Krumboltz's theory. In D. Brown, L. Brooks, and Associates (Eds.), *Career choice and development* (pp. 145-196). San Francisco, CA: Jossey-Bass.

Moles, O. C. (1991). Guidance programs in American high schools: A descriptive portrait. *The School Counselor, 38*(3), 163-177.

Moreno, J. L. & Kipper, D. A. (1968). Group psychodrama and community-centered counseling. In M. Gazda (Ed.), *Basic approaches to group psychotherapy and group counseling* (pp. 27-79). Springfield, IL: Charles C. Thomas.

Myers, J. E. (1991). Wellness as the paradigm for counseling and development: The possible future. *Counselor Education and Supervision, 30*(3), 183-193.

Myers, J. E., & Loesch, L. C. (1981). The counseling needs of older persons. *The Humanist Educator, 20*(1), 21-35.

Myers, R. S., & Pace, T. S. (1986). Counseling gifted and talented students: Historical perspectives and contemporary issues. *Journal of Counseling and Development, 64*(9), 548-551.

Myrick, R. D. (1977). *Consultation as a counselor intervention.* Ann Arbor, MI: ERIC Counseling and Personnel Services Information Center.

Myrick, R. D. (1987). *Developmental guidance and counseling: A practical approach.* Minneapolis, MN: Educational Media.

National Association of Certified Clinical Mental Health Counselors. *Code of ethics.* Alexandria, VA: Author.

National Board for Certified Counselors. *Code of ethics.* Greensboro, NC: Author.

National Board for Certified Counselors. (1993). *A work behavior analysis of professional counselors.* Greensboro, NC: NBCC & Muncie, IN: Accelerated Development Inc.

NCDA Professional Standards Committee. (1992). Career counseling competencies. *The Career Development Quarterly, 40*(4), 378-386.

Nelson, P. L. (1992, July). Lawsuits, legal matters and liability claims hit the profession. *AACD Guidepost,* p. 17.

Neulinger, J. (1974). *The psychology of leisure.* Springfield, IL: Charles C. Thomas.

Nicholas, D. R. (1988). Behavioral medicine and mental health counseling: An overview. *Journal of Mental Health Counseling, 10*(2), 69-78.

O'Bryant, B. J. (1992, Summer). Something's wrong. *The American Counselor,* p. 36.

Ohlsen, M. M. (1970). *Group counseling.* New York: McGraw-Hill.

Okun, B. F. (1987). *Effective helping interviewing and counseling techniques* (3rd ed.). Monterey, CA: Brooks/Cole.

Osipow, S. H. (1983). *Theories of career development* (3rd ed.). Englewood Cliffs, NJ: Prentice-Hall.

Page, R. C. (1985). The unique role of the Public Offender Counselor Association. *Journal of Counseling and Development, 63*(7), 455-456.

Pate, R. H., Jr. (1992, Summer). Student suicide: Are you liable? *The American Counselor*, pp. 14-19.

Pavlov, I. P. (1927). *Conditioned reflexes*. London: Oxford Press.

Peatling, J., & Tiedeman, D. (1977). *Career development: Designing self*. Muncie, IN: Accelerated Development.

Pedersen, P. (1985). *Handbook of cross-cultural counseling and therapy*. Westport, CT: Greenwood Press.

Pedersen, P. (1988). *Atland book for developing multicultural awareness*. Alexandria, VA: American Association for Counseling and Development.

Pedersen, P. B. (1991). Introduction to Part 4. Direct service delivery. *Journal of Counseling and Development, 70*(1), 205.

Pelsma, D. M., & Borgers, S. B. (1986). Experienced-based ethics: A developmental model of learning ethical reasoning. *Journal of Counseling and Development, 64*(5), 311-314.

Perry, W. C. (1970). *Forms of intellectual and ethical development in the college years*. New York: Holt, Rinehart and Winston.

Peterson, G. W., Otten, P., Burck, H., & Loughead, T. (1989). *A comparison of novice and expert perceptions of career maturity*. Paper presented at the annual convention of the American Educational Research Association, San Francisco, CA.

Peterson, G. W., Sampson, J. P., Jr., & Reardon, R. C. (1991). *Career development and services: A cognitive approach*. Pacific Grove, CA: Brooks/Cole.

Piaget, J. (1964). *Judgement and reasoning in the child*. Patterson, NJ: Littlefield, Adams & Co.

Pitz, G.F., & Harren, V.A. (1980). An analysis of career decision-making from the point of view of information processing and decision theory. *Journal of Vocational Behavior, 16*, 320-346.

Pope, K. S. (1988). How clients are harmed by sexual contact with mental health professionals: The syndrome and its prevalence. *Journal of Counseling and Development, 67*(4), 222-226.

Ramey, L., & Cloud, J. L. (1987). Relocation success: A model for mental health counselors. *Journal of Mental Health Counseling, 9*(3), 150-161.

Randolph, D. L. (1990). Changing the nonpsychology doctorate in counselor education: A proposal. *Counselor Education and Supervision, 30*(2), 135-147.

Remley, T. P., Jr. (1988). More exploration needed of ethical and legal topics. *Journal of Mental Health Counseling, 10*(3), 167-170.

Remley, T. P., Jr. (1992a, Spring). You and the law. *The American Counselor,* pp. 33-34.

Remley, T. P., Jr. (1992b, Summer). You and the law. *The American Counselor,* pp. 31, 33.

Riker, H. C. (1981). Preface. In J. E. Myers (Ed.), *Counseling older persons Volume III Trainer's manual for basic helping skills* (pp. xvii-xx). Washington, DC: American Personnel and Guidance Association.

Riker, H. C., & Myers, J. E. (1988). Older persons. In N. A. Vacc, J. Wittmer & S. DeVaney, *Experiencing and Counseling Multicultural and Diverse Populations* (2nd ed.) (pp. 189-219). Muncie, IN: Accelerated Development.

Rinas, J., & Clyne-Jackson, S. (1988). *Professional conduct and legal concerns in mental health practice.* Norwalk, CT: Appleton & Lange.

Ritchie, M.H. (1989). Enhancing the public image of school counseling: A marketing approach. *The School Counselor, 37*(1), 54-61.

Robinson, S. (1991). Ethical and legal issues related to counseling: Or its not as easy as it looks. In D. Capuzzi & D.R. Gross (Eds.), *Introduction to counseling perspectives for the 1990s* (pp. 447-468). Boston, MA: Allyn and Bacon.

Robinson, S. E., & Gross, D. R. (1989). Applied ethics and the mental health counselor. *Journal of Mental Health Counseling, 11*(3), 289-299.

Roe, A. (1956). *The psychology of occupations.* New York: Wiley.

Rogers, C. (1970). *Carl Rogers on Encounter Groups.* New York: Harper & Row.

Rogers, C. (1971). Facilitating encounter groups. *American Journal of Nursing, 71*(2), 275-279.

Rowe, W., Murphy, H. B., & De Csipkes, R. A. (1975). The relationship of counselor characteristics and counseling effectiveness. *Review of Educational Research, 45,* 231-246.

Ruiz, R. A. (1981). Cultural and historical counseling in Hispanics. In D. W. Sue (ed.), *Counseling the culturally different* (pp. 186-215). New York: John Wiley.

Sacks, J. S. (1992, May). AACD to become ACA. *Guidepost*, pp. 1, 10.

Saltmarsh, R.E., Jenkins, S.J., & Fisher, G.L. (1986). The TRAC model: A practical map for group process and management. *Journal for Specialists in Group Work, 11*,30-36.

Sampson, J.P., Jr. (1986). *Preliminary technical manual for the NBCC career counselor certification examination.* Washington, DC: NBCC.

Sampson, J. P., Jr. (1990). Ethical use of computer applications in counseling: Past, present, and future. In B. Herlihy & L. B. Golden (Eds.), *Ethical standards casebook* (4th ed.) (pp. 170-176). Alexandria, VA: American Association for Counseling and Development.

Sampson, J. P., Jr., & Krumboltz, J. D. (1991). Computerassisted instruction: A missing link in counseling. *Journal of Counseling and Development, 69*(5), 395-398.

Sampson, J. P., Jr., & Pyle, K. R. (1983). Ethical issues involved with the use of computer-assisted counseling, testing, and guidance systems. *Personnel and Guidance Journal, 61*(5), 283-287.

Sandberg, D.N., Crabbs, S.K., & Crabbs, M.A. (1988). Legal issues in child abuse: Questions and answers for counselors. In W.C. Huey & T.P. Remley, Jr. (Eds.), *Ethical and legal issues in school counseling* (pp. 173-181). Alexandria, VA: American School Counselors Association.

Schein, E. (1969). *Process consultation.* Reading, MA: Addison-Wesley.

Schepp, K. F. (1986). *Sexuality counseling: A training program.* Muncie, IN: Accelerated Development.

Scher, M. (1981). Men in hiding: A challenge for the counselor. *Personnel and Guidance Journal, 60*(4), 199-202.

Scher, M., & Good, G. E. (1990). Gender and counseling in the twenty-first century: What does the future hold? *Journal of Counseling and Development, 68*(4), 388-391.

Schwab, R., & Harris, T. L. (1981). Personal growth of counselor trainees. *Counselor Education and Supervision, 20*(3), 219-224.

Shaffer, J. B., & Galinsky, M.D. (1989) *Models of group therapy*. New York: Prentice Hall.

Sharf, R. S. (1992). *Applying career development theory to counseling*. Pacific Grove, CA: Brooks/Cole.

Sheeley, V. S., & Eberly, C. G. (1985). Two decades of leadership in measurement and evaluation. *Journal of Counseling and Development, 63*(7), 436-439.

Sheeley, V. L., & Herlihy, B. (1989). Counseling suicidal teens: A duty to warn and protect. *The School Counselor, 37*(2), 89-95.

Shertzer, B., & Linden, J. (1978). *Principles and purposes of assessment and appraisal.* Boston: Houghton Mifflin.

Shimberg, B. (1982). *Occupational licensing: A public perspective*. Princeton, NJ: Educational Testing Service.

Skinner, B. F. (1938). *The behavior of organisms: An experimental analysis*. New York: Appleton-Century-Crofts.

Slimak, R. E., & Berkowitz, S. R. (1983). The university and college counseling center and malpractice suits. *Personnel and Guidance Journal, 61*(5), 291-294.

Smith, R. L., Engels, D. W., & Bonk, E. C. (1985). The past and future: The National Vocational Guidance Association. *Journal of Counseling and Development, 63*(7), 420-423.

Smith, R. L., Piercy, F. P., & Lutz, P. (1982). Training counselors for human resource development positions in business and industry. *Counselor Education and Supervision, 22*, 107-112.

Solomon, C. (1982). Special issue on political action: Introduction. *Personnel and Guidance Journal, 60*(10), 580.

Stadler, H. A. (1988). Marketing counseling: Caveat emptor. *Counselor Education and Supervision, 27*(4), 320-322.

Stadler, H. A. (1990). Counselor impairment. In B. Herlihy & L.B. Golden (Eds.), *Ethical standards casebook* (4th ed.) (pp. 177-187). Alexandria, VA: American Association for Counseling and Development.

Stadler, H. A., Willing, K. L., Eberhage, M. G., & Ward, W. H. (1988). Impairment: Implications for the counseling profession. *Journal of Counseling and Development, 66*(6), 258-260.

Strein, W., & Hershenson, D. B. (1991). Confidentiality in nondyadic counseling situations. *Journal of Counseling and Development, 69*(4), 312-316.

Sue, D., Ino, S., & Sue, D. M. (1983). Nonassertiveness of Asian-Americans: An inaccurate assumption? *Journal of Counseling Psychology, 30*, 581-588.

Sue, D. W., & Sue, D. (1985). Asian-Americans and Pacific islanders. In P. Pederson (Ed.), *Handbook of cross-cultural counseling and therapy.* Westport, CT: Greenwood Press.

Sue, D. M., & Sue, D. (1988). Asian-Americans. In N. A. Vacc, J. Wittmer, & S. DeVaney (Eds.), *Experiencing and counseling multicultural and diverse populations* (2nd ed.). Muncie, IN: Accelerated Development.

Sundel, M., & Sundel, S. S. (1975). *Behavior modification in the human services.* New York: Wiley.

Super, D. E. (1957). *The psychology of careers.* New York: Harper & Row.

Super, D. E. (1969). Vocational development theory: Persons, positions, and processes. *The Counseling Psychologist, 1,* 2-9.

Super, D. E. (1976). *Career education and the meaning of work.* (Monographs of Career Education). Washington, DC: Office of Career Education, U.S. Office of Education.

Super, D. E. (1977). Vocational guidance in mid-career. *Vocational Guidance Quarterly, 25*(4), 294-302.

Super, D. E. (1990). A life-span, life-space approach to career development. In D. Brown, L. Brooks, and Associates (Eds.), *Career choice and development* (pp. 197-261). San Francisco, CA: Jossey-Bass.

Super, D. E., Thompson, A. S., Lindeman, R. E., Jordaan, J. P., & Myers, R. A. (1979). *Career Development Inventory.* Palo Alto, CA: Consulting Psychologists Press.

Talbutt, L. C. (1988). Libel and slander: A potential problem for the 1980s. In W. C. Huey, & T. P. Remley, Jr. (Eds.), *Ethical & legal issues in school counseling* (pp. 131-136). Alexandria, VA: American School Counselor Association.

Talbutt, L. C., & Hummel, D. L. (1982). Legal and ethical issues impacting on counselors. *Counseling and Human Development, 14*(6), 1-12.

Tarasoff v. Regents of the University of California, 529 P.2d. 553 (S.C. Cal. 1974).

Tennyson, W. W., Miller, G. D., Skovholt, T. G., & Williams, C. (1989). Secondary school counselors: What do they do? What is important? *The School Counselor, 36*(4), 253-259.

Tennyson, W. W., & Strom, S. M. (1986). Beyond professional standards: Developing responsibleness. *Journal of Counseling and Development, 64*(5), 298-302.

Thornburg, H. D. (1986). The counselor's impact on middle-grade students. *The School Counselor, 33*(3), 170-177.

Thorndike, E. L. (1932). *The fundamentals of learning.* New York: Teachers College.

Tiedeman, D.V., & O'Hara, R.P. (1963). *Career development: Choice and adjustment.* New York: College Entrance Examination Board.

Tinker v. Des Moines, 393 U.S. (1969).

Trotzer, J. P. (1989). *The counselor and the group: Integrating theory, training, and practice.*(2nd ed.) Muncie, IN: Accelerated Development.

Truax, C. B., & Carkhuff, R. R. (1967). *Toward effective counseling and psychotherapy: Training and practice.* Chicago: Aldine.

Trussell, J. (1988). Teenage pregnancy in the United States. *Family Planning Perspectives, 20,* 262-272.

Tyler, L. E. (1969). *The work of the counselor* (3rd ed.). Englewood Cliffs, NJ: Prentice Hall.

Usdansky, M. L. (1992). 'Diverse' fits nation better than normal. *USA Today,* pp. 1A, 7A.

Vacc, N. A. (1990). Changes and continuity for counselor education. *Counselor Education and Supervision, 30*(2), 148-155.

Vacc, N. A. (1992). An assessment of the perceived relevance of the CACREP standards. *Journal of Counseling and Development, 70,* 685-687.

Vacc, N. A., & Loesch, L. C. (1983). Research as an instrument for professional growth. In G. R. Walz & L. Benjamin (Eds.), *Shaping counselor education programs in the next five years (Conference Proceedings, Association for Counselor Education and Supervision)* (pp. 25-38). Ann Arbor, MI: ERIC Counseling and Personnel Services Clearinghouse.

Vacc, N. A., & Loesch, L. C. (in press). A content analysis of opinions of the National Counselor Examination. *Journal of Counseling and Development.*

Vacc, N. A., Wittmer, J., & DeVaney, S. (1988). *Experiencing and counseling multicultural and diverse populations* (2nd ed.). Muncie, IN: Accelerated Development.

Van Hoose, W. H. (1986). Ethical principles in counseling. *Journal of Counseling and Development, 65*(3), 168-169.

Vander Kolk, C. J. (1985). *Introduction to group counseling and psychotherapy.* University of Michigan: Books on Demand.

VanZandt, C. E. (1990). Professionalism: A matter of personal initiatives. *Journal of Counseling and Development, 68*(3), 243245.

Vasquez, M. J. T. (1988). Counselor-client sexual contact: Implications for ethics training. *Journal of Counseling and Development, 67*(4), 238-241.

Vasquez, M. J. T., & Kitchener, K. S. (1988). Introduction to special feature. *Journal of Counseling and Development, 67*(4), 214-216.

Wagman, M., & Kerber, K. W. (1984). Computer-assisted counseling: Problems and prospects. *Counselor Education and Supervision, 24*(2), 142-154.

Watson, J. B. (1930). *Behaviorism* (2nd edition). Chicago: University of Chicago Press.

Wattenberg, B. J. (1991). *The first universal nation: Leading indicators and ideas about the surge of America in the 1990's.* New York: The Free Press.

Weikel, W. J. (1985). The American Mental Health Counselors Association. *Journal of Counseling and Development, 63*(7), 457-460.

Weikel, W.J., & Palmo, A.J. (1989). The evolution and practice of mental health counseling. *Journal of Mental Health Counseling, 11*(1), 7-25.

Westervelt, E. M. (1978). A tide in the affairs of women: The psychological impact of feminism on educated women. In L. W. Harmon, J. M. Birk, L. E. Fitzgerald, & M. F. Tanney (Eds.), *Counseling women* (pp. 1-33). Monterey, CA: Brooks/Cole.

Wetzel, L., & Ross, M. A. (1983). Psychological and sociological ramifications of battering: Observations leading to a counseling methodology for victims of domestic violence. *Personnel and Guidance Journal, 61*(7), 423-427.

Wheeler, P.T., & Loesch, L.C. (1981). Program evaluation and counseling: Yesterday, today, and tomorrow. *Personnel and Guidance Journal, 59*(9), 573-577.

Whiston, S. C., & Emerson, S. (1989). Ethical implications for supervisors in counseling of trainees. *Counselor Education and Supervision, 28*(4), 318-325.

Whiteley, J. M., & Resnikoff, A. (Eds.) (1978). *Career-counseling.* Monterey, CA: Brooks/Cole.

Wiggins, J. D., & Weslander, D. L. (1986). Effectiveness related to personality and demographic characteristics of secondary school counselors. *Counselor Education and Supervision, 26*(1), 26-35.

Wilcoxon, S. A. (1987). Ethical standards: A study of application and utility. *Journal of Counseling and Development, 65*(9), 510511.

Wilcoxon, S. A., & Hawk, R. (1990). Continuing education services: A survey of state associations of AACD. *Journal of Counseling and Development, 69*(1), 93-94.

Williamson, E. G. (1939). *How to counsel students.* New York: McGraw-Hill.

Wilson, E. S., & Robinson, E. H. III. (1985). Association for Humanistic Education and Development: Leadership and diversity. *Journal of Counseling and Development, 63*(7), 416-419.

Wittman, P. P. (1988). Marketing counseling: What counseling can learn from other health care professions. *Counselor Education and Supervision, 27*(4), 308-314.

Wittmer, J., & Loesch, L. C. (1990). Roses, ducks, and doctoral degrees in counselor education. *Counselor Education and Supervision, 30*(2), 156-162.

Wittmer, P. J., & Loesch, L. C. (1986). Professional orientation. In M. D. Lewis, R. L. Hayes, and J. A. Lewis (Eds.), *An introduction to the counseling profession* (pp. 301-330). Itasca, IL: Peacock.

Wittmer, P. J., & Myrick, R. D. (1974). *Facilitative teaching: Theory and practice.* Pacific Palisades, CA: Goodyear.

Yalom, I. D. (1985) *Theory and practice of group psychotherapy,* 3rd Ed. New York: Basic Books.

Zahner, C. J., & McDavis, R. J. (1980). Moral development of professional and paraprofessional counselors and trainees. *Counselor Education and Supervision, 19*(4), 243-251.

Zunker, V. G. (1986). *Career counseling: Applied concepts of life planning.* Pacific Grove, CA: Brooks/Cole.

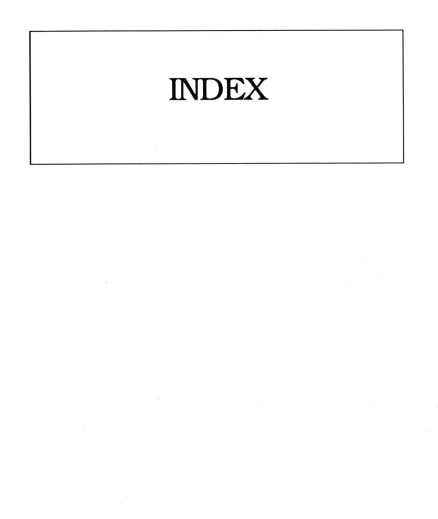

INDEX

INDEX

A

Abused persons, trends in ones
    served 133-4
ACA plans revision of ethical
    standards 202, 509
Access to records 161-2
Accident theory 312
Accountability 346-8
    counseling 50-1
Accreditation
    by other agencies 112
    procedures 110-112
Acquired Immune Deficiency
    Syndrome (AIDS) 147,
    183-5
Adams, Q. 41
Adler, A. 243, 509
Adolescence
    development 220-2
    physiological changes 221
    sociological changes 222
Adulthood, development 222-4
Adults, older
    development 222-4
Advertising 154-6
Affective domain, assessing 343-6
Affeman, M. 120, 514
African-Americans 230
Agency 308
Alexander, M.D. 144, 146, 147, 150,
    151, 156-7, 161, 162, 163,
    166, 519
Allen, V.B. 175, 509
Alonso, W. 226, 514
Alternatives 304
Ambrose, D.M. 154, 509
Amelioration 78
American Association for Counseling
    and Development (AACD) 36

American Association for Counseling
    and Development (AACD),
    Ethics Committee 199, 200,
    509
American Association for State
    Counselor Boards (AASCB)
    60
American Association of Colleges
    of Teacher Education
    (AACTE) 31
American Association for Marriage
    and Family Therapy (AAMFT)
    55, 69, 112, 136
    Clinical member 69
American College Counseling
    Association (ACCA) 31, 37,
    40
American College Personnel
    Association (ACPA) 31, 100,
    118
American College Testing Program
    (ACT) 340
American Counseling Association
    (ACA) 25, 55, 179-80, 186,
    193, 196, 199, 201-2, 281,
    509
    branches 59
    corporate affiliates 59
    former names 29
    governance structure 58
    international convention 58-9
    legal defense fund 58
    number of members 37, 56
    plans for revision of ethical
        standards 202, 509
    political involvement system 58
    types of membership 56
American Counseling Association
    (ACA) Ethical Standards
    174-8, 190, 198-9, 201-2,
    Appendix I, 377-92

consulting 177
counseling relationship 176
general measurement and
    evaluation 176
personnel administration 177
preparation standards 177
private practice 177
research and publication 176
American Counselor 58
American Educational Research
    Association (AERA) 55
American Mental Health Counselors
    Association (AMHCA) 35, 37,
    40, 449-66
American Personnel & Guidance
    Association (now ACA) 32
American Psychiatric Association
    347, 509
American Psychological Association
    (APA) 25, 55, 112
American Rehabilitation Counseling
    Association (ARCA) 33, 37,
    40
American School Counselor
    Association (ASCA) 32, 37,
    40, 100, 407-14
American Vocational Association
    (AVA) 55
Americans, native 232
Analyses
    addressing relationships 370-1
    applied behavior 248
    statistical 367-71
    transactional 253-5
Anderson, B.S. 148, 149, 150, 151,
    165, 166, 167, 185, 518
Appraisal
    definition 334
    of the individual 18
Apprenticeships 327
Aptitude tests
    group administered 341
    multifactor 341
Arreondo, P. 190, 519
Artistic personality characteristics
    318, *Figure* 319
Asian-Americans 231-2
Assessment 189, 333-52
    affective domain 343-6
    definition 333

goal 334
process 334, 348-52
Assessment in counseling 335-46
    affective domain 343-6
    cognitive domain 338-43
    purposes 335-7
    standardized tests 337-8
Assessment within empirical
    counseling 346-52, *Figure*
    349
Association of Colleges and Schools
    61
Association for Counselor Education
    and Supervision (ACES) 31
Association for Adult Development
    and Aging (AADA) 35, 37,
    40
Association for Assessment in
    Counseling (AAC) 33, 37
Association for Counselor Education
    and Supervision (ACES)
    37, 40, 99, 439-47, 509
Association for Humanistic
    Education and Development
    (AHEAD) 31, 37,40
Association for Multicultural
    Counseling and Development
    (AMCD) 34, 37, 40
Association for Religious and Value
    Issues in Counseling (ARVIC)
    34, 37, 40
Association for Specialists in Group
    Work (ASGW) 37, 40,
    481-493
Association for Measurement and
    Evaluation in Counseling
    & Development (AMECD) 33
Association for Measurement and
    Evaluation in Guidance
    (AMEG) 33
Association for Specialists in Group
    Work (ASGW) 34
Atkinson, D.R. 229, 231, 232, 233,
    510
Attitude assessment 345-6
Autonomy 171, 308
Avocational 296
Axelrad, S. 320, 516
Axelson, J.A. 229, 232, 234, 510

B

Bacon, C.L. 233, 510
Bandura, A. 211-12, 305, 311, 510
Bardon, J.I 20, 21, 339, 510
Barlow, D.H. 22, 372, 510
Barriers 233-4
Bartlett, W.E. 34, 510
Baruth, L.G. 230, 231, 232-3, 234, 510
Base for counseling, theoretical 45-6
Baseline
  in research 357
  multiple 358-9
BASIC ID 249
Bayer, G.A. 121, 515
Behavior analysis, applied 248
Behavior modification, cognitive 248
Belkin, G.S. 1, 19, 21, 510
Beneficence 171, 198
Benjamin, L. 529
Bennett, V.C. 20, 21, 339, 510
Bergland, B.W. 306, 510
Berkowitz, S.R. 150, 527
Bernard, J.M. 192, 510
Bias 233-4
  in group composition 363
Bindman, A.J. 262, 510
Bioland, P.A. 296, 511
Birk, J.M. 520
Bishop, J.B. 118, 510
Blake, R.R. 275, 511
Blocker, D. 262, 511
Bloland, P.A. 296, 511
Bonk, E.C. 30, 527
Borders, L.D. 76, 193, 510, 511, 513
Bordin, E.S. 313-4, 511
Borgers, S.B. 173, 524
Boundaries, culture and social class 311
Brammer, L.M. 329, 511
Brooks, D.K. 137, 511
Brooks, L. 79, 137, 511, 515, 522
Brown, D. 152, 159, 511, 522
Brown, M.B. 125, 518
Bumpass, L.L. 227, 511, 512
Burck, H. 297, 524
Burn, D. 190-1, 511

Burnout, prevention 78
Burns, C.F. 119, 511
Business and industry
  trends in work settings 121-2
Butler, R.N. 226, 511

C

Cabral, A.C. 311, 512
California Association for Counselor Education and Supervision (CASES) 101
Callanan, P. 84, 187, 192, 193, 282, 513
Campbell, D.T. 362, 363, 512
Caplan, G. 262, 267-8, 512
Capuzzi, D. 525
Career counseling 298
Career development
  counseling 293-331, Table 5
  definition 296
Career development skills 18
Career education 298
  definition 324
Career guidance 297
Career Information System (CIS) 328
Career management 297
Career maturity 297, 323
Career-education model
  employer-based or experience-based 326
  home/community-based 326
  rural/residential 326
  school-based or comprehensive 325
Carkhuff, R.R. 20, 21, 239, 512, 529
Carroll, M.R. 34, 512
Case illustration
  individual consultation 271-5
  John 24
  Keith 11-6, 41
CASEVE model 306
Castro Martin, T. 227, 512
Catholic Guidance Council in the Archdiocese of New York 34
Certification 62-9
  definition 62
  history 62-3

T 287
task 286
transactional analysis (TA)
287-8
Growth early 216-8
Grunwald, B.B. 138, 516
Guidance Information System (GIS)
328
Guidelines for Doctoral Prep in
Counselor Education 101
Guidelines, ethical
See Code of Ethics
See Standards, ethical
Guidepost 58
Guiterrez, F. 132, 513
Gysbers, N.C. 294, 299, 328, 516,
521

H

Hanson, T. 284, 516
Harding, A.K. 184, 516
Harding, S.S. 194, 520
Harmon, L.W. 530
Harren, V.A. 306, 524
Harris, T.A. 288, 517
Harris, T.L. 86, 526
Harris-Bowlsbey, J. 77, 517
Harvill, R. 282, 519
Havinghurst, R.S. 22, 517
Hawk, R. 75, 531
Hawthorne effect 363
Hayes, B.A. 121, 520
Hayes, R.L. 531
Hayes, S.C. 22, 372, 510
Health Maintenance Organizations
(HMOs) 120
Healy, C.C. 298, 517
Healy, M. 200, 517
Helwig, A. 33, 522
Herlihy, B. 144, 145, 164, 166, 175,
200, 509, 514, 517,
519, 520, 526, 527
Herma, J. 320, 516
Hernandez, H. 229, 517
Herr, E.L. 32, 36, 226, 231, 295,
296, 297, 299, 300, 304,
305, 308, 310, 321, 323,
326, 329, 330, 510, 517
Hershenson, D.B. 187, 528

Higher education, student
development practice 3
Hispanic-Americans 230
History, lessons from 37-44
HIV 183-4
HIV-positive 147
Hock, E.L. 25, 517
Hohenshil, T.H. 125, 518
Holdsworth, R. 518
Holland classifications of modal
personal orientations 317
Holland's theory 317-20
Holland, J.L. 317, 319, 320, 516,
518
Hollis, J.W. 88, 89, 93, 94, 136,
518
Holmes, Oliver Wendell, Jr. 38, 518
Hopkins, B.R. 148, 149, 150, 151,
165, 166, 167, 185, 518
Hopson, B. 241, 518
Hotelling, K. 195, 518
Hoyt, K.B. 324, 325, 518
Hudson, P. 200, 517
Huey, W.C. 157, 512, 528
Human capital theory 312
Human growth and development 16
Human resource development (HRD)
121
Hummel, D.L. 144, 146, 147, 150,
151, 156-7, 161, 162,163,
166, 167, 519, 528

I

Ibrahim, F.A 190, 519
Id 207, 242
Idiographic 24
Improvement of counseling 346
Individual tests 339
Individual with marital and/or
familial problems
trends in ones served 136-8
Individuals with sexual problems
trends in ones served 135-6
Induction 308
Influence
pretest 364
Information
computer-based 189
qualitative 338

Informed consent 141-3
Initiate plan 352
Ino, S. 232, 528
Inquiry
    research 354
Instruction
    computer-assisted 189
Instrumentation 363
Insurance programs 58
Integration 308
Intellectually gifted
    trends in ones served 129-30
Interference
    multiple-treatment 364
International Association for
    Addictions and Offender
    Counselors (IAOCC) 35, 37,
    40
International Association of
    Counseling Services (IACS)
    59, 118
International Association of Marriage
    and Family Counselors
    (IAMFC) 36,37, 40, 137,
    429-38,519
Interpretation, definition 334
Intervention
    counselor 189
    in research 357
Interviews 327
Investigative personality
    characteristics 318, *Figure*
    319
Investment 305
Involvement
    political 48-9
Iowa Tests of Basic Skills 342
Issues
    ethical 236
    ethical related to group counseling
    291
    legal related to group counseling
    291
Issues concerning counselors

cultural 225-36
social 225-36
Ivey, A. 240, 519

J

Jackson, G.G. 233, 519
Jacobs, E. 282, 519
Jaeger, R.M. 66, 519
Jenkins, S.J. 285, 286, 526
Job 295
Johnson, C. 46, 513
Johnson, C.S. 31, 519
Johnson, D.W. 286, 519
Johnson, F.P. 286, 519
Jones, B.G. 307, 520
Jordaan, J.P. 323, 528
Journal of Counseling 43
*Journal of Counseling and
    Development* 58
Jung, C. 244
Justice 171

K

Kagan, N. 240, 519
Kain, C.D. 184, 519
Kemp, C.A. 277, 280, 519
Kendall's tau 371
Kerber, K.W. 77, 530
Kerlinger, F.N. 365, 520
Kern, R. 226, 514
King, P.M. 214, 520
Kipper, D.A. 287, 522
Kirby, J. 263, 520
Kirchner, R. 19, 522
Kitchener, K.S. 172, 194, 195, 520,
    530
Knefelkamp, L. 520
Knowledge 16-8

time-series designs 357-9
type of scale 367-8
Median 368
Mehrens, W.A. 80, 338, 341, 522
Membership
types in ACA 56
Mental health
counseling 2, 44-5
consultation 267-8
counselor 14
service delivery, *Table* 12
Metropolitan Readiness Tests 343
Meyer, D. 33, 522
Micro-counseling 240
Micro-skill 240
Middle childhood
development 219-20
Middle school age children
trends in ones served 127
trends in work settings 115-6
Military Educators and Counselors
Association (MECA) 35, 37,
40
Miller Analogies Test (MAT) 340
Miller, G.D. 114, 529
Miller, G.M. 114, 522
Miller-Tiedeman, A. 308-9, 522
Milliken, R.L. 19, 522
Minkoff, H.B. 32, 522
Minority 229
Misconduct, sexual 164
Mitchell, A.M. 307, 520
Mitchell, L.K. 307, 522
Mitmenschen 243
Mitwelt 257
Mode 368
Model 263
career-education 325-6
CASVE 306
Holland's hexagonal, *Figure* 319
RIASEC/Holland's 317-9
Models
affective 255-8
analytical psychotherapy
244-5
behavior therapy 247-9, 290
behavioral 247-50
client/person-centered 246-7
cognitive 250-5
existential psychotherapy
256-8

Freudian psychoanalytic theory
241-3
gestalt therapy 255-6, 289-90
group 285-90
multimodal therapy 249-50
psychoanalytic 241-5
rational-emotive therapy 250-2,
288
reality therapy 252-3, 289
theoretical 240-58
transactional analysis 253-5,
287-8
Moles, O.C. 114, 522
Moreno, J.L. 287, 522
Mortality, experimental 363
Morten, G. 229, 510
Mouton, S.S. 275, 511
Multiple correlation analysis 371
Multiple regression analysis 371
Multiplicity 215-6
Muro, J.J. 80, 514
Murphy, H.B. 85, 525
Myer, J.A. 226, 514
Myers, J.E. 129, 135, 235, 522, 525
Myers, R.A. 323, 528
Myers, R.S. 130, 523
Myrick, R.D. 116, 117, 270-1, 523,
531

N

Nachmann, B. 313, 511
National Academy of Certified
Clinical Mental Health
Counselors (NACCMHC) 63
National Association of Counselor
Supervisors and Counselor
Trainers (NAGSCT) 99
National Association of Appointment
Secretaries (NAAS) 31
National Association of Certified
Clinical Mental Health
Counselors 467-480,523
National Association of Deans of
Women (NADW) 30
National Association of Guidance
Supervisors (NAGS) 31, 99
National Association of Placement
and Personnel Officers
(NAPPO) 31

ABOUT THE AUTHORS

Nicholas A. Vacc, Ed.D.

Nicholas Vacc, Professor and Chairperson of the Department of Counseling and Specialized Educational Development at the University of North Carolina at Greensboro, received his doctorate in counseling from the State University of New York at Albany in 1967. He is a National Certified Counselor, Certified School Counselor, Certified Clinical Mental Health Counselor, member of the ACA, and Fellow in the American Orthopsychiatric Association. Nicholas' special interests include teaching counselor education courses, providing clinical supervision, and working with the NBCC as an Examination Consultant, in particular, and consultant, in general. He has consulted with and conducted in-service training and supervision workshops for counselors and other mental-health professionals throughout the world. He has authored or co-authored more than 80 professional publications. In addition, his prior employment experience includes work in student residence life, counseling with veterans and their families, and directing a university counseling center.

Nicholas is a former editor of *Measurement and Evaluation in Counseling and Development*, Chairperson of the AACD Council of Journal Editors, and President of the North Carolina AMECD. Also, he has served as Member at Large at the Association for Assessment in Counseling (AAC) and President of Chi Sigma Iota, which is the Counseling Academic and Professional Honor Society International. He was a co-recipient of the 1992 AACD (now ACA) Arthur A. Hitchcock Distinguished Professional Service Award, primarily for his work on the development of the NBCC's National Counselor Examination.

Larry C. Loesch, Ph.D.

Larry Loesch, Professor and Graduate Coordinator in the Department of Counselor Education at the University of Florida, received his doctorate in counselor education from Kent State University in 1973. He is a National Certified Counselor and serves as the NBCC Evaluations Coordinator. He is a member of ACA. Larry's interests include teaching counselor education, doing clinical supervision, and consulting in the professional practice of counseling. He regularly conducts training workshops for counselors, other mental-health professionals, and personnel in public and private agencies. His prior employment includes work in student residence life, secondary school teaching and counseling, and computer programming.

Larry is a former President of Association for Measurement and Evaluation in Guidance (AMEG) and of Florida ACD, a past editor of *Measurement and Evaluation in Guidance,* Chairperson of the AACD Council of Journal Editors, editorial board member for *Counselor Education and Supervision,* AMEG representative to CACREP, and recipient of the 1986 AMECD Exemplary Practices Award. More recently, he was the 1990-91 President of Chi Sigma Iota (Counseling Academic and Professional Honor Society International) and a co-recipient of the 1992 AACD (now ACA) Arthur A. Hitchcock Distinguished Professional Service Award, primarily for his work on the development of the NBCC's National Counselor Examination. He has authored or co-authored more than 90 professional publications.

Please remember that this is a library book,
and that it belongs only temporarily to each
person who uses it. Be considerate. Do
not write in this, or any, library book.

DATE DUE

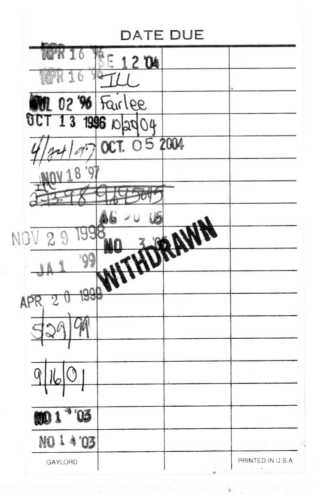